TRANSECT THROUGH TIME

THE ARCHAEOLOGICAL LANDSCAPE
OF THE
SHELL NORTH WESTERN ETHYLENE PIPELINE

(ENGLISH SECTION)

Janet Lambert

Nick Hair
Christine Howard-Davis
Rachel Newman
Tove Oliver

1996

Published by
Lancaster University Archaeological Unit
Storey Institute
Meeting House Lane
Lancaster LA1 1TH
Phone 01524 848666, *Fax* 01524 848606

Distributed by
Oxbow Books
Park End Place
Oxford OX1 1HN
Phone 01865 241249, *Fax* 01865 794449

Printed in Great Britain by
The Short Run Press, Exeter

This publication has been funded by Shell Chemicals UK Ltd

ISBN 0 901800 74 0
ISSN 1343-5205

A catalogue record for this book is available from the British Library

Editors
Janet Lambert, Rachel Newman, Adrian Olivier
Design
Robert Middleton, Janet Lambert
Layout
Val Tomlin, Ruth Parkin

To Robin and Noël

Front cover: Lune gorge, Tebay, Cumbria
Back cover: Tombstone of *Aelia Sentica*

is the publication series of Lancaster University Archaeological Unit. The series covers the full range of archaeological work undertaken by the Unit and associated organisations.

Contents

Tables

Abbreviations and conventions

AP	Aerial photograph
CFHS	Cumbria Family History Society
CRO	Cumbria Record Office
DOE	Department of the Environment
EC	European Community
GPS	Global Positioning System
LRO	Lancashire Record Office
LUAU	Lancaster University Archaeological Unit
NGR	National Grid Reference
NWEP	North Western Ethylene Pipeline
NWWS	North West Wetlands Survey
OD	Ordnance Datum
OE	Old English
ON	Old Norse
OS	Ordnance Survey
PGM	Permanent Ground Marker
PRO	Public Record Office
RCHAMS	Royal Commission on the Ancient and Historic Monuments of Scotland
RCHM (E)	Royal Commission on the Historical Monuments of England
SCUK	Shell Chemicals UK Ltd
SM	Scheduled Monument
SMR	Sites and Monuments Record

Throughout the text, sites on the pipeline route are referred to by their assigned numbers in the gazetteer, and are printed in bold, thus: **825**. Excavation context numbers are consistently referred to by the use of italics, thus: *103*. Object record numbers in the excavation reports correlate to the archive numbers in the finds catalogues (*on microfiche*), and are expressed as plain numbers, thus: 10.

Abstract

In 1988 the Lancaster University Archaeological Unit was commissioned by Shell Chemicals UK Ltd to carry out a phased archaeological assessment of the English sector of a proposed pipeline route. The North Western Ethylene Pipeline was designed to carry ethylene from Grangemouth in Scotland to the existing Shell refinery facilities at Stanlow in Cheshire.

The archaeological studies commenced with desktop assessments in 1988–1989, followed by intensive field-work in 1990–1991, post-excavation analysis in 1992, and a written synthesis in 1993–1994. The earlier phases of work comprised archive research, fieldwalking, and aerial photography, and further work at selected sites included topographical survey, geophysical survey, trial trenching, and excavation in several key areas. Construction of the pipeline took place between May and November 1991, and was monitored by archaeological line inspectors conducting a continuous watching brief, supported by a rapid response team equipped to survey or excavate features discovered during construction.

The pipeline route traversed all five counties of North West England, but the main thrust of the work programme focused on Cumbria, where four sites of local, regional, and national significance were exca-vated prior to construction, at Hadrian's Wall, Fremington, near Penrith, Powsons, and Low Borrowbridge, both in the Lune gorge south of Tebay. In addition, the intersections with two Roman roads were recorded during pipeline construction, at the Stanegate, south of Hadrian's Wall, and the main road north from Ribchester to Carlisle, at Sproatgill near Orton.

This monograph presents a chronological account of the phased work programme and techniques em-ployed (*Chapter 1*), describes all the sites briefly in relation to the topography of the pipeline route (*Chapter 2*), and provides a more detailed study of the Lune gorge, an area substantially affected by the pipeline and other major routeways (*Chapter 3*). There are full reports of the excavations at Hadrian's Wall (*Chapter 4*), the Roman cemetery at Low Borrowbridge (*Chapter 5*), an early medieval settlement at Fremington (*Chapter 6*), and a medieval farmstead at Powsons (*Chapter 7*).

Contributors

Denise Drury — Lancaster University Archaeological Unit
Paul Gibbons — Archaeological Field Unit, Exeter Museum
Nick Hair — Lancaster University Archaeological Unit
Louise Hird — Carlisle Archaeological Unit
Philip Howard — Department of Archaeology, University of Durham
Christine Howard-Davis — Lancaster University Archaeological Unit
Jacqueline P Huntley — Ancient Monuments Laboratory, University of Durham
Janet Lambert — 18 Storey Avenue, Lancaster
Jacqueline I McKinley — Osteoarchaeologist, 12 Victoria Road, Warminster, Wiltshire
Rachel Newman — Lancaster University Archaeological Unit
Tove Oliver — Hendra House, Nanquidno, St Just in Penwith, Cornwall
David Shotter — Department of History, University of Lancaster
John Williams — Kent County Council Planning Department
Deirdre Winstanley — Archaeologist, 42 Balmoral Road, Lancaster

Acknowledgements

The accomplishment of such a major project is only possible with the willing cooperation and assistance of a great number of people, and I would like to thank all those who provided all kinds of information, support, and specialist advice, including the landowners and farmers, especially Mr J Wilson and Mrs Wilson of Low Borrowbridge, Mr G Allen of Brockholes, Mr G Wilcox of Fremington, Mr Wannop of Linstock Castle Farm, Mr Thornton of Little Crimbles, and Mr Newsham of Banton House Farm; the specialists, John Anstee, Bob Bewley (RCHM (E)), Sally Cottam (University of Durham), Jim Cherry, Ken Dark (University of Cambridge), Anthony Ellwood, Vanessa Fell, Andrew Fitzpatrick, Helena Hamerow, Anthony Harding (Professor of Archaeology, University of Durham), Jennifer Jones, Maureen McHugh, Ailsa Mainmann, Sue Mills, Chris Sparey-Green, Vivian Swan, and Angus Winchester (University of Lancaster); staff of the Cumbria Record Offices in Carlisle and Kendal, and of the Lancashire Record Office; Nick Smith (Bechtel), and SCUK's NWEP project team, especially Alan Ryder, head of environmental affairs, Mike Stanistreet, head of quality assurance, safety, and environment, the late George Duxbury, chief safety officer, and John Brown, head of public affairs; Paul Dibb, Chris Henson, Stuart Dunn, and Chris Pritchard, surveyors; David Maynard, pipeline archaeologist; Tom Brown, Jack Buckham, and Willie Colville, land agents (Bell-Ingram); Brian Bateson, pilot (Blackpool Air Centre), Ray Steel and Chris Birbeck, JCB operators; Tom Clare (Cumbria), Ben Edwards (Lancashire), Ron Cowell (Merseyside), Phil Mayes (Greater Manchester), Rick Turner and Adrian Tindall (Cheshire), county archaeological curators; Bette Hopkins (Cumbria), Peter Iles (Lancashire), Gail Falkingham (Merseyside), Norman Redhead (Greater Manchester), and Jill Collens (Cheshire), county SMR officers; Peter McKeague and Jamie Hamilton, line inspectors (Centre for Field Archaeology, University of Edinburgh); Jayne Close, Sarah Mason, and Jane Hodgkinson, LUAU secretaries; Jill Pollard and Sarah Fitchett, LUAU administration; and Sue Fiddler, Marie Hale, Rachel Street, Natalie Williams, Ben Wilson, and Joy Wilson, excavation volunteers.

In the course of a six-year project, staffing and structural changes are inevitable. John Williams set up the project in the summer of 1988, and managed it for a year, until he left the Cumbria and Lancashire Archaeological Unit (as LUAU was then known) to become the county archaeologist for Kent. His successor, Adrian Olivier, maintained overall responsibility for the project until he in turn departed, in December 1993, to become manager of the Central Archaeology Service at English Heritage. Project management was then taken over by Rachel Newman, assistant director of LUAU. The initial assessment stage of the NWEP project, in 1988–1989, was directed by Peter Iles, and the first phase of fieldwork was co-directed, in the spring of 1990, by Jamie Quartermaine and Janet Lambert. From May 1990 until publication the project was directed by Janet Lambert. The two seasons of trial excavations, in 1990–91, were directed by Katharine Buxton, and the excavation site directors in 1991 were Denise Drury (Hadrian's Wall), Tove Oliver (Fremington), and Nick Hair (Powsons and Low Borrowbridge). The post-excavation programme was co-ordinated by Rachel Newman. The success of the project relied on the 60 members of LUAU staff involved, and remembered with thanks are the survey and excavation staff: Austin Ainsworth, Glyn Barrett, Denise Buckley, Robert Chester, Shona Connolly, Judith Driver, Colin Forcey, Robert Foreman, Steven Haig, Richard Harrison, David Hodgkinson, David Johnson, Philip Kibberd, Robin Lambert, Ian Miller, Michael Peace, Sarah Peacock, Fiona Pitt, Peter Redmayne, Matthew Robinson, Ian Scott, Trevor Simmons, Jonathan Smith, Jenny Swift, Andrew Thompson, Patrick Tostevin, Michael Wane, Angela Whitworth, and Chris Wild; Prince Chitwood, Denise Drury, and Mark Leah, line inspectors; Mick Krupa and Jamie Quartermaine, surveyors; Helen Quartermaine, archivist; Chris Cox, aerial photographer; Malcolm Harrison, photographic plotting and interpretation; Ruth Parkin, desktop publishing; Sonia Ely and Richard Harrison, gazetteer compilation and office administration; Robert Middleton and Colin Wells, North West Wetlands Survey; Peter Iles and John Dodds, computer management; and Michael Trueman, industrial archaeologist.

The principal author of this monograph is Janet Lambert, the co-authors of the excavation reports for Fremington, Low Borrowbridge, and Powsons are Tove Oliver, Rachel Newman, Christine Howard-Davis, and Nick Hair, and contributors to the Hadrian's Wall report are John Williams, Philip Howard, Paul Gibbons, and Denise Drury. David Shotter provided the section on the Romans in the Lune Valley, and reports on the tombstone and Roman coins. Other specialist contributors were Sally Cottam and Louise Hird (Roman pottery), Jacqueline I McKinley (human bone) Deirdre Winstanley (animal bone), and Jacqueline P Huntley (palaeoenvironmental analysis).

Aerial photographs are by Bob Bewley (2:16, 3:8, 5:1) and Chris Cox (7:8). Photographs of Fremington are by LUAU (6:8, 6:11); the rest are by Janet Lambert, who also produced the maps in Chapters 2 and 3 using Micrografx Designer 4.1. Site plans and historic maps were prepared for publication by Richard Danks, and finds illustrations are by Peter Lee. Figures 2:2, 2:5, 2:7, 2:8, 2:9, 2:13, 3:12, 4:1, 7:2 (Carlisle), and 2:14, 2:19, 2:22, 2:24, 2:25, 3:13, 3:14, 3:15, 3:18, 3:19, 3:20, 3:22, 3:24, 7:3, 7:4, 7:5, 7:6 (Kendal) are reproduced by permission from the Cumbria Record Office, and Figures 2:28, 2:32, 2:33, 2:35 by permission from the Lancashire Record Office; Crown copyright map extracts are reproduced by courtesy of the Ordnance Survey.

Foreword

The North Western Ethylene Pipeline was conceived as a solution to an ethylene feedstock supply problem. By safely transporting this versatile chemical from operations in Scotland to our manufacturing plants in the North West of England, we were able to underpin our own future development plans and play an integral role in stabilising the UK chemical industry.

However, as well as the commercial value of this extensive project, it also serves to demonstrate my company's attitude to environmental management.

Before beginning the construction of this 411km long pipeline, an extensive environmental assessment took place. As well as defining our intentions to the government's Department of Trade and Industry, that document gave us a baseline of data from which to plan construction and manage effective reinstatement.

The statement covers many aspects of environmental impact including ecology, agriculture, geology, geography, and archaeology.

By rerouteing the pipeline wherever possible and approaching the crossing of certain Scheduled Monuments with sensitivity, it has been possible to avoid having a significant detrimental effect on the archaeology of the North West and Border counties. Indeed, aerial photography, geophysical surveys, trial and detailed excavations have added to the understanding of the area's archaeological heritage.

In particular, careful excavation, carried out with the help of consultants and experts from the Lancaster University Archaeological Unit, has revealed new and important evidence regarding the early colonisation of land traversed by the pipeline. The body of information that has been investigated and collated by LUAU clearly indicates that a significant contribution has been made to the archaeological record for the UK.

I feel that this document prepared by LUAU is a valuable by-product of the Shell North Western Ethylene Pipeline project.

W A Colquhoun

General Manager, Shell Chemicals UK Ltd

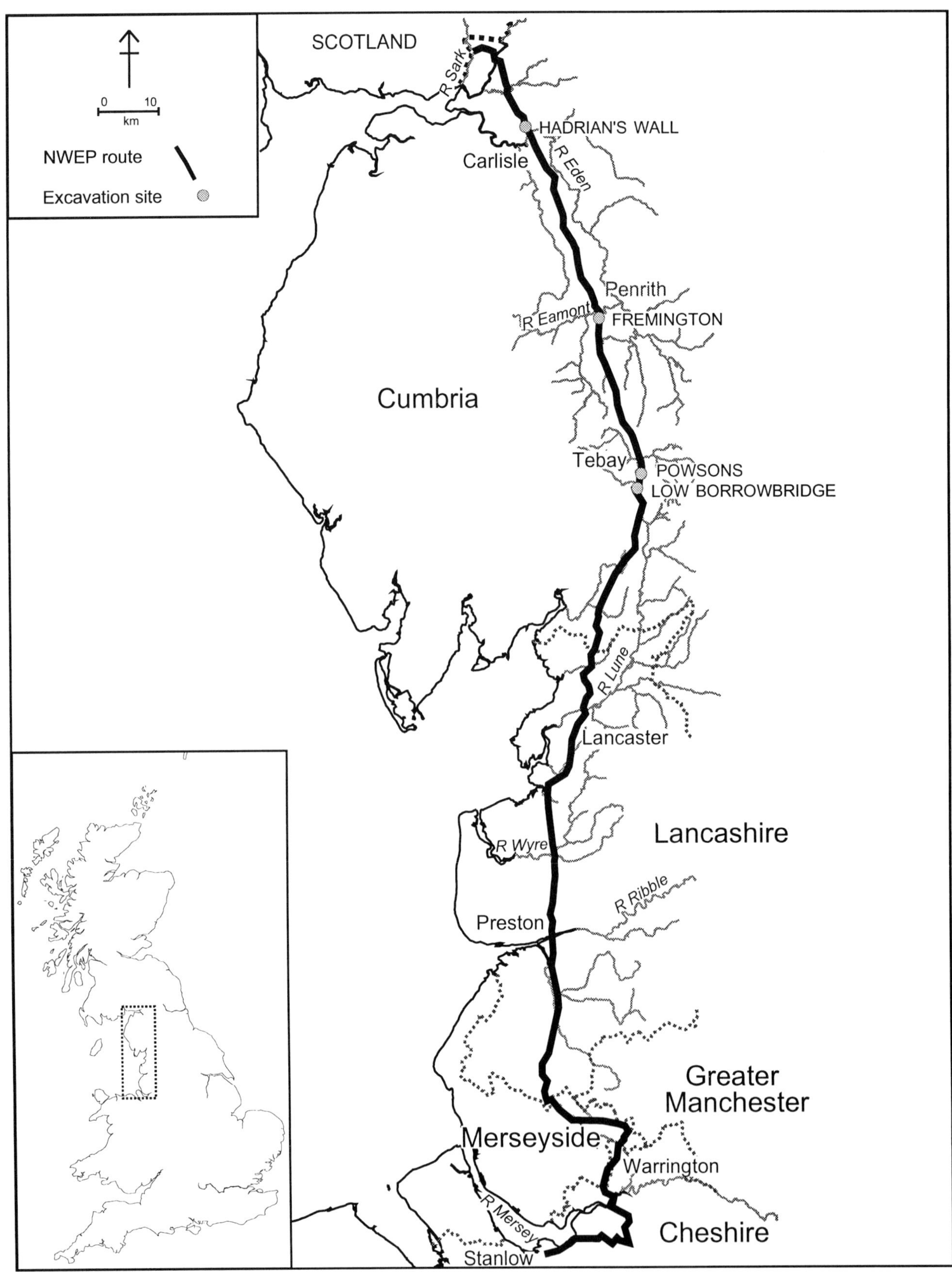

Fig 0:1 North West England and the pipeline route

Introduction

In July 1988 the Lancaster University Archaeological Unit began the phased archaeological assessment of a proposed pipeline route on behalf of Shell Chemicals UK Ltd (SCUK). The North Western Ethylene Pipeline was designed to carry ethylene from Grangemouth, on the Firth of Forth west of Edinburgh, to the existing Shell refinery facilities at Stanlow, on the River Mersey in Cheshire (Fig 0:1). North of the border, the Scottish section of the route was evaluated by staff of the Centre for Field Archaeology at the University of Edinburgh. The LUAU studies were concerned entirely with the 253km of the pipeline route in the English counties of Cumbria, Lancashire, Merseyside, Greater Manchester, and Cheshire.

The detailed archaeological management policy originally put forward by LUAU was subsequently adapted for incorporation in SCUK's Environmental Statement, as part of its planning application. The initial desk-top assessment, in 1988–1989, formed part of an overall environmental impact assessment, encompassing also the geology, hydrology, ecology, and landuse of the proposed route, as prescribed by EC regulations. The results of these studies imposed constraints which were taken into account in the routeing of the pipeline, and SCUK then published an Environmental Statement, in September 1989, in support of their application to the Department of Energy for Pipeline Construction Authorisation (SCUK 1989). Following the identification of statutory archaeological constraints for the purpose of the planning application, LUAU was requested to design a project for the further investigation and recording of sites and areas of archaeological interest along the chosen route.

The pipeline route passes through one of the archaeologically lesser known areas of England, providing a cross-section of many of the widely varying landscapes to be found in the North West, and affecting, or passing close to, a number of important archaeological sites. The aim of the study was to preserve sites, wherever possible, by avoidance; where this was not feasible, a management plan was devised to mitigate the impact of construction on each site affected. Approximately 500 sites were evaluated, in a structured process designed to identify and record every site at a level appropriate to its archaeological value. This major investigation of a corridor 253km long consisted of a review of existing records, field validation, aerial photography, and selective survey or excavation where necessary, while a watching brief was maintained throughout pipeline construction. The fieldwork was accompanied by a synthesis of all the information into a computerised database and gazetteer, and a series of 17 progress reports to SCUK.

This transect through North West England, from the Solway to the Mersey, crossed upland areas of marginal agricultural value, rich arable lowlands, a busy communications corridor, bleak moorlands, and relatively densely populated river valleys and estuaries. The greatest contrast in landscapes lay between the remote Westmorland fells, and the conurbations and industrial horizons of Merseyside and North Cheshire. The range of sites recorded reflects these contrasts in North West England, and while the preponderance of field system elements indicates the rural nature of much of the route, the many linear obstacles, including rivers, Roman and later roads, canals, and railways, demonstrate the importance of transport arteries crossing the area over many centuries. The NWEP project has contributed to our knowledge and understanding of the contrasting development of these landscapes.

LUAU routinely applies professional standards in accordance with the stated policy of English Heritage and the Code of Conduct of the Institute of Field Archaeologists. The aims of the NWEP project were to advise the developer on the best means of protecting archaeological features, to record all threatened sites and areas of archaeological interest, and to publish the results of the project. The primary objective was to seek to preserve archaeological remains *in situ*, and so excavation was considered an action of the last resort, when all protective strategies had been exhausted. Every effort was made to identify and record sites of archaeological importance prior to pipeline construction to avoid the necessity for detailed recording under difficult construction conditions, and to avoid costly delays to the construction timetable. A change in procedures was generated by the major policy revision expressed in the English Heritage publication, *The management of archaeological projects*. The fieldwork was conducted according to the provisions of the first edition of this manual (English Heritage 1989), while the revised methodology of reporting and archiving (English Heritage 1991) was followed in the post-excavation phase.

1

METHODOLOGY AND CHRONOLOGY OF THE STUDY

LUAU's involvement in the NWEP project began in July 1988, when the route design was still at the conceptual stage of development within a broadly defined corridor 2km wide. SCUK's approach to this major linear development was innovative in that considerable importance was attached to the archaeological landscape, within the context of an overall environmental assessment methodology. The NWEP became the first pipeline project in the UK to be subject to the new EC regulations regarding environmental impact assessments for large construction projects, and furthered SCUK's declared policy of caring for the environment (SCUK 1993b). In the first instance, the pipeline route was designed to avoid 'obviously unsuitable areas such as areas of high relief and urban conurbations' (SCUK 1989).

The archaeological studies were ultimately divided into four successive phases, with separately negotiated funding, over a period of six years. Phase I (1988–1990) was concerned with the identification of sites from existing records, aerial survey, and fieldwalking, and assessment of the appropriate archaeological response to the construction of the pipeline. Phase II (1990) comprised a selective programme of survey and trial excavation, and Phase III (1991) included additional fieldwork in previously inaccessible areas, more extensive excavation immediately prior to pipeline construction where no other mitigation measures were possible, and the archaeological watching brief carried out during construction (May–November 1991). The ensuing phase of post-excavation analysis (1992) was designed to process the accumulated data and artefacts, and finally texts were prepared for publication (1993–1994).

The phased programme of archaeological investigation progressed from the collation of previously recorded data on all known sites within a broad corridor, followed by reconnaissance in the field, to a selection of sites for further recording and investigation, within a much narrower corridor. Results were rapidly collated, analysed, and transmitted to SCUK, primarily as an aid to further planning and refinement of the route. About half the archaeological sites within the scope of the evaluation were identified and located by the desktop search, while the other half were identified by means of field survey, aerial photography, and the watching brief during construction.

Phase I

The archaeological assessment in the first instance addressed the identification of Scheduled Monuments (SM) and strategies for their management, and was completed in August 1988 (Williams 1988a). The 2km wide corridor was screened for all SMs, which are of national importance and afforded a measure of statutory protection. This first level of assessment was applied to a broad corridor within which the outline route could be modified, in respect of the specific monuments. Within the designated corridor, there were 32 scheduled sites, of which 28 were in Cumbria, three in Lancashire, and one in Cheshire. Eight of these were located on, or immediately adjacent to, the proposed centre-line.

Prehistoric monuments included three stone circles on Hardendale Fell, two round cairns on Windrigg Hill and at Seal Howe, a long barrow on Trainford Brow, and two Iron Age or Romano-British settlements near Brougham, all in Cumbria. An additional site of national importance, albeit lacking statutory protection, was a Bronze Age cairn at Manor Farm, near Borwick in North Lancashire. Scheduled sites of the Roman period included Hadrian's Wall and forts at Old Penrith, Brougham, and Low Borrowbridge, as well as a fortlet, six marching camps, and a Roman road, again all in Cumbria. Medieval sites included the gatehouse at Wetheral Priory, Norman motte and bailey earthworks at Tebay and Halton, and a deserted medieval village at Dalton near Burton-in-Kendal. Among the post-medieval sites were the Countess Pillar by the A66 road at Brougham, Wetheriggs

Pottery in the same area, Rufford Old Hall in South Lancashire, and Ince Manor house, the only SM potentially affected in Cheshire.

The provision of such a wide corridor of interest allowed for the elimination, by careful routeing, of the threat to identified sensitive sites, and in only one area other than Hadrian's Wall did it seem that a scheduled site might be unavoidable. In the environs of the Roman fort at Low Borrowbridge (**1137**), near Tebay, the route came extremely close to the southern boundary of the scheduled area, across a field likely to contain remains of the Roman extra-mural settlement (**1139**).

The archaeological constraints of the scheduled areas were considered by SCUK prior to extensive rerouteing. Once the corridor of interest had been narrowed to 500m, and subsequently to 400m, only four SMs were potentially affected. Two of these were Iron Age/Romano-British settlements, one on Lazonby Fell (**934**, Cu 194a), affected as a result of a reroute to avoid the Roman marching camps in the vicinity of Old Penrith, the other at Sceugh Farm, near Brougham (**998**, Cu 388). The remaining two were Hadrian's Wall (**825**, Cu 28 (16)), and the extramural settlement associated with the Roman fort at Low Borrowbridge (**1139**, **1137**, Cu 33). With the exception of the line of Hadrian's Wall, it eventually proved possible to avoid all the scheduled sites during pipeline construction.

Consideration was also given to the fact that associated features might survive outside the limits of the scheduled areas, as proved to be the case at Low Borrowbridge (*see Chapter 5*). The presence of SMs was regarded as a crude measure of the archaeological landscape values of the surrounding area, providing some general indication of the archaeological potential along the pipeline route and highlighting, at this early stage, the comparatively high density of sites in Cumbria. The relative importance of such areas, and the existence of additional archaeological sites, could only be established from a more detailed assessment of all known sites and monuments.

Record search

Once the constraints of the scheduled areas had been defined, it was necessary to consult the existing records of all other known sites, the majority of which have no statutory protection. The Sites and Monuments Records for the counties of Cumbria, Lancashire, Merseyside, Greater Manchester, and Cheshire were searched, and the advice of the five county archaeologists was sought. The Department of the Environment's Listed Building Schedules, available aerial photograph collections, and the North West Wetlands Survey archive were also consulted. A subsequent reroute meant that the county of Greater Manchester was only affected by a fringe of the broader corridor, and once the corridor was finally reduced to 40m, it became logical to exclude the county from further study.

From the existing records 240 known archaeological sites were identified within the 500m corridor specified by SCUK, ranging from individual chance findspots to complex field systems. The information relating to these sites was collated in a computer database, to which all subsequent textual data, from all sources, was added for the duration of the project. Many of these sites were avoidable by minor reroutes of the pipeline within the established corridor. Strategies for recording the sites remaining within the corridor were proposed, and emphasis was laid on the clear identification, at an early stage, of their nature and extent, in order to minimise the number of excavations required (Williams 1989).

In response to numerous environmental and archaeological constraints, the pipeline route was subject to extensive revision in 1989, involving a reappraisal of 63km of the corridor (Iles *et al* 1989). At the same time, the corridor was narrowed from 500m to 400m, the effects of which also entailed numerous adjustments to the gazetteer. The need for field reconnaissance was stressed, to define the extent of known sites on the ground, and to validate sites derived from aerial photographs or documentary evidence. The amount and type of detailed recording necessary could be rapidly assessed in the field, and it was also anticipated that fieldwalking would result in a substantial increase in the number of known archaeological sites.

The other non-destructive techniques proposed were aerial photography, of the entire pipeline route south of the Scottish border, and detailed topographical and geophysical survey of selected sites. The need for excavation was predicted at Hadrian's Wall, at Brougham (an area of exceptional archaeological potential), and in the Lune gorge near Tebay, where topographical constraints made it inevitable that important sites would be affected. The pipeline route would also cross several Roman roads, including the Stanegate south of Hadrian's Wall, and it was recommended that these should be located and examined in section by controlled excavation.

Rapid field scan

The rapid field scan, accompanied by outline topographical survey, was restricted to a 40m wide corridor, while record searches and aerial photography still covered the full 400m corridor width. The rapid field scan started in late January 1990, and, covered 210km in seven weeks, an average of 3km per team per day. All available areas of the pipeline corridor were examined, with the exception of certain heavily industrialised areas. Excluded areas, where access was denied until shortly before construction began, amounted to 32km of the pipeline route, and included known sites of archaeological significance on Lazonby Fell, Orton Low Moor, and Tebay Fell, all in Cumbria. The number of records in the gazetteer of sites was nearly doubled by the rapid field scan: 193 new sites were identified, of which 117 were in Cumbria, 63 in Lancashire, six in Merseyside, and seven in Cheshire (Lambert and Quartermaine 1990a, 1990b), a distribution reflecting that of the scheduled sites.

Aerial survey

Five flights for oblique aerial photography were made simultaneously with the rapid field scan in the spring of 1990, with three further flights that summer. The aerial photographer and navigator flew with a qualified pilot from the Blackpool Air Centre, in a Cessna 172 high-winged single-engined aircraft.

The aim of the aerial survey was to record and illustrate known sites of archaeological interest, and to locate new sites which were later subject to field validation. The pipeline route was flown in the spring, while vegetation cover was low, to record upstanding earthworks, and in summer to record buried archaeological features which might show as cropmarks caused by differential crop growth, or parchmarks in pasture. Relatively few cropmark sites were observed during the summer of 1990, which was not a particularly dry season in the North West.

Photographic coverage was extended by examination of recent photographs from the National Monuments Record, Sites and Monuments Records (SMR), Potato Marketing Board, and Bechtel's archive of 1:10,000 vertical aerial photographs. Computer plots to aid interpretation were produced using the Bradford Aerial Photograph Rectification Programme.

On completion of field and aerial survey, information from the survey record forms was synthesised with the existing records in the gazetteer, to describe each site from the documentary, field survey, and aerial perspectives. The extents of all known archaeological features within the 400m corridor were plotted onto 1:10,000 scale strip maps of the route. Revised 1:2500 scale alignment sheets were then annotated with scale drawings of the survey data and plots from aerial photographs, together with the locations of all sites previously recorded.

Hadrian's Wall

A strategy for crossing Hadrian's Wall (**825**, Cu 28 (16)) was the subject of a separately timetabled assessment from the earliest stage of the project (*see Chapter 4*). An accelerated programme of work began in the winter of 1988, to determine the optimum route through the designated area north-east of Carlisle.

Scheduled Monument Consent was obtained from the DOE for evaluation designed to locate the area of least survival of the various elements of the Hadrianic frontier, and a programme of further work was then formulated to investigate and record any surviving remains at the revised crossing point.

Previous excavation reports relating to the section of Hadrian's Wall between Tarraby and Walby indicated that the Wall, although in a ruinous state, survived in Brunstock Park but not in the fields to its east. Field reconnaissance confirmed that immediately east of Brunstock Park Hadrian's Wall was not visible above ground, and that arable farming and localised quarrying had destroyed most of its associated features (Williams 1988b).

By means of geophysical and contour survey, in May 1989, efforts were made to determine the actual line of the Wall, Wall-ditch, and *vallum*. The work included investigation of a hollow-way, which crossed the fields from east to west, approximately on the projected line of Hadrian's Wall. As this lane, unlike the adjacent fields, had not been levelled by ploughing, it was considered that it might preserve archaeological deposits relating to Hadrian's Wall. Geophysical survey confirmed that the locations of the Wall-ditch and *vallum*, as shown on the current 1:2500 scale map (OS 1973), were essentially correct (Williams and Howard 1989).

Trial excavation, in November 1989, demonstrated that no Roman stratigraphy or features survived in any of the trenches, which traversed the quarried area favoured for the crossing point (Gibbons and Olivier 1989). On the basis of these investigations, the pipeline route in this location was planned to coincide with an area frequently ploughed and subject to recent quarrying and landfill. Further Scheduled Monument Consent was obtained, to excavate along the proposed pipeline trench within the scheduled area.

This excavation, in April 1991, confirmed that most, but not all, of the area had been rendered archaeologically sterile by recent quarrying. Sealed archaeological deposits were present under the hollow-way, although their significance was unclear in the narrow trench, and the southern end of the trench lay outside the quarried area, revealing the *vallum*, in section, as a broad, deep ditch (Drury 1991) (*see Chapter 4*).

Recommendations

The combined results of the archive search, aerial survey, and rapid field scan provided an overview of the entire route, which in turn would allow a standard set of recommendations for the treatment of archaeological sites to be applied to each site identified as at risk (Lambert *et al* 1990a, 1990b). All sites were assessed for their archaeological value, and a strategy suggested, as appropriate, from a predetermined list of recommendations. Several of these strategies involved the protection of important sites, and included rerouteing the pipeline or narrowing the corridor, avoidance and fencing of discrete monuments, and reinstatement of earthworks following construction. Where avoidance was clearly not feasible, investigation and recording by means of geophysical or topographical survey and trial or full excavation were recommended. For many sites of limited archaeological significance the recommendation was for no further action. Finally, it was advised that a general watching brief should be held on the pipeline corridor throughout construction, and that this should be intensive in areas of known archaeological significance or previously established archaeological potential.

Phase II

The fieldwork campaign extended over two seasons, with topographical surveys, geophysical surveys, and trial excavations, as well as three additional flights for the aerial survey, in the summer of 1990. The second season, in the spring and summer of 1991, included two trial excavations and two area excavations. Several additional topographical surveys, and fieldwalking in areas where access was now permitted, completed the investigative programme prior to construction.

Topographical survey

The outline surveys completed in Phase I provided accurate locations for the sites recorded during the rapid field scan. More detailed survey was now required for earthwork sites that would be affected by pipeline construction. Twenty-four sites were recorded by detailed topographical survey, nineteen in July to September 1990 (Lambert 1990), four in January to March 1991, and one during construction, in August 1991 (Lambert 1991).

Of the surveyed sites, eighteen were in Cumbria, and six in Lancashire, but the scarcity of upstanding earthwork features in the two southern counties meant that no sites were surveyed in Merseyside or Cheshire. The distribution of the surveys reflects the survival of earthworks in the rural sector of the pipeline route, and particularly in the Cumbrian uplands, where there was widespread occurrence of features representing former settlements and field systems.

Surveys were conducted by means of a Zeiss Elta–4 total station and Husky Rec–500 datalogger, with respect to the PGM survey control installed by SCUK throughout the pipeline route, and tied into the National Grid. Computerised plots of the detailed topographical survey results were used to produce site drawings at a scale of 1:500. Each site was then redrawn at a reduced scale of 1:2500, to provide a set of acetate overlays for the alignment sheets at the same scale. The original plots and drawings are deposited with the project archive.

Geophysical survey

Sixteen sites were subjected to geophysical survey, three in Lancashire, the rest in Cumbria. The work was subcontracted to the University of Durham, and carried out in July and September 1990 (Howard 1990), with the exception of the survey of Hadrian's Wall, which took place in May 1989 (Williams and Howard 1989).

The resistivity surveys were carried out using a Geoscan RM4 resistivity meter and DL10 datalogger, employing the twin-electrode configuration. For the magnetic surveys a Geoscan FM18 fluxgate gradiometer was used. The results were processed on a portable IBM-compatible computer using Geoplot software supplied by Geoscan, to produce dot-density plots, and on a Sun workstation at Durham, where the UNIRAS graphical system was used to produce grey-scale shaded contours and three-dimensional plots.

The surveys were designed around a series of 20m squares, within which measurements were normally taken at the nodes of a grid of 1m. Where the suspected nature of the archaeological deposits warranted a closer scan, a grid of 0.50m was used, and the Roman cemetery at Brougham (**1004**) was covered by a 0.25m grid, as it seemed unlikely that a less intensive search would be productive. An exception to the usual grid layout was made for the Stanegate (**831**), where single long transects were used, in an attempt to locate the road, whose course was only projected in this area (Howard 1990).

Trial excavation

A series of fifteen trial excavations was carried out in August and September 1990, at eleven sites in Cumbria, and four in Lancashire (Buxton *et al* 1990). Trenches were excavated using JCB or CASE backactor mechanical excavators, fitted with toothless buckets varying from 0.70–1.55m in width, and the turf, topsoil, and subsoil were separated to ensure correct backfilling and returfing. Standard methods of recording included scaled section drawings, context records, and photography, and a Zeiss Elta–4 total station was used to locate the centreline of the pipeline route, and to survey the trenches and relevant topography.

There were two further trial excavations in April 1991, one in Cumbria, at Sceugh Farm (**998**), the other in North Lancashire, at Farleton (**12504**) (Lambert 1991). None of the sites south of the River Ribble, of those identified prior to construction, merited excavation. This reflects the higher rate of destruction of sites in the arable lowlands of West Lancashire, and the industrial areas of South Lancashire and North Cheshire.

The negative outcome of most of these excavations eliminated a number of archaeological hazards within the pipeline corridor. None of the sites with a negative archaeological result subsequently revealed features during construction, leading to the conclusion that the sites may not have survived below ground. As the overall aim of the project was to avoid archaeological sites rather than to confront them, this must be considered as a successful result of the careful planning.

At this stage, only three sites subject to trial trenching displayed potential for further investigation. At Fremington, near Brougham, a stone-lined circular pit and other features, in association with coarse pottery, were recorded in the trial trench sections (**1008**). In the Lune gorge, south of Tebay, a rectangular stone building was sectioned at Powsons, a hitherto unrecognised settlement site (**1132**). A short distance down the valley, the supposed site of a *vicus* associated with the Roman fort at Low Borrowbridge produced a small pit containing Roman pottery and iron nails (**1139**). There was a clear case for further excavation at these three

locations, which had the greatest archaeological potential of all the sites located during field evaluation prior to construction.

Palaeoenvironmental survey

From the early stages of the project, the importance of wetland sites in North West England had been stressed (Williams 1989). Wetland areas containing peat are known to be of considerable archaeological potential, as they were prime settlement locations in prehistoric times due to the coincidence of economic resources, including wildfowl, fish, and grazing for animals. The unique conditions found in wetland locations allow for the preservation of sites and artefacts, as well as plant microfossils and macrofossils.

The North West Wetlands Survey, sponsored by English Heritage, is based at LUAU, and was involved in consultation and practical intervention throughout the project. The wetlands were considered at all stages, and integrated in the programme of fieldwork. During the rapid field scan, in February and March 1990, two members of the North West Wetlands Survey were responsible for fieldwalking in the known wetland areas, and as a result, a closer assessment was made of the potential of wetlands likely to be affected by pipeline construction. The areas of concern known to contain deep, well-preserved, peat deposits, with a high potential for archaeological remains, were Cockerham, Winmarleigh, and Rawcliffe Mosses in the Fylde, and Croston, Hoscar, and Rainford Mosses south of the River Ribble (Lambert *et al* 1990b).

Several wetland sites were recorded during the rapid field scan in 1990, at Knells (**811**) and Drybeck Moss (**1183**) in Cumbria, and Hall Green (**1601**) and Marsh Moss (**1611**) in Lancashire. Palaeoenvironmental sampling, in the form of gouge auger transect coring of the peat, was carried out in October 1990 near Hall Green on Croston Moss (**1601**), where a sand island was located adjacent to deep peat deposits. During topsoil removal, near Nook Farm in the Fylde, a small hollow in the boulder clay containing immediately post-glacial peat to a depth of 5.8m (**1446**) was investigated by auger traverse.

None of these wetlands subsequently fulfilled their potential, at least within the limited areas affected by the pipeline. Despite the appointment of a wetlands specialist as line inspector for the southern section (Spread 4) which contained the majority of wetland areas, little evidence was gained, as the method of peat removal during construction was not conducive to palaeoenvironmental recording.

The main programme of exploratory fieldwork had been completed in Phase II, while certain mitigation measures were deferred until immediately prior to or, in the case of Roman roads at the Stanegate (**831**) and Sproatgill (**1091**), during construction. Whilst every effort had been made to identify and record sites in the earlier phases, it was recognised that inevitably some sites would only be revealed during the topsoil strip and pipeline trenching. Agreement was consequently reached with SCUK for a watching brief throughout the construction process.

Excavations at Fremington and Powsons

The late spring of 1991 was designated by SCUK for two of the area excavations where trial excavation the preceding summer had demonstrated the need for further work. These were both in Cumbria, at Fremington (**10014**), south-east of Penrith, and Powsons (**1132**), in the Lune gorge south of Tebay (Lambert 1991). Both excavations were unavoidably delayed until 7 May, a week after construction began, and there was therefore a timetable constraint to complete the archaeological work without any disruption to the construction schedule. In the event, the fencing and construction crews did not reach these sites until the excavations were complete.

Once the complex nature of the site at Fremington (**10014**) was revealed, the excavation was extended until 19 July, to allow full recording of this early medieval rural settlement with Anglo-Saxon attributes, of a form hitherto uninvestigated in the region (*see Chapter 6*). The features excavated at Powsons (**1132**), primarily a stone building belonging to a farmstead of late medieval to post-medieval date, proved to be less complex, and the excavation finished on schedule by 21 June (*see Chapter 7*).

Recording system

Adaptations of the recording system and Delilah database developed by the English Heritage Central Archaeology Service were used for the open area excavations at Fremington, Powsons, and Low Borrowbridge. Information from the trial excavations was incorporated in each case, and a single sequence of numbers was used for contexts (1–999), and another for finds (1000+). The records were input in the field on a Toshiba 8086 portable computer, and the supplementary paper record was later incorporated in the database. Exceptionally, under rescue conditions at Low Borrowbridge, where the time constraint did not allow for on-site data input, a paper record was kept and transferred to computer in the post-excavation phase. A Zeiss Elta–4 total station and Husky datalogger were used for three-dimensional recording of the finds, and the data was processed using ACAD Microsurveyor software and output to an A3 plotter. Turf and topsoil were stripped under archaeological supervision by JCB mechanical excavators, using toothless buckets, and the surfaces were cleaned manually to reveal features and finds.

The watching brief on construction

A watching brief was conducted over the full length of the pipeline route. For the duration of construction, 1 May to 1 November 1991, three members of LUAU staff were seconded to the SCUK project team as archaeological line inspectors. They covered Spread 3 (Penrith to Cockerham) and Spread 4 (Cockerham to Stanlow), while the line inspector for Spread 2 (Moffat to Penrith) was employed by the Centre for Field Archaeology at Edinburgh University (the consultant for the Scottish section of the NWEP) and likewise seconded to SCUK. Spread 2 extended 40km south of the Scottish border, to Penrith, and for consistency of recording and further analysis, the results of the watching brief were forwarded to LUAU, for processing and archiving with the other records from the English section.

The inspectors monitored work at previously identified sites, and noted how they were affected by pipeline construction, and the watching brief also contributed 65 new sites to the gazetteer. The inspectors recorded sites to a basic field survey level, referring those which warranted more detailed investigation to SCUK's pipeline archaeologist. A rapid response team was maintained on standby by LUAU, to excavate or survey at short notice, as deemed appropriate and whenever required by SCUK. On two occasions, when circumstances required rapid intervention for rescue excavations, at Low Borrowbridge and Sproatgill, the response team was expanded to include many other members of LUAU staff.

Excavations during construction

Of the nine excavations carried out by the rapid response team during pipeline construction, five were brief investigations, of one or two days' duration, of defined features revealed as a result of topsoil stripping (Lambert 1991).

The sites excavated included three ditches containing evidence of burning to the north-west of Scotby Shield farm (**853**); several features, probably representing traces of a small-scale industrial site, north of Oak Bank, near Aiketgate (**9202**); and a linear feature, probably a hedge line, at Watson's Wood, near Nateby (**1451**). A trench was excavated to record linear ditches and gullies in the vicinity of the fenceline between the two excavation areas at Fremington, and an isolated fire-blackened sandstone flag was recovered some 90m south of the same site (**10014**).

Three more excavations, each of approximately a week's duration, provided brief opportunities to investigate two Roman roads in Cumbria and an industrial site in Cheshire. The Stanegate, south of Hadrian's Wall, yielded structural evidence for the road linking the principal forts along the original Roman frontier and, on a later occasion, parallel ditches were recorded to either side of the road surface previously located (**831**). The main north-south Roman road, linking Manchester and Carlisle, was excavated at Sproatgill (**1091**), west of Orton. An industrial site in Cheshire, at Beckett's Wood, near Aston, proved to be a brick clamp kiln (**1957**), probably associated with the construction of canals or other industrial structures in the vicinity.

The Roman cemetery at Low Borrowbridge (**11318**), in the Lune gorge, was excavated in the first instance by the rapid response team, following its discovery during topsoil stripping. In the south-east corner of the field thought to contain the extramural settlement associated with the nearby Roman fort, the archaeological line inspector observed five discrete burnt areas, containing charcoal, Roman pottery, and metalwork. Topsoiling of the remainder of the area was monitored, and construction activity was suspended by SCUK later the same day. The response team was called out the following day to evaluate the site, and as the work progressed it rapidly became clear that the site was undoubtedly a Roman cemetery. Additional funding was provided by SCUK to continue the intensive rescue excavation, between the contractors' running track and the edge of the pipeline corridor, for seven weeks until 2 August (*see Chapter 5*).

Artefacts recovered during the watching brief

Christine Howard-Davis

At Old Grove, near Hadrian's Wall, a shallow pit was briefly investigated, and found to contain more than 50 fragments of handmade, decorated, ceramic vessels (**827**). These were later identified as Peterborough Ware, which is conventionally dated to the later third millennium BC, and is a ceramic tradition well known elsewhere in Britain, although an uncommon find in Cumbria. Isolated sherds, usually in poor condition, have, in recent years, been found at Brougham (Fell 1972), on Crosby Ravensworth Fell (Cherry and Cherry 1987), and at Shap (Ellwood pers comm), all areas in the vicinity of the pipeline route. Such a large quantity, however, was hitherto unknown from an inland site in the North West.

Small pits such as the one at Old Grove are thought to have been rubbish or storage pits, associated with domestic settlement sometimes located some distance away. Funerary and ritual monuments of Neolithic date are recorded from the Eden Valley, but domestic sites are virtually unknown, and thus the discovery of such a site is of regional significance. The pottery was in good condition, although examination of the edges suggests strongly that the vessels were broken and incomplete prior to deposition, presumably the reason why they were discarded. There were, however, enough fragments to suggest that at least three different vessels were represented. No other finds of Neolithic date were associated with the pottery.

Finds recovered from the watching brief were otherwise unexceptional, and largely fell into two clearly defined groups: struck flints, and post-medieval domestic ceramics; nonetheless, two fragments of medieval ceramic (**11317, 1151**) indicated activity of that period in the Lune gorge. Small fragments of post-medieval ceramic and glass domestic vessels and clay tobacco pipes often appear in appreciable numbers on agricultural land, and derive largely from the practice of nightsoiling, and the localised clearance of domestic middens.

Final phase

Following pipeline construction, assessments were made, in accordance with English Heritage management guidelines (English Heritage 1991), of the post-excavation requirements for analysis, and the appropriate level of publication.

Post-excavation analysis

Fieldwork was followed by processing the primary site records, plans, photographs, and finds, to provide a comprehensive archive of the sites investigated. Each site was then assessed to place it in its correct archaeological context, and to determine the level of analysis required.

At the conclusion of each excavation, finds and raw data were returned to LUAU for preliminary processing. Finds were washed, marked, and stored in archivally stable bags and boxes. To facilitate further analysis, context, object, plan, and photographic records were input to a Delilah database. Following initial post-excavation assessment, three sites were accorded further detailed analysis: the Roman cemetery at Low Borrowbridge (**11318**), the post-Roman settlement at Fremington (**10014**), and the rural farmstead at Powsons (**1132**).

Gazetteer of archaeological sites

From the inception of the project in 1988, a customised database held information on all sites within the pipeline corridor, in a readily accessible format. Southdata's Superfile software was run on IBM AT and Opus 286 computers, with the flexibility to assimilate and order data, initially from the record search, but eventually from many different sources. The product of this meticulous record-keeping was a gazetteer of sites, which went through four major revisions before final editing and selection produced a definitive record of all archaeological sites affected by the pipeline. This basic reference tool, in conjunction with the annotated 1:10,000 scale maps and 1:2500 scale plans, enabled SCUK to vary the route of the pipeline in full knowledge of the archaeological hazards, and to discuss the selection of sites meriting further fieldwork. The final version of the gazetteer contained 329 archaeological sites, and represents the sum of the knowledge gained of each site, from many sources, during the NWEP project.

The secondary purpose of the gazetteer was to enhance the county SMRs. At the outset records of known archaeological sites were obtained from the county SMRs and the updated information has now been deposited with them on completion of the project. A register of sites provides a one-line summary of the gazetteer (*see Appendix 1*), while the full gazetteer of sites can be found on microfiche (*see Appendix 2*).

Project archive

The project generated a considerable volume of data of many types. The results of the fieldwork and analysis have been synthesised to provide a detailed assessment of each site investigated (Lambert 1993). These results include the processed records of the rapid field scan, the watching brief, 24 detailed topographical surveys, 16 geophysical surveys, one palaeoenvironmental survey, and 28 excavations, of varying scale and extent. The archive also incorporates flight logs and photographic interpretations of the aerial survey, documentary and cartographic evidence, catalogued survey data, photographs, plans, finds records and illustrations, and specialists' reports.

The archive of original documentation and plans is deposited with the Cumbria Record Office (Kendal). Copies of this publication, including the microfiche section, are deposited with the National Archaeological Record, the Cumbria, Lancashire, Merseyside, and Cheshire County Record Offices, and the museums receiving the finds. The microfiche section contains the full gazetteer of sites, the finds catalogues for the Low Borrowbridge, Fremington, and Powsons excavations, and the bone tables for Low Borrowbridge and Fremington excavations. Artefacts are deposited, with the agreement of the landowners, with museums at Carlisle, Kendal, Lancaster, and Chester.

Health and safety

One of the project's finest achievements was an excellent safety record. Rigorous safety regulations were adhered to, in line with the most recent directives from the Health and Safety Executive, the manual produced by the Standing Conference of Archaeological Unit Managers (Allen and Holt 1986), which defines standards for safe archaeological practice, and SCUK's policy regarding safe working practices on the linear construction site. As a result of the importance accorded to personal responsibility for safety, only four minor accident reports were filed in the six-year life of the project.

2

ARCHAEOLOGY AND THE LANDSCAPE

The primary planning constraint of the pipeline route was the avoidance of urban areas and mountainous terrain (SCUK 1989, 3), and it therefore traversed a rural landscape in the north-western counties of England, skirting towns, villages, and the higher fells. The archaeological sites recorded reflect the characteristics of this landscape, and may be considered as broadly representing the types of feature associated with rural settlement and agriculture in the North West. In order to draw out the significance of these features, they are considered briefly here in their wider landscape context, geographically from north to south. This chapter provides a summary account of virtually all sites recorded within the pipeline corridor, and the basic information given here is supplemented by the full gazetteer entries on microfiche (*see Appendix 2*). In contrast, a more detailed interpretation of changing settlement patterns in the Lune gorge, selected for its high concentration of archaeological sites, is presented in Chapter 3.

This overview is important because the area investigated is a very narrow strip through the landscape of North West England, nearly all the sites referred to falling at least partly within a corridor only 40m wide. During construction, normally only a 20m width was actually topsoiled and excavated for the contractors' vehicle running track and the pipeline trench, although this was exceeded in places, as at Low Borrowbridge (**11318**), and reduced elsewhere, as at Hadrian's Wall (**825**). Many of the recorded features were elements of larger sites, especially former field systems, which in their entirety extended far beyond the corridor. Many more sites, not described here, lay within the 400m wide corridor originally assessed, but just outside the final corridor, and these were considered at an early stage of the study.

The uneven distribution of sites is clearly demonstrated by the accurately plotted locations of all archaeological sites recorded within the 40m corridor (Figs 2:1, 2:6, 2:11, 2:17, 2:23, 2:30, 2:34, 2:37, 2:38, 2:39).

The distance covered by the pipeline route, from the Scottish border at the River Sark, north of Longtown in Cumbria, to the Stanlow refineries east of Ellesmere Port in Cheshire, is approximately 253km. South of the border, it crossed the Solway Plain and traversed the Cumbrian uplands between the Lake District and the Pennines. From north of Carlisle down to Lancaster, the pipeline was routed through a pastoral farming landscape, roughly parallel to and east of the M6 motorway, which was crossed at Galgate. The route continued at some distance to the west of the M6 through the arable farmland and former wetlands of the Lancashire Fylde, before turning east again to avoid the urban and industrial conglomerations of West Lancashire and Merseyside. Finally, after crossing the River Mersey, it turned to the west on the approach to Stanlow, in North Cheshire.

It was anticipated that the great contrasts in landuse, between the rural uplands in the north and the industrial lowlands of the south, would have influenced the nature of the archaeological remains, and that their survival would also be in proportion to the amount of post-medieval activity. This contrast between the northern uplands, where many earthwork sites were recorded, and the southern lowlands, where such sites were comparatively scarce, probably bears little relation to the distribution of settlement in prehistoric, Roman, or medieval times, but is a direct consequence of post-medieval events which have had a devastating effect on the landscape. These were the Parliamentary Enclosures of the eighteenth and early nineteenth centuries, contemporary with the Industrial Revolution and accompanying developments in transport and communications, and the later nineteenth and twentieth century expansion in population leading to urban sprawl and conurbations in the industrial areas. The combined destructive effects of these processes on the landscape have obliterated many of the earlier field systems, and subsequent intensive ploughing of surviving fields has reduced earthworks to insubstantial cropmarks, which on investigation appear in many instances to have no subsoil existence at all.

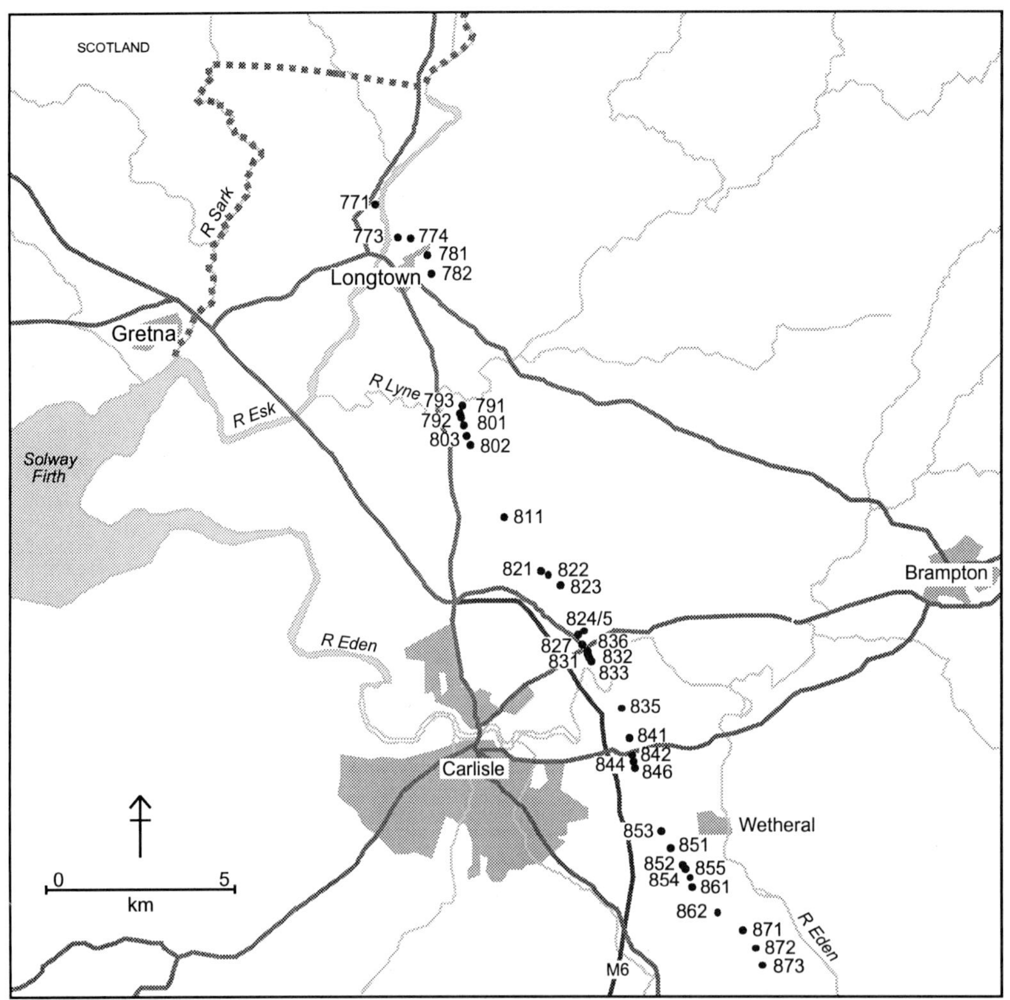

*Figure 2:1 NWEP sites in the Carlisle area (**771–873**)*

Cumbria

Solway

The Carlisle Basin is a relatively level expanse of
Carboniferous sediments, including limestones,
sandstones, and shales. The area (Fig 2:1), from the
River Sark at the Scottish border to the River Lyne
at Barrockstown, is mainly pastoral farmland, with
some arable, deciduous woodland, and peat moss
under commercial exploitation. A single prehistoric
flint waste flake was found north-west of Barrockstown (**792**). Elements of former field systems were
recorded in this area (**774, 782, 802**), including widespread expanses of ridge and furrow of medieval
or post-medieval date (**773, 791, 801**), generally associated with headlands and field boundaries. Post-
medieval pottery scatters, probably the result of
manuring, were found at several locations during
fieldwalking, and subsequently during construction
(**781, 793, 803**), at which time the embankment of

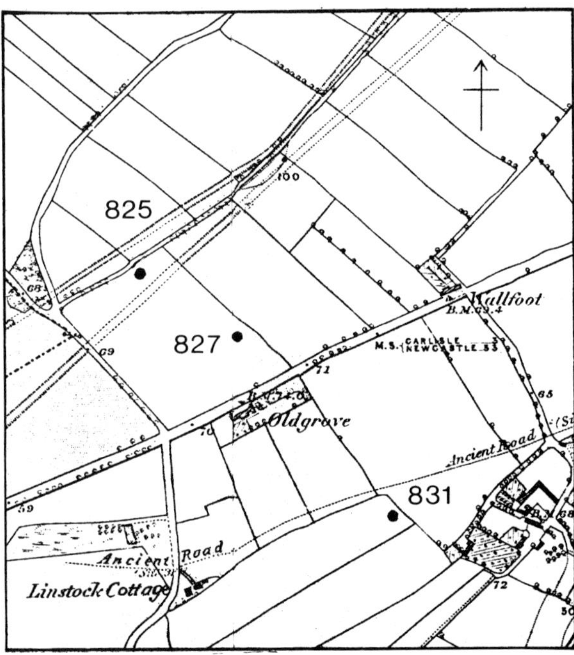

*Figure 2:2 Hadrian's Wall (**825**), Old Grove (**827**),
Stanegate (**831**), OS 1st edn 6″ map extract (1865–6)*

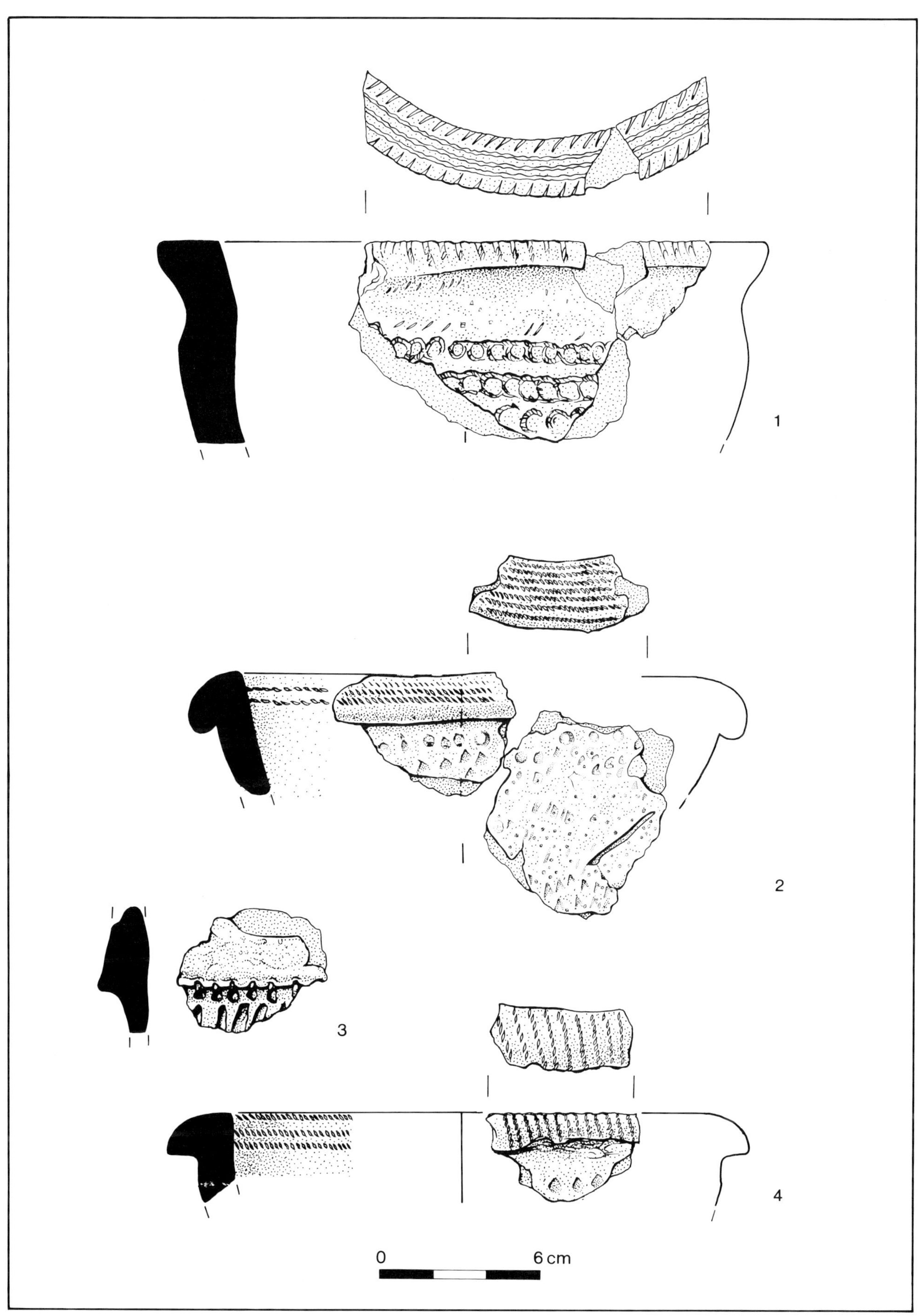

*Figure 2:3 Old Grove (**827**), Neolithic pottery*

11

the disused North British Railway from Hawick to Carlisle was sectioned near Longtown (**771**).

Carlisle

North-east of Carlisle, the area bounded to the south by the River Eden is mainly grassland, with an area of waterlogged pasture containing some peat at Knells (**811**), and some cereal cultivation around the Hadrian's Wall complex east of Brunstock Park. North of Hadrian's Wall (**825**) the only sites recorded were field boundaries (**821, 823**) and one instance of medieval ridge and furrow (**822**), while near Old Grove, in the field immediately south of the Wall a significant assemblage of Neolithic pottery was recovered during construction (**827**). At Park Broom the main focus of interest was the projected alignment of the Stanegate (**831**), the Roman road between Carlisle and Corbridge, and other sites included medieval ridge and furrow (**833**), a ditch of recent origin (**836**), and a field boundary (**832**).

Hadrian's Wall

There are no upstanding remains of Hadrian's Wall (**825**, Fig 2:2) in the level ploughed fields east of Brunstock Park, where a hollow-way of some antiquity crosses the ploughland on the approximate line of the Wall, as shown on the OS 1:2500 scale plan (OS 1973). The loose red sandy soils here have been quarried and are currently under arable tillage. Survey and excavation revealed no surviving trace of the Wall footings, although the *vallum* which runs parallel to the Wall was recorded in a section of the pipeline trench (*see Chapter 4*).

Old Grove

A shallow pit containing a quantity of sherds of Peterborough Ware (**827**, Fig 2:3) was observed during the topsoil strip in a field at Old Grove (Fig 2:2), south of Hadrian's Wall, and less than 1km north of the River Eden. The proximity to the river and other recently discovered sites, in conjunction with the presence of the pottery here, is a likely indicator of Neolithic activity in the vicinity.

Stanegate

South of Hadrian's Wall, the pipeline also crossed the Stanegate (**831**, Fig 2:2), the Roman road which marked the earlier frontier, and continued to provide an important supply route for the garrisons stationed on the Wall. The intersection of the pipeline with the projected line of the Stanegate was 350m north of Linstock Castle, and 200m west of Park Broom Farm. Despite attempts to locate the Roman road during fieldwalking and by geophysi-

*Figure 2:4 The Stanegate intersection (**831**), cobbled surface*

cal survey, the first indication of its survival was revealed during the topsoil strip preceding pipeline construction in July 1991. A cobbled surface (Fig 2:4) was briefly excavated and, subsequently, two ditches exposed by the pipeline trench on either side of this surface were recorded in section.

A scatter of pebbles revealed the location of a road surface on an east-west alignment, only 0.30m beneath the present turf level. A very broad stony surface was exposed under the topsoil and a silt layer, apparently orientated east-west. The depth of the make-up varied between 0.17m, where up to four layers of cobbles were distinguished, and 0.07m, where the surface comprised a single uniform layer. The cobbles, of similar size throughout the layers recorded, did not appear to have been carefully laid, but to have been deposited and roughly spread out. The original road surface, which had not survived, may have been composed of smaller pebbles or gravel. There was no indication either of the use of kerbstones, or of larger broken stones forming a road foundation. Two ditches were subsequently exposed in section during excavation of the pipeline trench in September 1991, running parallel to the cobbled surface. A shallow ditch (0.70m wide, and 0.20m deep) was aligned 2m to the north of the road, and a more substantial ditch (2.70m wide and 0.90m deep) was aligned 4m to the south of the road.

The surface was almost double the width, at 16.40m, of other sections of the Stanegate previously excavated. Within the limits of the narrow 1m strip excavated across the road surface, it was not possible, however, to determine whether there was any variation in width. Near Gilsland the road had previously been found to be 3.65–4.88m wide (Haverfield 1899), at Haltwhistle Burn 5m wide (Margary 1957), and west of Over Denton 7–8m wide (Richardson 1976).

Wetheral and Cumwhinton

There was no sign of remains associated with the Bronze Age cemetery discovered near Aglionby in the 1920s (Cumbria SMR 483), and a single flint dressing chip (**841**), recovered during fieldwalking, was the only indicator of prehistoric activity in the vicinity. Two further flint waste flakes were collected during pipeline construction some distance further south at Wetheral Shield (**862**) and near Cotehill (**873**).

South of the River Eden, dairy and stock farming in the open valley landscape are ubiquitous. Around Cumwhinton, the extensive medieval strip field system survives in the form of small linear fields, with many hedgerow trees (Fig 2:5). A trackway running along a former lynchet (**844**) was removed by construction west of Aglionby, and a field boundary was noted during fieldwalking at Scotby Shield (**851**). Geophysical survey found no trace of the medieval chapel between Wetheral and Cumwhinton (**852**). The only other artefacts found in the area were a nineteenth century lead seal (**842**) and domestic glass and pottery (**846**).

During construction, several stone hearths (**854, 855**) and charcoal spreads resulting from fire (**861, 871, 872**) were found to the east and south-east of Cumwhinton, and on pastureland 200m north-west of Scotby Shield Farm, three ditches (**853**) were cut by the pipeline trench, and were briefly examined in September 1991. The ditches had been backfilled with charcoal and other burnt material, but no dating evidence was recovered. This cluster of fire-associated sites may be of significance in the history of the area, but as there were no surface remains to indicate their presence, their late discovery during construction precluded any extensive investigation.

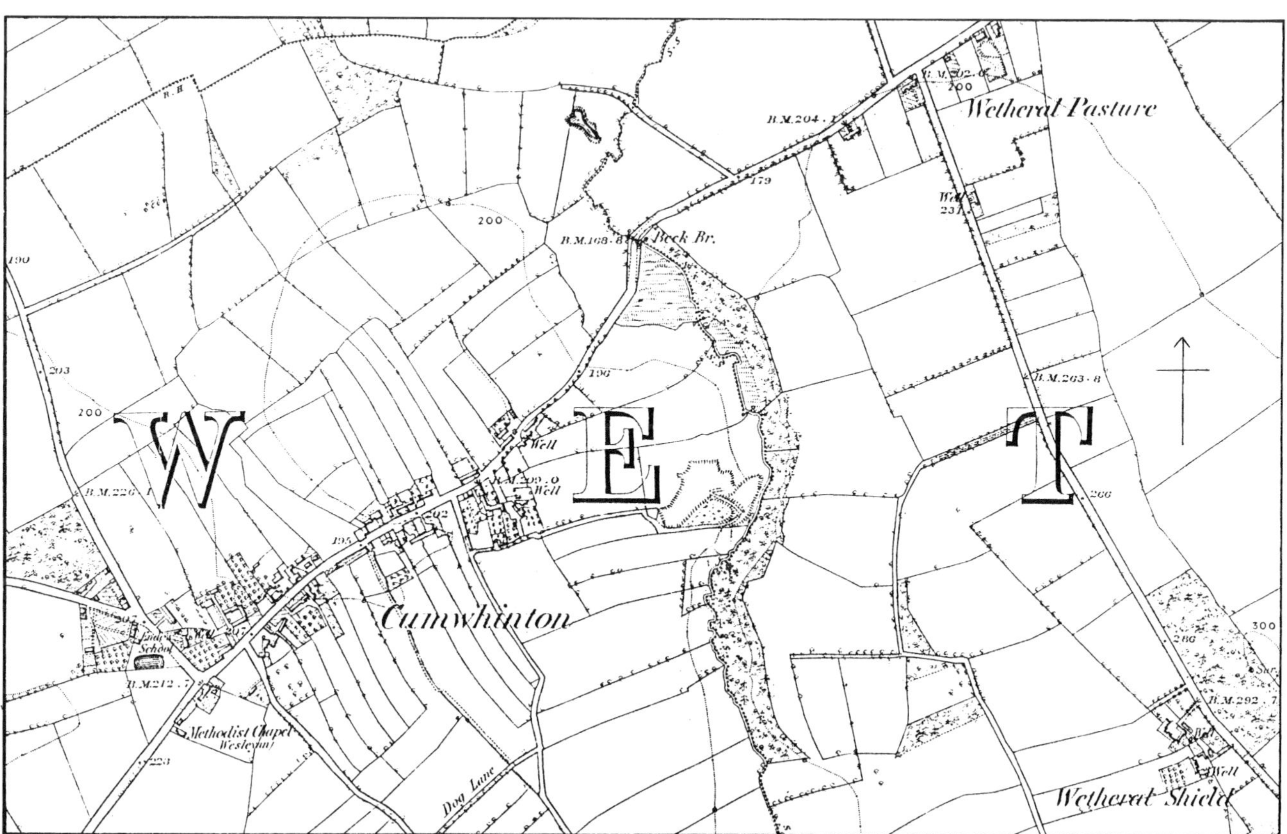

Figure 2:5 Cumwhinton field system, OS 1st edn 6" map extract (1868)

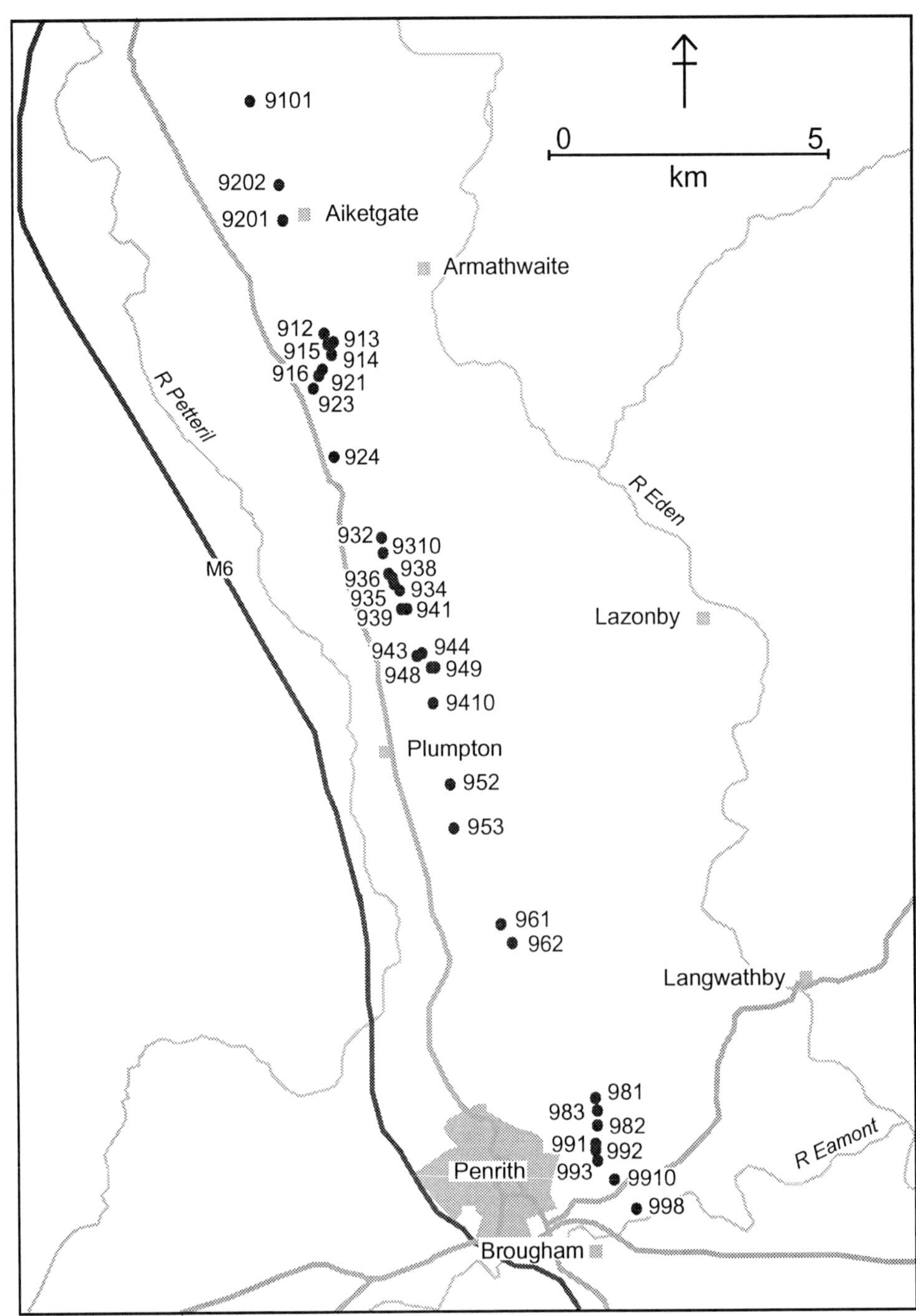

*Figure 2:6 NWEP sites from Carlisle to Penrith (**9101–998**)*

Aiketgate

A post-Enclosure landscape of large squarish fields, under cereal and silage crops, extends over Barrock Fell and Blaze Fell, but around Aiketgate the medieval strip field system survives, defined by hedged field boundaries. The pipeline route cut through many of these small linear fields, but only in one was broad medieval ridge and furrow noted (**9201**).

On level ground, to the north of the slope rising from Oak Bank, two pits containing undated vitrified industrial residues (**9202**) were investigated during construction in August 1991. The summit of the prominent hill immediately east of Aiketgate is the site of Castle Hewen (NY 48544627), a medieval stronghold associated with the legendary giant king, Ewain Caesarius (Parker 1909, 34). Excavations revealed the remains of a settlement of two hut circles with palisade walls, and rectangular buildings with a stock enclosure (Cumbria SMR 709). Later structures, thought to be the foundation walls of the castle, faced with large ashlar stones and 2.5m thick, were described in 1794 (Hutchinson 1794,

14

492), but had completely vanished a century later (Graham 1909, 211).

Tarn Wadling

South of Castle Hewen is the site of Tarn Wadling (**912**, Fig 2:7), now a shallow depression 0.5km across, but formerly a lake scooped from the boulder clay by glacial action (Walker 1964, 232). The tarn is likely to have been a focus of prehistoric settlement, and was certainly a significant reference point in the landscape by the medieval period. In 1088 William Rufus granted to the prioress and nuns of Armathwaite 217 acres of land at Nunclose, on the northern shore of Tarn Wadling (Nicolson and Burn 1777, 2, 343), and it appears also to have been a meeting place of the Inglewood Forest Court (Cumbria SMR 6513).

The pipeline cut through the bed of the former tarn, once 100 acres in extent (Hutchinson 1794, 491) and noted for its 'very fine carp' (Jefferson 1840, 218). The tarn was drained from the late eighteenth century onwards, but not entirely successfully until the Second World War (Walker 1964, 232). Trial excavation in 1990 revealed deposits indicating the shallow silted edge of the former tarn, but was otherwise unproductive. On the shoreline of the tarn was a building said to have been a boathouse, but named on the OS 1st edn 6" map (OS 1868, Fig 2:8) as Tarnwadling Cottage (**914**), with a smaller, unnamed, building to the north, now a complete ruin (**913**). During construction a scatter of post-medieval pottery and glass (**915**) was located adjacent to these buildings.

A charcoal spread was also recorded nearby, at the foot of Blaze Fell (**916**), within 100m of the findspot of a prehistoric flint waste flake (**921**) collected during fieldwalking. Cropmarks previously recorded on the western flank of Blaze Fell (**923**, **924**) were not visible at any time during fieldwork.

Lazonby Fell

The line of the A6 road north of Penrith coincides with the main Roman north-south route, and along this straight stretch are traces of marching camps and settlements, as well as the Roman fort at Old Penrith (*Voreda*), near Plumpton. The probable presence of further unknown Roman sites in the area, as well as the likely extent of the known sites beyond their scheduled areas, implied that unless the pipeline route was radically changed the high archaeological potential of the area would dictate a need for considerable amounts of detailed evaluation and investigation. A reroute was strongly recommended to avoid the five SMs which would have been

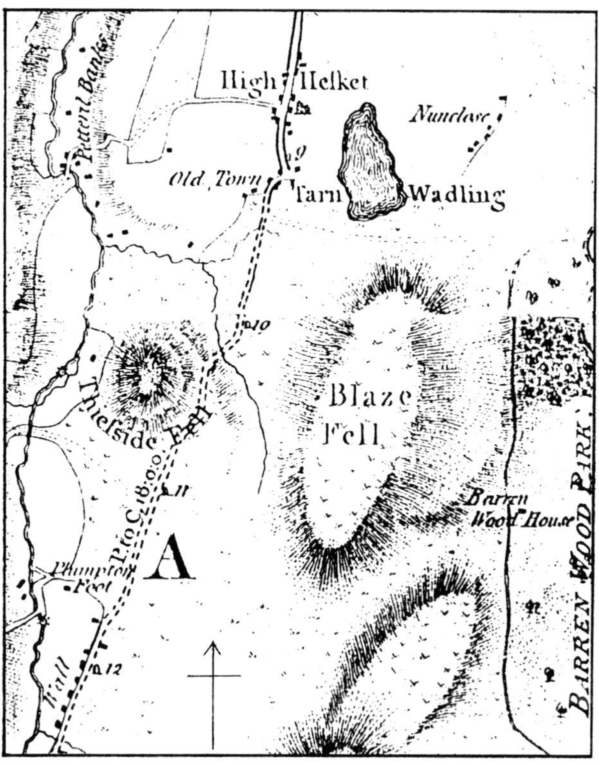

*Figure 2:7 Tarn Wadling (**912**), Hodskinson and Donald's map of Cumberland, 2nd edn (**1802**)*

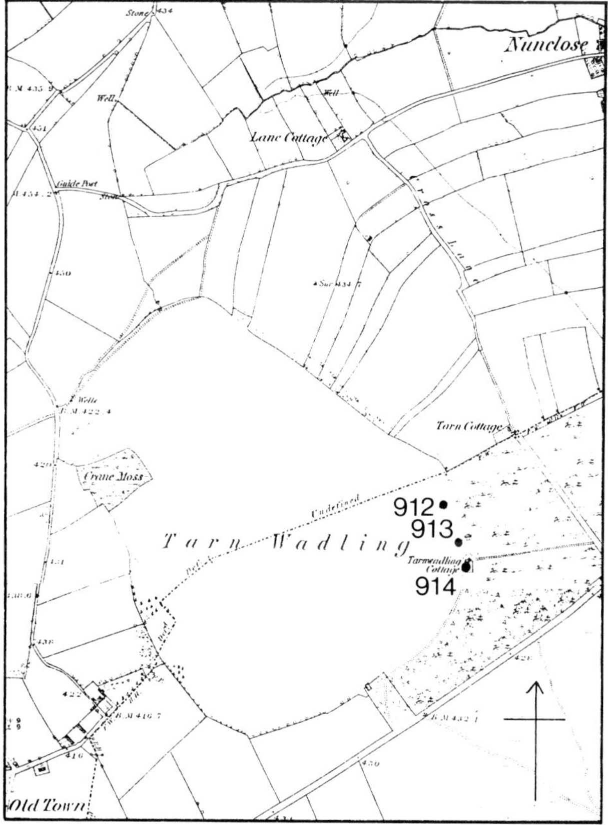

*Figure 2:8 Tarn Wadling (**912**), OS 1st edn 6" (1868)*

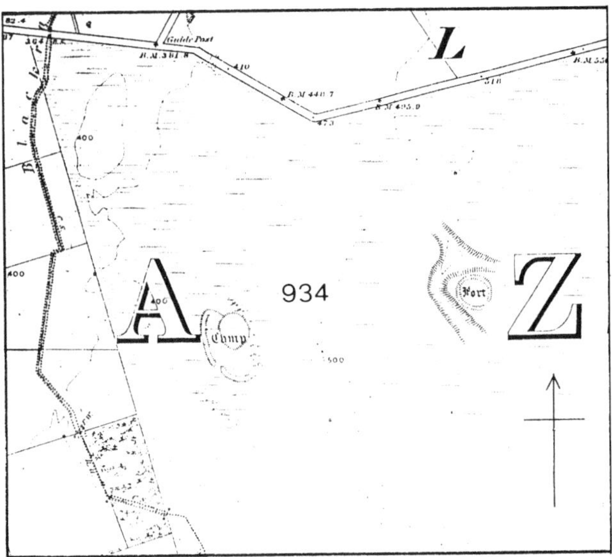

*Figure 2:9 Lazonby Fell settlement (**934**), OS 1st edn 6" (1868)*

directly affected, and the pipeline was subsequently diverted east over Lazonby Fell, avoiding the Roman camps. Ironically, this diversion affected sites of an earlier period on Lazonby Fell, notably a scheduled Iron Age settlement (**934**, SM Cu 194a, Fig 2:9), and its associated boundary features.

Lazonby Fell is formed of Penrith Sandstone, which is at present quarried for sand east of Pears Gill (NY 49984032), although there are many disused flagstone quarries on the fell. Part of the fell is a Site of Special Scientific Interest, in recognition of the rich variety of species supported by the mature heath overlying the sandstone, and the pipeline route crossed the most sensitive areas utilising wherever possible the line of an existing trackway.

Much of the fell is unploughed heathland, and this management has allowed many prehistoric earthworks and artefacts to survive in good condition. In the eighteenth and nineteenth centuries, antiquarians identified grooved or sculptured stones (**935**, **936**) and a cairnfield with burial urns (**941**), as well as collecting a stone axe (**943**) and flint arrowheads (**944**; Cumbria SMR 940, 941) from the fell. This cluster of prehistoric sites and findspots, some of which lay within the pipeline corridor, represents the highest concentration of known prehistoric sites along the English section of the route.

Other sites located during fieldwork include elements of a field system, to the north, south, and west of the Iron Age settlement (**934**). A glacial esker, with a trackway running the length of its narrow summit, appeared to form the settlement's natural northern boundary, although later ridge and furrow was visible to either side (**938**). A circular cairn, possibly of prehistoric origin (**9310**), was situated on a small rise to the north-west, and other cairns were noted in the vicinity (**949**).

The upstanding remains of the Lazonby Fell settlement (**934**, Fig 2:10) comprised the footings of a stone-walled enclosure and large hut, with associated field boundaries. The site was immediately bounded by a small marsh to the north, east, and south, and its position and nature are suggestive of a late prehistoric defended farm. Topographical survey of the area before excavation revealed a series of previously unrecorded platforms and trackways outside the scheduled area. The major features surveyed consisted of a discontinuous curvilinear bank and ditch with an external counter bank to the south and east.

A minor reroute avoided the scheduled area, as did the trial trenching in September 1990. The only features of any archaeological significance noted during the excavation were two pits or hollows, both of which were cut from below the subsoil, approximately 1.20m in diameter, and filled with a dark, burnt orange sand containing many small pebbles. The pits did not contain identifiable material, and

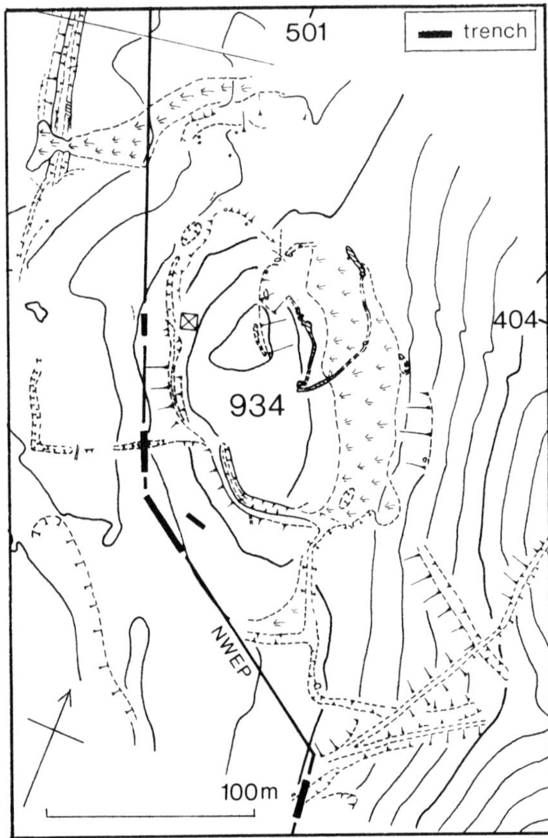

*Figure 2:10 Lazonby Fell settlement (**934**), surveyed features and trench locations*

appeared to have silted up naturally. During construction, the working width was restricted in the vicinity of the scheduled area, and the running track for vehicles was located to the west of the pipeline trench, to avoid outlying features of the settlement.

A double linear bank (**939**), similar in form to other banks associated with the settlement, ran in a south-easterly direction 250m to the south, continuing beyond the field wall which divides the open moorland to the south from the improved pasture to the north. This was surveyed before its removal during construction.

Three deeply incised parallel trackways (**948**) ascended the western slope of Lazonby Fell, broadly following the line of a track shown on the OS 1st edn 6″ map (OS 1868). The sections of these trackways which lay within the fenced pipeline corridor were surveyed during construction. These multiple hollow-ways were probably variants of the route which climbs the slope from the general direction of the Roman fort at Old Penrith towards the quarries above Scratchmill Scar. The pipeline route left the open heath, descending the slope to avoid Scratchmill Scar, and entered a post-Enclosure landscape of regular walled fields. These are in striking contrast to a sinuous, turf-covered, stony bank and ditch (**9410**) located in the valley bottom at Scarfoot, which separated an area of low-lying bog from rising ground to the east.

A bank and ditch (**952**) of quite different character were recorded south of the Plumpton to Lazonby road (B6413) at West Brownrigg and, on the western flank of Wan Fell, a complex of trackways (**953**) crossed the open moorland towards the east, perhaps marking an earlier route to Lazonby. The only other features in this section of the route were faint ridge and furrow in the fields east of Bowscar (**961**, **962**). South of Bowscar the route descended gradually towards the River Eamont, and the few disparate sites recorded from the area east of Beacon Hill near Penrith were a charcoal spread (**983**), a sheep-wash (**982**), a terraced trackway (**992**), and a lynchet (**993**).

Brougham

The Eamont Valley has been a favoured location for settlement since prehistoric times, forming an east-west corridor in the short course of the River Eamont from the foot of Ullswater to the River Eden. It has long been an important junction between the main north-south road from Carlisle (A6) and the road along the Eden Valley (A66). The latter connected the Roman forts at Brougham and Brough, and the later Norman castles, before crossing the

north Pennine hills by the Stainmore pass. At this important crossroads, a fort was established by the Romans at Brougham, and the Roman cemetery (**1004**; SM Cu 154) has been located to the east of the fort, although to date there is no firm evidence for any associated nuclear settlement. A concentration of fairly small native farmsteads in the valley, including the settlement at Sceugh Farm (**998**), has been interpreted as a dispersed civilian settlement associated with the Roman fort (Higham and Jones 1975).

Sceugh Farm

A scheduled Iron Age or Romano-British settlement (**998**; SM Cu 388) is located in the field immediately east of the Sceugh Farm buildings. It consists of a series of ditches, stone banks, and enclosures on the raised, relatively level ground, above a steep scarp slope overlooking the River Eamont to the south. Although the pipeline avoided the settlement nucleus, peripheral elements of the field system, and possible trackways visible on aerial photographs, lay within the corridor. A complex of enclosures and banks was recorded by topographical survey, and the outlying features were plotted from aerial photographs (Fig 2:12).

Trial excavation, in April 1991, investigated two possible trackways, shown as cropmarks on aerial photographs, and a field boundary. Other than a steeply sloping horizon suggestive of terracing, there was no evidence to confirm the presence of trackways, such as metalling or wheel ruts. The profile of the upstanding field boundary was not reflected in any variation to the underlying natural strata and, indeed, it was commonly found during the course of work on the pipeline that the insubstantial earthworks and cropmarks encountered in upland areas were not visible in the subsoil. Opposite Sceugh Farm, on the floodplain south of the River Eamont, a faint linear bank and ditches (**999**) were investigated by geophysical survey and trial excavation in August 1990 but, as with the previous site (**998**), these did not survive in section as identifiable stratigraphic units.

The survival of a combination of fort, cemetery, settlement sites, and field systems in the Brougham area is unusual for the North West. The density of sites in the vicinity of the Roman fort and civil settlement was such that not every site could be avoided, although the pipeline was rerouted to the east of the area in order to skirt the eastern edge of the Roman cemetery (**1004**). The latter had been subject to disturbance during the A66 road improvements in the late 1960s, when over 200 burials and many artefacts were recovered during the excavation

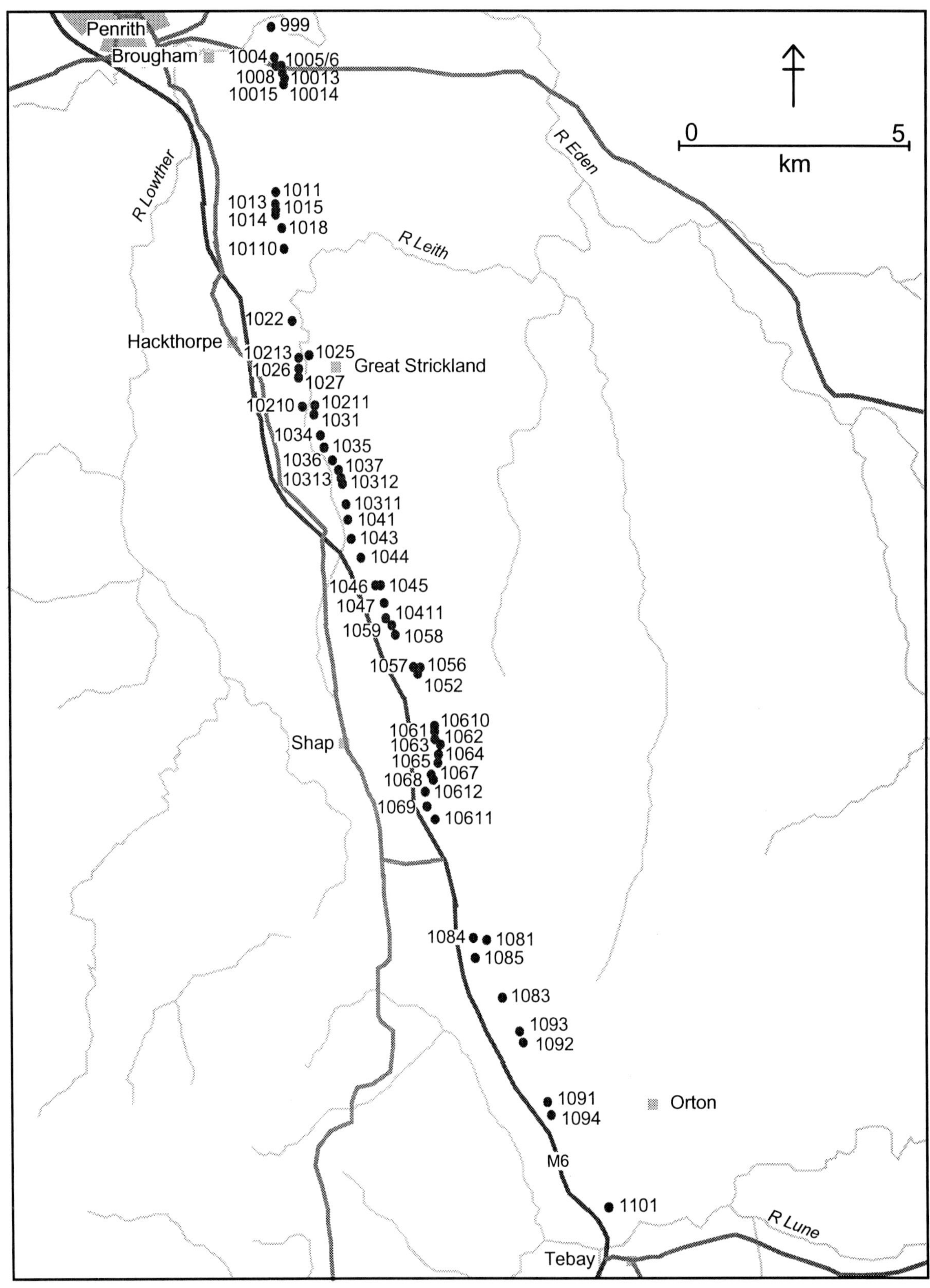

*Figure 2:11 NWEP sites from Penrith to Tebay (**999–1101**)*

18

preceding the roadworks (Ministry of Public Buildings and Works 1967, 12; 1968, 17). Neither geophysical survey nor trial excavation in 1990 revealed archaeological features along the revised route. There was no indication of the cemetery during topsoil removal, and it may be assumed that it did not extend this far eastwards.

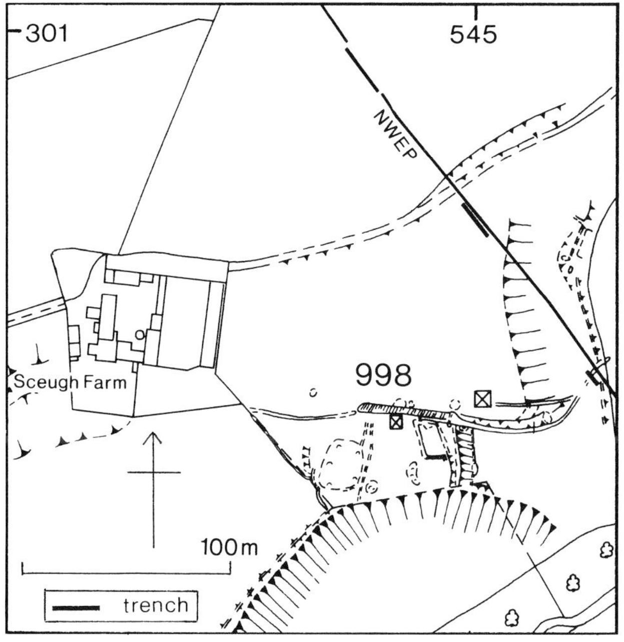

*Figure 2:12 Sceugh Farm (**998**), surveyed features*

A railed enclosure on the verge of the A66 road near Brougham contains the Countess Pillar, another scheduled site (**1005, 1006**; SM Cu 410) which was carefully avoided by the pipeline route. The octagonal stone pillar is surmounted by a square block, painted with coats of arms and sundials, and was erected to commemorate the last parting, in 1656, of Lady Anne Clifford and her mother. Nearby, a post-medieval pottery scatter was located during construction (**10013**).

Fremington

Prehistoric funerary monuments also cluster in the Brougham area, the closest known site to the pipeline route being a stone cist (**1008**; Cumbria SMR 2865) discovered in the nineteenth century, which contained a contracted skeleton together with a beaker and food vessel. The supposed location of the cist was near the top of a low hill north-east of Fremington Farm, less than 1km from the Roman fort at Brougham (Fig 2:13). Trial excavation here in September 1990 revealed a pit containing fragments of very coarse pottery, and a small quantity of Roman pottery was also found nearby. These finds suggested possible prehistoric and Roman activity in the area, and prompted further excavation from May to July 1991 (**10014**) (*see Chapter 6*).

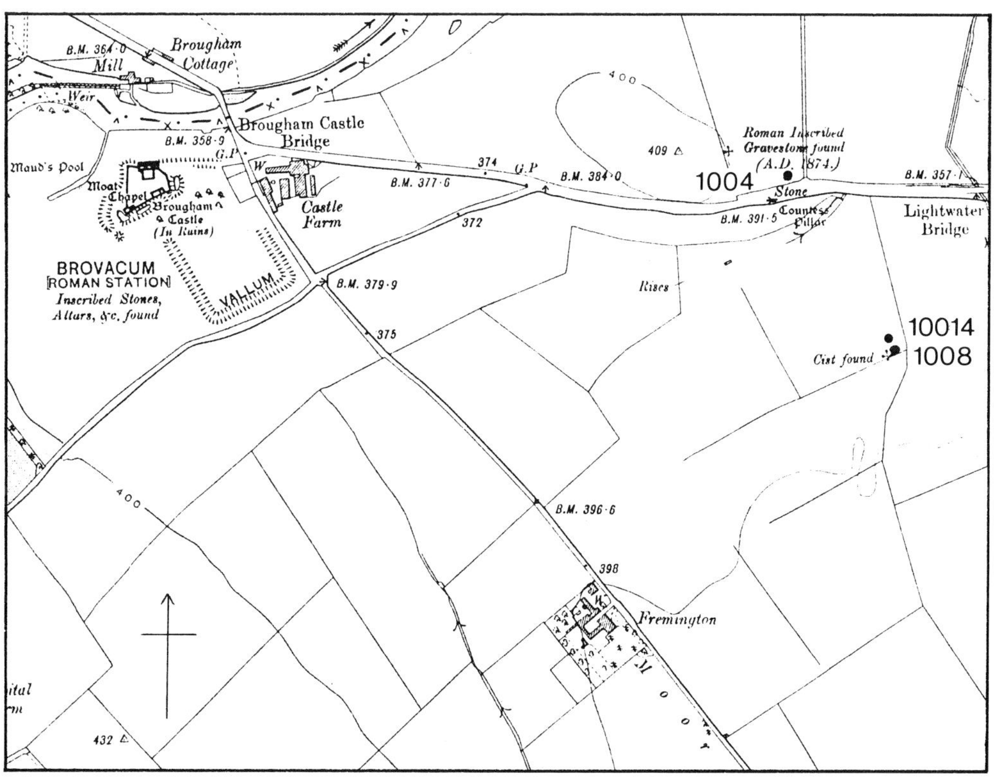

*Figure 2:13 Brougham (**1004**, **1008**, **10014**), OS rev edn 6″ (1920)*

Traces of a settlement (**10014**) were first seen as dark patches of soil filling several large sub-rectangular features measuring 5 x 4m, cut into the sand and gravel subsoil. These were identified as sunken-featured buildings, which seemed to have been in use over a long period, as all showed signs of refurbishment. A post-built timber structure containing a sandstone hearth was associated with the sunken buildings. Close by was a shallow pit lined with fire-cracked stones, apparently protected by some sort of superstructure or windbreak. In and around the pit was a large quantity of hand-made pottery characterised by extreme coarseness and heavy grit tempering (Figs 6:16, 6:17). Finds associated with this settlement date mainly to the seventh and eighth centuries AD, and indicate that it is probably associated with the expansion of Northumbrian control into Cumbria at this time. Many small fragments of Roman material, all dating to the second and third centuries AD, were also found, reflecting the existence of earlier Roman settlements in the area, and perhaps also the later collection of Roman goods by the people of this settlement. The small number of coins and metal artefacts may suggest that Roman artefacts were acquired as heirlooms. The settlement was largely domestic in character, with evidence of small-scale blacksmithing scattered across the site. Textile manufacture was indicated by a quantity of spindle whorls and loomweights, some of which were made of reused Roman pottery, and others of stone (Figs 6:18–6:21, 6:26). Traces of grain and legumes were recovered from the site, as was a fragment of a rotary quern (Fig 6:27).

During pipeline construction a possible hearth, consisting of a blackened flagstone, charcoal, and other burnt debris (**10015**), was found slightly to the south of the excavated site (**10014**) and, if broadly contemporary, may represent a shift in the location of the settlement. The Fremington settlement was not excavated in its entirety, and the area lying beyond the pipeline corridor may survive beneath the ploughsoil. The site appears to reflect an integration of Anglian settlement with a community which had occupied the area continuously since the Roman period.

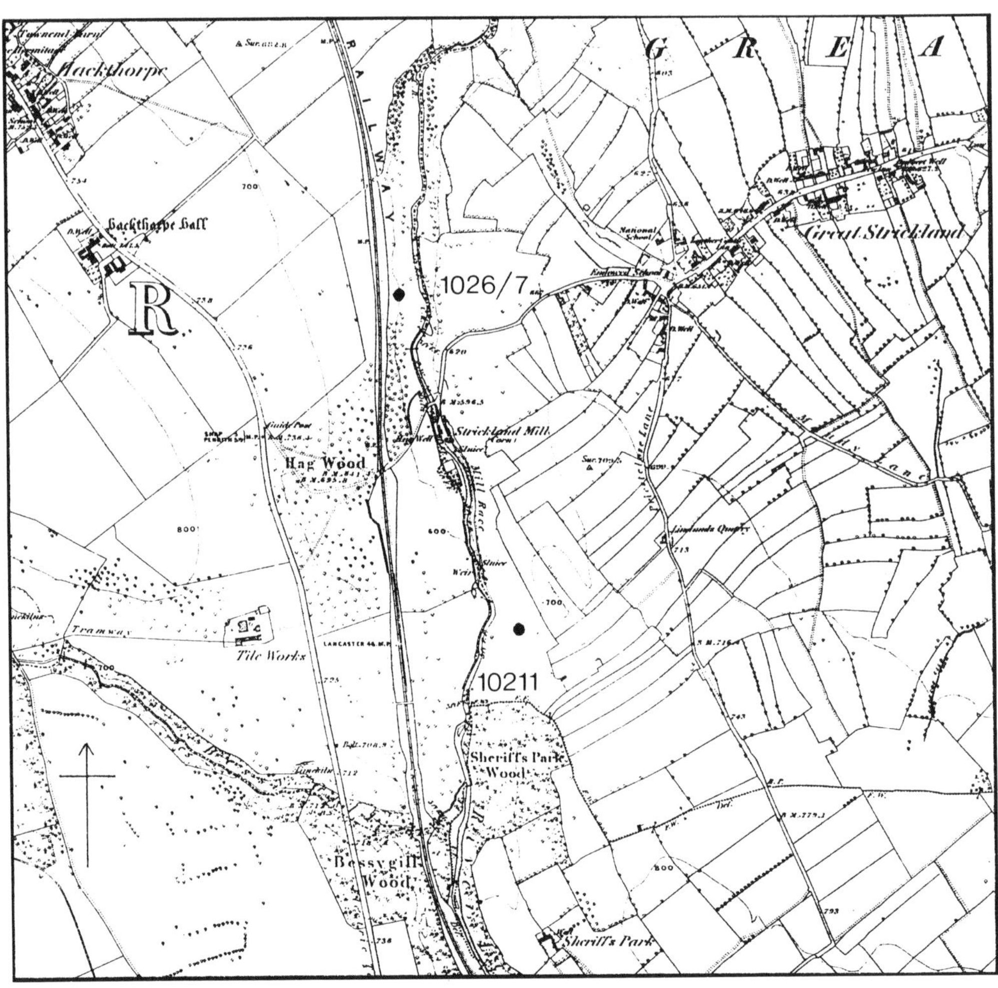

*Figure 2:14 Great Strickland field system (**10211**), OS 1st edn 6″ (1863)*

Clifton

The pipeline route left the Eamont Valley beyond Fremington, rising gradually through the large arable fields on red sandy soils to Clifton Dykes, where a ditch and boundaries of the medieval strip field system survive (**1011, 1014**). In the field adjacent to the disused Eden Valley Railway (**1015**), a fragment of volcanic greenstone (**1013**), thought to be a waste flake from a retouched Langdale Neolithic stone axe, was found during fieldwalking. A pattern of small, squarish fields lies to the south of the strip fields, and in one of these, broad medieval ridge and furrow and a bank and ditch (**1018**) were noted.

Great Strickland

Beyond Melkinthorpe, the pipeline route joined the steep-sided valley of the River Leith, which cuts through the limestone topography north of Great Strickland. Medieval ridge and furrow was visible in most of the fields, and lynchets on the eastern valley slope (**10213**) were not affected by the pipeline. To the south-west of the village, the curving strips of the medieval field system are still defined by stone walls (Fig 2:14). On the west bank of the river, the modern boundaries do not reflect the pattern of the medieval fields associated with Hackthorpe. Well preserved areas of medieval ridge and furrow, separated by headlands, a terraced trackway, banks, and a linear stone revetment (**1022, 1025**) were, however, located during fieldwalking north-east of Hackthorpe Hall.

Downstream from Strickland Mill, terraced trackways, banks, and a building platform (**1026, 1027**) were surveyed between the river and the railway. South of the mill, post-medieval ridge and furrow and field boundaries (**10210**) were intersected by the pipeline in its descent to the River Leith, which was crossed at this point. On the eastern slope of the valley, aerial photography revealed a complex pattern of lynchets, ridge and furrow, field boundaries, and trackways (**10211**), which were surveyed in detail in February 1991 (Fig 2:15). The pipeline ascended the slope along the northern boundary of Sheriff's Park Wood, traversing many more elements of the medieval field system (**1034, 1035, 1036, 1037**) and skirting the boundary of the former deer park.

Little Strickland

Fieldwalking of the pipeline route by J Cherry, following reinstatement of the topsoil, resulted in the collection of a number of prehistoric flints on the limestone uplands, including a blade and a scraper from the eastern slope opposite Thrimby Hall (**10312, 10313**).

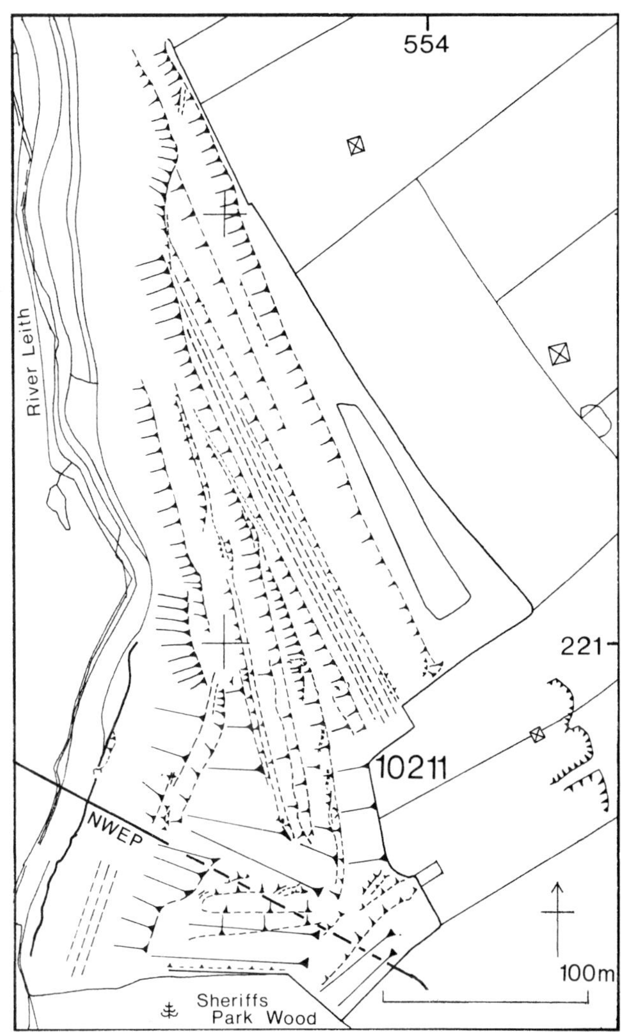

*Figure 2:15   Great Strickland lynchets (**10211**), surveyed features*

A former field system was surveyed on the western edge of the Little Strickland fields, above Thrimby Bridge (**10311**), and similar features were traversed as the pipeline passed close to the village (**1041, 1044**). Geophysical survey of earthworks south-west of Little Strickland (**1043**) did not reveal evidence of features associated with deserted house plots nearer to the village (**10412**). The whole area between Great and Little Strickland displayed a high density of earthworks associated with earlier land management and lines of communication, whether medieval or prehistoric in origin.

Hardendale

Between Towcett and Hardendale, an area of early prehistoric funerary and ritual monuments was traversed below Windrigg Hill. Extensive cairnfields and field systems, sometimes associated with settlements, are found on these limestone uplands. A basalt hand axe (**1046**) had previously been recorded near the prehistoric stone circle at Gunnerkeld, which lay outside the corridor, and two prehistoric flint scatters (**1058, 1059**) were found by J Cherry after reinstatement south-east of the stone circle.

Field boundaries (**1045, 1047**) and narrow post-medieval ridge and furrow (**10411**) were observed in this area, and an oval mound (**1052**), possibly prehistoric, near the Cross Stone of Keverigg, was fenced off and protected during construction, together with several nearby subrectangular enclosures of unknown date (**1056, 1057**). On the outcropping limestone escarpment at Trainriggs, which has in the past been subject to extensive small-scale quarrying, enclosures and pits (**10610**) visible on aerial photographs were investigated by trial excavation in August 1990. Although a pit and linear bank were observed in section, the very slight cropmark features did not yield further evidence of occupation, and the features could not be dated. South of Trainriggs Farm, field boundaries, post-medieval ridge and furrow (**1061, 1063, 1064**), and a derelict stone structure (**1062**) were recorded, on the outskirts of a field system (**1065, 1067**) which is likely to have been an outfield of the deserted medieval village at Hardendale. A group of banked enclosures and building platforms, with lynchets and ridge and furrow nearby (**1068**), probably indicate a long deserted farmstead, and further elements of this field system (**1069**) were found below Hardendale Nab. In this stony area west of the extensive modern Hardendale quarries, a number of flints and fragments of chert (**10611, 10612**) were recovered during fieldwalking by J Cherry.

Crosby Ravensworth Fell and Orton Low Moor

The high density of sites associated with prehistoric or medieval occupation and landuse between Great Strickland and Hardendale is in contrast to the almost complete lack of earthworks recorded on the inhospitable open moorlands of Shap summit. Around the western shoulder of Crosby Ravensworth Fell, a late reroute to the west on the limestone escarpment left two derelict stone structures (**1081, 1083**) untouched, but a third walled enclosure (**1084**), not previously recorded, was identified only during construction, when it was destroyed. These structures may have been shelters or bields, built for protection from the prevailing south-westerly winds. A prehistoric flint and a concentration of chert fragments (**1085**) were found near a disused quarry on the same limestone escarpment following reinstatement of the topsoil. Further south, towards the Orton to Shap road, two flint waste flakes (**1092, 1093**) were found during topsoil re-

moval in an area which had previously yielded many flint artefacts (Cherry and Cherry 1987, 9–12).

Sproatgill

The pipeline route crossed Orton Low Moor to follow the boundary wall between the moorland and the enclosed fields, which marks the line of the main Roman road from Ribchester to Carlisle for several kilometres across the moor (Fig 2:16). This road once linked the forts at Ribchester, Overburrow, Low Borrowbridge, Brougham, Old Penrith, and Carlisle. The predicted intersection of the Roman road with the pipeline was 400m north of Sproatgill Farm where, during topsoil removal in August 1991, a 42m length of the Roman road (**1091**) was disturbed. Rapid excavation over the next six days demonstrated that the road surface was approximately 10m wide, with a discontinuous central line of stones, and a stone kerb at the western edge, beyond which was located the western ditch. The boundary wall overlay the eastern edge of the road, and presumably obscured the corresponding kerb and ditch. The finds from this site were mainly post-medieval, and the only other artefacts recorded from the vicinity of the Roman road were two potsherds, likewise post-medieval (**1094**).

Figure 2:16 Sproatgill, Roman road, aerial photograph, looking north

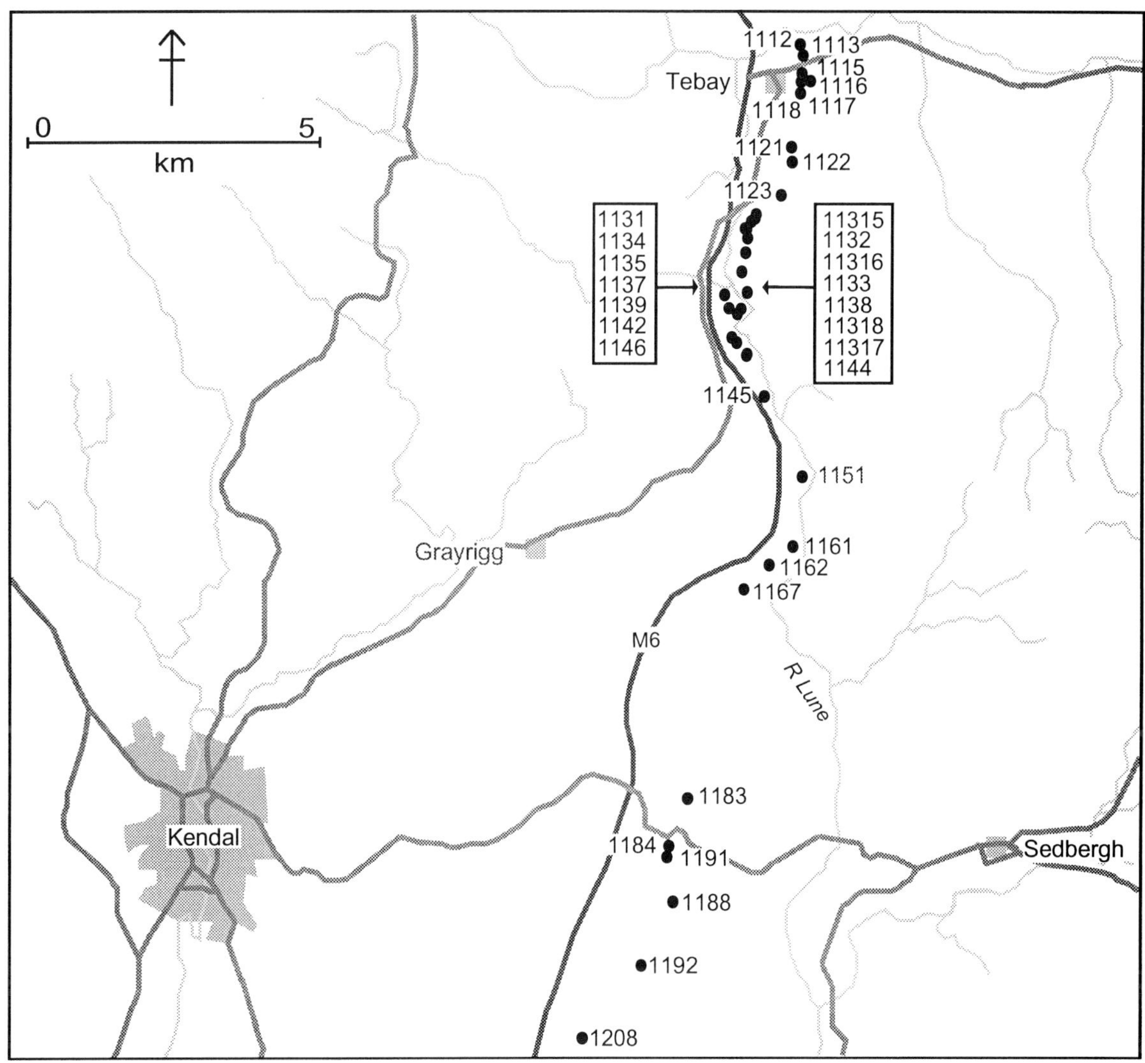

*Figure 2:17 NWEP sites in the Tebay area (**1112–1208**)*

Tebay and the Lune gorge

No further sites were encountered on the rough moorland south of Sproatgill, until the route turned southeast to descend into the upper Lune Valley, where ridge and furrow was visible on either side of the river (**1101, 1112**), and a hollow trackway, High Beck Lane (**1113**), probably a route formerly of some importance, was sectioned. One of the fields adjacent to this trackway was named Hollow Gate Road on the Tebay tithe apportionment (WDRC/8/110).

Crossing the River Lune for the first time above Tebay Bridge, the pipeline traversed a number of field boundaries (**1115, 1117, 1118**) west of Cocklake Farm, and skirted the edge of an extensive possible Romano-British settlement and field system (**1116, Fig 2:18**) identified from aerial photographs. Trial excavation in August 1990 at the edge of the site revealed no features, and the pipeline was subse-

quently rerouted further east, avoiding the settlement altogether.

On the open moorland of Tebay Fell, a substantial reroute left undisturbed narrow post-medieval ridge and furrow and a trackway (**1121, 1122**) in the enclosed fields at Tebaygill Farm. The revised route ran parallel to the farm track over the rough fell grazings to Roger Howe where, at the saddle on the ridge, it turned south-west to descend the steep valley side. On the saddle, low linear features (**1123**) were faintly visible, and these stony banks, tentatively thought to define enclosures and even possible building platforms, were surveyed in 1991. The indistinct earthworks were not identified during topsoil removal, which affected much of the site. Whatever the nature of this site, it appears to have been linked with the farms in the valley by a narrow trackway ascending the fell obliquely from the farmstead at Powsons (**1132**).

23

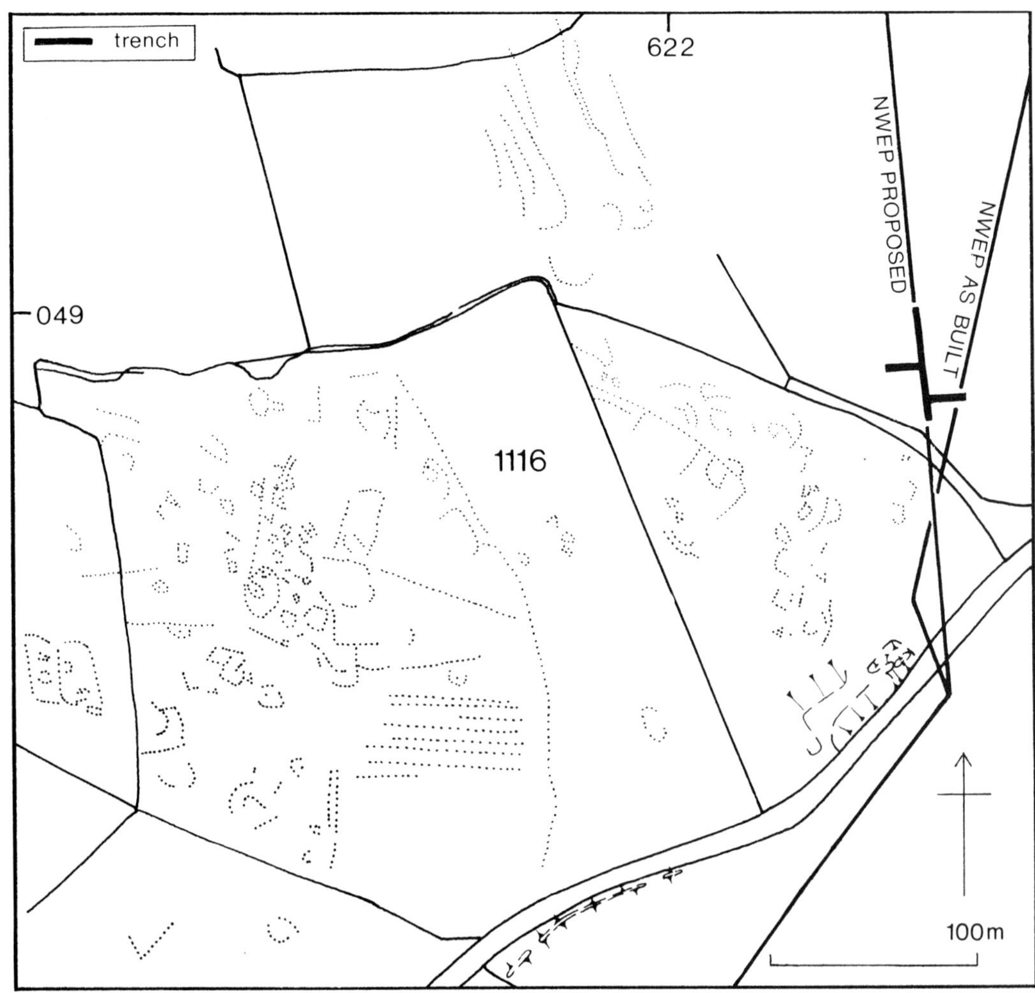

*Figure 2:18 Tebay settlement and field system (**1116**), aerial survey features, trench locations, and pipeline routes*

The route descended into the Lune Valley at its most constricted point, where the motorway (M6), the Kendal to Tebay road (A685), and the main line railway are terraced into the flank of Jeffrey's Mount above the river. East of the river, enclosed pastures extend up to the intake wall, and the farm track to Brockholes provides the only means of access to the eastern side, which remained relatively undisturbed prior to pipeline construction. The pipeline crossed many earthworks of earlier field systems and trackways, including field boundaries and narrow ridge and furrow (**1131, 11315**) north of the Powsons settlement (**1132**), and further walls, banks, and a trackway to the south (**1133, 1134**).

Powsons

A line of settlements is strung along the eastern valley side from Tebay to Lowgill, ranging from the long-deserted subcircular enclosures of Iron Age or Romano-British date, to the present-day farms, whose buildings generally date from the eighteenth century. Several of the abandoned settlements survive as visible earthworks, and one of these, of unknown date, was crossed by the pipeline in a boulder-strewn field below Powson Knott (**1132**, Fig 2:19) (*see Chapter 7*). A cluster of features was surveyed here, including field boundaries, trackways, enclosures, and a rectangular stone structure (Fig 2:20). Excavations in August 1990 and May–June 1991 investigated several features which lay within the corridor, although much of the extensive site was left undisturbed. A rock outcrop adjacent to the principal excavated feature was removed by blasting during construction.

A rectangular stone building was located by survey, tested by trial excavation, and recorded by full excavation, prior to its disappearance during construction. The building as excavated (8.5 x 4m) was built across the slope at 185m OD. The well built drystone walls survived up to three courses high, and an original entrance faced uphill at the eastern end. The building was modified in a later phase,

24

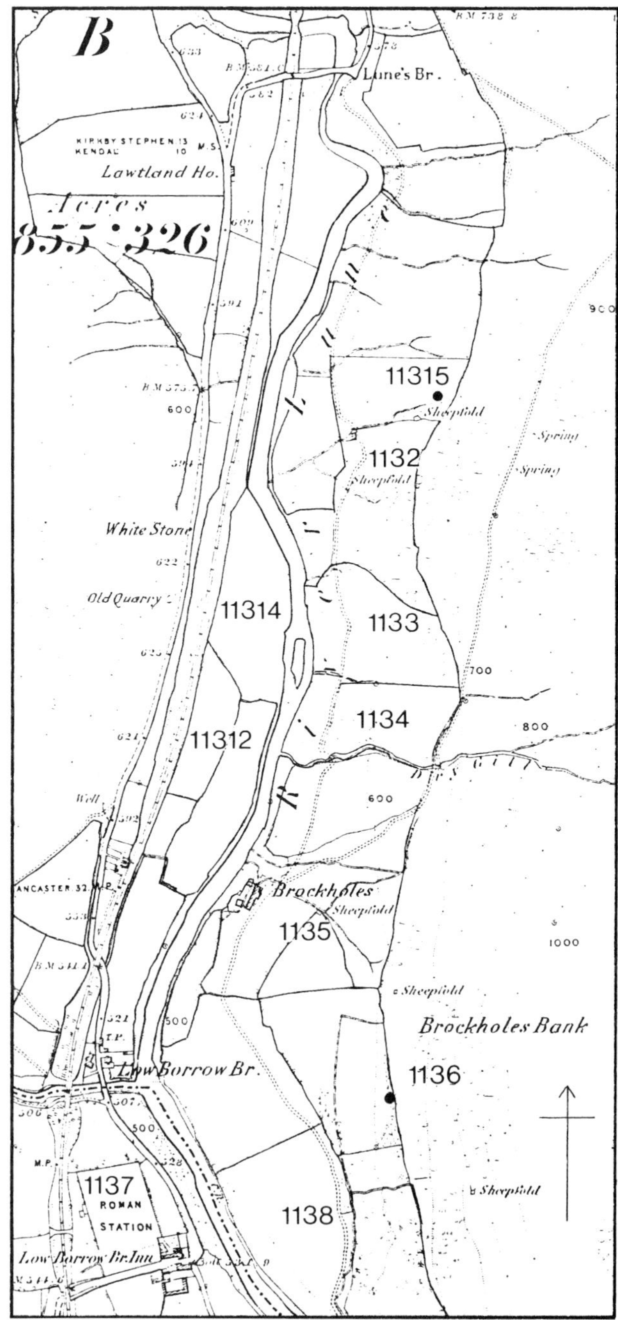

*Figure 2:19 The Lune gorge from Powsons (**1132**) to Low Borrowbridge (**1137**), OS 1st edn 6" (1858)*

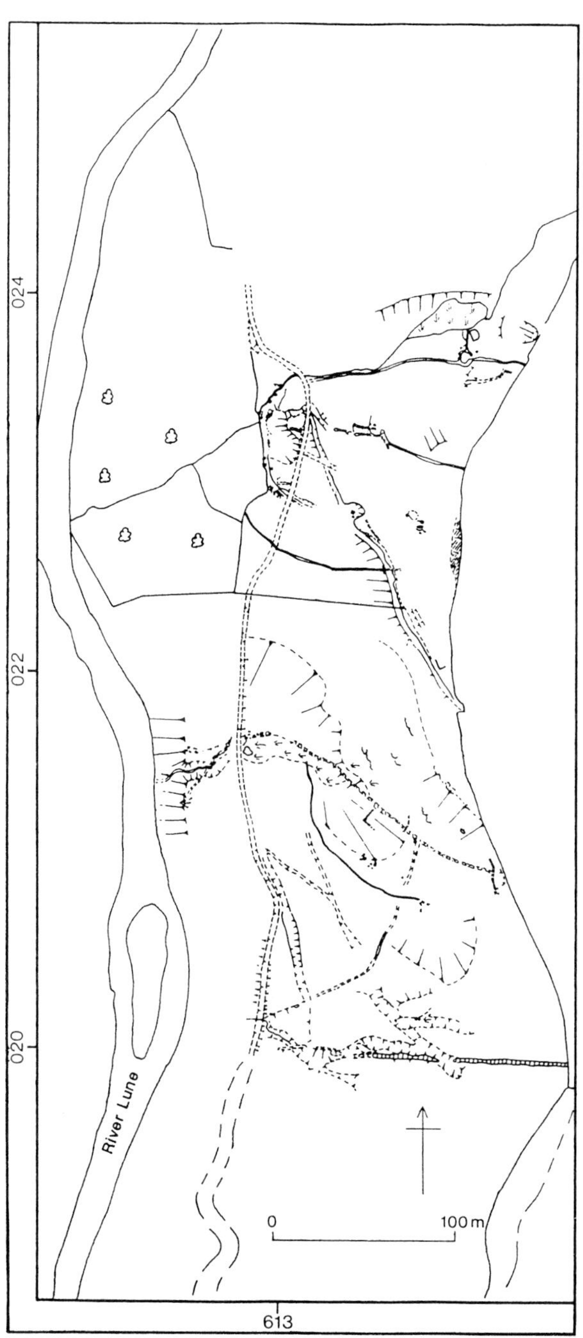

*Figure 2:20 Powsons (**1132, 1133**), surveyed features*

with a platform to level the floor at the western end, and additional entrances in the west and north sides were blocked up. Finally the building and associated field walls decayed and became turf-covered and forgotten. A possible yard at the north end of the building was the only external enclosure identified by excavation, although a relic field wall abutted the south-east corner of the building, and many other relic boundaries have been recorded within the adjoining modern fields.

Although three worked flints (**11316**, Fig 7:14), probably of Bronze Age date, were found at Powsons during the excavation, their significance is limited, as they are likely to have arrived at the site in hillwash from the fells above, known to have been used by prehistoric man. The building was quite empty of the type of rubbish generated by human or animal use, and no datable or diagnostic artefacts were recorded, perhaps reflecting the very basic living conditions of the later medieval period, when the few utensils were commonly of wood or leather, which decay without trace in the wet climate. It can nonetheless be surmised that this was either a shieling hut, used only in the summer season by herdsmen, or part of a more permanent farm. There is firm documentary evidence, from the mid sixteenth century, for a farmstead or smallholding at Powsons, which was finally merged with the next farm down the valley, Brockholes; in its later existence the excavated building was probably a dwelling or outhouse.

Stone-walled enclosures and a trackway, predating the present field boundary, were also surveyed in the field immediately to the south of Powsons (**1133**, Fig 2:20). Beyond Brockholes Farm the route passed through riverside meadows, with deeper soils more frequently ploughed. Earthworks would be more vulnerable here, and although elements of a former field system, including a boundary bank (**1135**), survived south of the farm, and a Romano-British settlement (**1136**) was only narrowly avoided by an unforeseen reroute upslope, little else was visible in the relatively lush meadows of the valley bottom. Towards the southern end of the meadows, cropmarks suggestive of another Romano-British site (**1138**) had been identified on aerial photographs, but on investigation by geophysical survey and trial excavation in August 1990, no subsoil features were found which might confirm the interpretation.

Low Borrowbridge

The pipeline's second crossing of the River Lune, above Salterwath Bridge, brought it into contact with the nucleus of Roman occupation in the valley. A Roman fort at Low Borrowbridge controlled communications and supply lines through the valley in conjunction with the Roman road, which crossed the river near Salterwath Bridge. This road was another section of the main north-south artery linking Ribchester and Carlisle, also encountered at Sproatgill near Orton (**1091**).

South of the Roman fort (Fig 2:21), in the large field running down to the river by Salterwath Bridge, aerial photographs revealed a number of indeterminate features (**1139**, Fig 5:1), thought to represent elements of the extramural settlement associated with the fort. Although the field is subject to occasional ploughing, detailed topographical survey recorded many slight earthworks, including faint ridge and furrow and possible lynchets, but

*Figure 2:21 Low Borrowbridge Roman fort (**1137**), looking east*

also banked enclosures and subcircular platforms (Fig 5:3).

Within the pipeline corridor at the south end of this field, geophysical survey in August 1990 assisted the location of trial trenches, one of which sectioned a small pit containing Roman pottery sherds, burnt material, and iron objects. During pipeline construction the following year, the archaeological inspector monitoring topsoil stripping noted five discrete burnt patches, with Roman pottery, charcoal, and iron nails at the surface of the subsoil. Construction was halted, and archaeological evaluation began the next day. It rapidly became clear that this was the site of a Roman cemetery (**11318**), and excavation continued for seven weeks to record the cremation burials, possible inhumation graves, and associated enclosures defined by shallow ditches (Figs 5:5, 5:6, 5:7).

A road surface, probably also Roman, had been identified in two parallel trial trenches, and a larger area of this road was uncovered during the main excavation, apparently oriented towards the postulated south gate of the fort. The end of the excavation was marked by the discovery of a splendid third century Roman tombstone, in almost perfect condition (Back cover, Fig 5:14; *see Chapter 5*).

Further damage was caused to the cemetery in early 1992, when preparation for a new farm access road beside the River Lune revealed more cremations perilously near the surface. A second rescue excavation was rapidly organised with the assistance of a grant from English Heritage, enabling the recording of numerous cremations and enclosures in the relatively small area between the 1991 excavation site and the river bank (Figs 5:5, 5:8).

Following the west bank of the river around the bend at the south-west corner of the field containing the cemetery, the pipeline took the only possible line on the steep slope below the motorway and railway. The gradient here may have been modified by railway construction in the nineteenth century, but the unfavourable terrain is in any case unlikely to have supported settlement. Two sites on this slope were subjected to topographical and geophysical survey. These were a former driftway, on the projected line of the medieval road, running obliquely upslope (**1142**), and a stone-walled enclosure to the south (**1145**). Other possible enclosures, and a conjectured Roman road alignment, visible on aerial photographs, were identified on the ground as natural watercourses, gullies, banks, and a river terrace (**1144, 1146**). Otherwise, no further sites were recorded until the pipeline reached Low Park, below Dillicar Common.

Lowgill

The Lune Valley has attracted settlement by virtue of its busy communications route, but in recent times the imperatives of transport have overtaken some of the settlements, which have become isolated by road or railway construction. At Low Park are the derelict remains of a once substantial farmhouse and its outbuildings, on a narrow shelf above the river (*see Chapter 3*). Occupation of this site over many centuries is evident in the enclosures, ridge and furrow, and deeply indented trackways below the farmstead. A single sherd of medieval green glazed ware (**1151**), found by a drainage inspector during construction, also hints at the longevity of the farm.

The pipeline crossed the River Lune twice between Low Park and Lowgill, to avoid the steep deciduous woodland on the west bank. The route climbed from the fourth Lune crossing towards Lowgill, crossing field boundaries and a terraced trackway (**1161**) in the field behind the railway cottages. Another field boundary (**1167**) was recorded south of Lowgill, but otherwise the only archaeological site affected was the embankment of the disused branch railway to Ingleton (**1162**, Fig 2:22). At an early stage of the project, the pipeline was actually routed between the arches of the railway viaduct, and so would have had a considerable impact on the complex of sites at Beckfoot and Lowgill, including the viaduct and a packhorse bridge, both Grade II Listed Buildings, and Davy Bank Mill (Fig 2:22). In consequence of a fortuitous reroute, these sites were in the end completely avoided, fulfilling the recommendation made by LUAU.

Firbank

South of Lowgill, the route rose past Birchfield to cross Firbank Fell, an upland area of acidic grassland and peat mosses with little modern settlement and few roads, and correspondingly few archaeological sites, although low earthworks may have been obscured by the rough vegetation. The disturbance by earlier drainage of peat deposits in Drybeck Moss had revealed organic material (**1183**), but although this was closely observed during pipeline construction, no further archaeological evidence was forthcoming. The only site identified in this area was a square enclosure, previously recorded, in the vicinity of Capplethwaite Moss (**1184**).

An early drove road, used from at least the twelfth century for bringing cattle south from Scotland and known as Scotch Lane or the Old Scotch road (**1191**), underlies the modern minor road over Lambrigg and Killington Parks (Farrer 1905b, 976–80). The

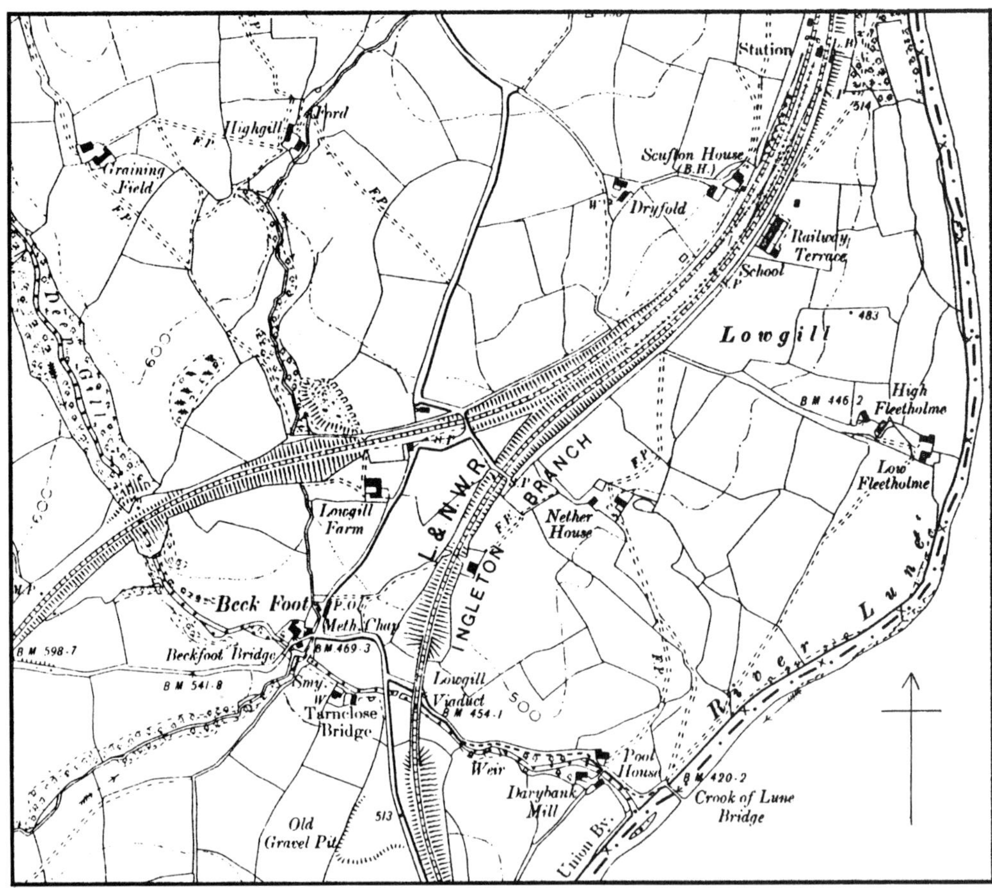

Figure 2:22 Lowgill, OS rev edn 6" (1899)

road was crossed by the pipeline east of Killington Reservoir, but nothing of archaeological significance was observed.

Two mounds of possible prehistoric origin (**1188**) near Mutton Hall were avoided during construction and, in a nearby field, ploughmarks (**1192**) were observed in the subsoil after topsoil removal. The route through the enclosed pastoral farmland of Old Hutton and Preston Patrick rural parishes avoided the known archaeological sites of the area, affecting only a lynchet and two low banks, possibly of medieval origin (**1223**), south-west of Gatebeck Reservoir. The route descended through fields to Hollins, where elements of a former field system, including lynchets, boundaries, ridge and furrow, and a trackway (**1241, 1242**) were surveyed. Places with 'Hollins' names characteristically were associated with packhorse and drove roads, denoting resting places along these routes (Atkin 1989, 77), in this case the continuation southward of the Galloway Gate.

Farleton

South of the Kendal to Skipton road (A65), near Dove House Farm, were terraced platforms, post-medieval narrow ridge and furrow, and a bank which appeared to dam a small valley (**1243**). The valley of Farleton Beck was crossed and the route ran alongside the Lancaster Canal to Farleton, where lynchets and post-medieval ridge and furrow (**12413**) were observed in the narrow fields running up the fell (Fig 2:24).

When the northern part of the Lancaster Canal was built in the early nineteenth century, it was diverted from its original route in order to serve the needs of the limeburning industry on the western slope of Farleton Fell. Barges bringing coal north from the Lancashire coalfield carried lime for land improvement and building purposes on their return journey south. Derelict limekilns, with associated trackways (**12501, 12502**) leading from the fellside quarries, lay on the periphery of the pipeline route behind Marsden and Townend Farms. The pipeline climbed the slope to the south, where parallel boundary banks defined a former field, or parcel of woodland, containing two small oval platforms and a trackway (**12503**).

Beyond the parish boundary wall the fellside, once tree-covered but now enclosed rough pasture, was

28

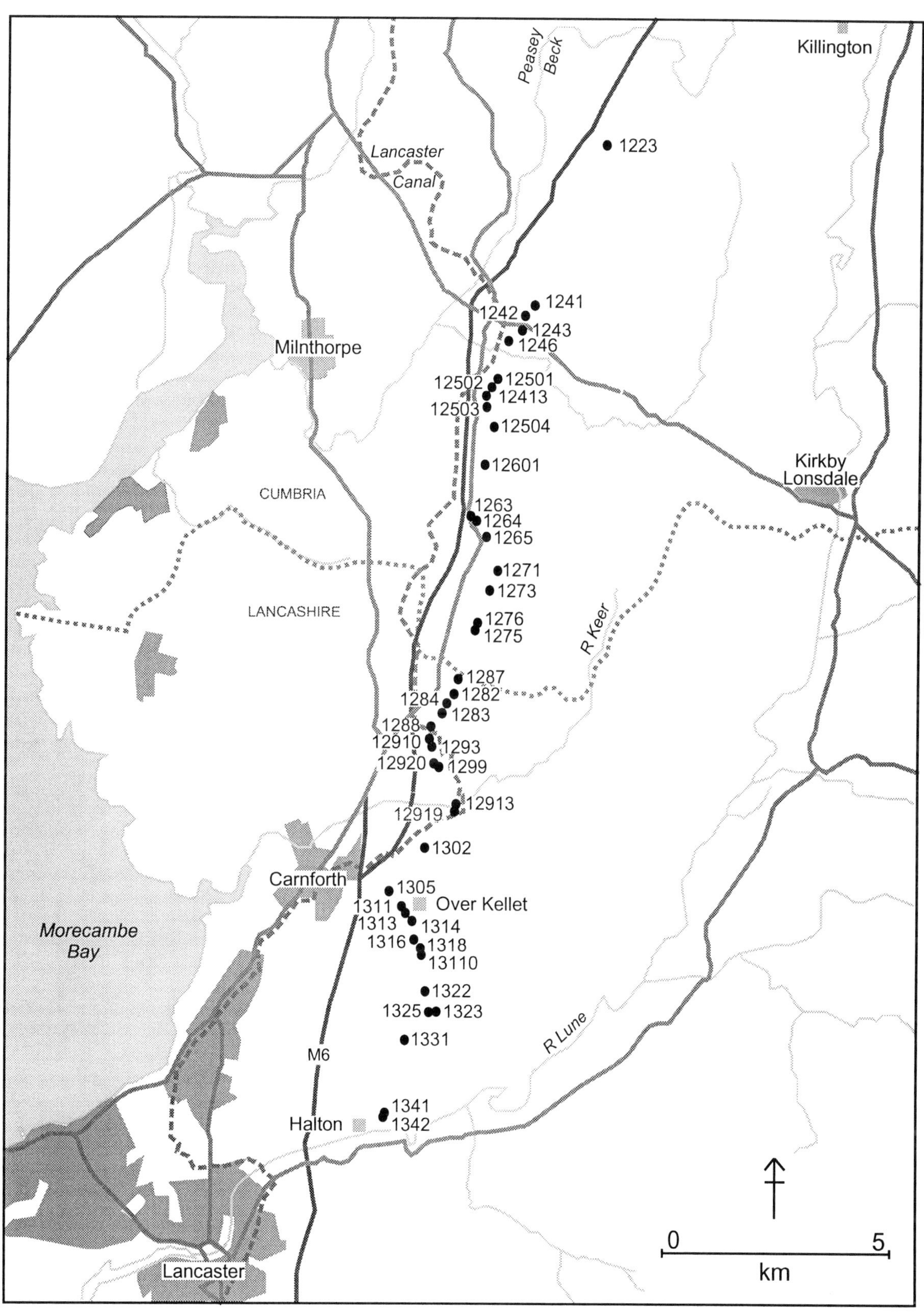

*Figure 2:23 NWEP sites from Killington to Lancaster (**1223–1342**)*

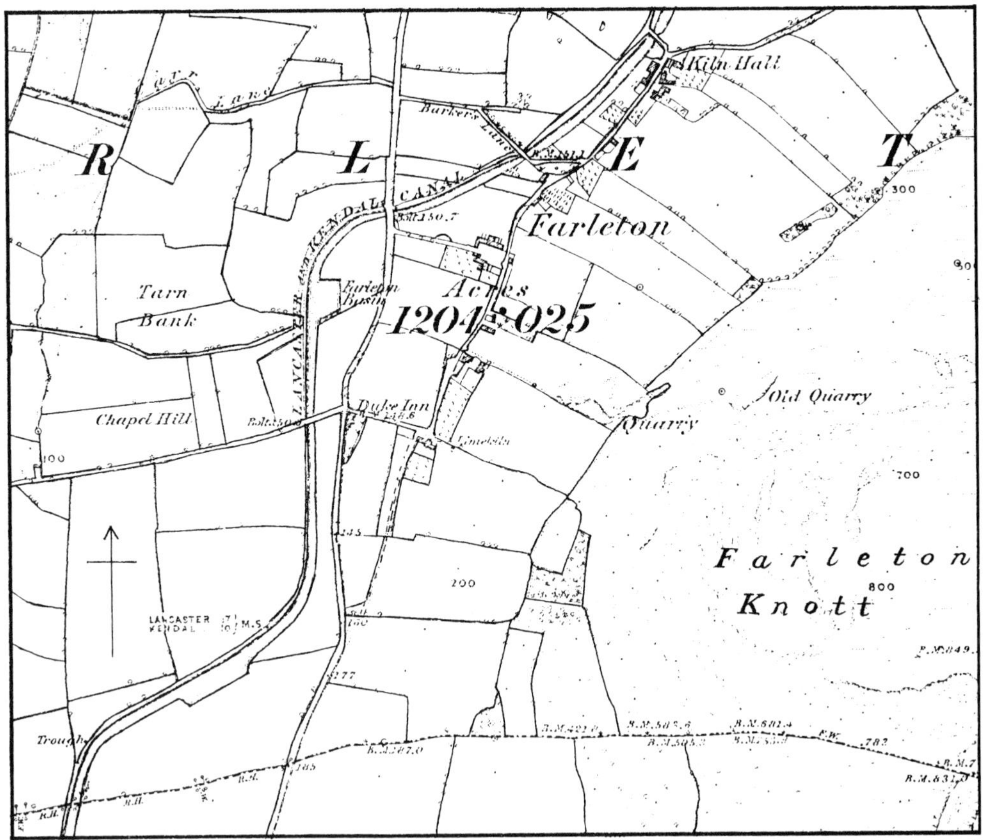

Figure 2:24 Farleton Fell and the Lancaster Canal, OS 1st edn 6" (1862)

scattered with similar platforms, terraced into the slope (**12504**, Fig 2:25). Fragments of charcoal were observed on the surface of several of these platforms, which were similar, in size and shape, to many charcoal burners' pitsteads recorded in woodlands in other parts of Cumbria (Lambert forthcoming). Two of the platforms lay directly on the pipeline route, and were excavated in April 1991, to ascertain whether they had been used for charcoal manufacture. A single charcoal-rich layer was located near the surface, confirming the interpretation, but no finds were forthcoming, and it seemed likely that the pitsteads had only been used for one season's work.

At the base of Holme Park Fell, beside the trackway leading up to the fellside quarries, a low turf-fast wall crossed the exposed limestone strata from east to west, in association with two small enclosures (**12601**). This small complex of features, which predates the existing field boundaries, was surveyed in August 1990. A considerable detour was necessary to avoid the large active Holme Park Quarry and much of the limestone pavement in Curwen Woods, where a mound, 22 x 12m (**1263**), similar in character to a Neolithic long barrow, fortunately remained undisturbed during pipeline construction.

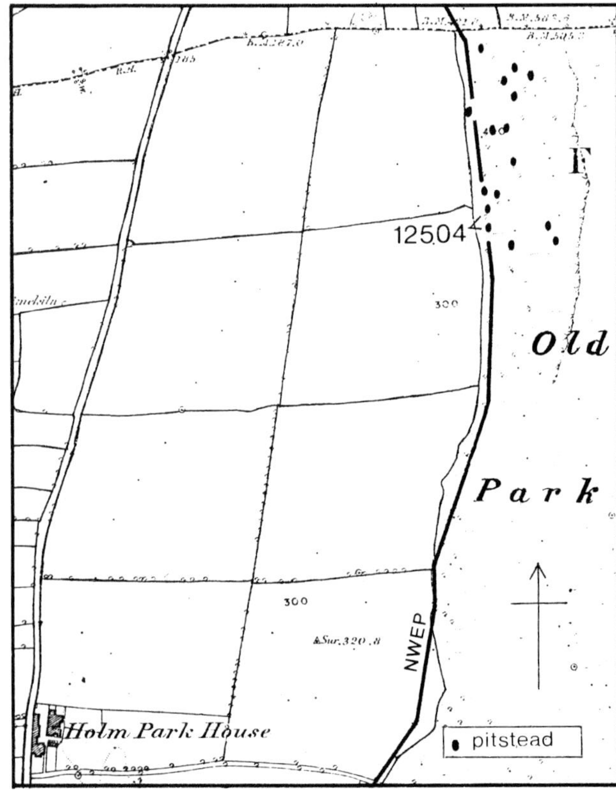

Figure 2:25 Farleton Fell (12504), charcoal burners' pitsteads superimposed on OS 1st edn 6" (1862)

The route for a short distance ran very close to the motorway (M6), which follows the base of the limestone escarpment here, and then turned east to take the least damaging line through Sexton Hagg broadleaved woodlands, which also overlie limestone pavement.

Burton-in-Kendal

There was no visible sign of the supposed deserted medieval village at Clawthorpe (**1265**), but to the east of Burton-in-Kendal elements of the medieval or early post-medieval field system were noted, including ridge and furrow, linear banks, and a trackway (**1273**). The route crossed these former townfields in a direct line between two boundary stones (**1271, 1276**), both in lanes leading to Dalton, one to the north of Burton, the other to the south, probably marking Burton's eastern boundary.

Immediately south of Dalton Lane, the pipeline route entered Dalton Park, where extensive earthworks of a medieval field system preserved in the parkland included lynchets, ridge and furrow, and enclosures (**1275**). This field system had been the subject of a small-scale survey in 1976 and, other than fieldwalking, there was no further opportunity for recording prior to construction. Many of the features were unaffected by the pipeline, but the remains of a wall, a field boundary, and a trackway in use as recently as 30 years ago, were observed during the watching brief on the topsoil strip.

The route was revised here during construction, taking a more westerly line through the park, and thereby giving a wider berth to the main area of earthworks. It then passed between Coat Green and Dalton Old Hall Farms, to cross the county boundary into Lancashire.

Lancashire

Priest Hutton

In the damp valley bottom of White Beck were several earthwork features of unknown date (**1282**), identified from an aerial photograph. Set into a low ridge at the edge of the wetland was a circular ditch, 15m in diameter and 1.5m wide, a low boulder wall forming an enclosure on a platform, a double ditch linking the enclosure to a small pond, and a raised trackway across the wetland. Post-medieval pottery was recovered from these features during construction.

The surviving boundaries of the medieval strip fields at Priest Hutton curve over a low ridge and down to White Beck. An impressive set of lynchets, stepped into the north-facing slope of the hill, lay beyond the pipeline corridor, but other elements of the earlier field system were affected during construction, including ridge and furrow associated with a headland (**1283**) in a field above White Beck. Three fields further south, levelling of the hillside to facilitate vehicle access during construction destroyed part of three parallel lynchets and a corresponding area of narrow ridge and furrow (**1284**), which had been surveyed in August 1990.

Borwick

The pipeline crossed the Lancaster Canal (**12910**) north of Borwick, where the remains of a small brick building (**1288**) were recorded during construction. Both broad and narrow ridge and furrow and a headland were recorded in the fields at Sander's Farm and Manor Farm (**1293, 12920**). The low-lying area west of Borwick has been exploited on a large scale for its gravel deposits, and in recent years quarrying has expanded east of Dock Acres to Kellet Lane and beyond.

Manor Farm

Previous fieldwork, in 1979, recorded two dished earthworks south of Manor Farm, and in 1982, in advance of further expansion of the gravel pits, excavation identified one of these as a Bronze Age funerary monument (Olivier 1987). This excavation of the larger earthwork revealed a substantial early Bronze Age funerary cairn that originally contained at least two inhumations associated with grave goods, lying below a cairn of smaller stones, with apparently inserted cremations suggesting reuse in the later Bronze Age. The second, smaller earthwork (**1299**) had not thus far been affected by gravel extraction, and fieldwalking in March 1990 revealed that the monument, consisting of a ring bank, 12m in diameter, defining a small subcircular enclosure, had an annex to the north, increasing the overall diameter to 25m. The pipeline was rerouted here to avoid the rise of the mound, but this did not account for any possible outlying features related to the monument. Geophysical survey in July 1990 confirmed the perimeter of the ring bank, but trial excavation the following month, at its eastern edge, failed to identify any associated features on the limestone bedrock, nor was any additional evidence recorded during construction.

At Capernwray, post-medieval lynchets and ridge and furrow (**12913, 12919**) were visible in the fields between the canal, the Leeds to Carnforth railway line, and the River Keer. The canal was bored for a second pipeline crossing east of Overhead Cottages, and the route then made a right-angled turn across Capernwray Road, to enter the Over Kellet field system.

Over Kellet

The Lancaster Canal formed the northern boundary of the field system, which extended over a low glacial ridge north of the village. Cropmarks plotted from aerial photographs showed two possible settlements (**1302**, Fig 2:26) of Iron Age type between the pipeline route and the canal. Geophysical survey and trial excavation in September 1990 at the edge of these features did not reveal any outlying elements of the settlements, or provide any dating evidence for them, and they were not disturbed by construction.

Curving round to pass Over Kellet on its western side, the route cut through fields containing many relic boundaries, lynchets, ridge and furrow, and a disused trackway (**1305**, Fig 2:27). The area was surveyed in detail, and further study demonstrated that many of the relic boundaries coincided with those shown on the tithe map of 1840 (DRB, Tithe 1840, Fig 2:28). A sherd of northern gritty ware was recovered from one of the boundaries, datable to the twelfth or thirteenth century.

Between Hall Farm and Leapers Wood Quarry, another extensive area of the medieval field system

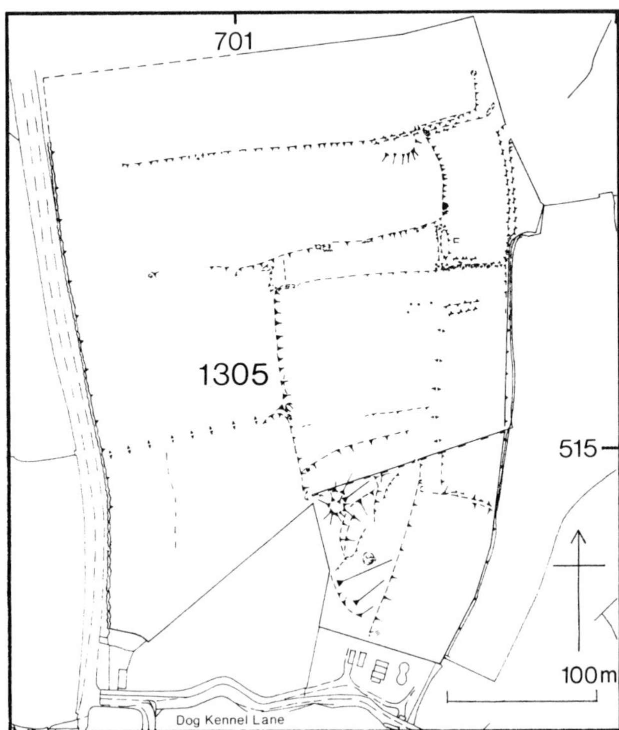

*Figure 2:27 Over Kellet field system (**1305**), surveyed features*

was surveyed (Fig 2:29), comprising strip fields, ridge and furrow, lynchets, and a building platform (**1311**, **1313**, **1314**). In both these areas (**1305**, **1313**), to either side of Kellet Road, nearly all the old boundaries had been removed to form large modern fields, and the current OS maps do not reflect the earlier field system recorded during the survey.

Small quarries and a possible limekiln, on the outcropping limestone at Slack's Wood, postdate the medieval field boundaries, but are long disused and in total contrast to the vast modern Leapers Wood and High Roads quarries just over the hill. The pipeline route veered to the east to avoid the quarries, and by Kit Bill Wood a stone wall along the base of a limestone outcrop was noted, together with a small post-medieval cairn (**1316**). On the western slope of Birkland Barrow a terrace appeared to define the area of a drained tarn, and partly encompassed an expanse of ridge and furrow (**1318**), which to the east was oriented north-south and was very broad, but to the west was narrow and oriented east-west.

Fieldwork and the watching brief failed to locate three parish boundary stones (**13110**) shown on the OS 1st edn 6" map (OS 1847), at least one of which would have been within the pipeline corridor, and it was therefore assumed that these were no longer *in situ*.

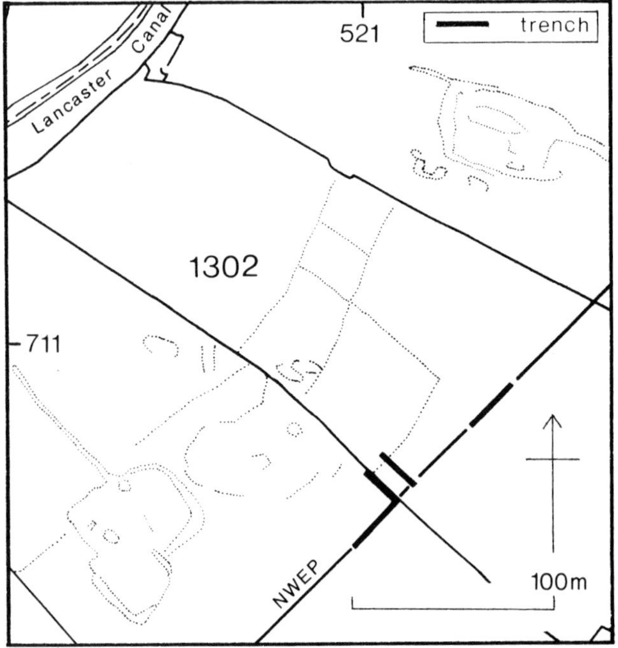

*Figure 2:26 Over Kellet Iron Age type settlements (**1302**), aerial survey features and trench locations*

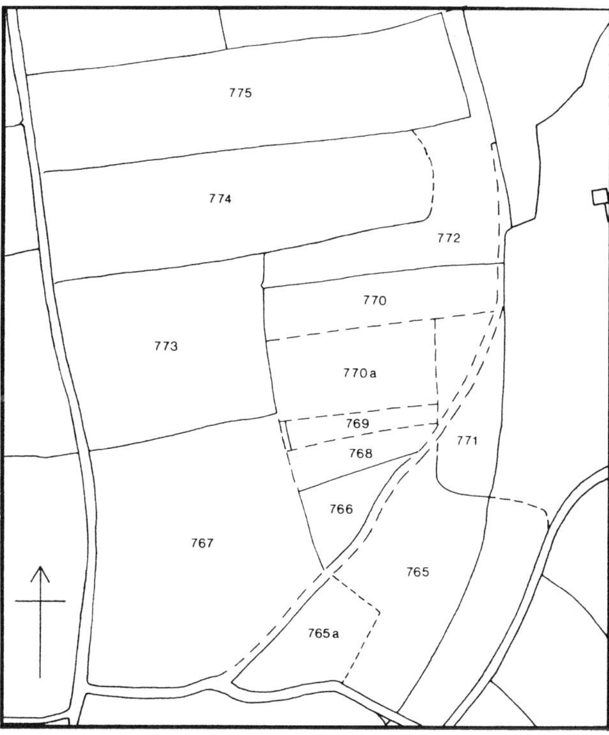

*Figure 2:28 Over Kellet field system (**1305**), tithe map extract (1840)*

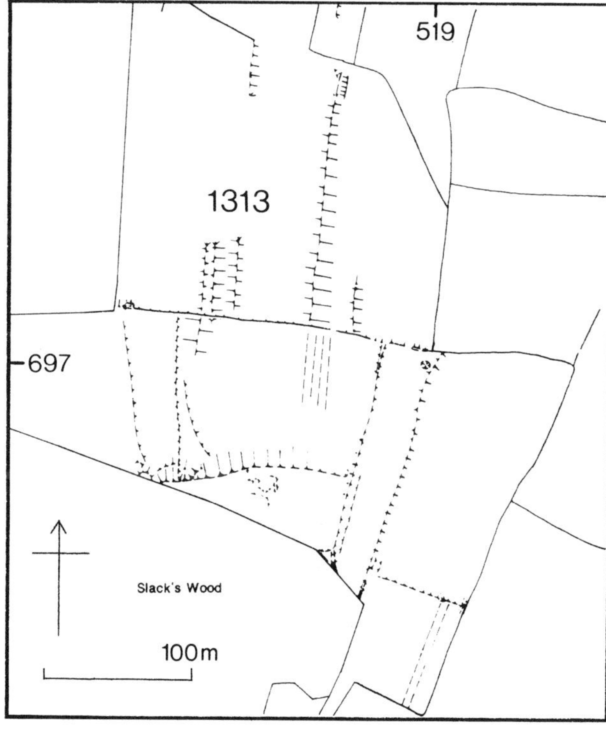

*Figure 2:29 Over Kellet field system (**1313**), surveyed features*

Nether Kellet

East of the Dunald Mill quarries and Intack Farm, a broad, low bank appeared to form a causeway across a marshy area, in which there were also two low mounds, 4m and 21m in diameter respectively (**1322**). Field boundaries, narrow ridge and furrow, and trackways (**1323**), overlain by modern lanes and walls in the fields adjoining Green Hill Lane, indicated the earlier post-medieval farming landscape, but former industry was also present in the form of quarries and a bellpit (**1325**). The upper part of the bellpit was sectioned by the pipe trench during construction, revealing spoil from the central shaft, but there were no finds.

Halton

Just over the parish boundary at Scargill Wood, aerial photographs showed earthworks of curvilinear banks and ridge and furrow (**1331**), overlain by modern field boundaries. No further sites were recorded south of the extensive Nether Kellet quarries, until the route began its descent to the Lune Valley east of Halton. Oakenhead pond, surrounded by a low bank (**1341**), was situated on the crest of a small hill, on the slopes of which were post-medieval narrow ridge and furrow, boundaries, and terraced trackways (**1342**).

The Lune Valley above Lancaster marked the southern limit of the limestone topography which had been followed intermittently since the pipeline left the Eamont Valley at Clifton, south-east of Penrith. East of Halton Mills, the pipeline crossed the River Lune for the fifth and last time, climbing the southern bank to cross the Little North Western Railway (**1343**), disused since 1967.

Scotforth

Farmland on the western side of Quernmore Park preserved extensive post-medieval narrow ridge and furrow, consistently 2.5–3m in width (**1347, 1353, 1354, 1356**), and terraced trackways and hollow-ways (**1353, 1361**). The route then traversed the long ridge east of Lancaster to Scotforth Heights, where a cluster of sites was recorded near Langthwaite and Blea Tarn Reservoirs. Former cultivation was again represented by field boundaries and post-medieval ridge and furrow 2.5–3m wide (**13701, 13703**). A derelict stone building incorporated in the field wall (**13702**) lay outside the corridor, and several trackways (**13706, 13708**) were recorded during construction.

Blea Tarn was originally partially moss-filled, and during peat extraction for construction of the reser-

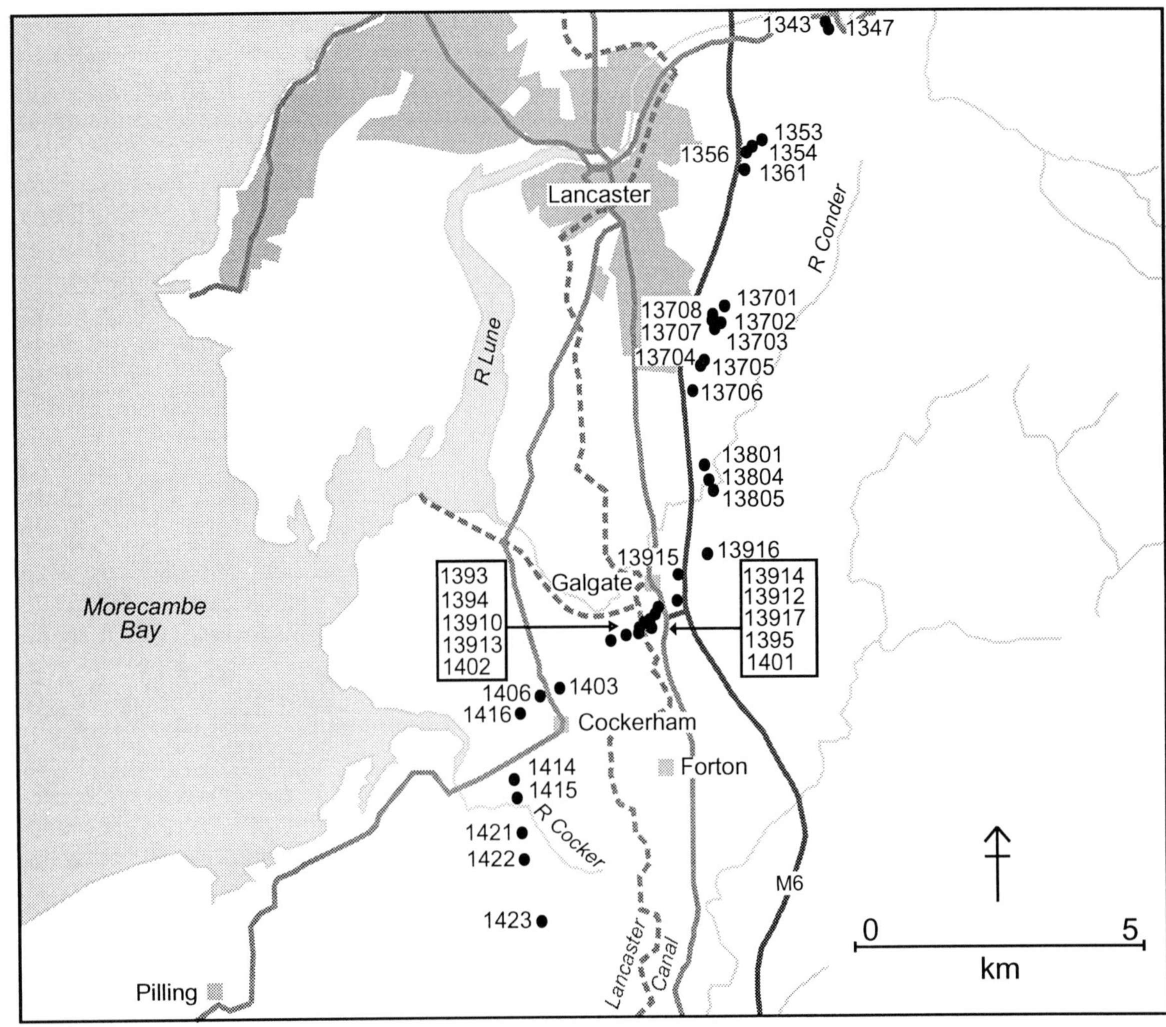

*Figure 2:30 NWEP sites in the Lancaster area (**1343–1423**)*

voir in the late nineteenth century, a prehistoric dug-out canoe was discovered (**13705**). The area was closely observed before and during pipeline construction, but the only tentative evidence for prehistoric activity in the area was a turfed oval mound measuring 3 x 4m (**13704**). Two patches of burnt ground on the subsoil immediately below the topsoil (**13707**) were, however, observed at the western edge of the corridor, during construction near Langthwaite Reservoir.

The route descended from the ridge to the River Conder, where the possible remains of an oval settlement enclosure had previously been recorded west of Banton House Farm (**13801**). Detailed topographical survey revealed a rectangular building platform within the enclosure, a further subcircular enclosure, and terracing of the slope, together with banks and trackways (Fig 2:31). Both the OS 1st edn 6″ map (OS 1848, Fig 2:32), and a plan of the Banton House estate dated 1858 (copy shown to LUAU staff

by Mr Newsham), show a row of cottages at the same location as the building platform. Trial excavation in September 1990 revealed several post-medieval features including a cobbled surface, and during construction this surface was observed to extend over a large area. The earthworks concentrated here may simply be the remains of nineteenth century farmworkers' cottages, but are quite likely to represent also a succession of settlement over many centuries, at this favourable spot with extensive meadows beside the River Conder.

Hollows in the fields adjacent to the present access road to Banton House Farm have been infilled over the years, using nightsoil and waste material from Lancaster (pers comm Mr Newsham), and the post-medieval pottery scatters found during fieldwork at this site are largely attributable to this source. On the adjacent floodplain was a network of drainage ditches, recently infilled, which correspond to field boundaries shown on the OS 1st edn 6″ map (OS

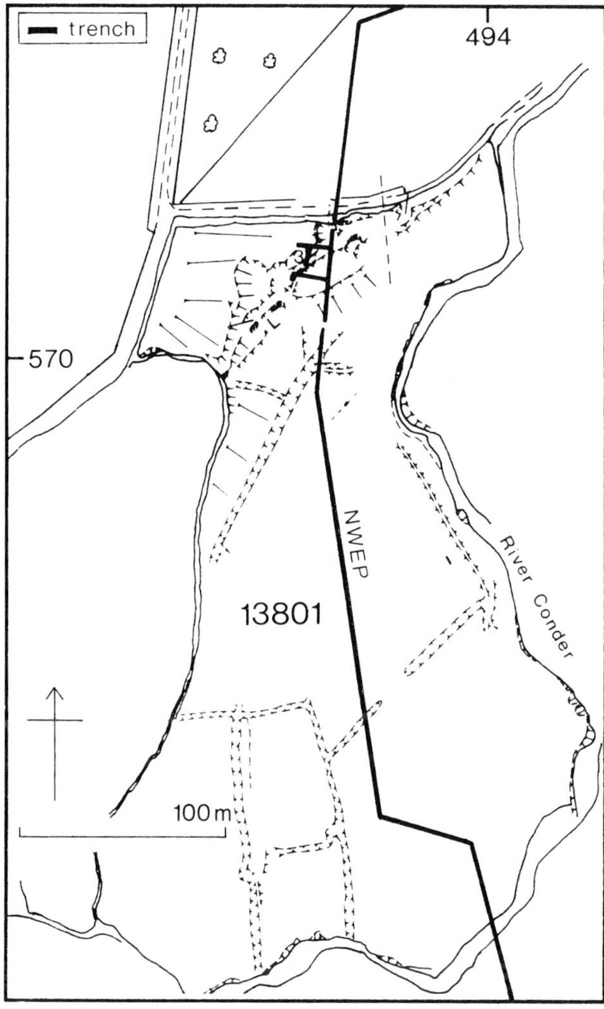

*Figure 2:31 Banton House Farm (**13801**), surveyed
features*

*Figure 2:32 Banton House Farm (**13801**), OS 1st edn
6" (1848)*

1848). Ridge and furrow was visible at the south side of the floodplain (**13804**) and on the steep bank of Kit Brow (**13805**).

Ellel

East of Galgate, undulating pastoral farmland, with occasional stands of deciduous woodland, occupies the catchment area of the River Conder. During construction, a stony hedgebank and ditch (**13916**) were sectioned near Whitley Beck, at the back of Cockshades Hill. Whitley Beck was the boundary of land at Cockshades which was the subject of a grant by Herbert de Ellel to the canons of Cockersand Abbey in 1190–1220 (Farrer 1905a, 779).

The motorway was crossed by auger boring between Galgate and Hampson Green, and to its west at Pennine Farm another stony hedgebank and ditch were intercepted (**13914**). A gravel and clinker surfaced trackway (**13915**) was observed after topsoil strip-ping for a temporary access road to the motorway crossing point here. On the low hill between the A6 road and the Lancaster Canal south of Lane House, a number of features were noted. A trackway, in part a hollow-way (**1393**), was overlain by modern field boundaries, and on the west-facing slope were a lynchet and a boundary bank (**1394**). Adjacent to Quarry Wood were two trackways (**1395**), one a hollow-way, both of which were probably associated with quarry pits and waste dumps in this area. A hollow-way some 2m deep, with a hedgebank on its western side (**13917**), led around the flank of the hill from the A6 to Double Bridge over the canal.

The Lancaster Canal (**13912**) was bored for the third time south of Double Bridge, and the route then entered the Ellel Grange estate, where a post-medieval field system seen on aerial photographs was visible during fieldwalking as a series of ditches, ridge and furrow, and a lynchet (**13910, 13913, 1401**). West of Home Farm was a terraced trackway (**1402**), which after topsoil removal was seen to have a cobbled surface overlying an earlier, narrower trackway.

Cockerham

West of the canal the landscape becomes characteristic of the Lancashire Fylde, which the pipeline route traversed from Thurnham south to the River Ribble, over or around reclaimed peat mosses, whose low-lying fertile soils are subject to relatively intensive cultivation. Ridge and furrow was observed in the fields north of Cockerham (**1403**, **1406**), but the reclaimed marshland to the west appeared featureless, and at Marsh Houses, circular cropmarks seen on aerial photographs (**1414**) were not confirmed during examination of the subsoil after topsoil removal.

Crimbles

South of the River Cocker, a succession of linear earthworks was recorded between Little Crimbles and Hardhead (Fig 2:33). Crimbles was mentioned in Domesday Book as a small manor within the lordship of Preston, but was absorbed into the manor of Cockerham in the mid twelfth century, when William de Lancaster gave the manor of Cockerham and 'the Hamlets of Great and Little Crimbles' to Leicester Abbey (Lancashire SMR 2528; Sharpe France 1955, 38). Crimbles was listed in a rental of the 1150s preserved in the abbey's cartulary, and subsequently featured in the manorial custumal of 1326. The custom of the manor required that the tenants of Cockerham as a whole should not 'dig more turves than they can conveniently and sufficiently use for burning', and specifically that the tenants of Great and Little Crimbles should 'maintain the dikes of the mill pond so that the pond does not burst for the lack of them' (Sharpe France 1955, 42).

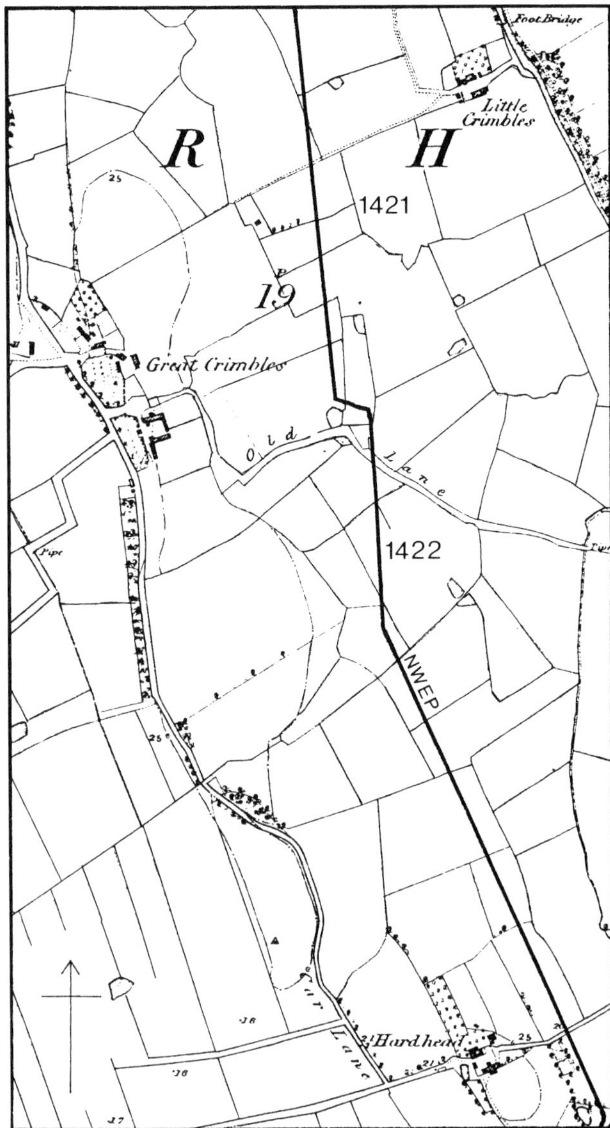

*Figure 2:33 Crimbles (**1421**, **1422**), near Cockerham, OS 1st edn 6″ (1848), with NWEP route superimposed*

Crimbles has been listed as a deserted medieval village (Lancashire SMR 2528), and there was reason to believe the site might be traversed by the pipeline route. The area was therefore closely observed, by means of aerial, geophysical, and topographical survey, prior to trial excavation in September 1990. South-west of Little Crimbles Farm, promising linear depressions turned out to be redundant watercourses (**1421**), and no archaeological stratigraphy or medieval artefacts were found here during either trial excavation or topsoil removal. It is suggested that the site of the medieval village is more likely to be to the west of the pipeline crossing, closer to Great Crimbles.

An extensive area of medieval or post-medieval field boundaries, ridge and furrow, hollow-ways, ponds, and platforms (**1422**) survived in the neighbouring fields of Middle Crimbles. A substantial boundary bank separated the upper part of one field, containing ridge and furrow, from the lower-lying section, quite different in character and once probably peat-covered, which contained linear ditches, ponds, and rectilinear platforms. During construction, peat was observed between Middle Crimbles and Hardhead, and peat-cutting and drainage of the moss, from the medieval period onwards, but particularly in the last two centuries, have contributed to the pattern of earthworks here. Cropmarks seen on aerial photographs, interpreted as ditched field boundaries overlying trackways (**1423**), were not visible on the ground or after topsoil removal.

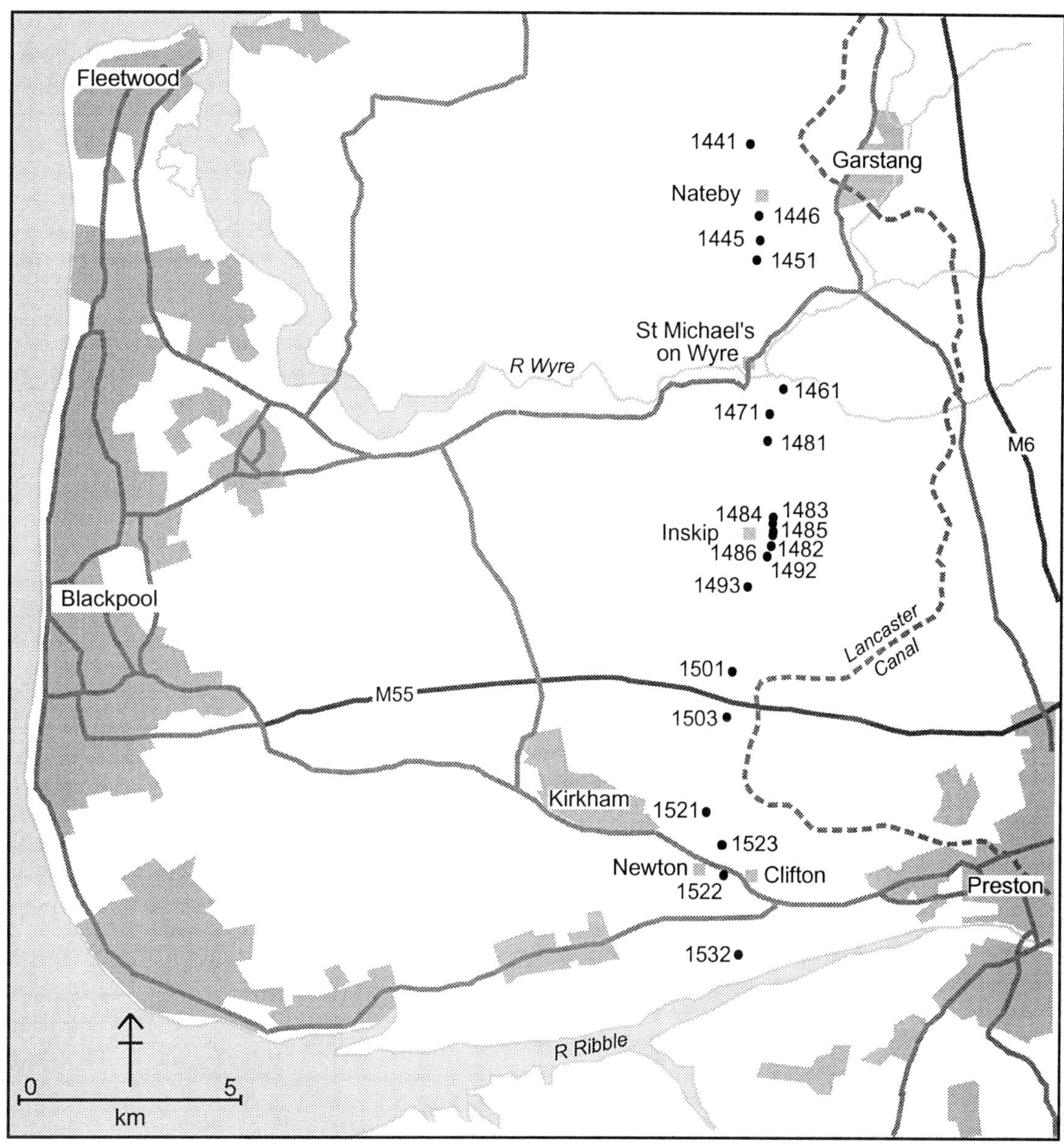

*Figure 2:34 NWEP sites in the Lancashire Fylde (**1441–1532**)*

Nateby

The embankment of the Garstang and Knott End Railway (**1441**), disused since 1965, was demolished at the crossing point of the pipeline. The route continued across the level farmland of the Fylde, from Nateby to St Michael's on Wyre, encountering few archaeological sites in this low-lying landscape of reclaimed mossland. During topsoil removal an exceptionally deep peat deposit (**1446**) south of Nook Farm was tested by auger traverse, which established its depth as at least 5.8m, originating in the immediately post-glacial period. A field boundary was recorded during construction west of Watson's Wood (**1445**) and another was briefly excavated (**1451**), but no features were seen on the extensive floodplain of the River Wyre east of St Michael's,

and south of the river boundaries seen on aerial photographs (**1471**) were not visible during construction.

Inskip

Broad medieval ridge and furrow, in a poor state of preservation as a result of later ploughing, was visible in most of the fields east of Inskip (**1482, 1483, 1484, 1485, 1486, 1492**), and south of Higham Side (**1493**), indicating intensive cultivation in the past. The route crossed the motorway (M55) between Stanley Lodge and Stanley Grange, where cropmarks of field boundaries seen from the air (**1501, 1503**) were not visible on the ground, or after topsoil removal.

Figure 2:35 *Newton-with-Clifton (**1522**), OS 1st edn 6" (1848)*

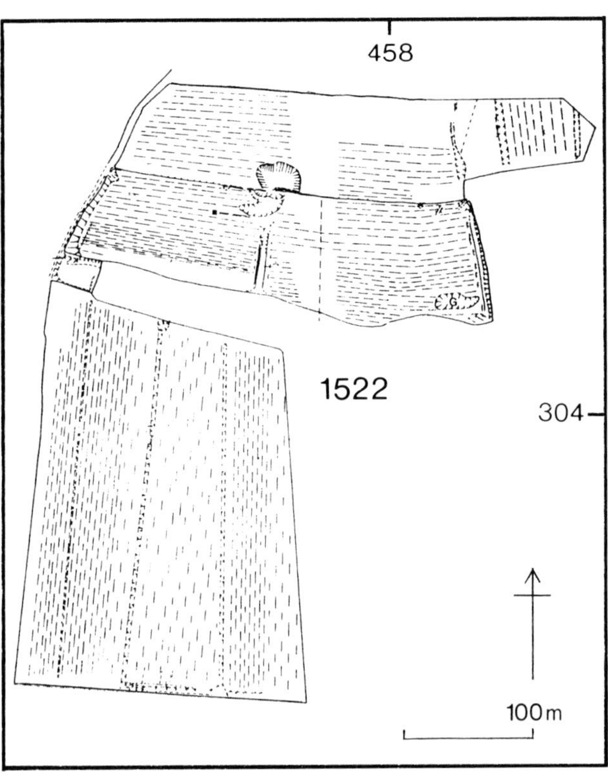

Figure 2:36 *Newton-with-Clifton field system (**1522**), surveyed features*

Newton-with-Clifton

East of Kirkham, at Dingle Farm, broad medieval ridge and furrow was again visible (**1521**) and, nearer to Newton, well preserved broad medieval ridge and furrow (**1523**) was not only over 1m in height, and up to 10m wide, but formed a clear pattern in the subsoil after topsoil was stripped.

The best preserved field system in the lowland sector of the route was recorded north of Hanging Banks Plantation, between Newton and Clifton (**1522**, Fig 2:35). The features covered a large area of the terrace above the plantation on a steep scarp, and also below on the floodplain of the River Ribble. The fields on the terrace (Fig 2:36) contained broad and narrow ridge and furrow 13m and 2.5m wide, with headlands, trackways, ditches, small quarries, and a building platform, of medieval and post-medieval date. The broad ridge and furrow here was also visible in the subsoil after the topsoil strip in the two fields north of the plantation. On the floodplain, ridge and furrow 4.5m wide was probably of later date.

The final site north of the Ribble was a sea bank at Clifton Marsh (**1532**) which was sectioned during construction. The bank was apparently the earlier of two dykes built successively to control floodwaters in the Ribble estuary.

Much Hoole

The Ribble was crossed by boring, and south of the crossing, at Hall Pool Bridge by Longton Marsh, was an isolated survival of narrow post-medieval ridge and furrow (**1551**). The West Lancashire Railway (**1561**), closed in 1964, was crossed at a cutting west of Much Hoole. Cropmarks of field boundaries (**1562, 1564**) on the alluvium east of the River Douglas, identified from aerial photographs, were not confirmed on the ground, but broad medieval ridge and furrow and headlands were visible in one field (**1563**). South of Much Hoole, a small, shallow pit, possibly of prehistoric origin, was observed after topsoil removal, cut into the clay subsoil and filled with a stiff, charcoal-stained, black clay containing a few burnt pebbles (**1565**).

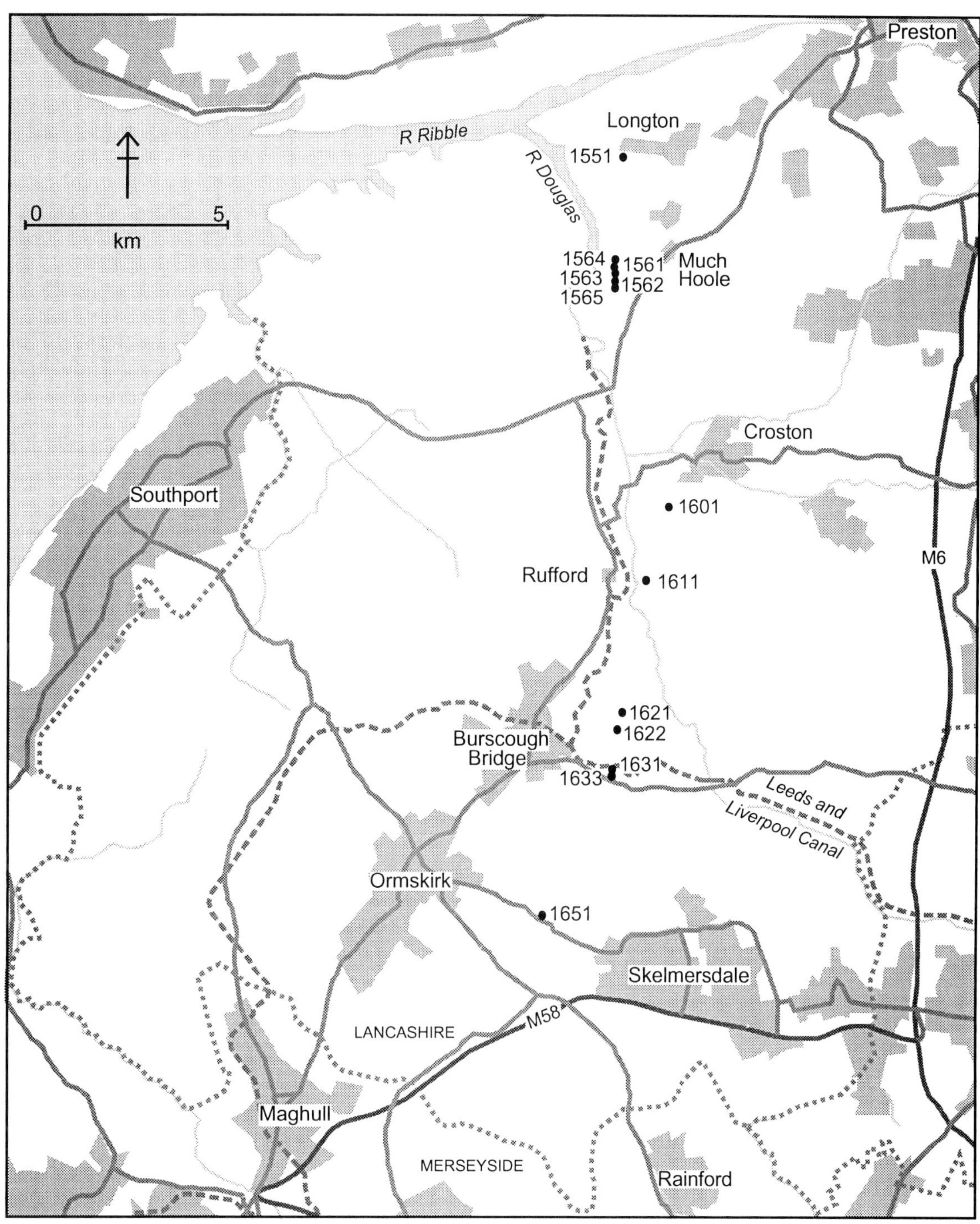

*Figure 2:37 NWEP sites in West Lancashire (**1551–1651**)*

Croston Moss

The farmland from Croston to Burscough is the result of large-scale reclamation of the peat mosses. Croston Moss is a former raised mire which retained deep peat deposits in places, while elsewhere the level of the peat had been lowered by agricultural activity, to the extent that the underlying non-peat deposits were exposed. A gouge auger core transect here confirmed the existence of a sand island, formed of Shirdley Hill Sand, which in prehistoric times would have been ideal for settlement, as a dry island surrounded by mosslands (**1601**). A prehistoric worked flint was recovered from the surface during the coring. Further south, on Marsh Moss, large fragments of bog oak had been brought to the surface of the glacial clay subsoil (**1611**).

Burscough

Linear and circular cropmarks near Bleak Hall Farm, shown on aerial photographs (**1621**), were not visible on the ground, but a linear feature, probably a drainage ditch (**1622**), was observed during construction nearby. The Leeds and Liverpool Canal (**1631**) was bored near Moss Bridge, east of Burscough, and associated features were not affected by construction. Cropmarks of linear features and a D-shaped enclosure (**1633**), in the nearby arable fields, were not visible on the ground. The Ormskirk to Rainford Junction branch of the Liverpool, Ormskirk and Preston Railway (**1651**), closed in 1964, was crossed by a section through the trackbed, but no associated features were affected.

Merseyside

The comparatively low survival rate for archaeological sites on Merseyside is attributable to the effects of intensive agriculture, succeeded by the spread of industry and housing. In complete contrast to the Cumbrian uplands, upstanding earthworks of any period prior to the Industrial Revolution are rare, and such structural remains as there are tend to be relics of that era.

Billinge

A trackway observed during construction near Shoot's Delph Farm (**1752**) was probably of fairly recent date, as the make-up included crushed brick and cinder. Further east, post-medieval ruins relating to Startham Hall (**1751**) were located during fieldwalking, and a row of rough sandstone blocks was seen during construction, but these were undressed and unmortared, and appeared to have been reused in a drain. To the east of Startham Hall, the pipeline passed through a narrow section of Goyt Hey Wood, which is classified as Ancient Woodland and contains mainly oak with some willow and alder carr in the valley bottom (SCUK 1989, 14.13).

Haydock

At Arch Lane, a brick tunnel *c*2.5m high (**1771**) was intersected during trenching, on a rerouted section which had not previously been investigated. No evidence was found for the possible medieval moated site at New Hall (**1791**), and the only other site north of the East Lancashire Road (A580) was a disused branch railway line, which once connected the Liverpool to Manchester Railway with the Liverpool, St Helens, and South Lancashire Railway (**1792**). The railway was crossed in a cutting, without damage to any associated features. The Roman road at Lodge Lane (**1801**) has been overlain by modern roads and other development, and there was no trace of the road make-up described in 1883 as 'about 200 yards in length... 14 yards in width and a yard in thickness. It was formed of earth, with a layer of rude blocks of red sandstone, and upon this a layer of gravel... it does not seem to have been paved' (Watkin 1883, 64–5).

Newton-le-Willows

The same branch railway line crossed at Haydock was crossed again at Newton-le-Willows (**1811**), where the embankment was bored without significant disturbance. Several other sites in this area were of very limited interest, resulting from fairly recent industrial activity, including a pond (**1812**), a field boundary or drain (**1813**), and an area of tipping bounded by a clay bank (**1814**). On Newton Common, however, slight earthworks may indicate the site of a spectators' stand adjacent to the former racecourse here (**1821**). The racecourse is shown on the OS 1st edn 6" map (OS 1872), and the stand is visible on photographs taken in 1887, seen in the Swan Inn (pers comm J Quartermaine). West of Penkford Bridge, a disused section of the St Helens Canal (**1822**) was crossed at a point where it had been infilled, only the towpath remaining as a public footpath.

Cheshire

Fiddler's Ferry

The area around Fiddler's Ferry was considered to have archaeological potential, as it is composed of waterlogged and riverine deposits likely to preserve organic remains (**1871**), but no evidence for prehistoric or later activity was recovered from any part of the Mersey crossing. The River Mersey here is flanked by the St Helens Canal (**1872**) to the north and the Manchester Ship Canal (**1881**) to the south. No new archaeological evidence was recovered at either of these canal crossings, or from the intersection, to the south-east, of the first modern canal built in England, the Bridgewater Canal (**1882**).

Daresbury

West of Daresbury Hall, post-medieval stone wall foundations, recorded during construction (**1895**), may represent the former boundary wall of the Hall.

Figure 2:38 NWEP sites in Merseyside (**1751–1842**)

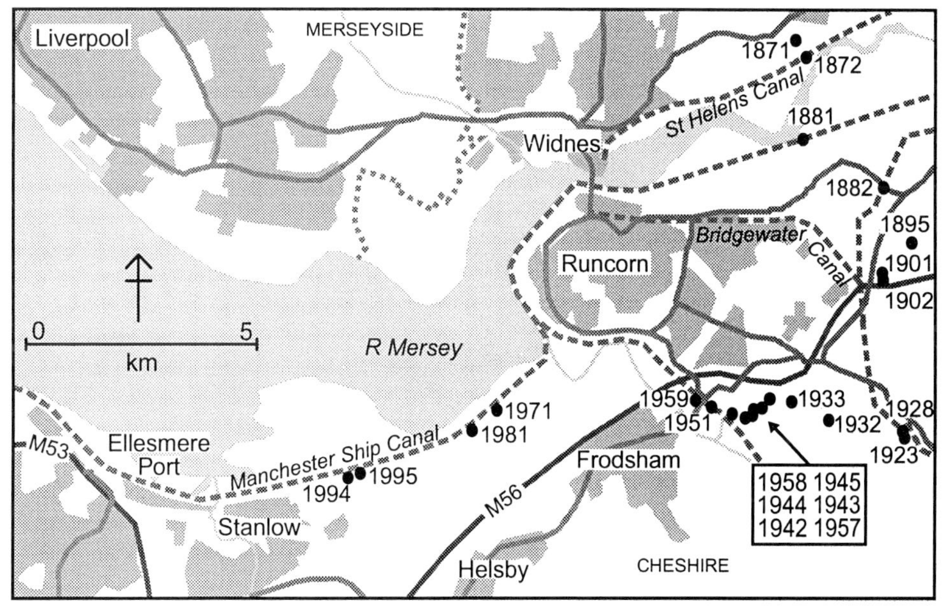

Figure 2:39 NWEP sites in Cheshire (**1871–1995**)

A pair of medieval lynchets (**1901**) survived west of Newtonbank Farm, near the motorway (M56).

Dutton

Near the north bank of the Trent and Mersey Canal (**1923**), which the pipeline crossed at Longacre Wood, a concentration of nineteenth and twentieth century debris, including pottery, brick, slate, and oyster shell, was noted during fieldwalking, and a pottery sample was collected from spoil heaps during construction. During cleaning and assessment of the pottery, all of which was discarded, a prehistoric flint waste flake was found (**1928**).

Aston

The low ridge north of the village of Aston had been highlighted as an area where evidence for prehistoric occupation may survive, but no sites were observed during fieldwalking of the ridge. Several flints were, however, found here during construction. An early Neolithic leaf arrowhead was found on the subsoil after the topsoil strip north of Aston Lane (**1933**), and a waste flake was found in the burnt fill of a ditch, exposed during topsoiling west of Bird's Wood (**1932**). Further west, near Sutton Hall, a prehistoric flint and two chert fragments were found following topsoil removal (**1958**).

Sutton

South of Sutton Hall, narrow post-medieval ridge and furrow, banks, and trackways (**1942**, **1943**), were recorded during fieldwalking. During construction close to Beckett's Wood, a pit containing post-medieval pottery (**1945**) was exposed, and a linear feature, probably a ditch (**1944**), was also recorded.

Beckett's Wood

On a steep bank above the Weaver Navigation, construction activity disturbed brick foundations, consisting of parallel rows of bricks laid end to end on the natural subsoil, with evidence of firing (**1957**). A brief excavation and survey of the site in June 1991 indicated that this had been a brick clamp, a temporary form of kiln used for producing bricks. Its period of operation was probably during the building of the nearby canals or railways in the eighteenth or nineteenth century, although the OS 1st edn and subsequent 6″ maps do not show any structures at this location (OS 1872, 1899, 1910). At the time when this part of Cheshire was undergoing rapid industrial development and population increase, bricks would have been in great demand. The temporary nature of clamp kilns, and the fact that they were designed to be dismantled after use, means that they are rarely found or recorded.

The Weaver Navigation (**1951**) was crossed near the Mill Cut, and further west near the south bank a brick chamber, probably a disused cesspit (**1959**), was located during construction.

Frodsham and Ince Marshes

Considerable disturbance of the alluvial deposits of Frodsham and Ince Marshes occurred during the construction of the Manchester Ship Canal in 1897, and a number of prehistoric artefacts were recovered from the alluvium at that time, including Bronze Age spearheads (**1971**) and a looped and socketed bronze axe (**1995**). The pipeline followed the southern bank of the canal for the last 6km of the route to the Stanlow oil refineries, through the area of major previous disturbance. Stratified finds were not, therefore, expected, although there was some potential for random finds of prehistoric artefacts, but an undated piece of scrap bronze (**1981**) discovered by a fencing crew was the only find recorded during the watching brief in this area. Finally, a series of rectangular platforms (**1994**) alongside the Ship Canal at Holme Farm may have been the foundations for a navvy camp, providing temporary accommodation for labourers during the construction of the canal in 1897.

The distribution of archaeological sites within the regional transect

---

In avoiding both the more rugged and urbanised areas, the pipeline transect largely affected land which has been intensively exploited for agriculture over many centuries, although where possible it crossed marginal areas of least agricultural value, revealing a palimpsest of prehistoric, medieval, and post-medieval rural settlement, with a later overlay of transport systems and associated industry. The choice of route also determined the presence within the transect of many sites relating to communications, for it followed closely the west coast corridor shared by a succession of routeways, including Roman, medieval, and turnpike roads, canals and railways, and most recently the M6 motorway.

Among the most frequent and widespread of all the archaeological remains encountered were the earthworks associated with rural settlement and landuse of all periods, from prehistoric times down to the Parliamentary Enclosures of the eighteenth and nineteenth centuries. In the uplands the environment has always been more hostile than on the coastal plain and in the lowland valleys, resulting in the dispersed settlement pattern produced by a subsistence economy based on pastoral farming. Although individual components of these historic landscapes may not necessarily have a high intrinsic archaeological value, their accurate survey for the purposes of the NWEP project has provided invaluable data for enhanced interpretation, in the future, of the farms and field systems to which they belong.

In the lowlands of the Eden Valley, the Fylde, West Lancashire, and North Cheshire, a milder climate and deeper fertile soils made arable farming viable, and consequently settlement has been more concentrated and prosperous, often resulting in the growth of nucleated villages. Upland sites are frequently preserved as earthworks because the marginal nature of the land precludes the destructive effect of repeated ploughing so common in the valleys, where cropmarks are often the only visible sign of earlier patterns of settlement and agriculture. The lowlands south of the River Ribble have been subject to intensive agricultural and industrial activity, and the survival of prehistoric earthworks is correspondingly low, although the abundance of finds of prehistoric date, over the last two centuries, confirms the early occupation of the region.

The evident disparity between the extensive surviving remains in the upland rural areas of Cumbria and North Lancashire, and the paucity of sites in lowland industrial and arable West Lancashire, Merseyside, and Cheshire, serves to emphasise the special nature of the northern uplands, where well-preserved earthworks abound. Although the large number of upland sites indicates a higher density of rural population in the past than is now the case, the relatively small number of sites recorded in the south indicates only a more intensive and disruptive subsequent landuse, which has served to obliterate most traces of earlier occupation.

3

ASPECTS OF SETTLEMENT IN TEBAY
AND THE LUNE GORGE

The Lune gorge is well known to travellers on the M6 motorway, the London to Glasgow railway line, and the A685 Kendal to Appleby road (Fig 3:1). The approaches from north and south are spectacular, as the Howgill Fells come into view before the plunge into the confines of the deep valley between Lowgill and Tebay. Settlement in the valley has been profoundly affected by the routeways, from the Roman road to the railways and motorway, all of which, like the NWEP, exploit this convenient north-south gap in the Pennine-Cumbrian range of hills.

A detailed analysis of all the areas traversed by the NWEP obviously was not feasible, and emphasis was naturally given to the four main excavation areas (*see Chapters 4, 5, 6, and 7*). Two of these excavations were, however, located at Low Borrowbridge and Powsons in the Lune gorge, where the pipeline route was impressed on a landscape which is highly visible from the M6, but about which very little of historical interest has been published. This valley, between Tebay in the north and Lowgill 9km to the south, was selected for more detailed appraisal because of the intense modification of the archaeological landscape that had already occurred. The NWEP represents merely the latest episode in the reshaping of a valley whose landscape reflects the powerful changes wrought by many centuries of territorial and political ambition, from the Roman military occupation, Anglian and Norse settlers, and medieval barons, to the enhanced communications by road and railway in the less turbulent post-medieval period.

A coherent picture of the settlement pattern during the post-Roman period could only emerge from study of a more extensive landscape than the actual pipeline corridor, which was only 40m wide. Consequently a revised area of study was defined by the documentary source material, parish boundaries, and the local topography, to coincide with the modern civil parish of Tebay, with reference, as appropriate, to adjoining parishes. The key documents used were the Lonsdale archive, which

includes the manorial records of Tebay from 1560 (D/Lons/L, Wharton Box 1), and the Tebay tithe map and apportionment (WDRC/8/110), in conjunction with estate, county, OS, and railway maps. The absence of modern county or parish histories necessitated the use of a great variety of published sources. Documentary evidence for the medieval period in Westmorland is notably sparse, in comparison with the southern counties, and its border location in long disputed territory led to land charters being granted relatively late. The first known land grants are recorded in Farrer's transcript of the Cockersand cartulary (Farrer 1905b) for the parishes adjoining Tebay to the south, and in the eighteenth century county history of Westmorland (Nicholson and Burn 1777) for Tebay itself. Documentary sources referring specifically to Tebay are

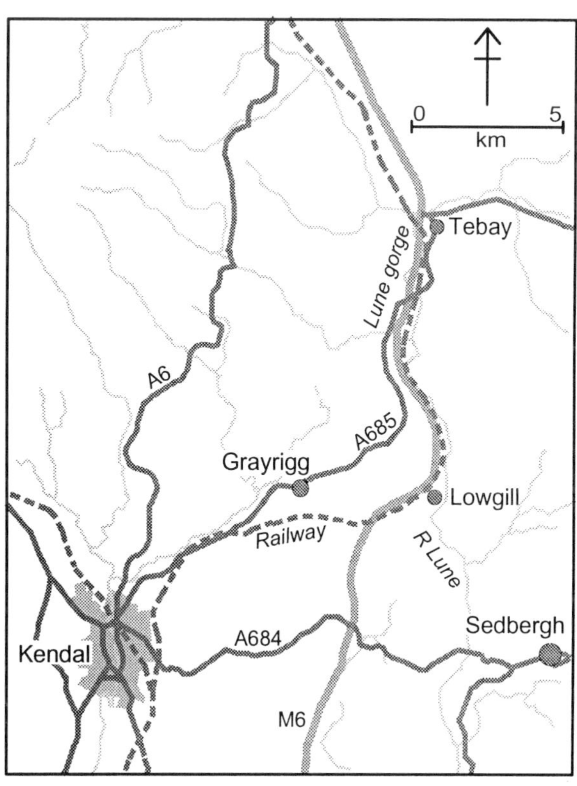

Figure 3:1 Location of Tebay and the Lune gorge

45

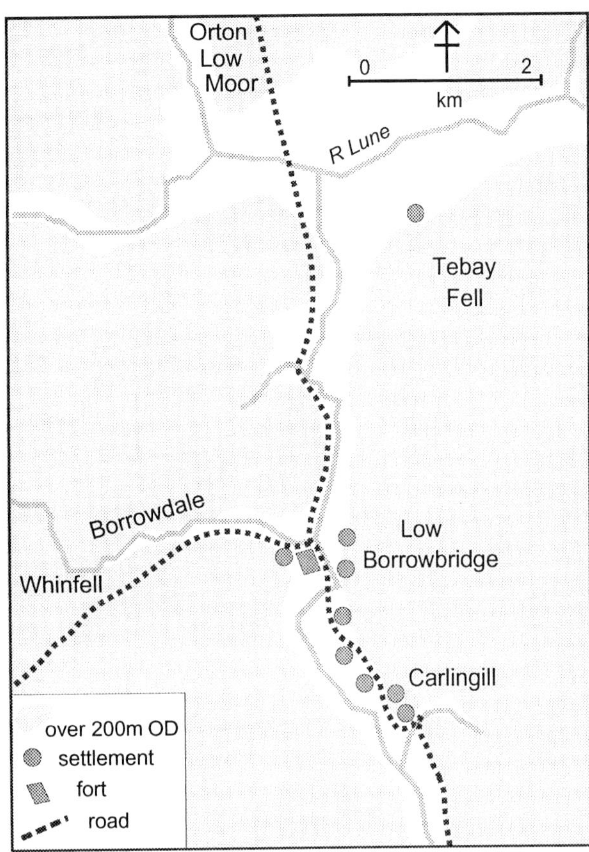

Figure 3:2 Roman fort, roads, and settlements in the Lune gorge

not readily available in the County Record Offices for the medieval period, and sources potentially relevant in the Public Record Office and elsewhere are as yet untapped.

A greater density of archaeological sites was intersected by the NWEP in the Lune gorge than in any other section of the pipeline route (Figs 2:17, 2:19). Independent fieldwork over the last 20 years has greatly increased the number of recorded sites, particularly settlements of probable Romano-British date, and features associated with the Roman fort at Low Borrowbridge (Fig 3:2). These sites typically survive as earthworks in the shallow topsoil, but with limited subsoil presence. Many sites have been disturbed in the past, with adverse effects on archaeological survival: neither the construction of three railway lines in the last century, nor that of the M6 motorway in 1967–70, was accompanied by any archaeological recording. Furthermore, in this narrow and steep-sided valley there is little scope for avoiding known sites, or for minimising damage, as rock-blasting and terracing have been an inevitable part of route engineering in the gorge for railways and roads, and indeed for the pipeline.

The record search, combined with fieldwork and aerial photography, identified a total of 29 archaeological sites lying at least partly within the pipeline corridor between Tebay and Lowgill. These sites were mainly associated with settlement and farming, and include several possible Romano-British settlements (**1116, 1136, 1138**) in the vicinity of the Roman fort (Fig 3:2). Two significant excavations took place in the Lune gorge during pipeline construction, at sites only 1.5km apart: the probable medieval shieling and later farmstead at Powsons (**1132**) (*see Chapter 7*), and the Roman cemetery associated with the fort (**11318**) (*see Chapter 5*). The concentration of sites here is striking in comparison with the low incidence of sites along the pipeline route both north and south of the Lune gorge. To the north, Crosby Ravensworth Fell and Orton Low Moor, crossed by the main Roman road, have historically been used as unenclosed upland grazings, and the field boundaries and settlement sites characteristic of the Lune gorge were not observed on these limestone uplands. They are, however, rich in evidence for prehistoric occupation (Cherry and Cherry 1987, 8–41), and this was represented in the pipeline transect by a modest number of flints collected during and after construction on Crosby Ravensworth Fell (**1085, 1092, 1093**). The notable lack of prehistoric earthworks of any kind in the confines of the Lune gorge suggests either that the valley was not in prehistory a major routeway, or that intensive use from the Romano-British period onwards has obscured the earlier pattern of use. South of Lowgill, where the valley broadens and the pipeline route climbs over Firbank Fell to Killington, the valley fields are again succeeded by rough moorland with little evidence, within the pipeline corridor at least, for past cultivation or field systems. It seems, therefore, that harsh as the environment might appear today, at various times in the past the Lune gorge has been a favoured location, by Westmorland standards, for fairly intensive settlement and landuse.

The climate and geology have been as formative on the landscape as human influence (Fig 3:3). This deeply cut valley seems to have its origin in the early Pleistocene, when the headwaters of a stream following a major fault in the Howgill Fells west of Sedbergh cut northwards through the watershed between Borrow Beck and Carlingill. The resultant breach eventually led to the formation of the upper Lune Valley north of the Howgills, as streams previously draining north to the Eden Valley were diverted to flow west with the infant River Lune as far as Tebay, before turning abruptly at the confluence with Birk Beck to flow due south through the breached watershed to Lowgill. Glacial activity subsequently deepened the valley, encouraging the capture of streams from the fells to east and north,

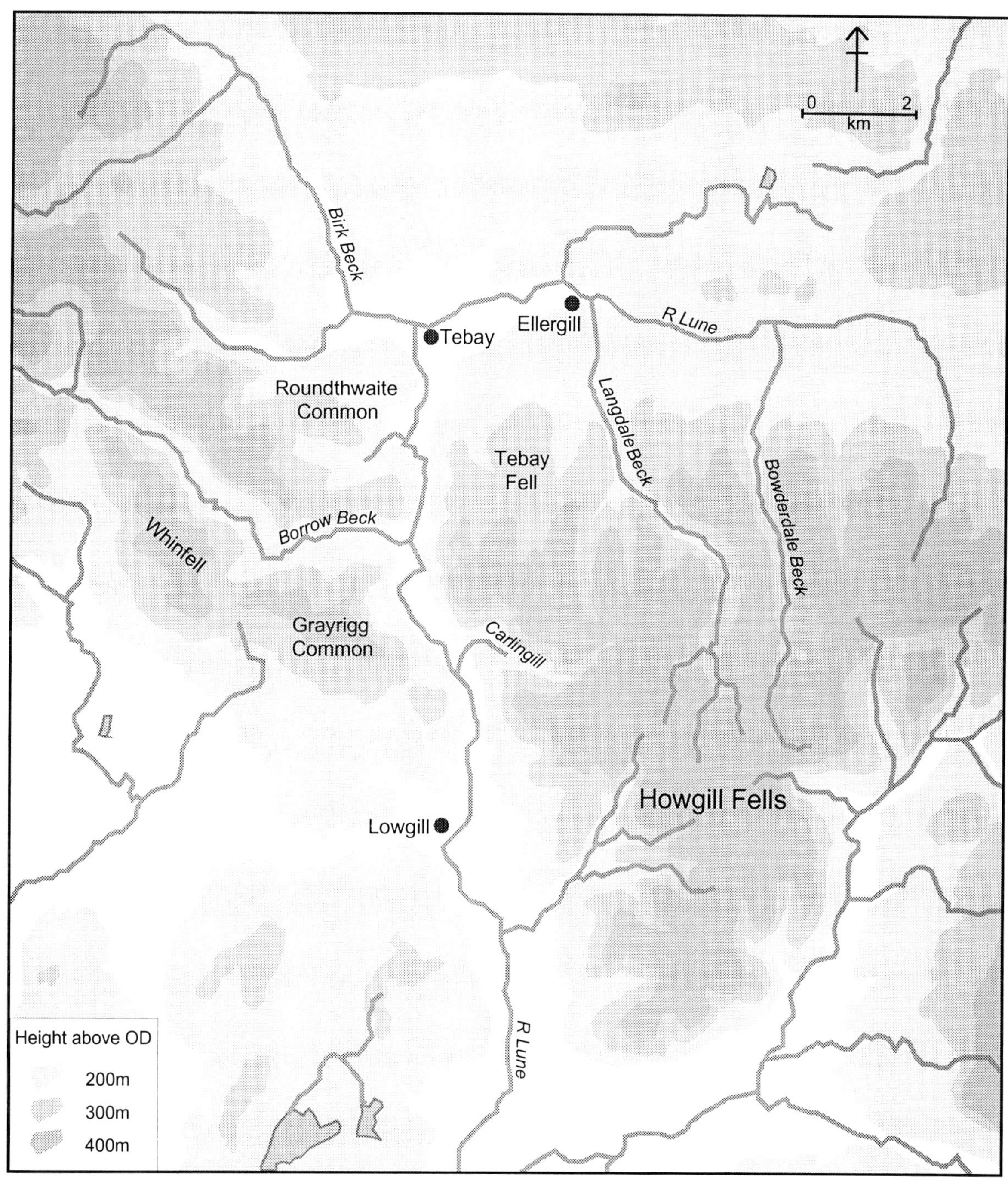

Figure 3:3 Lune gorge, relief and drainage

notably Birk Beck, Borrow Beck, and Carlingill Beck (Pringle 1990, 23–4, fig 2b).

The Howgills and Whinfell, which flank the Lune gorge, were formed by sedimentary processes in the Silurian period. Alluvium and gravels, influenced by fluvio-glacial activity, fill the valley bottom, and boulder clay, deposited by the glaciers flowing southwards from Scotland and the Lake District in the Devensian stage of the Quaternary era (Taylor *et al* 1971, 83–7) extends up the long tributary valleys immediately above the valley floor and onto Tebay Fell. The lower slopes are characterised by the mudstones and siltstones of the Bannisdale slates, and the fells, rising steeply on either side of the valley to a maximum height of 400–600m, are capped by Coniston Grits (both of the Ludlow Series). On the upland plateau stretching from Tebay Fell to Blease Fell, coarse moorland grasses cover eroded peat deposits up to 2m thick, which formed during the relatively mild climatic period between 7500–3000 BC (Taylor *et al* 1971, 90),

47

while occasional exposed rock outcrops show the near vertical bedding planes, often quarried in the past.

Tebay is an upland parish, with its lowest point at the Lune, which flows west and then south through the valley meadows, from 190m OD at Ellergill, falling to 160m at Low Borrowbridge, and 130m at Lowgill. The gradual elimination of trees from the fells, partly as a consequence of stock grazing, has destabilised the soils and hastened the process of gully erosion on the west-facing slopes, which are prone to occasional landslides following heavy rain. Although the valley lands are fairly extensive, especially around the village of Tebay, there is only limited scope for arable cultivation due to the high rainfall. Settlement in the valley has necessarily been based on pastoral farming, and this still predominates, despite the external pressures on the limited meadow land.

The Romans built a fort at the junction of the Lune and Borrow Beck, perhaps in recognition as much of earlier tribal boundaries as of the important routeway they needed to control. In the early medieval period the valley became a focus for the territorial conflict between the northern kingdoms of Strathclyde and Northumbria, and for centuries thereafter was affected by the unstable conditions of the fluctuating northern frontier. The divisions which finally became fixed, through the medieval pattern of feudal lordships, in the modern county and parish boundaries, spelt unrest and insecurity for many generations of the local population.

The Roman fort at Low Borrowbridge may have continued in use as a Dark Age stronghold, perhaps amid the gradual decay of the local farming economy, but little evidence has accrued as yet for the effects of the Roman occupation on settlement (*see Chapter 5: Romans in the Lune valley*). The remaining inhabitants may have drifted or been driven away once the economic benefits and protection of the fort ceased to exist, and only one of the settlement sites recorded on the eastern valley side between Tebay and Low Carlingill, perhaps contemporary with the Roman fort, gives any hint of later activity. The site (**1136**, Cumbria SMR 3525), close to the fort, has been excavated (Anstee 1986) and was dated by the finds to the first or second century AD. The embanked, stone-built enclosure, *c*15.25m square, with the main entrance facing north, is quite untypical of settlements in the valley, and may have been modified during the medieval period. The pipeline was unexpectedly rerouted onto the steep slope below the site, close to its western perimeter, and cut through a hollow-way rising from the fields in the valley bottom.

The Roman name for the fort at Low Borrowbridge remains uncertain, although a recent interpretation of the Antonine Itinerary advances the probability that it was *Galava* (Shotter 1993, 105–6). The name Borrowdale (*borg dalr*, 'the valley of the fortification') is of Norse origin (Smith 1967, 1, 138), and this implies structural survival into the medieval period; even a derelict fortification at this juncture would have fulfilled a useful defensive function in the unsettled frontier zone. The imprint of the two well engineered Roman roads which meet at Low Borrowbridge remains clear in the few places where these are not overlain by modern roads. The route through the main valley followed Howgill Lane, referred to in a mid thirteenth century grant to Cockersand Abbey as the *magnam stratam quae tendit de Lonnesdale versus Westmeriam* (Farrer 1905b, 961), and this is now the secondary road through the Lune gorge. The road up Borrowdale and over Whinfell towards Kendal and Watercrook fort is shown on nineteenth century maps (OS 1858), and survives today in the form of a broad terraced trackway as far as the summit of Whinfell. These roads appear therefore to have continued in use into the medieval period, perhaps influencing the later distribution of settlement in the valley.

Some of the present valley farms, such as High and Low Carlingill (NY 61400040, SD 62209968) and Whins (SD 63209743), are on or near the sites of possible Romano-British settlements (Fig 3:4), and other farms may overlie and thus obscure the earlier settlements. These farms, past and present, have probably always occupied preferred locations as regards aspect, water supply, and quality of land, and some may have been reoccupied during the later medieval expansion of settlement. Two upland peat deposits, one beneath an alluvial fan in Carlingill (SD 62759980), the other nearby but high up on Archer Moss (NY 63300062), have provided pollen samples, analysed by Cundill (1976). Although the sample sites lie to the east of the main valley, and the process of pollen deposition generally reflects the vegetation of the immediate vicinity, this can be modified by local conditions, and it is recognised that mires on upland plateaux can receive canopy component pollen by way of the updraft from local winds (Moore *et al* 1991, 15–16). In this case the prevailing south-westerly winds would blow pollen from the wooded Lune gorge up Carlingill and onto the fell above (Cundill 1976, 306). The evidence of pollen analysis points to the unlikelihood of continuity of settlement in the valley in the early medieval period, since the samples indicate a phase of woodland clearance during the Roman occupation, followed by many centuries of woodland regeneration (Cundill 1976, 308). The known abandoned farmsteads in the Lune

Figure 3:4 Romano-British settlement at High Carlingill

gorge north of Carlingill lie within the present field system, implying that the margin of settlement, as dictated by the topography, lay approximately on the 200m contour, which is followed by the present intake wall dividing the enclosed and improved fields from the open fell.

Britons, Anglians, and Vikings

The Lune gorge probably lay within the fifth century British kingdom of Rheged, whose territorial boundaries remain a matter of conjecture. It is thought to have extended from the Solway plain to Tebay, or perhaps Kirkby Lonsdale (Higham 1986, 253), although at some stage it may have reached as far south as the Ribble (Fell 1973, 237) or even the Mersey. In the later sixth century the Lyvennet Valley, 7km north of Tebay, seems to have been a chief estate centre of Urien, king of Rheged (Higham 1986, 266). After Urien's death, Rheged was challenged by the Northumbrian Anglian king, Aethelfrith, and was certainly under Northumbrian rule by about AD 638 (Kirby 1962, 80). Evidence from elsewhere in the region, however, suggests that Anglian control of the part of Rheged later to become Westmorland may not have been formalised until the later seventh century, perhaps around the time that the Northumbrian king, Ecgfrith, in AD 677 granted Cartmel, in North Lancashire, with

all the Britons therein, to St Cuthbert (Farrer and Brownbill 1914, 8, 254).

Place names with Anglian elements are concentrated in the lower Lune Valley between Kirkby Lonsdale and Lancaster, on land suited to arable farming. The slim evidence for an Anglian presence north of Killington in the Lune gorge rests on a few settlement names, none of which have the *ing* or *tūn* suffix. The blend of Old English and Old Norse place name elements, in fairly equal proportions with many cognates, makes it impossible to determine the sequence of occupation, especially as the local settlement names were first recorded between the twelfth and fourteenth centuries. This mixture of names may illustrate the relatively peaceful integration of a few Norse settlers alongside even fewer established Anglian farmers in an area where there was, as yet, little or no contest for farmland.

The choice of settlement location would presumably have been influenced by the availability of fertile riverside land, reflected in the place name element *ēg*, denoting an island or water meadow. Tebay, first recorded as *Tibeia* in *c*1160 (Smith 1967, 2, 50), is the only *ēg* settlement name in Westmorland, and one of only three in Cumbria (the others being Corney and Bardsea in the Furness peninsula) (Gelling 1984, 36), and this rarity emphasises its very specific location. *Tiba*, after whom the settlement was named, naturally selected the prime land, the alluvial meadows in the bend of the Lune. The neighbouring Anglian settlement to the north of the Lune, Orton, recorded as *Overton* in 1239 (Smith 1967, 2, 42), may even have been named in relation to Tebay if, as suggested by both Gelling (1984, 178) and Ekwall (1960, 351), it derives from the OE comparative adjective *ufer*, meaning higher or upper. Orton, at 230m OD, occupied the open fellside, in contrast to Tebay, on the valley floor by the river at 180m OD.

Fellows-Jensen concluded that 'names which originally denoted topographical features were among the first to be given by Anglian settlers to their habitation sites' (1985b, 77), and that 'settlements with English names are much more likely to have survived' (1985a, 397), implying that the earlier Anglian settlements were of higher status or situated on better land. If this were the case, then Orton and Tebay may have been of greater importance than their current status implies. Orton was in some respects more advantageously located than Tebay, on gentler south-facing slopes and fertile soils overlying Carboniferous limestone, in an area favoured for occupation since the Neolithic, as the many flint artefacts recently recovered demonstrate convincingly (Cherry and Cherry 1987, 28–41). Orton developed into the early church site and centre of the large ecclesiastical parish to which Tebay later belonged.

Although many of the farmsteads close to the Roman fort would have been forgotten and overgrown in the Anglian period, the nearby farm at Brockholes (*Brokhole*, 1377), on a favourable site with abundant riverside meadows, and Woodend, closer to Tebay, have names hinting at an Anglian origin. The location of Woodend, overlooking Tebay at the north end of the ridge, gives the impression that this farm marked the northern limit of woodland cover on Tebay Fell. The apparent absence of cereal cultivation or woodland clearance at this time (Cundill 1976, 308) points, however, to the abandonment of farming in the Lune gorge in the early medieval period. The lack of diagnostic pre-Conquest artefacts, typical of this period in Cumbria as a whole, is of note here in view of the major earthmoving associated with building roads, railways, and the NWEP, which might be expected to have produced some evidence of occupation. The absence of any such evidence hints at a prolonged lapse of settlement in the Lune gorge after Roman influence faded, and indeed the Roman cemetery near Salterwath Bridge fell out of use during the fourth century (*see Chapter 5*), although the strategic location of the fort at Low Borrowbridge may, as was elsewhere the case, have extended occupation of some sort well into the fifth century (Shotter 1993, 95–6).

The dearth of pollen and artefact evidence make it likely that only Tebay and Orton were of importance in the Anglian period. To the north, the site excavated at Fremington (**10014**) (*see Chapter 6*), near Brougham, was occupied during the Anglian expansion west along the Eden Valley in the seventh century, and may even in some respects be a parallel for the low-status Anglian rural settlement at Tebay, also on a major route and subject to outside influence.

While Anglian settlement was consolidated under Northumbrian rule, the powerful British kings of Strathclyde had territorial ambitions in the former kingdom of Rheged. The decline of Anglian Northumbria in the late eighth century made way for the annexation of Cumbria to Strathclyde by AD 900, by which time Norse settlement was beginning in Westmorland. The River Eamont, 25km north of Tebay, was probably the boundary between Strathclyde and Northumbria in 927, when the British king Owen paid homage to King Athelstan of Wessex here, following his invasion of Northumbria earlier that year (Stenton 1947, 328, 336; Kirby 1962, 86). The district south of the Solway was still part of Strathclyde when Edmund of Wessex ravaged Cumbria in 945. Westmorland was something of a cultural melting pot, as British, Anglian, and Norse settlers were caught up in the border disputes of their respective kings in these turbulent centuries. From being an insignificant and inhospitable backwater, Westmorland in the tenth century was thrust into the forefront of the struggles for domination of the North West. The Scandinavian settlement occurred at a time of population growth and pressure on existing farmland to expand, and the Norse settlers appear to have gravitated to the marginal uplands. Roundthwaite (*Runethweyt*, 'the clearing among the rowan trees'), recorded in 1256 (Smith 1967, 2, 51), is likely to have been created in the secondary colonisation of this area by early Norse settlers (Gelling 1984, 210), and remained subsidiary to Tebay, which by inference was still an 'island' in the woodland surrounding the floodplain in the river bend.

Although the place name element *þveit* 'woodland clearing', is fairly common, with 20 examples in Westmorland (Fellows-Jensen 1985a, 90), Roundthwaite is the only one in this locality (Fig 3:5). A sprinkling of *þveit* and *rydding* names in Sedbergh, Firbank, and Grayrigg nonetheless indicates woodland clearance in the surrounding area. The final phase of woodland regeneration seems to have lasted throughout the early medieval period, as the Norse settlers appear to have made little impact on the wooded slopes in the confines of the Lune gorge, and not until after the Norman Conquest was there a marked decline in tree cover (Cundill 1976, 308).

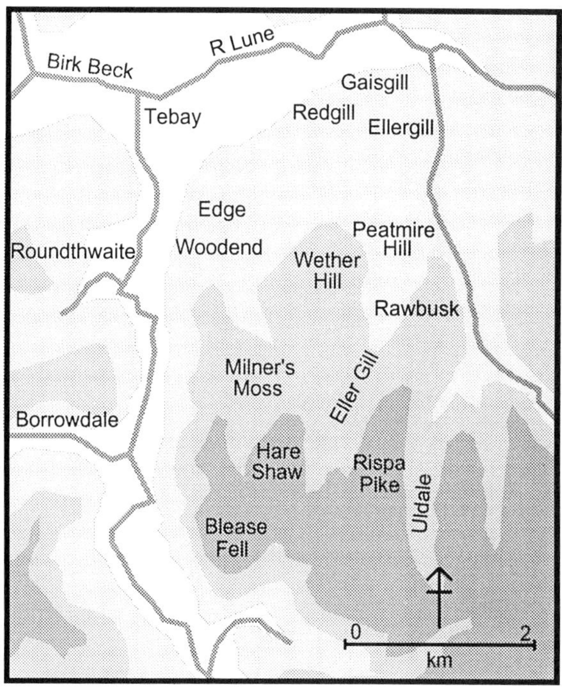

Birk Beck	birch stream
Blease Fell	*blesi,* hill with a bare spot
Borrowdale	*borg dalr,* dale with a fort
Edge	*ecg,* edge
Ellergill	alder-tree ravine
Gaisgill	ravine of the wild geese
Hare Shaw	*sceaga,* hare copse
Milner's Moss	the miller's peat moss or turbary
Rawbusk	*buskr,* bushes
Redgill	reed ravine
Rispa Pike	*hrispe,* brushwood hill
Roundthwaite	rowan clearing
Tebay	*Tiba's ēg,* water-meadow or island
Uldale	*ulfr,* wolf valley
Wether Hill	sheep hill
Woodend	*wudu,* wood

Figure 3:5 Place names indicating landuse in Tebay

During this last phase of woodland regeneration, the pollen diagrams from Carlingill and Archer Moss show the tree species to have been mainly birch, oak, and alder, with smaller numbers of lime, ash, pine, and holly while, among the shrubby vegetation, the predominance of hazel is striking. As some of the pollen may have been blown onto Archer Moss by the wind funnelling along the main valley and Carlingill, the tree species represented probably indicate those growing in the Lune gorge as well as on the surrounding fellsides (Cundill 1976, 306).

The threat of wolves was very real, as indicated by the valley name Uldale (OE *ulfr*), and stock could not be grazed in safety until this threat had been eliminated (Fig 3:5). The juxtaposition of such place names as Uldale and Wether Hill may record the transition from woodland (OE *sceaga*, Hare Shaw, and *wudu*, Woodend) to rough grassland cropped by sheep and cattle: a scrubby deteriorating woodland, still supporting bushes (ON *buskr*, Rawbusk) and undergrowth (OE *hrispe*, Rispa Pike) (Smith 1967, 2, 46, 53). Not until well after the Conquest did persistent grazing of stock finally inhibit woodland regeneration and encourage the growth of heather and coarse grasses on the Tebay fells. Whether or not the monasteries with a local interest were using these grazings, this array of place names suggests that the tree cover dwindled, and that the tenants increasingly used the commons for grazing. This activity presumably eliminated the last remaining trees on the fell tops and higher slopes, while advancing enclosure of fields did likewise on the valley floor, leaving perhaps only a belt of woodland, of which vestiges survive to this day, along the lower slopes.

Other than Tebay itself, which is in part a personal name, the settlement names are mainly topographical, and only a handful are recorded before 1400: Borrowdale (*Borgheredala*, 1154–89) (Farrer 1923, 231), Roundthwaite (1256), Ellergill (1310), and Gaisgill (*Gasegille*, 1310) (Smith 1967, 2, 50–1). If these are truly Norse settlements, they represent colonisation of the Lune gorge as far south as Low Borrowbridge. The *gil* names are characteristic of those given by Norse settlers (Gelling 1984, 99), and it is therefore possible that Gaisgill, Ellergill, Redgill, and Carlingill were all in existence much earlier than the records would suggest. These late recorded place names are typical of Cumbria in general, and are symptomatic of the paucity of documentation for the earlier medieval period in the North West.

Mottes, dykes, and boundaries

Armies, warbands, and raiders all used the gap of the Lune gorge, and probably the surviving stretches of the Roman roads, on their northward and southward campaigns. The local population no doubt had to contend repeatedly with the demands of raiding parties and armies in transit, and although the material requirements of the Roman garrison stationed at Low Borrowbridge had once stimulated the local economy, this may subsequently have been inhibited during the centuries of warfare over this disputed area. The shifting frontiers of war repeatedly challenged the local boundaries, as the kingdoms of Strathclyde and Northumbria battled for supremacy in Cumbria. This territorial conflict evolved into war between two emergent nations: Scotland and England. The Scottish kings ruled

Cumberland and the northern half of Westmorland until the early eleventh century, but their ascendancy was undermined by increasing numbers of English settlements (Kirby 1962, 93). The earls of Northumbria set about suppressing the Cumbrian Britons and took control of their territory in the first half of the eleventh century.

Malcolm III of Scotland invaded Cumbria in 1070, and Gospatric, earl of Northumbria, then plundered Cumbria in retaliation before coming to terms with the Scottish king in 1072 (Stenton 1947, 606). Malcolm then seems to have made Gospatric's son Dolphin lord of Carlisle. When Domesday Book was compiled, Malcolm was still in possession of Cumberland and much of Westmorland apart from Kentdale, and the Scottish border followed the boundary between the Kendal and Westmorland baronies south of Tebay. North Westmorland, including the Tebay area, was in consequence omitted from the Domesday survey, and may therefore have escaped the harrying of Mercia and Northumbria by William I in 1069–70. His son, William Rufus, came north in 1092, however, to evict Dolphin from Carlisle and claim the territory south of the Solway. Malcolm was killed during his invasion of Northumberland in 1093, and the Scottish border was pushed back to the Tweed-Solway line (Kirby 1962, 94). The whole of Westmorland was briefly part of England during Henry I's reign, but upon his death in 1135, the lands *inter Angliam et Scotiam*, that is Cumberland and North Westmorland, reverted to Scottish rule under David I (Poole 1955, 265). Henry II eventually annexed these northern counties to the Crown of England in 1157 (Ferguson 1894, 86; Poole 1955, 275), and this seems to be the point at which Norman rule finally reached this part of the North.

The predations of the Scots nonetheless continued unabated. The devastation caused by the renewed Scottish invasion of 1173 so drastically reduced the Westmorland revenues that no cornage rent was charged in 1175–6, and furthermore, for three years 'a lump sum of £45 2s 6d was allowed for restocking and restoring to culture lands that had been wasted' (Ferguson 1894, 92–3). It is perhaps significant that the first known land grants in Tebay date from 1189, some 12 years later. In a far-flung corner where Norman dominance was still precarious, Tebay can hardly have been a safe or profitable place to live. These first land grants were perhaps intended to establish a strong presence on the border, with one or more castles as a centre of lordship and defence.

To the south of Low Borrowbridge, the Lune Valley until 1974 marked the boundary between Yorkshire and Westmorland, coinciding here with the

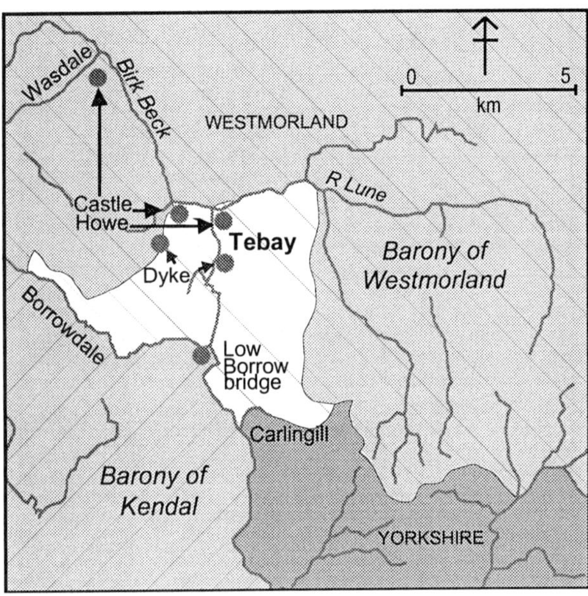

Figure 3:6 Westmorland baronies, pre-1974 counties, and Tebay civil parish

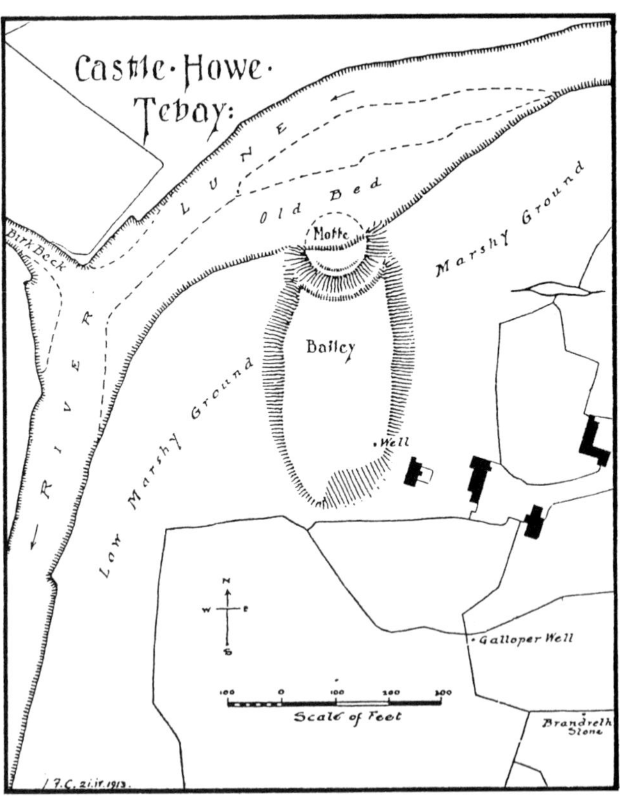

Figure 3:7 Castle Howe, Tebay, looking north (from Curwen 1913, 32)

division between the feudal baronies of Westmorland (Fig 3:6), and this critical location has had a profound effect on its history. The medieval boundary with Yorkshire followed the Lune north to Carlingill, where it turned east to follow the north-south watershed over the Howgills. The Westmorland and Kendal baronies were divided by a boundary following the Lune north from Carlingill to Low Borrowbridge, and thence north-west up Borrowdale. There is still a county boundary stone at Carlingill, and further north another well-known stone survived, built into a field wall, until the motorway was constructed south of Old Tebay. This, the Brandreth Stone (NY 61600490; SMR 4214), was a granite boulder incised with a cross, reputed to have been a boundary or mere stone between the English and the Scots (RCHM(E) 1936, 226). Although it was Borrow Beck, to the south, which marked the boundary between the Westmorland and Kendal baronies, three sites named Castle Howe, at Tebay (NY 61350520; SMR 1946), Greenholme (NY 60080532), and Salterwath (NY 57860910), emphasise the importance of Birk Beck as a medieval boundary.

Castle Howe at Tebay (Fig 3:7) may date from the twelfth century (Curwen 1913, 33), built perhaps by Herbert de Tybai on his land close by the village (Jackson 1990, 89). The strategic site, at the confluence of Birk Beck and the Lune, guarded the entrance to the Lune gorge, much as the Roman fort at Low Borrowbridge had formerly controlled traffic through the gorge. The motte of Castle Howe has been partially eroded by the Lune, whose course has wandered over this flat alluvial floodplain, and its outer bailey now rubs shoulders with the motorway (Fig 3:8). Its location at the head of the Lune gorge emphasises the importance of the route between Tebay and Lancaster, near which no fewer than eleven castles were built, the characteristic motte and bailey structures indicating nine of these (Harrison 1976, 3–4, 50–2, map 1). Clearly this route continued in use after the Conquest, and had not yet been superseded by the route from Kendal over Shap Fell, along which Norman castles are notably absent between Kendal and Bampton, north-west of Shap.

The supposed motte at Low Greenholme, at the confluence of Dorothy Beck and Birk Beck (Fig 3:6), is in the far north-west corner of Tebay parish, and appears unfinished (Curwen 1913, 29; Jackson 1990, 90). It occupies a natural scarp above Birk Beck, but has a remarkably even slope and flat top. The third site named Castle Howe, overlooking Salterwath ford near Wasdale foot, is a circular enclosure atop a natural drumlin with a ruined farmstead on its north side (OS 1864). These castles

Figure 3:8 Castle Howe, Tebay, aerial photograph, looking south

may have been built or refurbished as a line of defence on the shifting Scots border. Another medieval boundary, supposedly defensive, took the form of a *plessicium*, or slashed hedge, and is mentioned in a grant of *c*1180 concerning Borrowdale. William de Lancaster's grant of his land in Borrowdale to Byland Abbey refers to this hedge as part of the boundary, perhaps following the line of the Breasthigh Road, a track from Borrowdale Head over the fell to Bretherdale Head (Curwen 1913, 199–200).

Dyke Farm at Greenholme lies beside Mere Beck on the Tebay parish boundary at the foot of Bretherdale, about 1km from Castle Howe at Low Greenholme (Fig 3:6). The other farm in Tebay named Dyke was above the former railway station, where the land rises steeply to Roger Howe above the main road, at the edge of the still unenclosed commons. These two farms, 1.5km and 2km respectively from the

Figure 3:9 Carlingill

old village of Tebay, may be on the line of the ancient head-dyke, or ring-fence, marking the outer limit of Tebay's cultivated fields and pastures, beyond which was waste and woodland. Access to the commons would be through gates in the head-dyke, and the location of two of these is strongly indicated by the prominent scars of terraced trackways leading onto Roger Howe, and multiple deep hollow-ways from Mount Pleasant.

The dykes referred to in these names may thus indicate a transition as new farms were founded on the edge of the waste (Elliott 1973, 49), but another possibility deserves consideration. They may belong to a later period altogether, marking the boundary of the deer park for which William English was granted a licence in 1338/9 (Nicolson and Burn 1777, 1, 492). East of the modern railway village, the boundary between the enclosed fields and the common waste is also marked by two more farms, Edge and Woodend, both of which still lie at the limit of the commons.

Carlingill (Fig 3:9), below Blease Fell, was one of the most remote parts of the Lune gorge, and seems to have been at the interface of the southward expansion from Tebay, and a corresponding northward expansion from Sedbergh. The lowest part of Back Balk, on the south side of Carlingill at the county boundary, is known as Gibbet Hill, and is also the site of a large cairn or burial mound. This place, deep in the Lune Valley at the far corners of Westmorland and Yorkshire, still had macabre associations as late as 1684, when the corpse of William Smorthwaite, a notorious highwayman, was supposedly hung in chains on the gallows here (Macfarlane 1981, 172).

Lords and tenants after the Conquest

Expansion from Tebay, hard up against the Lune and the lands of Orton to the north, was necessarily to the south, into the Lune gorge and up onto the fells. Roundthwaite, on the opposite side of the river, and closer to the gorge than Tebay in the broad upper valley, was of secondary importance, but the two settlements were coupled in land grants of the earlier fourteenth century. A useful comparison can be made with the late thirteenth century colonisation of Derwentfells, in Cumberland, which has been characterised as 'an earlier core of settlement centred on a small village beside open-field arable land on the valley bottom to which was added a dispersed scatter of farmsteads, set in their own enclosed fields, along the lower skirts of the fells' (Winchester 1987, 40). Settlement in Tebay was perhaps delayed by the insecure conditions of the border zone but certainly by the early fourteenth century settlement radiated south, east, and west from Tebay village, encompassing the hamlets of Roundthwaite, Gaisgill, and Ellergill. Slightly further afield, there were smaller settlements at Woodend on Tebay Fell, in Borrowdale, west of Tebay at Greenholme on Birk Beck, and in the main valley at Borrowbridge, Brockholes, and Carlingill.

Westmorland was still held directly from the Crown at the accession of Richard I in 1189, the only exceptions being the manor of Crosby Ravensworth and some land at Tebay. Some 30 years after Henry II annexed Westmorland these were granted to Alan de Valeines. He received cornage rent of £1 6s 8d from these lands, as did his widow's second husband, Hugh de Hastings, until 1200 (Ferguson 1894, 93). The lordship of Tebay seems to have been divided by the earliest date for which records survive, for it was already held in severalty when in 1200/01 Hugh de Hastings, together with Herbert de Tibbay and his son Robert, paid 100 marks to the exchequer for lands here (Nicolson and Burn 1777, 1, 492). They held only part of the manor, for the English family of Little Asby had an interest here, and also a small part was held directly from the barons of Westmorland, the Veteriponts, and later the Cliffords (Nicolson and Burn 1777, 1, 492). King John granted the barony of Westmorland to Robert de Veteripont in 1201, and it later descended through the marriage of Isabel, daughter of the third baron, to her guardian, Roger de Clifford. She held the land in Westmorland directly from the king, and at her death in 1292 her estates descended to her son Robert de Clifford (HMSO 1912, 70). The barony remained in the same family for another 300 years, during which time the lords of Tebay were invariably tenants of the Cliffords.

In 1217/18 Hugh de Hastings was granted free warren in Tebay and Crosby Ravensworth. By 1302/03, this right had passed to Henry Threlkeld of Crosby Ravensworth, and was extended to Roundthwaite as well as Tebay. In 1338/39 William English was granted free warren with licence to impark 100 acres (Nicolson and Burn 1777, 1, 492), but whether the park was ever enclosed or stocked is unknown, nor are there any identifiable earthworks, in contrast to the sixteenth century deer park nearby in Ravenstonedale. Tebay and Roundthwaite were separate lordships at this period, and from 1341 both were subject to a fine, the proceeds of which were granted to William English during his lifetime (Nicolson and Burn 1777, 1, 511). To complicate matters further, his son, three years later, inherited a moiety of the two lordships. Thomas de Hastings held two carucates of land at Tebay from 1283, paying a quitrent of 5s a year (Nicolson and Burn 1777, 1, 492; HMSO 1908, 533), a sum which reappears unchanged in documents up to the seventeenth century, perhaps indicating the survival of this unit of arable land. The Wharton family, later to acquire the lordship in the mid sixteenth century, already had a foothold in Tebay, as the two ploughlands were held jointly until 1482 by the Whartons and the Ristewalds as underfeoffees of the Hastings family (Ragg 1908, 322–7).

By the later thirteenth century, some of the divided lands were held by the Dacres and Musgraves who each, in addition, had a moiety of the neighbouring manor of Orton. The Dacres continued to hold property in Tebay, and Humphrey de Dacre still had lands in Roundthwaite in 1491/92 (Nicolson and Burn 1777, 1, 493). Richard de Blenkinsop of Helbeck, near Brough, also acquired an interest in Tebay in the early fourteenth century, by conveyance of the lands and tenements of Richard son of Robert de Gaisgill, and of William de Ellergill's capital messuage at Ellergill (Nicolson and Burn 1777, 1, 492).

The first half of the fourteenth century is notorious for a disastrous sequence of events: cattle plague in the early years, followed by perhaps the worst of the Scottish raids in 1322, and the Black Death in the late 1340s. The sequel to this was a shrinkage of settlement and consequent neglect of farmland, and this must have been no less devastating in Tebay than elsewhere in the northern border zone. Yet despite these troubles, during this time it was, by Westmorland standards, a relatively prosperous settlement. The Lay Subsidy for 1332 records Tebay's taxable wealth as £60 and 18 taxable households, with broadly similar figures for Kirkby Stephen, Dufton, and Kirkby Thore, whereas in the whole of Westmorland, only the vast manor of Shap (£90, 29 taxpayers) paid more (Fraser 1966, 144). It seems likely, therefore, that colonisation of available land in the immediate vicinity of Tebay and the upper Lune Valley was well advanced. A setback may be inferred, however, from the fact that Cumberland and Westmorland were exempted from this taxation only two years later, in 1334, in recognition of the devastation ensuing from the renewed Scottish wars.

Peripheral monastic influence

There were many twelfth and thirteenth century grants to northern monasteries and priories of extensive lands adjacent to Tebay (Fig 3:10). This is of considerable significance, as monastic land management has been held largely responsible for the transition from cattle and pigs to sheep-rearing in northern England (Pearsall 1961, 79).

Orton's church was granted to Conishead Priory in Furness, while Sedbergh's church was granted to Coverham Priory in Yorkshire. Cockersand Abbey, a Praemonstratensian house at the mouth of the Lune near Lancaster, was granted many tenements and pieces of land in the first half of the thirteenth century, mainly in Kentdale and Lonsdale (Farrer 1905a, 1905b; Elphick and Lancaster 1989, 2–5). The Cockersand grants extended as far north as Carlingill, on the county boundary 5.5km south of Tebay, and Whinfell and Grayrigg to the west of the Lune. Bretherdale, Bannisdale, Fawcett Forest, and Borrowdale were granted to the Cistercian abbey of Byland in Yorkshire. At the death of Robert de Clifford (HMSO 1912, 70) in 1314, the grange and pasture of Bretherdale were held in fee farm by the abbot of Byland, with an annual income of 30s. The manors of Langdale, and later Ravenstonedale with Newbiggin, were granted to the Gilbertine Priory of Watton in Yorkshire (Nicolson and Burn 1777, 481–2, 491–2; Nicholls 1877, 17). The original cartulary of Shap Abbey, the only monastery in Westmorland and the nearest geographically to the Lune gorge, is unfortunately lost. The full extent of the abbey's possessions is uncertain as the seventeenth century transcripts are incomplete, but the known grants to the abbey were of Wet Sleddale, Shap, Reagill, and Milburn Grange (Colvin 1951, 169, 382). There is no reference to any grant in Tebay, and the neighbouring manor of Ravenstonedale, previously held by Watton Priory, was apparently Shap Abbey's only landholding in the Howgills.

While these lands peripheral to Tebay were clearly being exploited as monastic sheepwalks and vaccaries, no record of any grant to an abbey or priory has yet been found for Tebay itself. This may perhaps in part be explained by the fragmentation of tenure in the manor from an early date. After the dissolution of the northern monasteries in 1539–40, most of their former lands continued as sheepwalks in the hands of new tenants. Alan Bellingham of Helsington acquired Cockersand Abbey's land in Whinfell in 1552 (Farrer 1923, 228), and Byland Abbey's sheepwalk of Fawcett Forest in 1554. Bellingham's cattle and sheep already shared the grazings of these moorlands west of Tebay in the early sixteenth century, when a witness in a dispute over grazing rights claimed that 'two kyne were

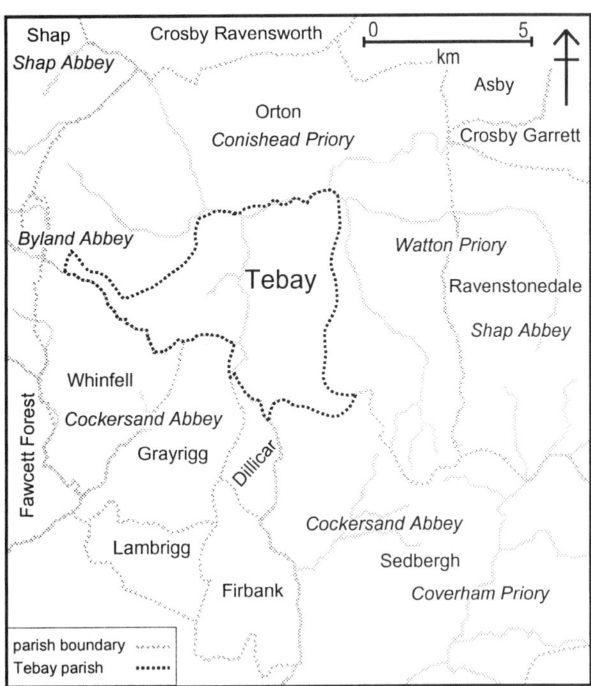

Figure 3:10 Monastic land around Tebay

slain by woundes besides shepe and lambs slaine'. Bellingham was the principal sheep farmer in the area, 'owning at his death in 1577, 4224 sheep and lambs' (Satchell 1989, 139), and Forest Hall is still one of the largest sheep farms in Westmorland (Wainwright 1988, 100). Alan Bellingham was one of Lord Wharton's Borrowdale tenants in 1560, paying 20s annual rent for sheep grazing rights (D/Lons/L, Wharton Box 1), but in 1570 Wharton conveyed to Bellingham his lands and tenements in Borrowdale and Crookdale (Farrer 1923, 238). These grazings in Borrowdale were, however, marginal to Tebay, and seemingly untypical of the manor, in most of which small herds of cattle were grazed by nearly all the tenant farmers.

The exceptionally wet climate of the Lune gorge may also have made the valley less suitable for sheep farming than for cattle. If, as becomes apparent from the later medieval period, the mainstay of the Tebay economy lay in cattle rearing, it would seem that the direct influence of monastic, and in particular Cistercian and Praemonstratensian farming practices, was not brought to bear in Tebay, in contrast to the peripheral manors and lordships.

Shielings

The advance of pastoral farming into the less hospitable uplands or wooded valleys can to some extent be measured by the distribution of shieling sites on these lands marginal to the permanent farms and hamlets. The words 'shieling' and 'scale' derive from the ON *skáli*, and the broad distribution of 'scale' as a minor place name, in the townships contiguous with Tebay, signifies the local importance of seasonal transhumance in medieval times. In the early summer the livestock was driven to upland pastures used only for summer grazing, and herded there while the village townfields were put under crops of hay, oats, and barley. The beginning of autumn was marked by the return of the cattle to the townfields and inbye pastures, to graze the stubble and manure the land. The shieling comprised both the summer pastures and the huts in which the herdsmen lived. As increasing populations pushed back the margins of settlement, these sites on the waste beyond the enclosed fields often became permanent farmsteads, sometimes retaining the name 'Scale' to the present day, as at High and Low Scales in Orton parish. At Cowperthwaite in Firbank, through which the pipeline runs alongside the Galloway Gate, a *scalinga juxta domum Willelmi le Turnur* (1186–1268) was given to Cockersand Abbey (Farrer 1905b, 975). This description does not accord with the definition of a shieling as an isolated hut or group of huts on the common grazings, but seems to indicate the interface between permanent settlement and seasonal shielings.

The colonisation of marginal land beyond the Anglian settlement of Tebay by Norse or later farmers gave rise to a string of settlements from Ellergill to Carlingill, whose topographical names illustrate their location at the foot of narrow valleys running deep into the Howgills. Further up these valleys, and on the fellsides surrounding the Lune gorge, there may have been shielings on the summer pastures, but pollen evidence from Archer Moss, in the col between Blease Fell and Hare Shaw, indicates continuing woodland regeneration during the Norse period (Cundill 1976, 308). This suggests that there may have been only limited exploitation of the Tebay fells for upland summer grazing until after the Conquest.

Parallels can to some extent be drawn with the rural uplands of North East Perthshire, where the RCAHMS has carried out landscape studies which identified three bands of settlement activity in Strathardle and Glen Shee, where shielings were integral to the farming system until a much later date than in Cumbria. The primary settlements were in the main valleys, permanent settlement and shieling activity overlapped in the tributary valleys and on the moors above, and the outermost zone contained only shielings (RCAHMS 1990, 5). The distribution of abandoned farmsteads and shielings in Perthshire provides a useful model for the Tebay

area, where survival is far more limited and the overall picture therefore less clear (Fig 3:11). All six of the known shielings in the south-west corner of Orton, four of them overlaid by post-medieval farms, are identified from place names. Fieldwork in Bland (Sedbergh) has located earthworks corresponding to four shielings mentioned in the Cockersand cartulary (Cleasby 1991, 2–9), as well as several likely sites hitherto apparently undocumented. With the exception of Cold Seat, a farm in Dillicar whose name derives from *cald, saétr* (Smith 1967, 1, 2), the place names which indicate shielings all come from the ON *skáli*, generally thought to denote higher or more marginal sites than those with *erg* or *saétr* names, and this implies Norse influence on local farming practices.

These *skáli* names, which must predate permanent settlement, cluster in Bland in the north-west of Sedbergh parish, and around Bretherdale and Orton Low Moor, but are almost completely absent from Tebay, where only one instance is known. Adam Slack's Gill (NY 63400303) is a miniature forked ravine close to the secluded and now uninhabited farmstead of Rawbusk, which may even occupy the former shieling site. The presence of only one known shieling in Tebay may indicate merely a lack of documentation, and it is quite possible that other marginal farms of the sixteenth century and later, the ruins of which are dotted over Tebay Fell (Fig 3:21), overlie former shieling huts of which there is no surviving written record.

The distribution of known shielings (Fig 3:11) not surprisingly often coincides with the grants of land to Cockersand Abbey and other northern monasteries, as the cartularies frequently provide the earliest records of landholding. If it is not a case simply of missing documentation, but of a genuine absence of monastic activity in Tebay, then the shielings recorded in the adjoining manors might be argued to have existed as a product of monastic influence on land and stock management. The evidence on the ground tends to suggest that in Tebay and the Lune gorge as far south as Carlingill, the pattern of management does vary from that of the neighbouring manors, but the recently excavated site at Powsons (**1132**) may lead to a revision of this perception (*see Chapter 7*).

Four shielings in Bland feature in grants to Cockersand Abbey in the early thirteenth century. The cartulary lists these *scalingas* at Castley, White Fell Middle Tongue, Bland, and between Nevelbeck and Carlingill (1220–1260) (Farrer 1905b, 955, 959). Only the shieling at Castley developed into a modern farm, but the ruins of the other three are still visible as earthworks and stone tumble on Back Balk and

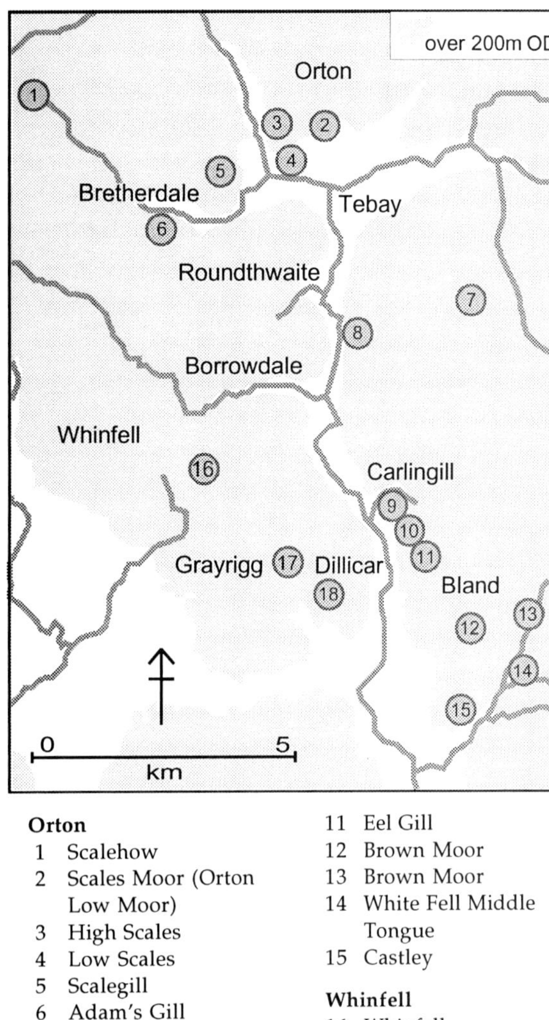

Orton
1 Scalehow
2 Scales Moor (Orton
  Low Moor)
3 High Scales
4 Low Scales
5 Scalegill
6 Adam's Gill

Tebay
7 Adam Slack's Gill
8 Powsons

Sedbergh
9 Back Balk
10 Back Balk

11 Eel Gill
12 Brown Moor
13 Brown Moor
14 White Fell Middle
   Tongue
15 Castley

Whinfell
16 Whinfell

Grayrigg
17 Grayrigg

Dillicar
18 Cold Seat

Figure 3:11 Shieling sites around Tebay

Brown Moor. Here, where the lower slopes of the Howgills remain unenclosed, are the footings of many ruined stone structures, some of which may have been peat huts, hogg houses, or simply sheepfolds. A good many, however, share some of the characteristics of stone shieling huts in other parts of northern England, as inventoried by Ramm (1970). Approximately 25 sites recorded in Bland are of the subrectangular type, typically 8 x 4.5m, with a single entrance in one side, and occurring singly except at Longrigg Beck (SD 64709638), where there is a group of nine huts (Cleasby 1991, 2–9). These dimensions are remarkably similar to those of the stone building excavated at Powsons (**1132**; *see Chapter 7*, Fig 7:12), which proved to measure at foundation level 8.5 x 4–4.8m. Powsons is located on the west-facing slope in the narrowest part of the Lune gorge, below the late eighteenth century intake wall; if, by analogy with the hut sites south of Carlingill in Bland, and by other criteria (*see Chapter 7*), it can be considered as a former shieling, this is the first such to be identified in the Lune gorge itself. Powsons, apparently overlain by a post-medieval farmstead, and Adam Slack's Gill, represented by the farm of Rawbusk in Ellergill, may perhaps be seen as illustrating the margins of pastoral farming in Tebay, in the centuries following the Conquest, and probably more closely datable to the climatic optimum of *c*1150–1300 (Steane 1985, 174). Furthermore, these two sites demonstrate the development of seasonal huts and pasture grounds in favourable locations into permanently occupied farmsteads, which survived respectively into the nineteenth and twentieth centuries.

The typical location for shieling huts on the western slopes of the Howgills is between two streams, at a confluence, or at least close by a beck, preferably in a hollow, or perched on a shelf just above the valley bottom. This choice of location is found elsewhere in Cumbria, for example at Scale Field in Eskdale, where a group of five or more subrectangular or oval huts, each *c*6 x 4m, has been recorded at the confluence of Scale Gill and the River Esk (Winchester 1984b, 267). In the lower Lune Valley, permanent settlement had overtaken former shieling sites by the twelfth century, but in the more remote upland valleys shielings continued in use until at least the late fourteenth century (Whyte 1985, 110), an observation confirmed locally by the record in 1360 of a shieling in Whinfell held by John, son of Roland de Patton, of the abbot of Jervaulx (Farrer 1923, 224).

The shieling system, having reached a peak in the heyday of sheep and cattle ranching in the thirteenth century, had become obsolete in the Lake District by the sixteenth century, many former shielings having developed into permanent farms. Winchester observed, on the basis of his research in West Cumbria, that 'if the fells were cattle country in the thirteenth century, they were sheep country by the sixteenth' (Winchester 1987, 96). This progression might equally be applied to the monastic sheepwalks on the periphery of Tebay, but perhaps is less typical of Tebay itself. The inventory of landuse contained in a sixteenth century manorial survey (D/Lons/L, Wharton Box 1) (*see below*) shows clearly that cattle farming was still predominant here in the later sixteenth century, and that large-scale sheep farming was only found in the upper reaches of Borrowdale.

The extraordinary proliferation throughout the Howgills of stone sheepfolds, often large and elaborate, nonetheless demonstrates the importance of sheep to the local economy, in later centuries at least. In this range of fells covering 40 square miles, virtually every valley head has a sheepfold, and it is perhaps reasonable to speculate that some of these might indicate, and obscure, the sites of earlier shielings. The distances between the upland grazing areas and the upper Lune Valley settlements are not great (2–3km at the most), and the deep scars of innumerable trackways leading onto the fells from these farms and hamlets testify to the use of the upland wastes for grazing over many centuries.

A Wharton manor in the sixteenth century

Friction between the feudal lords Dacre and Clifford erupted into open conflict in the early sixteenth century. The Dacres had for centuries held a moiety of Orton manor and part of Tebay from the Clifford overlords. The lesser tenantry became embroiled in the rivalry between these two dynasties, and in 1532 Sir Thomas Wharton's brother led rioters in an attack on Dacre tenants at Orton (Harrison 1981, 31). By 1536, the growing enmity between these lords and chief tenants had contributed to the unrest among the tenantry which brought about the northern rebellion known as the Pilgrimage of Grace. One of the rebels' most bitter complaints was the imposition of greatly increased gressoms, or entry fines, paid at the change of lord or tenant (Harrison 1981, 47). Sir Thomas Wharton raised the gressoms on his Cumberland estates in the 1530s, but Tebay, not yet a Wharton manor, had no grievance on this score, and did not play a major part in the ill-fated rebellion.

After the dissolution of the monasteries most of the Tebay lands and messuages, previously in assorted ownership, were brought together under the lordship of Sir Thomas, by now Lord Wharton. The manor was still not intact, however, for in 1571 the Blenkinsops held messuages at Gaisgill, Tebay, and Ellergill, and as late as 1614/15 the Dacre holdings included two tenements at Tebay and one at Roundthwaite (Nicolson and Burn 1777, 1, 488).

Sir Thomas Wharton was made a baron by Henry VIII in recognition of his service as Warden of the Western Marches and governor of Carlisle. Such was Wharton's unpopularity with his tenants that during the Pilgrimage of Grace he was a prime target for retribution, and was forced into hiding for the duration. Wharton's elevation was timely, as great tracts of monastic land were coming onto the market. He was granted the estates of Shap Abbey in 1545 (Whiteside 1904b, 179), and acquired numerous manors, including Ravenstonedale, adjacent to Tebay, in 1547. By 1560 he owned most of the manor of Tebay, and in that year he commissioned a survey of his Westmorland estates, which presaged an escalation of gressoms and fines. That there was little goodwill between Wharton and his tenants is not surprising, considering his treatment of the Ravenstonedale tenantry, many of whom he dispossessed at this time to enclose a deer park. The survey, notwithstanding, provides the earliest detailed account of tenure and landuse in Tebay (Fig 3:12).

The 1560 survey listed all Wharton's tenants in each of his Westmorland manors, described the holdings, and detailed the customary rents, leases, and entry fines or gressoms (D/Lons/L, Wharton Box 1). In Westmorland, as elsewhere in the north, labour services had largely been commuted to money rents by the end of the fourteenth century, but the system of border tenantright, operative in this still disputed frontier territory, conferred near freehold status on the tenants, in return for their service in the wars with the Scots. Some of the tenants, benefiting from their rights of inheritance and freedom from labour services, were moving towards yeoman status by industrious improvement and enclosure of land. Wharton had 65 tenants in Tebay, mostly farmers, although a few, such as Alan Bellingham, were clearly men of substance who had extensive properties elsewhere. One of these, Anthony Duckett, was lord of the manor of Grayrigg, but also held tenements at Carlingill and Woodend in Tebay. This external influence increased when Alan Bellingham married Anthony Duckett's daughter (Whitaker 1823, 2, 330).

The prominent local farming families of the sixteenth century were the Thornburrows and Atkinsons, and to a lesser degree the Whiteheads, Willsons, Crosbyes, and Gowthropps. Despite partible inheritance, an obvious hindrance to prosperity, one family in particular rose to become the most wealthy and influential in Tebay. The Branthwaites had been well established in the area at least since 1332, when Richard de Bramthwayte of Whinfell was assessed for the Lay Subsidy as having 37s 6d in goods (Farrer 1923, 223). They were numerous in 1560, four of them tenanting farms at Carlingill (probably the original farm subdivided, with new enclosures) and two others at Borrowbridge and Tebay. They held all the farms in the Lune gorge between Borrow Beck and Carlingill Beck, and became pillars of

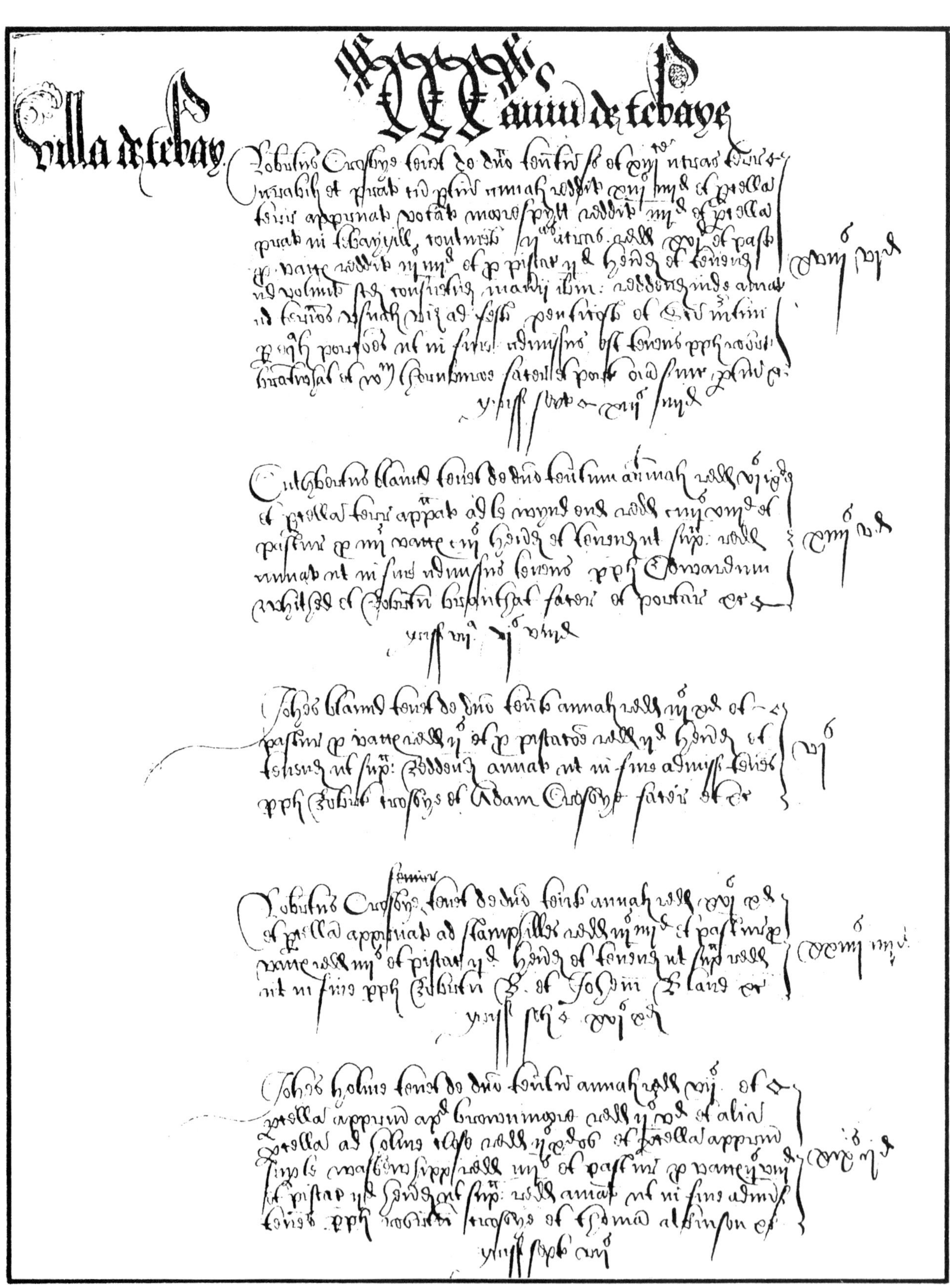

Figure 3:12 Survey of Lord Wharton's estates in Westmorland, 1560 (D/Lons/L, Wharton Box 1), first page of Tebay entry

local society, by the eighteenth century presiding over the manor courts. Their home at Low Carlingill appears on a 1765 plan of Grayrigg manor (D/Lons/L5/3), but by 1841 Low Carlingill had passed to Thomas Atkinson. Although they still owned three farms, with a total of 300 acres, at Tebay Town Foot, Low Borrowbridge, and High Carlingill, by the mid nineteenth century the Branthwaites were no longer resident in the township (WDRC/8/110).

Improvements

The earlier part of the sixteenth century saw a great deal of piecemeal enclosure, as is demonstrated by the substantial number of parcels of land described in the Wharton survey as 'improvements' (D/Lons/L, Wharton Box 1). In all, 75 recent enclosures are listed, of which by far the largest number were by the tenants of Tebay vill (27) and Roundthwaite (16), indicating that the two dominant settlements were thriving and expanding in due proportion to their long established importance. The two ploughlands held by Thomas de Hastings from the late thirteenth century were presumably on the fertile riverside meadows. The valley farms held strips in the townfield here, together with enclosed pastures and grazing rights on the commons. As enclosure progressed, access from these farms to their fell grazings was preserved by the creation of driftways, either in the form of narrow walled outgangs or, in the case of Tebay and Gaisgill, broad avenues of wet terrain, rutted with hollow-ways in the steep sections.

The Tebay farmers, once they had taken in the remaining waste between the old village and Mount Pleasant, were obliged to extend their holdings up the steep slopes of Tebaygill, while the Roundthwaite farmers expanded onto the flanks of Jeffrey's Mount. Some of these enclosures, particularly those closest to Tebay village and in the Lune gorge, reclaimed land which had been cultivated at a much earlier date, probably during the Roman occupation. To what extent the margin of settlement had shrunk after the disastrous events of the fourteenth century is unknown, but the present enclosed pastures along the valley side can in places be seen to overlie an earlier field system. This is particularly clear south of Powsons (**1132, 1133**) and in the fields of the neighbouring farm of Brockholes, where a number of earlier boundaries and trackways (**1135**) were crossed by the pipeline route.

The Tebay farmers were thus busy in the earlier sixteenth century enclosing and improving land on Tebay Fell and across to Carlingill. Although it appears to have been a family enterprise, colonisation of Carlingill did not fall to the Branthwaites alone, as the thirteen tenants of Ellergill, Gaisgill, and Redgill were also enclosing new land hereabouts. There must have been great pressure on land in the broader north-eastern section of the Lune Valley for the farmers to expand their holdings so far from home at Carlingill, where the land is poor and steep. The farmers of Gaisgill and Redgill were also making enclosures nearer home, and these subsequently developed into the upland farms of Rawbusk, High Cocklake, and Gill Hole, among others.

Cow pastures

The Wharton survey does not mention specifically the extensive manorial waste on the fells to either side of the Lune gorge, but the prevalence of stinted cow pastures, especially on Tebay Fell, indicates the economic importance of these common grazings to the farming community. Although there was abundant if poor quality grazing on the waste, the tiny proportion of cultivated townfields would provide very limited grazing after the harvest. The survey seems to illustrate the solution to this problem: improvement of new cattle pastures enclosed from the waste, some held individually, others as communal 'cowbounds'.

Two thirds of the 65 tenants in 1560 had cow pasture rights, nine of which were stinted. Six of the farmers at Ellergill and Gaisgill each had pasture for five cows, and one farmer each at Redgill, Roundthwaite, and Greenholme had pasture for seven, nine, and four cows respectively. Cow pastures were an important part of all the farms except Woodend and Borrowbridge. Borrowdale appears to have been managed differently, and in common with Fawcett Forest and Bretherdale (outside the manor) was largely given over to sheep.

The enclosed cow pastures certainly existed in 1588, when the manorial Book of Fines listed John Gowthroppe as tenant of 'certayne cow pasture in Langdaille Cowebound of the yearlie rente of 2s 2d', which he exchanged with Thomas Wylson for 'one other impro[ve]mente', or enclosure, with 3s 11d annual rent payable. This must have been a valuable transaction for both parties, to make it worth the fines of 12s and 8s levied by Lord Wharton on the exchange. That these stinted pastures continued to be fundamental to the local economy is clear from a rental 130 years later. A transaction at the manor court in 1718 records the transfer from Oliver Whitehead to Thomas Nelson of 'two Grasses or Cattle gates in Gaisgill pasture' (*ie* grazing for two cows), customary rent 8d. At the same court, Thomas Metcalfe, gentleman, was admitted tenant of 'One close and two cattle gates', rent 2s 6d (D/Lons/L, Wharton Box 1).

Rents and gressoms

The Wharton survey records the levels of the rents and fines before Lord Wharton began to increase the latter. The tenancies were regulated according to manorial custom, with rents payable at Pentecost (Whit Sunday) and the feast of St Martin (11 November). As was universally the case, the ancient fixed rents no longer represented the true value of the properties, and so it was from entry fines, payable by tenants at the death of the lord and at any transfer of tenancy, that the landlord obtained much of his revenue. Many tenants had several enclosures in addition to their original holdings, and the commissioners doubtless sought these out in order to extract new rents.

Eight of the nine farmers of Roundthwaite paid rent of over 20s a year in 1560, six of them paying more than 26s. John Atkinson of Roundthwaite paid the highest rent in the manor (35s), and also among the more substantial tenants were Robert Branthwaite of Carlingill (33s) and William Gowthropp of Brockholes (27s 9½d). At the other end of the social scale the lowest rents, ranging from 9s down to 6d a year, were paid by the few cottagers, and also, in several instances, by those such as Anthony Duckett whose main landholdings were elsewhere. The cottagers usually had a tenement with cattle grazing rights and one or two small enclosed parcels of land.

Gressom, or entry fine, was paid only by the 32 customary tenants, half of the total, and it seems that the later customary tenancies and the freehold tenancies were not subject to gressom. Tenancies established as a result of later expansion of the enclosed land seem to have been exempt from gressom, which was not being attached to new holdings. In every case, the gressom was equivalent to a year's rent, to within a few pennies, for the original tenement, excluding all additional parcels of land and other rights such as fishery and grazing. Twelve tenements subject to gressom were in Tebay vill, six at Roundthwaite, several at Carlingill, Gaisgill, Redgill, and Borrowbridge, and one each at Brockholes, Greenholme, and Woodend. No gressom was payable at Borrowdale, a side valley which was marginal to the manor, forming its south-western boundary. If these gressoms indicate the older tenancies, it becomes clear that Tebay had long been the most populous vill.

Sometimes tenants were behind with their payments, and faced dire consequences. In 1589 Thomas Atkinson of Ellergill owed the lord a 40s fine and was threatened, if he did not pay 6s 8d every Martinmas until the fine was quit, with forfeiture of his tenantright and all his farm 'savinge the peatemosse' (presumably on Peatmire Hill above Ellergill). The enhanced entry fines now imposed occasioned numerous pleas of poverty, not least because Lord Wharton appears, by the 1590s, to have increased these out of all proportion to the ancient gressoms recorded in the 1560 survey, which after all were only the equivalent of a year's rent. The proceedings of the manor court for Tebay and Langdale, held in 1588 and in 1595–7 at Greenholme, are notable for their frequent references to the poverty of the tenants, whose inability to pay the fines all at once was often recognised in a concession allowing them to pay by instalments.

In keeping with the trend throughout Westmorland, the new fines amounted to four or five times the annual rent, and even wealthier tenants like the Branthwaites claimed to have trouble in paying this inflated sum. When Robert Branthwaite took over his father Edward's holdings in 1589, he was required to pay a fine of £3 6s 8d on a tenement whose annual rent was only 14s 7d, and this was apparently quite a low fine 'in respecte of the great povertie of the yonge man and because his faither payed no moor and the ground newe impro[ve]-ment'. This consideration was evidently not sufficient, as the rental is annotated to the effect that Robert did not finish paying the fine until 1606, some 17 years later.

Many of the tenants, generally those whose land abutted the River Lune, paid a uniform 2d a year for fishing rights, but only one man is recorded as paying his rent in fish! In 1589 Myles Bownes was admitted tenant of 'fower Acres of ground comonlie called Lord waskewe of the yearlie rente of 8d... the said Myles to deliver for th[e] use of my lo[rd's] howse eighte dyshes fyshe ev[er]ye frydaie a dyshe till the same be Runn' (D/Lons/L, Wharton Box 1).

The post-medieval farming economy

The latter years of Elizabeth's reign were a time of renewed border warfare, and the plague again visited Westmorland in 1597, when the Orton parish register shows an unusually high mortality rate of 53 between May and November (Nicholson 1891, 258). Despite these setbacks, Westmorland was said to be over-populated, with 27,000 people in a county which could not support dense settlement on the produce of its wet upland terrain. The proliferation of marginal farms on the wastes of Tebay Fell testifies to the expansion of a vigorous community in the sixteenth to eighteenth centuries, to the viable limits of land exploitation. The far-reaching significance of the expansion is emphasised by the fact that the retreat from this margin has largely occurred only since the Second World War, leaving in its wake many ruined farmhouses which were renewed or first built in stone in the early eighteenth century (*see below*).

The Wharton era of lordship came to an end in 1728, when the Lowthers of Meaburn Hall bought up all the outlawed Duke of Wharton's Westmorland estates for £26,000 (Nicholls 1877, 49). The other main changes in the eighteenth century stemmed from improved housing, roads, and increased carriage of goods to wider markets, rather than from the revolution in agriculture experienced in lowland arable and stock farming. Tebay was unaffected by industry until the railway era. There was no mineral extraction, and hence no mine shafts or levels, nor limekilns or blast furnaces, nor miners' roads or tramways. The many industries which proliferated in the Lake District and North Pennines are simply not represented in Tebay, and even those which relied on an abundant water supply, such as fulling and textile mills, tanneries, and paper mills, are noticeably absent.

The local stone was of course quarried, for the farmhouses and field walls, but its poor quality as a building material meant that there was no market for it outside the immediate area, and so the quarries remained small. Even in 1851, there was only one resident family of stonemasons: three brothers at Mount Pleasant (CFHS 1991, 98), who were perhaps exploiting the quarries at Roger Howe and Gelstone. At this date, of the 90 heads of household listed in the Census, 67 were farmers or farm labourers, 10 were railway employees, and the only tradespeople other than the stonemason were two carpenters, two tailors, a blacksmith, a grocer, a tollbar keeper and cordwainer, a weaver's wife, and a lodging house keeper. Even the innkeeper of the Cross Keys was also a farmer (CFHS 1991, 93–106).

Arable land and the townfields

The lynchets, ridge and furrow, relic field boundaries, and deeply incised trackways still plainly visible in the Lune gorge landscape testify to the continuity of both arable and pastoral farming in the area over many centuries. The two ploughlands held by Thomas de Hastings from 1283 would amount to anything between 130 and 200 statute acres, and probably represent virtually all the arable and meadow land of the manor, a figure comparable to the 140 statute acres of arable noted in

the tithe apportionment of 1841 (WDRC/8/110). Although it has been considered from the evidence of plant names that there was an absence of arable cultivation in the central Lake District before 1400, and very little before 1600 (Pearsall 1961, 79), this rather circumscribed view does not allow for the attested, if small-scale, cultivation of oats and barley as part of the subsistence economy of upland farms. The bias, dictated by the rigours of the Westmorland climate, was nonetheless towards a primarily pastoral economy, based largely on cattle and pigs, with the emphasis shifting towards sheep in the later post-medieval period.

It has also been observed that 'although piecemeal enclosure... gradually created an enclosed landscape in the mountain valleys there occasionally remained the small bundle of strips' (Elliott 1973, 84), and this process can be recognised in Tebay, particularly at Roundthwaite, Gaisgill, and Ellergill, and around the original settlement of Tebay itself. The lynchets defining strips in the townfields, and patches of ridge and furrow delineating smaller, earlier, enclosed fields, are plain to see on a clear day. This field pattern is preserved best at Roundthwaite, where it has proved more durable on the boulder clay subsoil than elsewhere on the thin shaly soils of the Lune gorge, or on the ploughed alluvial silts of the floodplain. The sharpest evocation of these former fields and strips is, however, to be found on the tithe map (WDRC/8/110), which preserves in remarkable detail the boundaries of many narrow strips and tiny closes, gardens, and paddocks (Figs 3:13, 3:15, 3:18). The apportionment complements the tithe map, giving details of land ownership and tenure, which when transferred to the map provide a complete distribution of landholdings throughout the parish.

There is no indication of cereals in the pollen diagrams from Carlingill and Archer Moss (Cundill 1976, 304–5) and, while the sample sites are too distant to reflect accurately the vegetation in the Lune gorge, it is nonetheless highly unlikely that cereal crops were grown here in earlier centuries. The settlement and field names are also remarkable for their lack of references to cereal or other crops, although flax and hemp are specifically mentioned in 1535 as a small part of the tithes of Orton church, to the value of 3s 4d a year (Whiteside 1904a, 166). Dillicar, the former township which occupies the floor of the Lune Valley south of Carlingill, and through which the pipeline runs as far as Lowgill, is named after the herb dill: 'an acre of land growing with dill or vetches' (*Dylacre* 1190–1220, Smith 1967, 1, 31), although there is now no evidence for the cultivation of a culinary herb that is often, incidentally, associated with salmon, for which the Lune is famous.

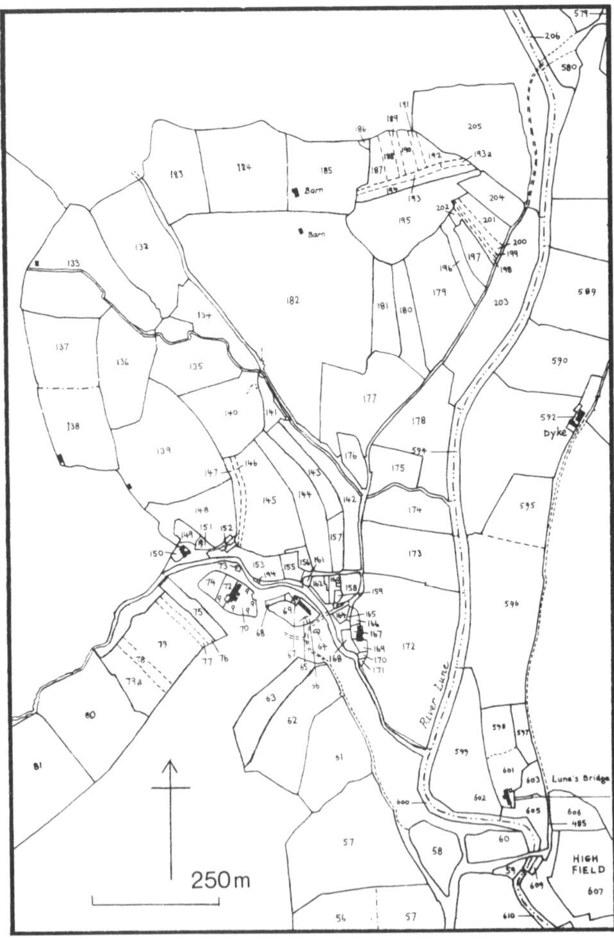

Figure 3:13 Roundthwaite, Tebay tithe map extract, 1841 (WDRC/8/110)

Cereal cultivation in Tebay was probably restricted to the townfields, which are found only in the upper part of the valley, from Roundthwaite to Ellergill. These lie well to the north of Carlingill, beyond the confines of the Lune gorge, and so would not be represented in the pollen record of Carlingill and Archer Moss, as the prevailing wind is from the south-west. The Roundthwaite townfield was eventually to be truncated by the railway and motorway, but the earthworks of the surviving fragment correspond to the divisions on the tithe map (Fig 3:13). The townfields of Gaisgill and Ellergill were likewise still divided into individually held riggs in 1841. Most of the Tebay townfield had by then been consolidated into larger holdings, with only a few long narrow fields remaining south of the village to indicate the earlier field pattern (Fig 3:18) (WDRC/8/110).

For the inconsiderable amounts of oats and barley which it was possible to grow on the townfields, a single manorial watermill was adequate and this, perhaps significantly, was located at Roundthwaite,

where in 1560 John Machell, clerk, held a mill by indenture for an annual rent of 20s. The 'mill rent' remained unchanged in 1633 (D/Lons/L, Wharton Box 1), and Miller Intack, on the west side of Roundthwaite, survived in name (WDRC/8/110), as did Milner's Moss (OS 1899, but not 1858) across the valley on the saddle of Powson Knott. By the nineteenth century, however, there were no mills at Roundthwaite or elsewhere in the township. In Orton manor, on the other hand, where there was a greater proportion of cultivable land, Thomas Blenkinsop tenanted the mill in 1395/96, there were two water corn mills in 1614/15 (Nicolson and Burn 1777, 488), and by 1885 there were three, at Bunflat, Raisbeck, and Coatflatt (Bulmer 1885, 265).

Upland pastures and expansion on the waste

In the medieval Lake District, the overall pattern was of cattle grazing in enclosures on the lower slopes, and sheep grazing on the upper slopes and waste (Denyer 1991, 78–9). While Tebay may have conformed to this practice, even as late as the mid sixteenth century sheep are barely mentioned in the Wharton survey, perhaps in part because the wastes did not attract rent, and the economy appears still to have been largely based on cattle rearing. This may have been over-emphasised in the Wharton survey because some of the cow pastures were by this time stinted, and hence under pressure of use. Place names throw a little light on the question: while the domestic animals referred to are cattle, sheep, and pigs, wild animals include goose, badger, hare, wolf, and weasel. It is interesting to note the relative values placed on vermin for which the churchwardens paid bounties as late as the seventeenth century: a fox head and a brock head were then each worth a shilling, ravens' heads a penny apiece, and a hedgehog or a wild cat twopence (WPR/9/01).

Tebay's common grazings were not enclosed for sheep, a major cause of settlement desertion in areas more favourable to arable farming (Fellows-Jensen 1985a, 394). The extensive commons amounted, even in the mid nineteenth century, to two thirds of the township's land, and were a precious resource for the tenant farmers. Some of the identifiable sixteenth century enclosures were on land not far from the townfields, which suggests that exploitation of the fellside lands was then only just beginning. Fields of the sixteenth century and later in the Lune gorge and Borrowdale are large and squarish in shape, and there is no evidence for townfields in the Lune gorge south of Roundthwaite.

The present intake wall on the eastern side of the

main valley coincides broadly with the 200m contour, and defines the upper limit of cultivation, or at least the potential for drainage and improvement of pasture. Above the farms of Castley and Crosdale, 3–5km south of Carlingill, there are remains of ridge and furrow, lynchets, and boundary banks indicating cultivation above the intake wall, but north of Carlingill the cultivated fields appear always to have been below this wall. There does not appear to have been a retreat from the more marginal land, although at Powsons (**1132**) the intake wall blocks access to the fell of two earlier trackways, interrupting an earlier pattern of management (*see Chapter 7*). The recent abandonment of farmhouses and barns is a result of consolidation into larger modern farms and has not brought about a reduction in the enclosed pastures.

All the known settlements in the Lune gorge and Borrowdale lie between the 200m contour and the valley floor, but the farms on Tebay Fell reach up to 300m. Waskew Head and Gelstone (Fig. 3:14) were the highest farms, at 310m OD, and represent the zenith of settlement in the seventeenth century, but neither of these still functions as a farmstead, although their fields continue to provide enclosed pastures. Waskew Head was referred to in 1560, not as a tenement, but as parcels of land or enclosures, and 'Le Waskew' or the 'lord's waskew', seems to have been an area of fell. By 1718, however, Hugh Tebay and Thomas Blamire each held a messuage and tenement at 'Waskah Head', at customary rents of 6s 6d and 4s 6d, and the messuage and tenement at 'Gellstall', later Gelstone, was rented at 2s 8d (D\Lons\L, Wharton Box 1). The farm appears to be a late foundation, and the farmhouse, built in the eighteenth century (RCHM(E) 1936, 225) and now partly ruined, was probably the first permanent dwelling on the site.

Enclosures

Enclosure benefited the lords of the upland manors by releasing the common land from customary rights, and thus making it available for 'capitalist development'. The wealthier freeholders, who were profiting from increased opportunities for livestock rearing, could develop this independently of the 'collective constraints imposed by the manorial courts'. To the majority of smaller landholders in Cumbria, however, enclosure was a lesser evil, and on balance preferable following the erosion of their customary rights as a result of the decline of the manorial system (Searle 1993, 152). In the later eighteenth century, however, falling stock prices curbed economic growth, and doubtless contributed to the delay in fencing the townfields and common pastures at Tebay until the middle of the following

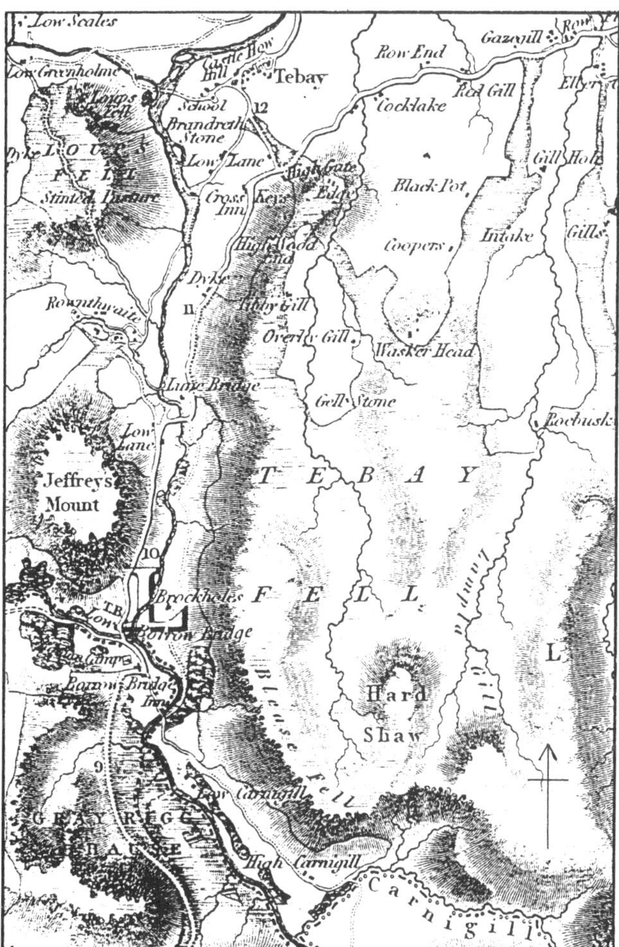

Figure 3:14 Westmorland, extract from Hodgson's map (1824)

century. This is remarkably late, in view of the contemporary observation that virtually all the cultivated land in Westmorland, including the former townfields, was enclosed by 1800 (Pringle 1805, 309).

Orton's commons were enclosed following an Award of 1769 (WPR/9/Z10), but a century then passed before Parliamentary Enclosure of the commons and waste of Dillicar (1853; WPR/9/25), Grayrigg (1868; WPR/9/31), and Fawcett Forest (1870; WPR/9/90). The regular field patterns in these parishes show little regard for the lie of the land, in sharp contrast with Tebay, where piecemeal enclosure had long been pursued with great vigour by the tenants, and the older fields spread more harmoniously up the fellsides. The lower slopes in the main valley, and in Borrowdale, Tebaygill, and Ellergill, were fenced for pasture long before Parliamentary Enclosure reached this area and unlike the adjacent parishes, most of Tebay's upland grazings, except the cowbounds, have never been enclosed.

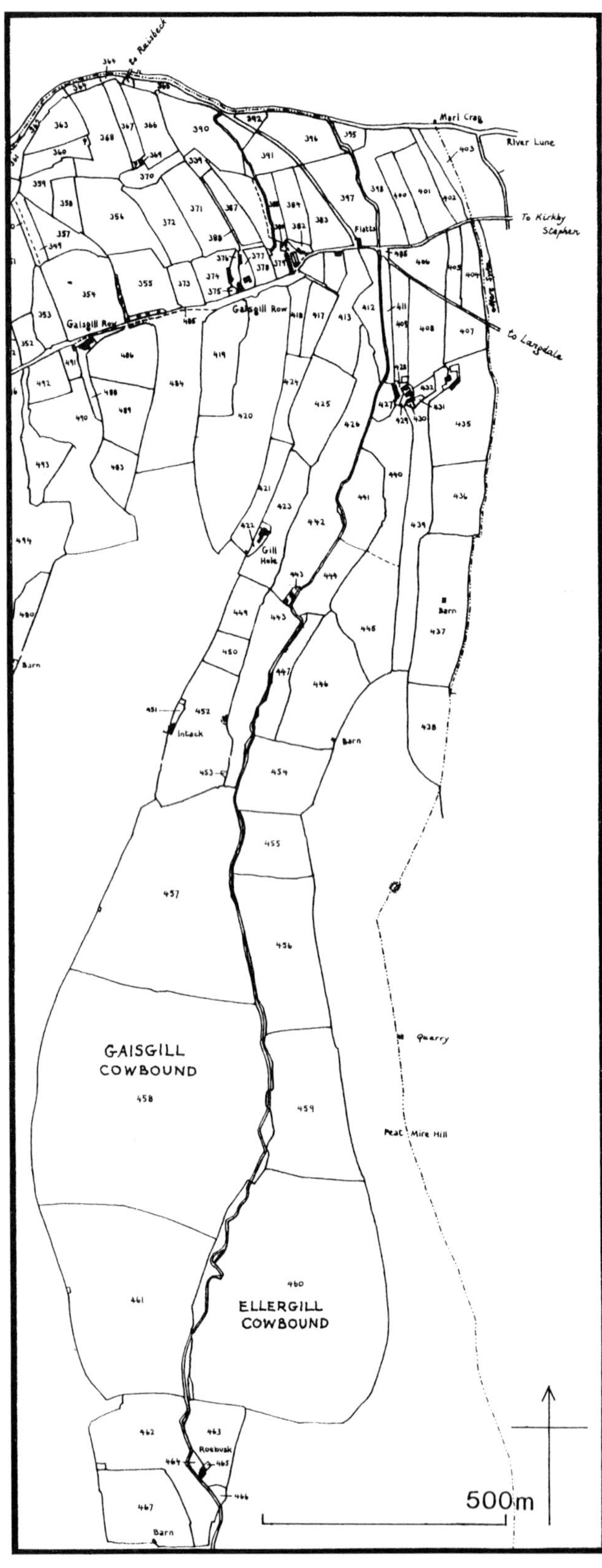

Figure 3:15 Gaisgill, Tebay tithe map extract, 1841
(WDRC/8/110)

The lower slopes were enclosed by agreement, mainly by tenants fencing, draining, and ploughing small parcels of the waste, over several centuries. This was clearly happening by the mid sixteenth century, and even as late as 1833 Michael Branthwaite applied to the manor court to take in a parcel of eleven acres from the commons and waste adjoining his estate at Carlingill (D/Lons/L, Wharton Box 1). Such enclosures also nibbled away at Loups Fell and Roundthwaite Cowbounds in the west of the township, and Gaisgill and Ellergill Cowbounds to the east. These huge enclosed cow pastures were still held by the tenants in common in 1841, and Roundthwaite (274 acres) and Loups Fell (233 acres) Cowbounds were both stinted (WDRC/8/110). All the cowbounds had good access to water: Loups Fell ran down to the west bank of the Lune below Tebay, Roundthwaite bordered on Roundthwaite Beck, and Gaisgill and Ellergill Cowbounds shared the watering of Ellergill Beck (Figs 3:13, 3:15). Roundthwaite Cowbound was still not divided in 1858, but Loups Fell by that date was encroached on by up to 20 fields and the Lancaster and Carlisle Railway, although a large central area remained open (OS 1858). Ellergill High Cowbound was the only one to be enclosed by Award, in 1867 (WPR/9/29), but all are now completely enclosed.

The progress of enclosure can be followed in Gaisgill Cowbound, which in 1841 comprised 53 acres (WDRC/8/110), but seems to have shrunk to that size from a much greater expanse, perhaps including at one time all the land within the intake wall as far as the boundary with Rawbusk (Fig 3:15). In 1841, John Brunskill, the freeholder who farmed Gaisgill Row, had parts of the former townfield near the Lune, two fields north of the turnpike road, a separate, relatively recent farm at Intack, which he rented out, and a large field abutting the cowbound. George Hogarth, the freehold farmer at Waskew Head, had the top field between the cowbound and Rawbusk. The pattern was clearly for the established farms to expand at the expense of the common enclosed pastures. Only on Gaisgill Cowbound, however, was an entirely new farm founded, at some date between 1858 and 1913. The OS 6″ map of 1920 shows the cowbound divided into four fields and a paddock, with a farmhouse called, appropriately, New Field. Today this short-lived farmstead is reduced to a small heap of stone tumble.

The road network

The settlements in Tebay and the Lune gorge are almost all associated with major routeways

(Fig 3:16). Carlingill, Low Borrowbridge, Round-thwaite, and Greenholme lay astride the main Roman road (Ross 1920, 1–3; Margary 1957, 2, 113, 117), which is visible at various places between Fairmile, south of Carlingill, and Sproatgill (**1091**) on Orton Low Moor (Fig 2:16) (*see Chapter 2*). Cockersand Abbey grants refer to the *magna via* and to a boundary *sequendo le waingate versus le North* (Farrer 1905b, 955, 963). This road is presumably Howgill Lane, which runs from Low Borrowbridge to Low Carlingill, across Fairmile, and as a deep hollow-way in Bland between the fields granted to the abbey in the early thirteenth century. It is still a vital link between Tebay and Sedbergh, and may have been used continuously since Roman times, as it was the only road for local traffic to avoid the higher fells.

Low Borrowbridge, Tebay, Redgill, Gaisgill, and Ellergill are aligned on the medieval route from Kendal to Appleby. This road descended to Low Borrowbridge from Grayrigg Hause, then followed the Roman route north for 2km, before turning east to cross the river at Lune's Bridge, which appears as the *pontem inter Tybay et Routhwayt* in 1380 (Ferguson 1893, 143), and is named as 'Lonesbrig' in 1379 (Smith 1967, 2, 51). Only Brockholes, of the medieval set-tlements, was relatively remote from any road, al-though connected to Howgill Lane by a trackway north from Salterwath Bridge, following the base of the fellside. Another trackway was, probably later, driven south through the steep gullied terrain from Lune's Bridge to Brockholes, providing an alterna-tive through route, via Powsons, for local traffic on the eastern bank down to Salterwath Bridge.

Packhorse routes

The absence of engineered and metalled roads, with the exception of surviving sections of the Roman roads, meant that the medieval trading routes of this region were simply packhorse tracks. One of the earliest commodities requiring transport from the source of manufacture to all communities, how-ever remote, was salt, essential primarily for pre-serving food. Sea salt was carried inland from the Solway by packhorse trains over a network of trackways, occasional place names providing clues to the routes taken, and in the Tebay area two Salterwaths refer to former fords over the Lune and Birk Beck. One of these is now replaced by a bridge carrying Howgill Lane over the Lune south of Low Borrowbridge (NY 61180090), and the other is at Wasdale foot (NY 58230918) where the ford, still in use, is supplemented by a nearby packhorse bridge spanning Birk Beck (Fig 3:16).

The medieval route south from Penrith over Shap to Kendal climbed Packhorse Hill after crossing Wasdale Old Bridge, where a track branched north-east across the flank of Birkbeck Fells Common to Salterwath below Castle Howe farm, continuing east to meet the Shap–Orton road a short distance south of the Galloway Stone (NY 58801000). Several trackways followed Birk Beck to its confluence with the Lune at Tebay, where all roads south were fun-nelled into one route through the gorge, diverging again at Salterwath Bridge.

Goods were invariably carried by packhorse until the later eighteenth century, and pack routes radi-ated from Kendal, the focus for the wool and cloth trade, with cross-Pennine trackways linking Kendal with other important medieval markets such as Richmond and Lancaster. The routes used by the packhorse trains characteristically ascended steep valley sides in sharp zigzags, and spread out on the felltops, making diversions around boggy ground. Deep hollow-ways scar the slopes of Blease Fell and Uldale Head (Fig 3:17), and less distinct grooves can be found on the northern slope of Wether Hill. These mark the line of 'the old packhorse track that forded the Lune between Dillicar and Low Carlingill and thence passed up Tebay Gill where a bridal [*sic*] road still exists, past Cooper's Land to the west of Gaisgill station' (Curwen 1926, 15). This account conflates several variants of the well-worn route over Tebay Fell. The routes diverge on Hare Shaw, the western branch continuing past Gelstone to join the main driftway from Tebay at Overcluegill. Multiple hollow-ways are carved deep into the steep, wet slopes as far as High Gate (now Mount Pleasant) on the turnpike road. The last stretch of the driftway to Old Tebay is now obscured by the roundabout linking the motorway and the modern road to Kirkby Stephen (A685), which from this point eastwards is laid on the trackbed of the former South Durham Railway. The main pack route, how-ever, continued north past Cooper House and down the less steep, but even wetter driftway to Gaisgill. Here it turned eastwards and crossed the Lune, continuing by way of Smardale Bridge and Waitby to Kirkby Stephen, and thence eastwards over Stainmore to Barnard Castle.

The packhorse routes were also used by broggers, who bought small packs of wool from the farms for sale to clothiers in Halifax or Kendal (Raistrick 1967, 118–9), and as the market network developed, these routes increasingly saw corn badgers, who traded from one market town to another, and to farms remote from markets, and butter badgers, who took butter from the farms to the larger towns (Nicholls 1877, 74). Low Borrowbridge Inn was a meeting point for routes and travellers of all types, and a stopping place for the packmen and cattle

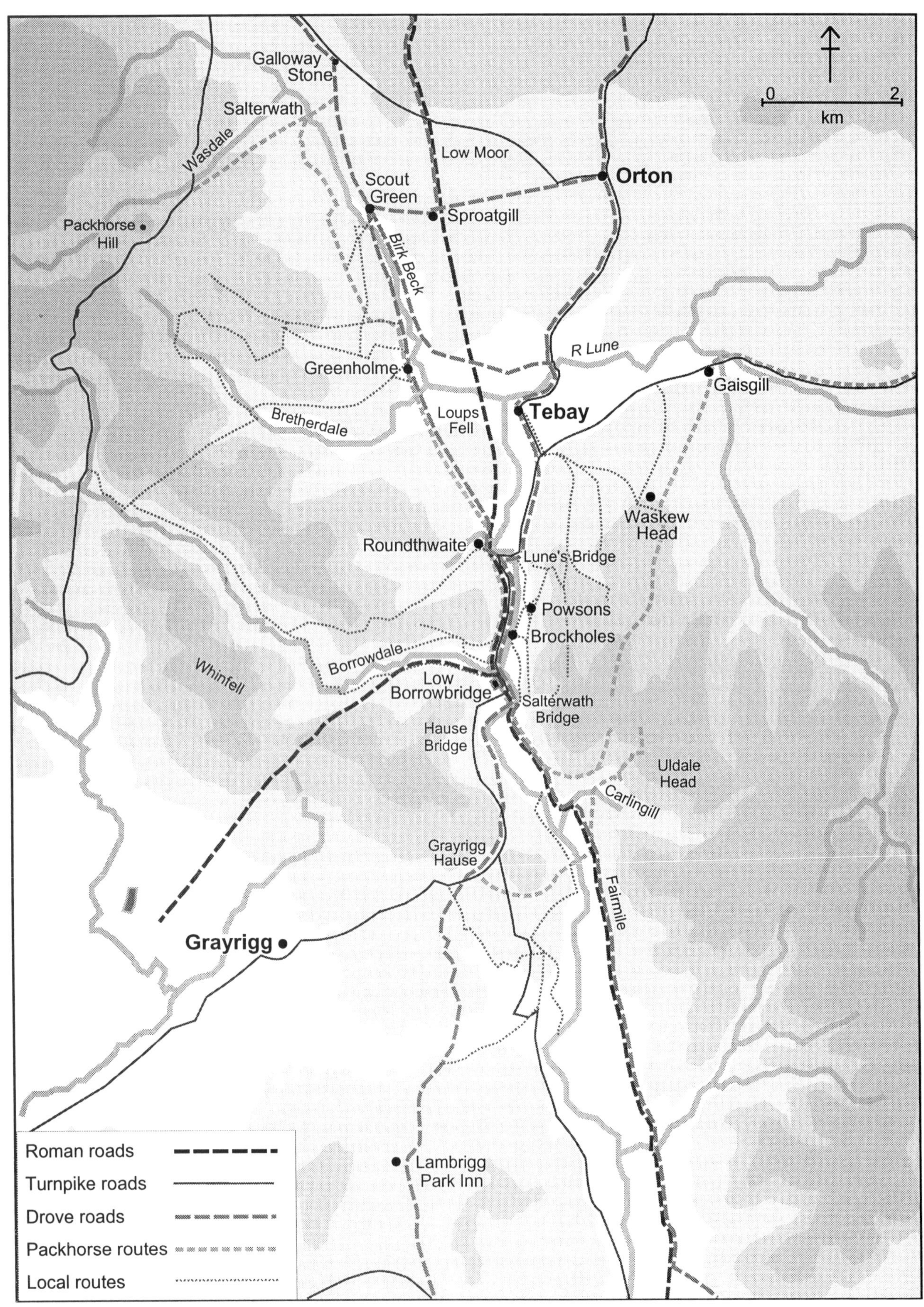

Figure 3:16 Roads in the Tebay area

Figure 3:17 Uldale Head, above Carlingill, hollow-ways formed by pony traffic

drovers. Like other inns on the main packhorse routes, it provided outbuildings for safe overnight storage of packs, and closes for the ponies. As wheeled traffic began to carry goods on the improved roads of the later eighteenth century, however, the steep gradients of the packhorse tracks proved unusable for wagons and carts, and they fell gradually into disuse.

Drove roads

The three main drove routes south from the Scottish Borders converged on Carlisle (Bonser 1970, 154, map; Hindle 1984, 99), continuing as a single route to Penrith and Eamont Bridge. Here the routes diverged, one heading for the Eden Valley and Stainmore, the other two going south. One of these followed the Lyvennet Valley to Crosby Ravensworth, continuing over the fell to Orton and Tebay. The other followed the line of the Galloway Gate from Eamont Bridge to Kirkby Lonsdale by way of Shap Thorn, over Birk Beck to Greenholme and Roundthwaite (Bonser 1970, 155–6). Galloway Gate was named by the late twelfth century in the Cockersand cartulary, and was primarily a drove route for Scottish cattle, but was also used by invading Scottish armies in the turbulent fourteenth century (Farrer 1924, 417), and perhaps its alternative name of Scotch Lane was attributed long before the Scottish drovers began to bring cattle south from Galloway. Much of this route is now overlain by modern minor roads, but the section south of Grayrigg Hause survives as a quiet bridleway between stone walls, with generous grass verges. The junction at Lune's Bridge south of Roundthwaite reunited the drove roads, which then passed over Low Borrowbridge (Bonser 1970, 155–6), and continued together to Salterwath Bridge, where they separated. The drove route to Sedbergh lay along Howgill Lane, while the Galloway Gate (**1191**) continued to Kirkby Lonsdale over Firbank Fell. These routes met again at Ingleton, from where one headed south-east through the Aire Gap to Doncaster, while the other followed the Lune Valley south-west to Lancaster (Bonser 1970, 162–3, map), and on through Galgate, a village whose name also evokes the former drove road.

At Salterwath Bridge, which was ruinous in 1811 and rebuilt in 1824 (Curwen 1926, 128), instead of crossing the river the Galloway Gate turned sharply to the west along the top of the river bank, parallel to the pipeline route, before bearing south-west obliquely up the fellside to meet the turnpike road. This route is visible in a good light, except where it is overlain by the motorway, from the bend in the Lune west of Salterwath Bridge as far as its junction, at SD 61379971, with the Kendal–Appleby road (A685). When the Lancaster and Carlisle Railway was built, an underpass was provided for the road, and adjacent to this the section surveyed within the pipeline corridor (**1142**) was still in use as a local driftway until the motorway was built in 1967–70. The route is shown on the revised OS 6" map (OS 1899) although, oddly, not on the first edition (OS 1858). Higher up the pass, deep hollow-ways on Grayrigg Hawse (SD 61339898) also demonstrate the line of the medieval route.

The drove route was crossed by, but remained distinct from, the later Kendal to Appleby turnpike road (Hindle 1984, 104–5). Roadside grazing was restricted once turnpike roads were enclosed within stone walls, and as these were incompatible with the needs of drovers and their cattle, the drove routes tended to remain separate, even if following the same general direction. The droving traffic needed inns every few miles on the Galloway Gate, notably in this area at Low Borrowbridge and Lambrigg Park (Farrer 1924, 417), as well as grazing for the large herds of cattle passing through the Lune gorge, and farmers with land adjacent to the road doubtless supplemented their income by supplying this need.

The drove road was also used by less innocent travellers. The Smorthwaite gang of highwaymen refreshed themselves in 1682 in alehouses along the Galloway Gate, at Clifton, Shap, Greenholme, Roundthwaite, Hawse House, and Lambrigg Park (Macfarlane 1981, 124–7, 139–40). Moreover, a letter from Richard Braithwaite to Colonel James Grahme of Levens recounts that a few years later 'at the regulation of the coin, the mob at Kendal threatened to burn Lowther, which put him in great fright. I then joined him at Rownthwaite, with above 200 horse to supress the mob, he having not above 40' (Nicholson 1891, 251).

The turnpike road

From 1676 the quarter sessions were held alternately at Kendal and Appleby (Bouch and Jones 1961, 162), and the courts travelled between the two towns. Daniel Fleming of Rydal was one of the judges on the northern Assize circuit, and in his *Description of Westmorland*, written in 1671, he mentioned Grayrigg Hawse as one of three 'common, but not very good' passes in Westmorland, the others being Crookdale, on the old Kendal to Shap road, and Kirkstone,

linking Ambleside with Penrith (Duckett 1882, 2). Whatever the state of the road in the Lune gorge at that time, it was to get worse before it was improved in the turnpike era. Low Borrowbridge, which spanned the boundary between the two divisions of Westmorland, was dilapidated in 1712, and a stretch of the highway 'adjoining to the Hause house field' was 'dirty, founderous and in decay' (Curwen 1926, 127).

In 1745, the Duke of Cumberland ordered the road down Grayrigg Hawse to be broken up 'in order to make the roads from Kendal and Appleby impassable for artillery and wheel-carriages', and so frustrate the retreat of the Jacobite rebels. At the same time, Wasdale Old Bridge on the Kendal to Shap road was ordered to be demolished (Ferguson 1889, 193). Whether or not this military vandalism was taken into account, it was nonetheless the inhabitants of Grayrigg who were liable to repair the road, when in 1749/50 the 200-yard section between Hausefoot Gate and Borrow Bridge was, not surprisingly, reported to be 'very ruinous, miry, deep broken and in such decay that the liege subjects of the King cannot pass ride or labour over it without great danger of their lives' (Curwen 1926, 127–8).

The contemporary solution for these foundering lines of communication was to set up a turnpike trust for the road from Kendal over Shap to Eamont Bridge, but although this was in hand by 1753, not until 1760 was a trust established for 'the road from Kendal through Grayrigg and Orton to Appleby and another from Tebay through Kirkby Stephen to Brough'. The following year an Act was passed for the road from 'Grayrigg Hause through Firbank to Marthwaite' (Bouch and Jones 1961, 279), completing the local network of turnpike roads. A toll bar was established on the Tebay–Grayrigg parish boundary at Low Borrowbridge farm, north of the inn, and a plan of 1765 depicts the turnpike house and a five-barred gate across the road (D/Lons/L/5/3). A later generation of judges on the northern circuit, among others, must have welcomed the road improvements, which undoubtedly made the journey from Kendal to Appleby less hazardous.

Tebay and the Lune gorge in the nineteenth century

Of all the early farms and vills, only Tebay developed into a village and a manor, but neighbouring Orton was the early church site which developed into a market centre, even though it never had a

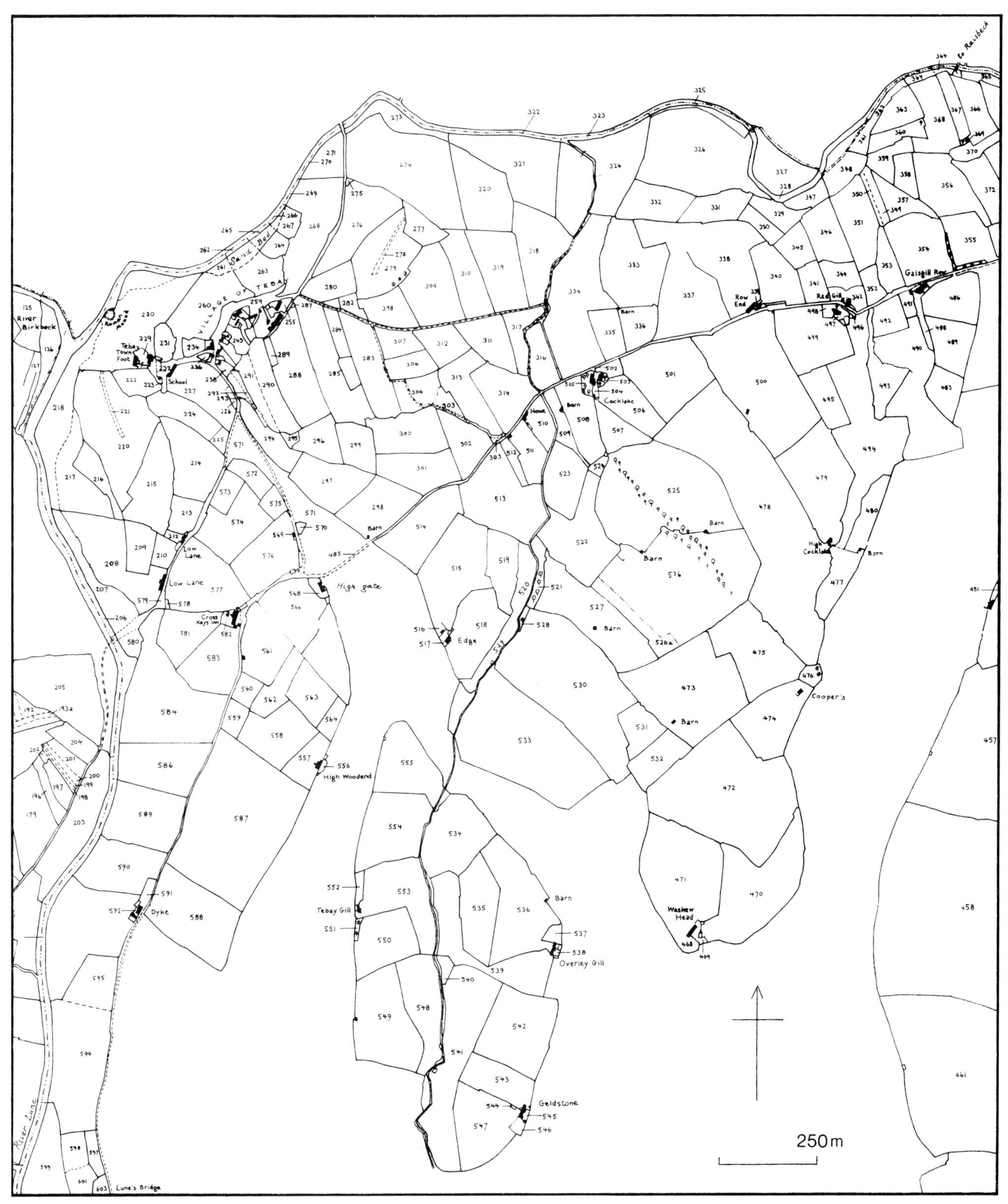

Figure 3:18 Tebay tithe map extract, 1841 WDRC/8/110)

borough charter. Tebay, by contrast, a constituent township of Orton parish, had neither church nor market until the late nineteenth century, and only became a parish in its own right at the height of railway expansion and its concomitant, prosperity. Great changes took place in the landscape and econ-omy of Tebay from the 1840s. The tithe assessment of 1841 was the last survey of landowners, tenants, and field systems before the railway cuttings and embankments sliced through the fields and a new village sprang up to accommodate an incoming population of railway employees and tradesmen.

Given the adverse topography and climate, the quantity of arable land is unlikely to have increased significantly over the centuries. Only 140 acres were under wheat, barley, and oats in 1841, as opposed to the 2492 acres of meadow and pasture, which with 100 acres of woodland and 4100 acres of common land, gave a total of 6832 acres for the township (WDRC/8/110). The tiny proportion of arable, distributed among fifty or sixty farmers, cannot have produced more than a bare sufficiency. Woodland had long been under great pressure, as can be inferred from sixteenth century references to enclosures in 'le Knot wode' (probably Birk Knott on Roundthwaite Common) (D/Lons/L, Wharton Box 1), and would tend to decline wherever regeneration was prevented by grazing animals. Above all, the acreage of pasture had greatly increased at the expense of the common land, since the late medieval enclosures were beyond the arable townfields, on marginal land won from the waste.

The number of tenants seems to have been remarkably consistent between 1560 and 1841. The Wharton survey (D/Lons/L, Wharton Box 1) lists 65, of whom several were absentee tenants renting grazing rights, and to these should be added a small number of tenants whose landlord was Blenkinsop or Dacre, rather than Wharton. By comparison, in 1841 there were 77 tenants including owner-occupiers, of whom six held two or more tenements, so that the number of individuals (not all of whom were farmers, nor indeed local residents) was actually 67 (WDRC/8/110). There was no significant difference between the boundaries of the manor and the later township, and so it appears that the number of families sustained by the farms and smallholdings of Tebay remained much the same over three centuries.

The sixteenth century improvements by Tebay farmers can be seen to have evolved into the marginal farms of Edge, Waskew Head, Intack, and Tebaygill. As always, the earliest farms on the best land were better equipped to survive than the later foundations on the waste. Several farms established on Tebay Fell perhaps as late as the eighteenth century, such as Coopers, High Cocklake, Gelstone, and Overcluegill, are now deserted and to varying degrees ruinous. On the other hand, Low Carlingill and Brockholes, two of the oldest farms in the Lune gorge, had consolidated their holdings by 1841 and were among the largest farms in the township. The tithe apportionment lists 52 separate farms, varying in size from five to 124 acres, and averaging 43 acres, although twelve farms had under 20 acres, while the marginal farms had an average of 36 acres each. Among the largest landowners in Tebay at this time were the Atkinsons and Wilsons, but still predominant were the Branthwaites, who held the two most extensive farms, at Low Borrowbridge and High Carlingill. Even these 'major' landowners did not hold huge amounts of land: the Branthwaites owned three farms with land totalling 305 acres, the Atkinsons six farms with 249 acres, and the Wilsons (including two vicars) seven farms with 244 acres.

Although the decline of the yeomanry was not hastened in Tebay by Parliamentary Enclosure, the effects are clear in the consolidation of holdings and a greater social divide in the nineteenth century. The successful farmers held larger farms, while the poorer farmers had become their tenants. Tenants finally became freeholders by enfranchisement in the earlier nineteenth century, and so the landowners in 1841 are in some measure comparable to the tenants of 1560. The Branthwaites, for example, resident tenants in 1560, were absentee landowners in 1841. Of the ten landowners of the largest farms in 1841, only three were owner-occupiers, and of the smaller farmers, only ten owned the freehold. The vast majority of farms were tenanted by dispossessed free tenants. Of the tenants in 1560, the ten paying the lowest rents (ranging from 1s 4d to 7s 6d) usually had, in addition to their tenement, a close and cow pasture rights, with perhaps another enclosure, and fishing rights. At the bottom of the social scale in 1841 were 11 cottagers, each renting a house, garden, and garth, within an acre or less of land. Some of these were tradesmen, and others may have held land outside the manor or township, but they were a tiny minority. Yeoman farmers were the mainstay of the population in Tebay, where there was no manor house, hall, or substantial landed estate. This could not be more different to the status of landholdings in the Lune Valley only a few kilometres further south. Within 5km of the Lune, between Sedbergh and Kirkby Lonsdale (14km), 17 halls are named on the current OS 1:50,000 scale map (OS 1987), and in the next stretch downstream to Hornby (10km) there are again 17 halls, as well as two castles. In Tebay, other than the Castle Howe earthworks, there are none.

The tithe apportionment lists 16 owner-occupiers, with holdings ranging from six to 76 acres (and four more with three acres or less), among the 67 tenancies, a proportion of approximately 26% of all landholders (WDRC/8/110). Based on trade directory listings, by their nature incomplete, the figures for Westmorland East Ward as a whole, in 1829, give a proportion of 40.8% of owner-occupiers, or yeomen farmers (Bouch and Jones 1961, 335). In 1849, of the 41 directory listings of farmers in Tebay township, only eight, or 19.5%, were identified as owners (Mannex 1849, 187), while in 1885 14, or

31.8%, were still described as yeomen, out of a total of 44 farmers (Bulmer 1885, 266–7). Although the steady erosion of the owner-occupied farm was well under way, these slim statistics nonetheless indicate the survival of the yeoman farmer here throughout the nineteenth century.

The rise of a railway village

As late as 1858, Tebay was described as 'a small village, consisting of farmhouses, most of which present an antiquated appearance' (Kelly 1858, 63). The focus of the village soon shifted a kilometre to the south, and the original nucleus remained little changed until the 1920s, by which time the world had passed it by and it was known as 'Old Tebay' (OS 1920). The almost exclusively farming community was rocked by a brief influx of navvies during railway construction. By 1849 railway employment was becoming the main occupation other than farming, and alien names arrived with railwaymen such as Daniel Barnes, stationmaster, and Peter Merry, engineer (Mannex 1849, 87). At first they accounted for only ten households out of 90 (CFHS 1991, 100, 103) and all lived in purpose-built cottages alongside the Lancaster to Carlisle line, but the transformation thereafter was rapid and the new village soon had 'a resident population of nearly 1000, chiefly railway employees and their families' (Bulmer 1885, 259). The service trades were based here, close to the station and the market hall. The neglect and partial destruction of Old Tebay have been finalised by the motorway, whose access road and roundabout conclusively separate the remains of the old village from the new.

Railway employment mushroomed when the junction with the South Durham Railway, opened in 1861, was sited at Tebay. Coal trains headed westwards from Barnard Castle over Stainmore and through the Lune gorge, linking the Furness iron industry with the Durham coalfield. That this had a very localised effect is apparent from the trade directories, which list no railway employees for Orton or the other townships in the parish. In Orton itself, there were many tradespeople and shopkeepers, but outside the village most people were still farmers, whereas at Tebay, the new village near the railway junction and station catered for the needs of the growing population with two shopkeepers, two blacksmiths, and a grammar school master (Mannex 1849, 187). The school founded in 1672 was replaced in 1863 by the building at Mount Pleasant (Bulmer 1885, 259), itself now superseded. A market hall supplied butter, eggs, and other local farm produce (Bulmer 1885, 258), until it was demolished in 1963 (Joy 1967, 62). A Methodist chapel (1865) and seven rows of houses (1880–1910) also catered for the railway workers and their families (Joy 1967, 60), and the parish church of St James (1880) was largely funded by the railway companies and employees (Wainwright 1988, 425). Low Borrowbridge and the Cross Keys at Tebay were the only inns in the Lune gorge, although beerhouses later opened for the railwaymen at Scufton House near Lowgill station (Fig 3:21), and Dyke Farm above Tebay station. Occupations by 1885 were evenly divided between farmers and railway employees together with shopkeepers and tradesmen. The importance of the railway to the local community at this time is emphasised by the directory listing of a platelayer, a locomotive superintendent, station masters at Gaisgill and Tebay, two railway line inspectors, a clearing house clerk, two locomotive foremen, and a refreshment room proprietor, bookseller, and manageress (Bulmer 1885, 266).

The expanding population and facilities at Tebay not only opened up distant markets for farm produce, but enabled a few local farmers to pursue a secondary occupation, as licensee, butcher, or limeburner, serving the needs of this community with an urban character in a rural location. The railways had 'greatly enhanced the value of the property, and produced a considerable increase in the material wealth of the district' (Bulmer 1885, 258). Livestock no longer travelled on the hoof, but in railway cattle trucks, and even the fell ponies now went by train to Brough Hill Fair and Kendal Horse Fair (Joy 1967, 62). The other hamlets, except Gaisgill which had its own station, were less directly affected by the railways than Tebay. Railway activity had a less subtle presence than nowadays. Steam trains taking up water at speed from the Dillicar troughs, stopping at Tebay to attach banking engines for the climb over Shap, or clanking through the gorge, laden with coke, on the downhill run from Stainmore, probably generated more noise and air pollution than the motorway does today.

At the southern end of the Lune gorge, Lowgill once had two railway stations and was also located at a junction, near the viaduct carrying the now disused Ingleton branch line (**1162**) (Fig 3:22). Lowgill had a single row of railway cottages and a school, where previously there had been only scattered farms, but it never developed into a village on the scale of Tebay.

The transient populations of Low Borrowbridge

Located in an unavoidable position between two sharp bends in the turnpike road around the raised site of the fort was Low Borrowbridge Inn, until

recently in Grayrigg parish. The parish boundary
has been changed, now following the railway rather
than the river, presumably to integrate Low Borrowbridge Inn, which previously occupied a remote
corner of Grayrigg parish (Fig 3:20), with the rest of
the dwellings in the Lune gorge in Tebay parish.
The Kendal to Appleby road (A685) (Fig 3:16)
passed between the farmhouse and buildings until
it was rerouted to the west to make room for the
motorway. There is no longer an inn at Low
Borrowbridge, but it remains a farm in whose fields
lie both the Roman fort (**1137**) and the associated
cemetery (**11318**) which was excavated during
construction of the NWEP (Figs 2:21, 5:1, 5:2) (*see
Chapter 5*).

On the far side of the bridge over Borrow Beck, now
dwarfed by the railway and motorway bridges tow-
ering over it, is the other farm of Low Borrowbridge,
where for many years in the eighteenth century, the
manor court was held at the house of William
Branthwaite (D/Lons/L, Wharton Box 1). The
tollbar keeper in 1851 lived at Bridge Gate, adjacent
to the farm, and also plied his trade as a shoemaker
(CFHS 1991, 99). In front of the inn, the turnpike
joined the Roman road to run north alongside the
fort. The needs of travellers contributed to the destruction of the fort walls at Low Borrowbridge, for
in 1827 the walls were largely removed (Birley
1947, 4) to provide building stone for the inn.

The proposed line of the Caledonian Railway
through the Lune gorge would have cut straight
across the fort (WQ/R/DP/15) (Fig 3:19), but fortunately the line eventually taken by the Lancaster
and Carlisle Railway in 1844 skirted the fort to the
west (WQ/R/DP/45). One or more of the fort's
ditches was nonetheless destroyed, and what was
left of the western fort wall was used as a stone

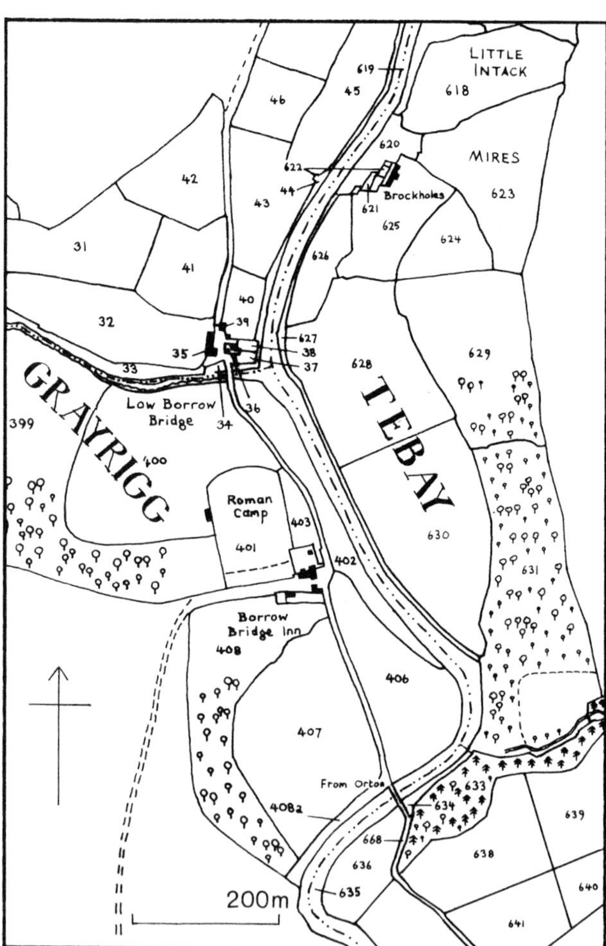

Figure 3:20 *Low Borrowbridge, Grayrigg and Tebay
tithe map extracts, 1835 and 1841
(WQ/R/C/5, WDRC/8/110)*

quarry for railway cottages (Ferguson 1894, 43). The
environs of the inn were also host to the navvy
camps established here for the duration of railway
construction in the 1840s, and it was then that the
navvies built their own bar from the stones of the
Roman bathhouse (J Anstee pers comm).

The droving and packhorse trades declined as transport was taken over by the railways, which effectively bypassed Low Borrowbridge, said in 1858 to
be 'little frequented, except once a year during a
fair which is held there' (Kelly 1858, 58). The inn
was the hub of activity during this annual stock fair
held on the fort from 1841 until about 1902. In September 1841 '1700 sheep were on view and large
numbers of cattle and horses. By 1849 this fair was
well established and was looked upon as one of the
best for sheep and young stock; the following year
there were over 5000 sheep exhibited' (Garnett
1912, 136). The decline of the fair was hastened by
the new system of auction marts, and by the railway which began to transport stock to distant markets, rendering the drove roads redundant.

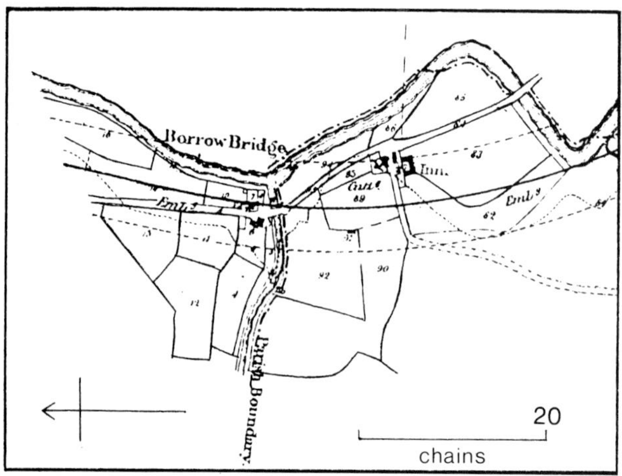

Figure 3:19 *Low Borrowbridge, proposed Caledonian
railway map extract, 1842 (WQ/R/DP/15)*

Motorway construction brought a new encampment of caravans in 1967–70, in the field between the railway and the former inn. For the three years that the motorway builders were resident, they trebled the number of children attending Tebay school (Westmorland Gazette, 28 January 1994).

The last retreat from marginal farmsteads

Several Tebay farmhouses are of late seventeenth century date, namely High Carlingill, High and Low Borrowdale, two houses at Roundthwaite, Town Foot at Old Tebay, Ellergill, and Waskew Head. Tebaygill and Low Greenholme are perhaps slightly later, while Brockholes, Lune's Bridge Farm, Overcluegill, Gelstone, Town Head Farm and another house at Old Tebay, and Gaisgill Row together with a nearby cottage, were built in the early eighteenth century (RCHM(E) 1936, 225–6). Prosperity came to Tebay after the Restoration of 1660, sufficient to build new farmhouses of dressed stone, some of which were on sites long used for successive houses, and the rebuilding here spanned less than a century. There are no recorded upstanding stone buildings which predate this period, despite the fact that stone appears always to have been the main building material, as demonstrated by the tumbled shieling and other hut foundations on the fellsides, and indeed the stone house or farm building at Powsons (**1132**, *see Chapter 7*).

Many farmsteads have succumbed to the renewed retreat from marginal agricultural land, and this trend is of course not particular to the Lune gorge. Hill farms throughout the area were deserted, many of them since the Second World War, their buildings and field walls falling into decay, while their enclosed fields were absorbed into the more successful neighbouring farms. All the deserted settlements are more or less isolated farmsteads, often settled late on marginal land. The post-medieval farms on Tebay Fell testify to the success and continuing growth of a community which pushed colonisation to the topographical limit. Life on these remote farms was undoubtedly hard, but perhaps not unhealthy; Thomas Morphet of Gelstone, for example, lived to the age of 103 (Bulmer 1885, 250). Several farms on Tebay Fell, Traildike, High Cocklake, and Gelstone, have post-medieval dialect names (Smith 1967, 2, 52–3), confirming their late foundation, and are among the eight fell farms now abandoned (Fig 3:21). There was no equivalent expansion of permanent settlement in other parts of the township; new farms were not founded in the Lune gorge or in Borrowdale and, except at High Borrowdale, there is less evidence of subsequent desertion.

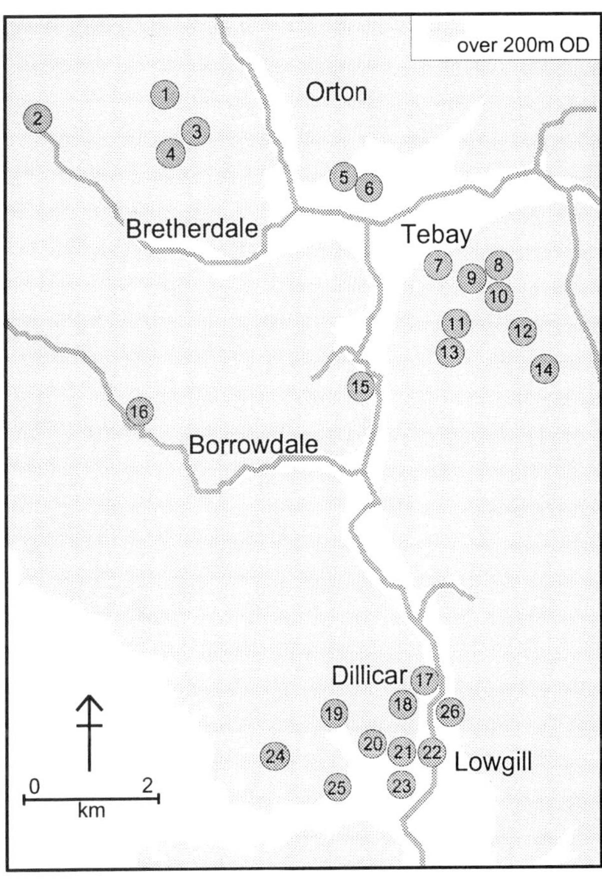

Orton	Dillicar
1 Eskew Head	17 Low Park
2 Scalehowe	18 High Park
3 High Crag	19 Lummer Head
4 Winster House	20 Highgill
5 Daniel Hill	21 Dryfold
6 Raisbank	22 Scufton House
	23 Nether House
Tebay	
7 Leagate House	**Grayrigg**
8 High Cocklake	24 Lambert Ash
9 Traildike	
10 Cooper House	**Firbank**
11 Overcluegill	25 Cowperthwaite
12 New Field	
13 Gelstone	**Sedbergh**
14 Rawbusk	26 Midgehole
15 Lawtland House	
16 High Borrowdale	

Figure 3:21 Post-medieval deserted farmsteads in the Tebay area

The desertion of farms on Tebay Fell is paralleled around Lowgill, at the southern end of the Lune gorge. A string of abandoned settlements here includes Highgill, supposedly the site of a deserted medieval village (Cumbria SMR 3673), but in 1636 simply a messuage with six acres of land (Farrer 1923, 212). Cowperthwaite Farm, whose lands were granted to Cockersand Abbey in 1220–40 (Farrer 1924, 418), has only recently ceased to be a working farm, its former access road and land having been

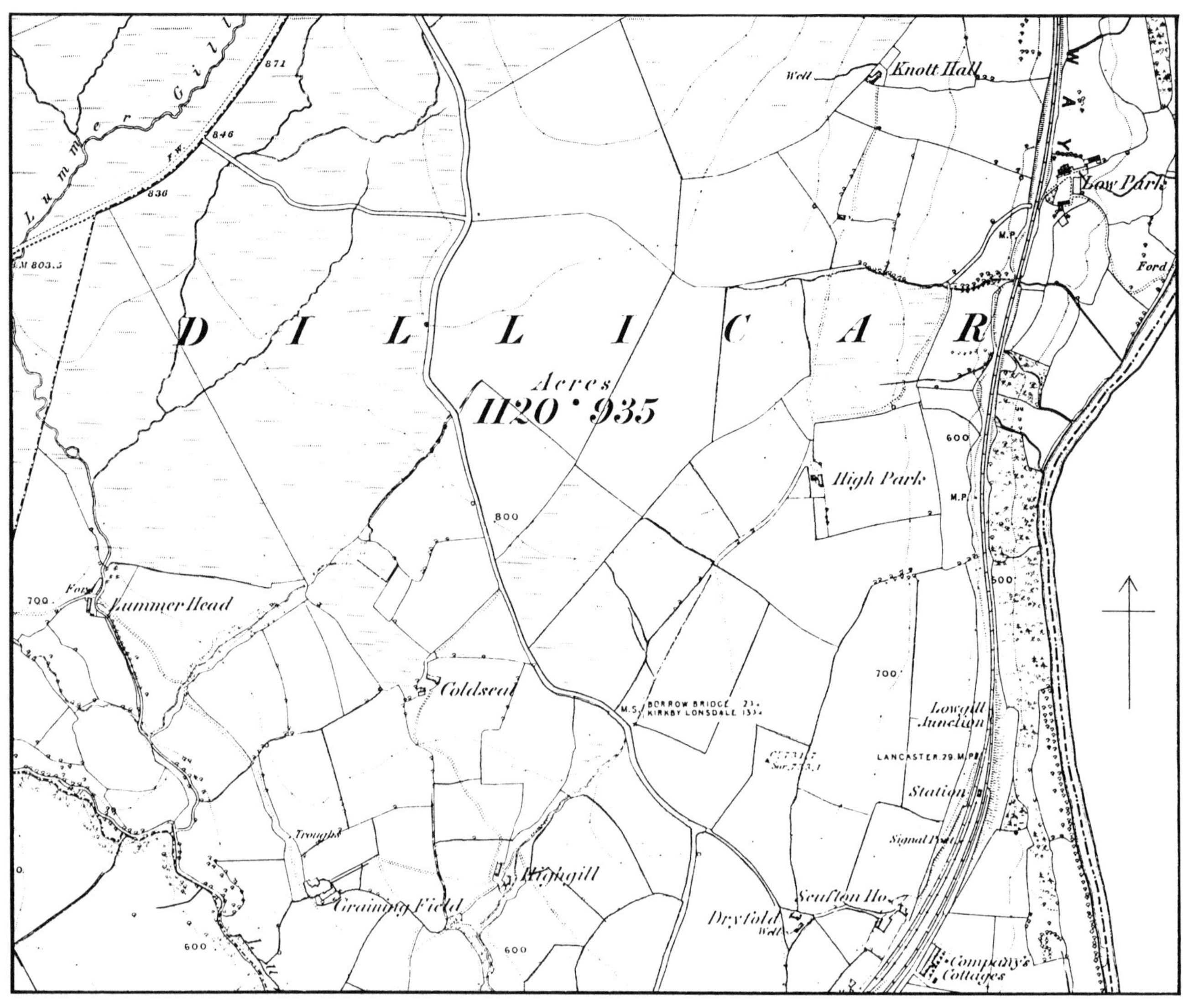

Figure 3:22 Dillicar and Lowgill, OS 1st edn 6″ map extract, 1858

sectioned by the motorway cutting directly below the buildings. Most of the ruinous farmhouses will eventually share the fate of the few, such as Lummer Head, which were deserted between 1897 and 1912 (OS 1899, 1920) and which, like Powsons (**1132**) higher up the valley, are now visible only as turf-fast tumbled masonry and trackways. Dryfold does not even survive to this extent, as it now lies beneath the northbound carriageway of the M6. The tiny population of Dillicar was drastically reduced this century by the loss of at least seven farms in an area less than 2km square (Figs 3:21, 3:22).

The process of change in the Lune gorge landscape is epitomised by High Park and Low Park, which owe their names to medieval parkland in Dillicar. 'Dillaker Parke' (Low Park) in 1641 was a messuage and tenement with 'eleven acres arable land, six acres meadow, fourteen acres pasture, thirty acres furze and heath', tenanted by Francis Warde,

gentleman, while 'High Howse' (High Park) had six acres of land in 1636, and was tenanted by James Travers, yeoman (Farrer 1923, 212–3). These linked farms had a rude awakening when the railway was pushed through the Lune gorge, and were dealt a mortal blow with the construction of the motorway. Low Park (Figs 3:21, 3:22, 3:23) is on the west bank of the Lune, the only recently deserted farmstead to be traversed by the pipeline. During topsoil removal a single sherd of green glazed pottery (**1151**) was recovered here, the only medieval pottery found during the NWEP project in the Lune gorge. The pipeline at Low Park followed a similar alignment to the proposed Caledonian Railway route of 1842 (Fig 3:24). In the event, the railway was built not between the farm and the river, but immediately above the farm. An underpass was provided for the lane to High Park, now also abandoned. By the time the pipeline was built, the damage to these farms had long been done.

Figure 3:23 Lowgill, Low Park deserted farm

Trains and cars and planes

The Romans made Low Borrowbridge the focal point of the Lune gorge, controlling and stimulating local productivity and traffic. Tebay, at the head of the valley, was an ideal site for Anglian settlement, and the Normans recognised its strategic importance, creating a castle at the centre of this minor lordship. Everyday life in the Lune gorge has frequently been disrupted since Roman soldiers arrived to build their road and fort. Tribal warriors, border raiders, and retreating or advancing armies succeeded one another through the ensuing centuries. Drovers and packmen followed their various routes through the valley and across the fells, until the turnpike road and then the railway put paid to their trade.

The community was less isolated than its location would suggest, and witnessed not only the passage of judges on the northern circuit, but even the occasional gang of highwaymen. Late on Whitsun Eve in 1684, Lancelot Arey and Thomas Crosby, his wife's son, were approaching home at Roundthwaite

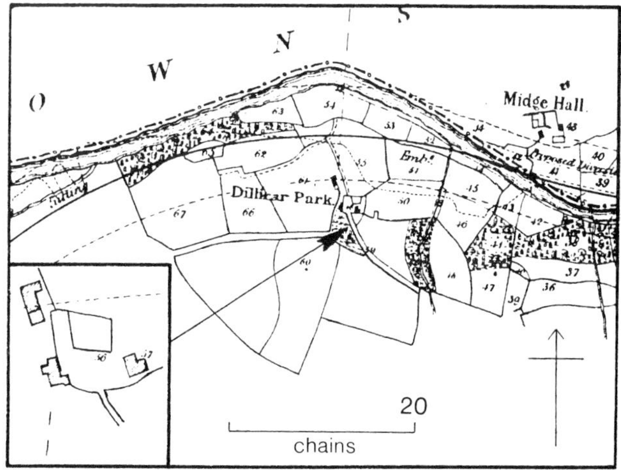

Figure 3:24 Caledonian railway proposal, 1842, Low Park (WQ/R/DP/15)

on their return from Kendal, when 'three men came riding furiously on the highway', seized Lancelot and took thirty shillings, all his money save sixpence. Meanwhile Thomas 'alighting from off his horse and leaping over a wall got into the house, the said robber pursuing him to the very door' (Macfarlane 1981, 140). These notorious highwaymen, on their travels in 1682 and 1684 between Penrith and Kirkby Lonsdale, seem to have followed both the Galloway Gate through Shap and the Roman road over Crosby Ravensworth Fell, these being the two roads which converge in the Lune gorge (Macfarlane 1981, 125, map).

The most dramatic recent episodes in the history of the Lune gorge have been the construction of the railway and motorway, bringing the valley back into focus as the main west-coast transport artery. The east and west valley sides have different histories, emphasised recently by the wholesale destruction of any archaeological sites which may have existed along the 200m contour on the western slopes, occupied by the railway, the rerouted Kendal to Appleby road, and the motorway. The relatively undisturbed eastern slopes have a string of settlements along the same 200m contour.

Major routeways have a compelling effect on settlement and economic development. Settlement here has been both attracted and repelled, the economic attraction apparently outweighing the attendant hazards during the Roman occupation. Since 1970 the local economy has been blighted, on the one hand, by the closure of Tebay station and the South Durham branch line, and also by the noise and pollution generated by the motorway. On the other hand, it has been regenerated by the improved communications and the motorway services which provide local employment, and these factors have recently stimulated new housing development at Tebay. The motorway's unending drone ended tranquillity, and the late twentieth century has made its own contribution, putting the Lune gorge in the regular flight path of low-flying jets on NATO training exercises. The farming community's resilience to these forces of change can be measured in its adaptation to difficult conditions imposed from outside. It has fed Roman soldiers, grazed drovers' cattle, supplied the railway population with meat and dairy produce, and managed its own motorway services. The most significant structures, all of which served to provide refuge and accommodate travellers, have been the Roman fort, Norman castle, inns, railway stations, and motorway service areas. The impact of the roads and railways here has been enormous—that of the 1991 pipeline, shortlived and relatively insignificant.

4

CROSSING HADRIAN'S WALL

Hadrian's Wall is a monument of outstanding national and international importance; as such it has statutory protection as a Scheduled Monument and is designated a World Heritage Site. Clearly the optimum route for crossing Hadrian's Wall, from the archaeological perspective, should cause the least amount of damage to the monument and any associated stratigraphy. In the immediate vicinity of the proposed pipeline crossing there were no visible remains of the Wall, and the exact positions of its various elements were unknown. For the purposes of the NWEP, the archaeologically sensitive area of the Wall was, therefore, subject to an accelerated programme of survey and trial excavation to ensure minimal disturbance by the pipeline at the proposed crossing point (NY 4285059400). In the light of the results of this evaluation, the pipeline route was revised and ultimately crossed the Wall some 225m further west (NY 4267059280) (Fig 4:1).

The construction of Hadrian's Wall, begun in AD 122, marked the consolidation of the province's northern frontier within its existing boundaries. The pre-existing Tyne-Solway frontier followed by the Stanegate road was strengthened and fortified by Hadrian. The Wall was designed to separate the tribesmen to the north from Roman occupation to the south, facilitating taxation on the movement of goods, and regulating the movement of people, through the numerous fortified gateways. Changing frontier policy led to its replacement by the Antonine Wall, and the subsequent reoccupation and reconstruction of Hadrian's Wall in the AD 160s (Breeze and Dobson 1987, 28, 40, 127–8). As originally planned, the Wall ran from Newcastle to Carlisle and then along the Cumbrian coast to Bowness-on-Solway, a distance of 76 Roman miles (113km) (Breeze and Dobson 1987, 28). From Newcastle to the River Irthing (45 miles) a stone wall was built, 10 Roman feet wide and c15 feet (c4.5m) high, on a foundation of stone and puddled clay (Bergstrom 1984, 6). The section west of the River Irthing (31 miles), was constructed of turf, on a broader foundation 20 feet (6m) wide, despite the availability of building stone, probably because of the lack of suitable limestone for mortar. The turf wall seems to have been similar in height to the stone wall (Breeze and Dobson 1987, 32, 74). Our knowledge of the various schemes for different styles of wall-building is based on the relatively small number of sites excavated, and the dimensions may in fact have been applied less rigidly than the figures given here might imply.

At every Roman mile a fortified gateway, or milecastle, was provided, and between these, at intervals of a third of a mile, were turrets built into the Wall (Breeze and Dobson 1987, 33, 36). The Wall was backed up by a series of forts connected by the Stanegate, at varying distances to the rear, but in the revised scheme these forts were relocated on the line of the Wall, replacing some of the milecastles. In conjunction with this second scheme, the *vallum* was built to the rear of the Wall (Breeze and Dobson 1987, 83), perhaps defining a military zone, and maybe with a secondary purpose of enabling covert lateral communications. The *vallum* was essentially a ditch 20 feet (6m) wide and 10 feet (3m) deep with a flat bottom 8 feet (2.45m) wide. The upcast from the ditch was piled into two continuous banks set 30 feet (9m) back from the ditch on either side, which were normally revetted with kerbs of turf-work.

The section of the turf wall between Walby and Tarraby (milecastles 62–65) was originally constructed between AD 122 and c126 (Breeze and Dobson 1987, 82) of cut turves laid in courses, and was 6m thick at the base. To the north was a berm c2m wide, in front of which was a V-shaped ditch averaging 8m wide and 2.75m deep. A final revision of the Wall structure occurred perhaps before AD 140, but more probably after 160, when the turf wall was replaced by an intermediate stone wall, 9 feet (2.75m) wide. Reconstruction of forts and other works took place as late as the fourth century but the Wall structure remained essentially the same, although its function as a linear barrier may have declined in consequence of some demilitarisation in the third century.

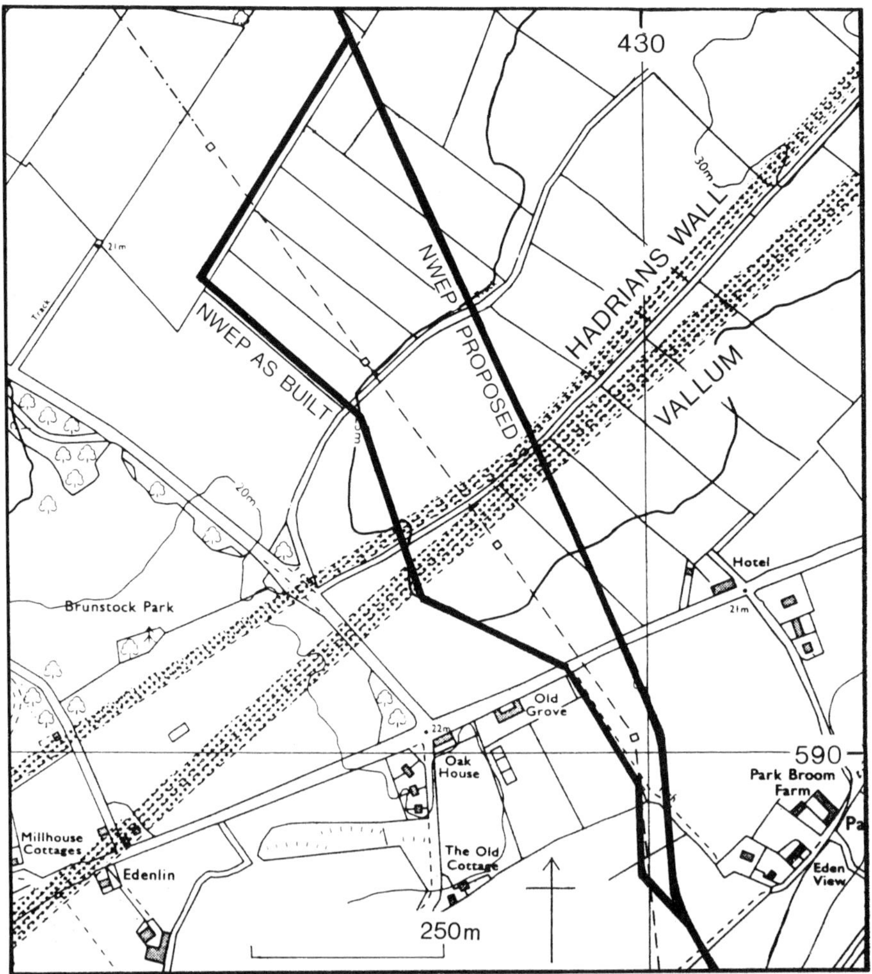

*Figure 4:1 Hadrian's Wall (825), east of Brunstock Park, with location
of proposed and revised NWEP routes*

Initial assessment

John Williams

While there were no upstanding remains of the Wall complex in the fields near the proposed NWEP crossing, the likelihood of buried structural elements could be assessed by reference to previous archaeological excavations on the line of the Wall to the east and west. The closest comparison was provided by Haverfield, who in 1894 excavated elements of the Wall complex in Brunstock Park (NY 424591). Here the Wall and *vallum* are only *c*30m apart, and the *vallum* and Wall-ditch were both still visible as earthworks. The excavations showed the *vallum* to be 9m wide at the top, 4.5m wide at the base, and 2.45m deep. The surviving fragments of the Wall were built of red sandstone with a little cement, on a foundation of cobbles. Haverfield, describing the stretch designated a century later for the pipeline crossing, noted that 'For about 2½ miles east of

Brunstock, Wall and *vallum* have almost wholly vanished before the plough' (Haverfield 1895a, 459).

Excavations in 1976 at Tarraby Lane (NY 40535755), east of the fort of *Petriana* at Stanwix, located various Wall components including a shallow, sinuous, linear feature approximately parallel to and 10m south of the Wall. This seems to have been an unmetalled hollow-way contemporary with the turf wall, but subsequently disused, since it was overlain by demolition debris. The Wall-ditch was found to be 6.5m wide at subsoil level, and the berm between Wall and ditch was 11.5m in width. Although, as elsewhere, the Wall itself had been robbed out, two foundation courses survived in places as slabs of red sandstone infilled with sandstone rubble and sandy mortar. The Wall at the base of its foundations was 3.2m wide, but there was no indication of the earlier turf wall apart from the hollow-way (Smith 1978, 23–4).

West of Walby (NY 435602) the line of Hadrian's

Wall was briefly examined during construction of the British Gas pipeline in 1975, but only indeterminate traces of the turf or stone wall were revealed under a farm road. The southern edge of the Wall-ditch was 16.4m north of the centre of this road, and here the ditch was 10.5m wide and 3.7m deep. The *vallum* was located 36m north of the line shown on OS maps, at NY 436600, and appeared to be 5.6m wide at the top, 3.7m wide at the base, and 1.8m deep (Richardson 1976, 10).

The landuse is arable, divided into large, relatively level, ploughed fields, an overgrown lane in the form of a hollow-way providing the only exception in the crossing area, and forming the boundary between fields to the north and south of the projected alignment of Hadrian's Wall. As Haverfield observed a century ago, to the east of Brunstock Park the remains have been ploughed over. The hollow-way ran eastwards from NY 42555922 along the approximate line of the Wall, flanked by earthen banks. The total width of the hollow-way and banks was up to 9m, and while the banks stood up to 1m above the level of the adjoining fields in places, elsewhere the hollow-way was 1m below field level.

On the current OS 1:2500 scale map (OS 1973) the Wall and Wall-ditch lines are plotted to the north of the hollow-way. At Wall Knowe, however, the Wall had been mislocated by the OS (Smith 1978, 21), and at Walby also the *vallum* was misplaced 36m to the north (Richardson 1976, 10). There was no certainty, therefore, of the exact position of the Wall, Wall-ditch, or *vallum* in the area immediately east of Brunstock Park. As the hollow-way followed closely the projected Wall alignment, there was a strong possibility that it might overlie the Wall or Wall-ditch. This uncertainty emphasised the need to fix the line of the Wall, Wall-ditch, and *vallum* by geophysical survey, and by contour survey of the hollow-way. This would define the area of the Wall complex which had suffered the most damage by the creation of the hollow-way and ploughing, through which the pipeline could most satisfactorily be routed.

Geophysical survey

Philip Howard

The geophysical survey was designed to locate the positions of the Wall-ditch and *vallum* on either side of a length of the Wall in arable farmland belonging to Linstock Castle Farm. Eight survey transects were set out in positions which were calculated to cross the likely line either of the Wall-ditch to the north-west of the Wall or of the *vallum* to the south-east, while avoiding the areas of magnetic interference from the barbed wire fences forming the field boundaries. The transects were all 20m wide, and 40–100m long (Fig 4:2).

The Wall-ditch

The Wall-ditch showed well in Transects 3 and 4, with clear positive and reverse anomalies, but Transects 1 and 2 showed little sign of any anomaly that could be linked to it. Activities postdating the use of the Wall-ditch may have masked or destroyed it, but the strength of anomaly produced by any ditch depends on the circumstances in which it was filled, and deliberate backfilling often produces only a slight anomaly. Transect 2 was positioned over a quarry pit which had been backfilled this century, according to information received from Mr Wannop, of Linstock Castle Farm. The edges of this depression were still visible. The orientation of the anomalies observed was very close to that indicated on the OS 1:2500 scale map (OS 1973), although the Wall-ditch seemed to be slightly further to the north-west than the map indicates.

The *vallum*

Transect 6 contained a single very strong anomaly running at right-angles to the line of the *vallum*, subsequently confirmed to be an iron water pipe (pers comm Mr Wannop). The clearest anomaly which can be ascribed to the presence of the *vallum* was in Transect 8. A strongly-marked positive anomaly ran from north-east to south-west, with a less continuous negative anomaly to the north-west; to the south-east the arrangement of contours produced a rather faint line running parallel to the positive anomaly. Taken together these features indicated the existence of a structure of an appropriate size and shape to be the *vallum*; once more, the position was very close to that shown on the OS map.

In Transect 5, to the extreme south-east of the survey area, a faint line could be seen in the centre, on an alignment varying only slightly from that shown on the OS map. This transect was, however, close to the quarry, which may have affected the survival of archaeological features. The anomalies contained in Transects 3 and 4 (Wall-ditch), and Transects 5 and 8 (*vallum*), indicated that the locations of the Wall-ditch and *vallum* on the OS map were essentially correct. The strongest anomalies occurred in the north-eastern part of the survey area. To the south-west, the *vallum* produced only a faint trace,

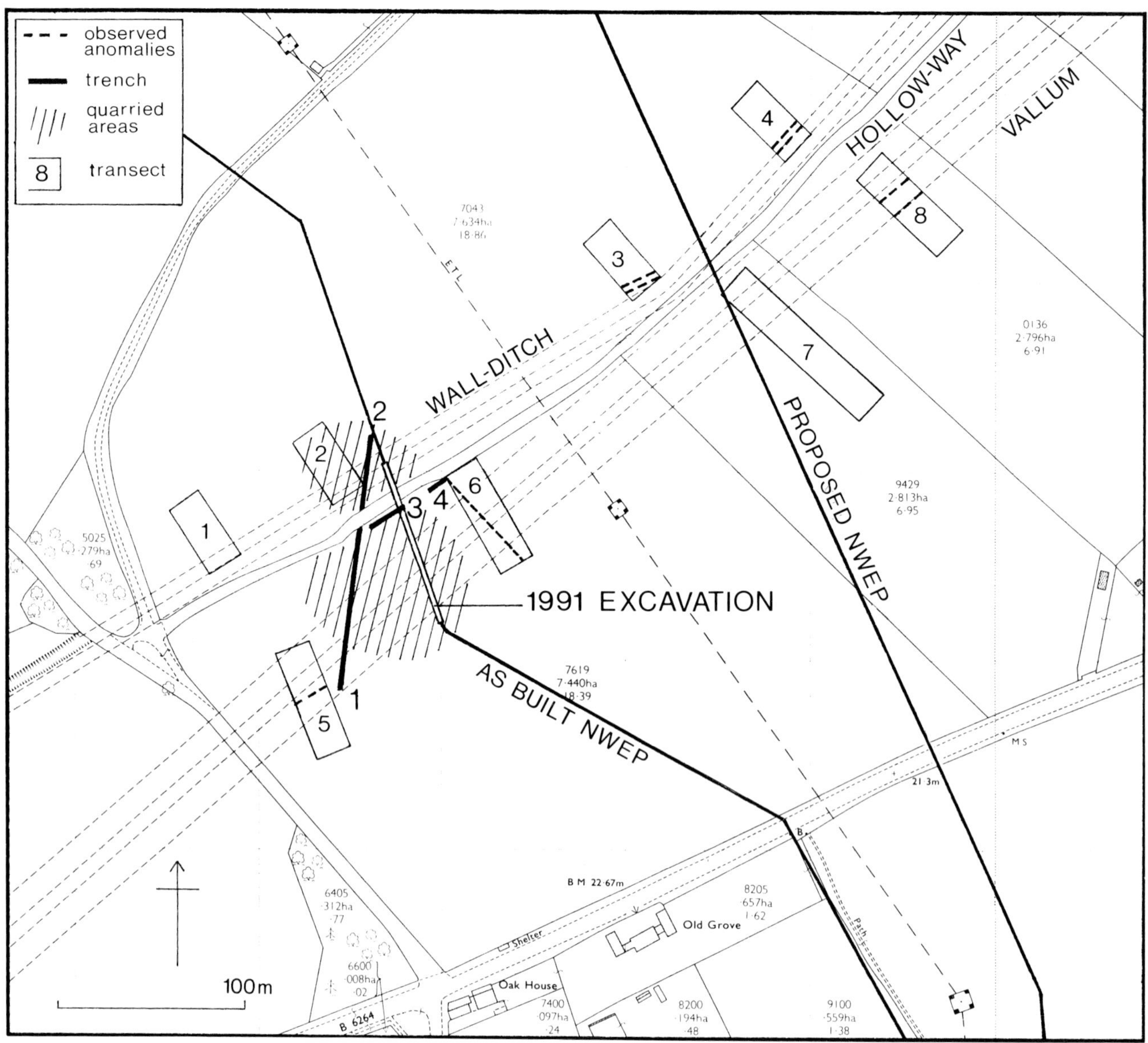

*Figure 4:2 Hadrian's Wall (**825**), NWEP routes, geophysical survey transects, and trench locations*

while the Wall-ditch did not appear in either Transect 1 or 2; from the projected line of the Wall on the OS map it may seem that Transect 1 missed the Wall-ditch, but the evidence of Transects 3 and 4 suggests that the line given by the OS is actually a little too far to the south-east. The survey demonstrated that the archaeological features were less well preserved in the south-western part of the area than in the north-east.

Contour survey

John Williams

Thirteen profiles were surveyed at intervals of 20–50m across the hollow-way, over a total distance of 500m. In about half of these profiles the fields on either side of the hollow-way were at the same height as each other, while in most of the rest the ground sloped upwards from north-west to south-east, particularly at the east end of the section of hollow-way surveyed. The base of the hollow-way was generally on the same level as the lower of the adjacent fields, but in a few places it dipped below the field level. The hollow-way had clearly cut some way into the natural slope of the ground and could have eroded or otherwise damaged archaeological deposits. Two of the profiles were anomalous, in that the slope was downwards from north-west to south-east, and there was a sharp drop from the bank on the south-east of the hollow-way into the field. A quarry in this area was filled in earlier this century, and a further probable area of quarrying, of uncertain depth, was subsequently indicated immediately to its north-west (pers comm Mr Wannop). The extent of this quarrying was estimated by plotting changes of slope which appeared to be inconsistent with the natural lie of the land. In the area of the two anomalous profiles the *vallum* seemed to have been either partially or totally destroyed by quarrying.

Trial excavation

Paul Gibbons

The Wall and *vallum* were probably better preserved in the area originally designated by SCUK as the preferred crossing point than immediately to the west, and it was considered that the bank forming the north-western side of the hollow-way within the surveyed area might in part overlie and protect the remains of the Wall structure. Two substantial hollows, located either side of the hollow-way, were identified during the geophysical survey as areas of backfilled quarrying. These hollows interrupted the projected line of the Wall and *vallum*, partially or wholly destroying a section of the monument. A reroute of the pipeline through the hollows would probably cause minimal damage to Hadrian's Wall, but to validate this judgement trial excavation was proposed. The recommended reroute was 230m to the south-west of the original route.

Following discussions between SCUK, LUAU, and English Heritage, the reroute was approved in principle, and Scheduled Monument Consent was sought and obtained. It was proposed to establish, by machine excavation, the nature and depth of the possible quarrying, in order to assess the damage sustained by the monument. The excavation was subject to constraints by English Heritage: only topsoil, ploughsoil, and post-Roman deposits could be removed; any *in situ* Roman deposits were to be left intact and their state of survival assessed; the hollow-way was not to be excavated; a trench was to be excavated on the eastern side of the quarry, parallel to the hollow-way, to assess the damage caused by the water pipe located by geophysical survey. Excavation of the trenches to a depth of 1.5m was considered sufficient to assess the degree of disturbance that the pipeline trench would cause.

The two hollows (NY 42665924, NY 42665930) were separated by the hollow-way, whose typical profile consisted of a double bank delimiting a central path, the base of which was always lower than, *ie* eroded into, the natural slope of the land. In the area between the two hollows the profile was atypical: the double banks were of a reduced height in relation to the base of the central path, which lay above the slope of the adjacent land, giving the general impression that the path lay on a raised causeway. This suggested that the two hollows had never been linked, but that the land had been quarried on either side of the hollow-way, leaving the path intact. Neither quarry is shown on the OS 1st edn 6″ map (OS 1865). It appeared that earlier this century both hollows had been deeper, and in order to facilitate cultivation the ground surface had been raised by making over both areas as temporary landfill sites (pers comm Mr Wannop).

The geology of the area consists of Triassic sandstone overlain by glacial till, and the topsoil is of the Clifton Series, consisting of a relatively stone-free grey-brown sandy loam.

The trenches were excavated with a Komatsu tracked excavator fitted with a 0.9m ditching bucket. Trenches 1, 2, and 3 established that the two hollows overlay at least two substantial intrusions into the natural subsoil which had been partially filled with ploughsoil and, more recently, landfill material. The northern quarry was some 32m wide, with a landfill of demolition debris. The base of the quarry was deeper than the trench. The southern quarry was at least 70m wide, with a landfill of domestic refuse that was loose and unstable. The base of this quarry was for the most part deeper than the trench. Trench 3 revealed the northern face of the southern quarry extending eastwards, and located its eastern edge (Fig 4:2).

The steep and unweathered nature of the edges of the quarries suggested that they had been immediately backfilled on cessation of quarrying. It appeared that the quarrying was concerned with the extraction of the finer sand and gravel occurring in substantial pockets and bands within a glacial till of more varied constituents. It was clear that the quarrying had removed all positive archaeological features associated with the Wall complex. With regard to the survival of the Wall-ditch and *vallum* ditch, it was not possible to determine whether the quarrying was of sufficient depth to have removed all traces of these negative features. As the surface of the subsoil forming the base of the quarries was uneven, it was possible that any high areas of subsoil remaining might preserve the lowest sections of the two ditches, which had previously been demonstrated to reach a depth of 2.45m (Haverfield 1895a, 457).

It was confirmed that the hollow-way had not been cut by quarrying activity in the area between Trenches 1 and 2, and there remained a possibility that the Roman ground surface, and even part of the foundations of the turf or stone wall, might be preserved beneath its banks.

Trench 4 established that the water pipe was located outside the quarried area, and in crossing the *vallum* may have disturbed areas of shallower Roman stratigraphy although, in comparison with the disturbance caused by the quarrying, the damage would be negligible.

No Roman stratigraphy or features were observed in any of the trenches and no artefact predating the twentieth century was recovered. The evaluation established that the least damage would be caused to the Wall complex if the pipeline were to follow a line through the two hollows as close as possible to the line of Trenches 1 and 2, in the area of maximum post-Roman disturbance.

The 1991 excavation

Denise Drury

Following recommendations to SCUK based on the findings of the evaluation, the pipeline route was substantially revised to cross the Wall complex at NY 4267059280, *c*225m west of the line originally proposed. Consent was granted under Section 2 of the Ancient Monuments and Archaeological Areas Act (1979) for further investigation comprising 'The excavation of one long narrow trench about 2m wide and 2m deep across the line of the hollow-way and the apparent line of the ditch and *vallum*'. The purpose of the excavation was to investigate and record any surviving archaeological features in advance of pipeline construction, within the parameters of the pipeline trench.

The 2m wide trench was excavated for a distance of 90m along the centre-line of the intended pipeline trench as it crossed the Hadrianic frontier. A Case mechanical excavator, fitted with a 1.55m wide toothless bucket, was utilised to excavate the trench to either side of the hollow-way, but the hollow-way itself was largely excavated by hand. The trench edges proved to be unstable, particularly in the deeper cut sections, leading to rapid collapse of the trench sides. This factor dictated the on-site practice of excavating, recording, and backfilling short sections of the trench, and to some extent limited the recording and sampling of the deeper sections. Across the area of the hollow-way the hedge, fencing, and overgrowth were mostly removed by machine. The hedgebanks, composed of fine sandy silts, also formed unstable sections and consequently, for reasons of safety, they were cut back wider than the trench.

For ease of reference the trench is described and discussed in three sections: the north field, the hollow-way, and the south field.

North field

To the north of the hollow-way a 13m long trench was opened across a pronounced hollow. At approximately 0.50m below the surface large blocks of reinforced concrete were encountered. Consequently the section was recorded and the trench was backfilled without further excavation. There was a greater depth (0.50m) of ploughsoil in this field, and it contained some modern material including reinforcing wire. Below the ploughsoil and immediately above the concrete blocks were lenses of a darker silty loam with small patches of red clay. These layers contained landfill material such as broken bricks, undecayed wood, and barbed wire. At the foot of the northern bank of the hollow-way it was evident that ploughing had partially eroded the outer edge of the bank, and it was in this area that a fragment of *mortarium* was retrieved.

The quarry to the north of the hollow-way had been investigated in Trench 2 of the trial excavation, with similar results. A marked change in ground level caused by the quarrying is still visible, despite more recent landfill activities. Taken with the results of excavation, this indicates that archaeological deposits would not survive in the area of the northern quarry, which may have included the line of the Wall and Wall-ditch.

Hollow-way

The banks of the hollow-way had protected a band of underlying stratigraphy approximately 10m wide, with apparently minimal damage caused by use of the trackway (Fig 4:3). At the base of the trench the irregular, truncated, natural subsoil profile revealed some form of disturbance. A series of intercutting features was observed, the form and dimensions of which could not be seen within the confines of the area available for excavation.

Overlying and effectively sealing the disturbed material was a depth of compacted sandy silt, apparently the remnants of a surface; the irregularities and shallow features could be ruts associated with that surface. Above this material was a patchy layer containing stones (*17*), almost certainly a feature of the hollow-way track base, which was partially obscured by material probably derived from the

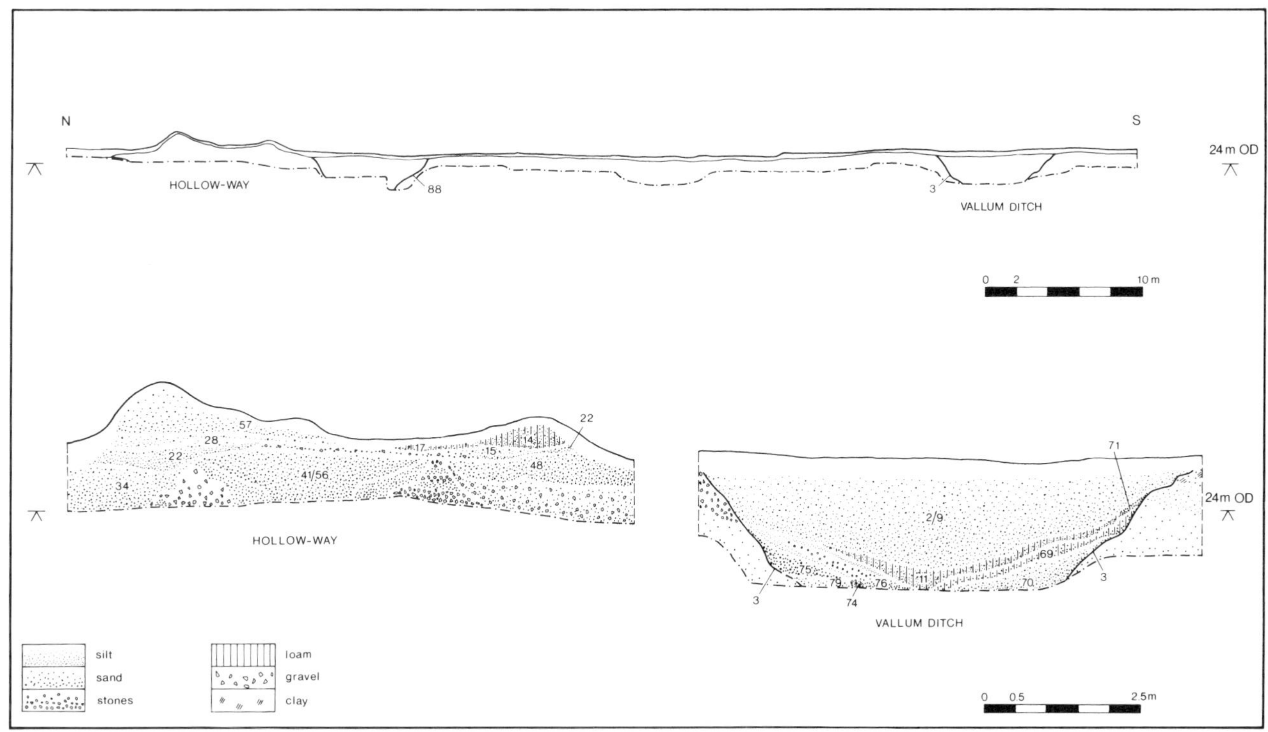

Figure 4:3 Hadrian's Wall (825), 1991 excavation, trench sections

adjacent banks. The quarrying, in combination with more recent ploughing adjacent to the banks, contributed to the truncation of any surviving archaeological features.

No evidence was found below the hollow-way for the Wall or Wall-ditch, which reinforces the likelihood, suggested by geophysical survey, that these elements were aligned slightly further to the northwest than the projected line shown on the current OS 1:2500 scale map (OS 1973; Fig 4:2).

South field

The trench to the south of the hollow-way was approximately 68m long; adjacent to the hollow-way it intersected Trial Trench 3, which had produced evidence of quarrying (Fig 4:2). The trench followed the eastern edge of the quarry hollow, except at the southern end, where it crossed higher, flatter ground. A deep-cut ditch was revealed below the ploughsoil, 40m south of the hollow-way, and approximately on the line of the *vallum* as estimated by the OS (OS 1973), and as indicated by the geophysical survey (*see above*, Transects 5 and 8). The trench was excavated, at this point, to the maximum permitted depth of 2m without revealing the base of the ditch. The sloping edges of the ditch, at an angle of approximately 40°, were clearly seen cut through natural sand; in both sections the northern edge of the ditch was the steeper, while the

southern edge appeared in profile to be partially stepped (Fig 4:3). The west-facing section was *c*8m wide at the top, and the east-facing section *c*9m wide, while at a depth of 1.70m the ditch was *c*4m wide. The form and dimensions of the *vallum* ditch, as seen in section, are comparable to other local excavated examples. Haverfield's excavations in Brunstock Park, for instance, recorded the *vallum* as having sides sloping at an angle of 30° from a width of 9m at the top to 4.5m at the flat base 2.45m below ground level (Haverfield 1895a, 457).

Despite the lack of opportunity to examine the stratigraphy in the deeper parts of the trench, distinct layers were observed at the edges and towards the presumed base of the ditch. Within the cut, towards its base and at the edges, the shallow layers represented tip lines or slumping of material into an open ditch. These layers were sterile and similar in composition to the natural subsoil. The upper part of the ditch was filled by different material apparently indicating silting (*11*) of the ditch, perhaps followed by deliberate backfilling (*2*). This material produced a single small sherd of degraded coarseware, possibly of second or third century date. The natural subsoil in the immediate area consisted predominantly of fairly coarse sand (*5*) interleaved with layers of gravel (*7*). At the northern edge of the ditch the natural subsoil was observed below the ploughsoil, while at the southern edge the ditch cut a moderately stony layer of reddish-brown sandy clay (*62*). To the south of the ditch an irregular profile was observed which included material similar to layer *62*, interspersed with areas and pockets of fairly stone-free pale reddish sandy clay and smaller areas, some of mottled appearance, of sand, sandy clay, and silty clay, which overlay layers of fine sandy silt and sand. Despite their mixed nature these were probably natural deposits.

North of the ditch, as the ground level dipped slightly towards the hollow-way, natural subsoil (*7*) was observed across the base of the trench, at a depth of *c*1.2m. Here the section revealed areas of disturbance over a particularly irregular sand and gravel profile. The material overlying the natural subsoil was mixed, consisting largely of light to red-brown sandy silts with lenses and amorphous patches of sands and gravels (*13, 20, 21*). There were, however, no discernible features and although this area had evidently been disturbed it did not yield any finds.

Immediately south of the hollow-way, where the trench intersected Trial Trench 3, a large intrusion (*88*) was recorded immediately below the plough-soil. The base of this feature was not reached by either of the excavations, the maximum depth of section here being 1.90m. The intrusion (*88*), measuring *c*12 x 7.80m, was cut through natural sands and gravels, and the main fill was a fairly uniform depth (1.30m) of medium brown, slightly plastic silt loam (*87*), disturbed in part by Trial Trench 3. The steep sand edge at the foot of the south bank of the hollow-way, which marked the northern edge of the intrusion, confirmed the eastern edge of the quarry previously identified in Trial Trench 3 (*see above*). At the southern extent of the quarry, approximately 0.40m from the top of the cut, a shallow, black, organic deposit (*82*) was observed which respected the edge of the cut, and increased in depth towards the base of the section.

The *vallum* ditch was located in the slightly higher ground outside the quarry hollow and was apparent immediately below the ploughsoil, where the ditch edges were clearly visible in section cutting through the sand and gravel subsoil. The *vallum* was approximately in the position indicated by the OS (OS 1973), reflecting the findings of the geophysical survey. The section to the south of the *vallum* ditch did not present a typical natural profile of sands and gravels: the profile was irregular

and included sandy and silty clays and mixed stony layers. Close examination did not reveal any evidence of the mounds and berms normally associated with the *vallum*. The original ground surface, including the uppermost part of the ditch cut, appears to have been disturbed by later activity, most obviously by ploughing, leaving evidence only of the deeper cut features. North of the ditch, the trench showed areas of relatively shallow but irregular disturbance to the slightly lower-lying ground at the eastern edge of the quarry.

The finds

One small abraded vessel sherd of reduced coarse-ware, of second to third century date, was retrieved from a fill (*2*) of the *vallum* ditch. A degraded fragment of *mortarium*, possibly of similar date, was found in an area disturbed by ploughing (*23*) adjacent to the outer face of the north bank of the hollow-way, where surviving archaeological layers had been truncated.

Conclusions

Within the confines of the pipeline trench, excavation established that archaeological features relating to Hadrian's Wall had survived, contrary to expectation. To the north of the hollow-way no evidence was found of the Wall or Wall-ditch within the quarried area, but the excavation did provide evidence of preserved archaeological levels beneath the hollow-way. The most significant discovery was south of the hollow-way, where the pipeline trench lay outside the quarried area, and the *vallum* ditch was recorded in section.

This sequence of archaeological work culminating in the excavation prior to pipeline construction has contributed towards the improved definition of the various elements of the Wall complex in this section of the Hadrianic frontier, while causing only minimal disturbance to the surviving stratigraphy relating to the Wall.

5

THE ROMAN CEMETERY AT LOW BORROWBRIDGE, NEAR TEBAY

The construction of the NWEP occasioned a series of three excavations, between 1990 and 1992, in the vicinity of the Roman fort at Low Borrowbridge (**1137**) in the Lune gorge, south of Tebay (NY 6113000910). The main Roman road from Ribchester to Carlisle passed through the gorge (Margary 1957, 2, 117–8; Ross 1920), then as now a major north-south communications corridor, and the fort at Low Borrowbridge was strategically positioned to control this narrow valley. The pipeline route was designed to avoid the scheduled area of the Roman fort (**1137**, SM Cu 33) (Fig 5:1) and other known archaeological sites in the vicinity, wherever practicable, but its course was also constrained by environmental factors including the River Lune, steep valley sides, and deciduous woodlands. It was therefore impossible to avoid completely the presumed location of the extramural settlement, thought to occupy the field to the south of the fort (**1139**). A previously unknown Roman cemetery (**11318**) was discovered during pipeline construction close to the present north-west bank of the Lune beside Salterwath Bridge (Fig 5:2).

Archaeological evaluation of the area commenced with fieldwalking and aerial photography in early 1990, when a number of degraded earthworks were recorded in the part of the field nearest to the fort. Aerial photographs taken some years previously under deep snow (J K S St Joseph, BLY 88–91) showed indeterminate amorphous features in the south of the field, although these were not confirmed by photography under less favourable conditions in the spring of 1990. Detailed topographical survey of the entire field the following summer, however, recorded numerous slight earthworks, including possible lynchets, subcircular platforms, ridge and furrow, and a trackway, in places almost ploughed out. Some of the terraces and mounds in the north of the field are probably associated with recently erected farm buildings, but other features further south may be traces of the Roman extramural settlement. Most of these earthworks, however, lay outside the pipeline corridor, which crossed only the southern edge of the field (Fig 5:3).

Geophysical survey identified several promising anomalies in the south-east of the field, including a rectangular and a subcircular feature, and was closely followed by trial excavation in August 1990. The same basic stratigraphy was consistent across the site. The lowest horizon consisted of a substantial layer of natural river gravels; these were sealed by orange-brown silty loam, which varied in depth and colour. Both these layers appeared to have been truncated by later plough damage. Three of the six machine-cut trenches revealed features of some significance. A metalled surface, 7m wide, was recognised in two parallel trenches (Trenches 2 and 3; Fig 5:3), and was probably part of a road, aligned north-south, leading towards the natural position for a south gate to the fort. No datable artefacts were found in association with this surface, and therefore the contemporaneity of fort and road could not be established.

Further to the east, near Salterwath Bridge, a small, circular, U-shaped pit, 0.50m in diameter and 0.20m deep, was sectioned in Trench 1. Its fill included carbonised material, several Roman ceramic vessel fragments, and iron objects including nails. Although the pit confirmed Roman activity on the site, this apparently isolated feature gave no indication of the cemetery, densely packed with cremations, which surrounded it. The remaining trial trenches added no further archaeological information.

In June 1991, during the removal of topsoil, the archaeological inspector noted five discrete patches of burnt material, each about 0.70m in diameter, with pottery fragments, charcoal, and iron nails visible at the surface. Pipeline construction in the immediate area was temporarily halted later the same day and the burnt patches, on investigation, were positively identified as cremation burials of Roman date. Complete archaeological excavation of the threatened area of the cemetery, under rescue conditions, was swiftly authorised by SCUK, and in the space of seven weeks, between June and August 1991, all accessible parts of the cemetery within the pipeline corridor were investigated. In this compact

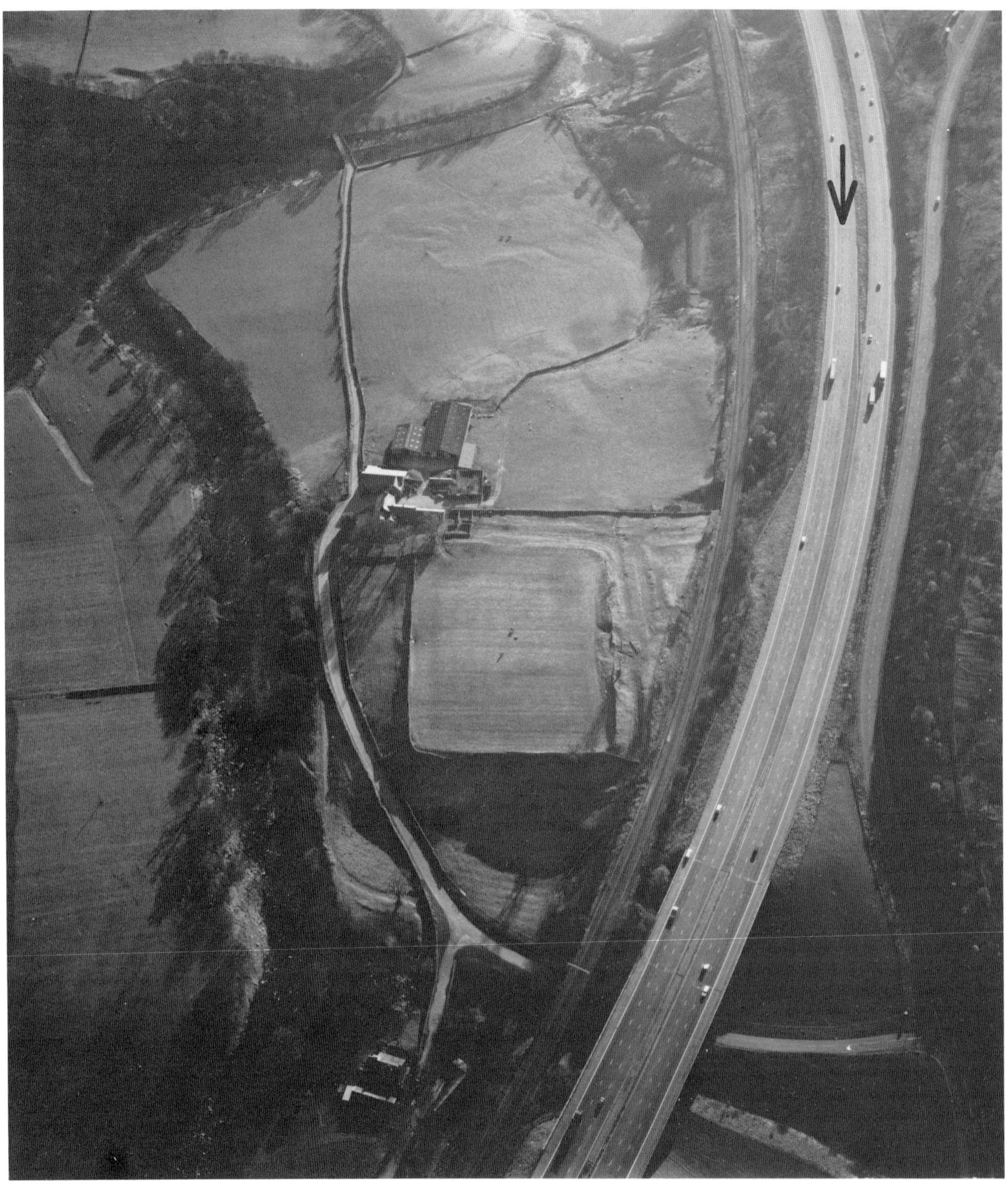

*Figure 5:1 Low Borrowbridge (**1137, 1139, 11318**), aerial photograph, looking south*

area, 20m north to south, and 30m east to west, 56 cremation burials, 16 possible inhumations, and a complex series of ditched enclosures were recorded.

Construction of a farm access road in March 1992, between the pipeline corridor and the top of the river bank, and slightly south of the previous exca-vations, revealed further cremation burials. Another part of the cemetery, a strip 4m wide north to south and 35m long east to west, had been exposed during topsoil removal prior to laying the road surface (Fig 5:4). On this occasion, English Heritage was able to provide funding for a further three weeks of excavation.

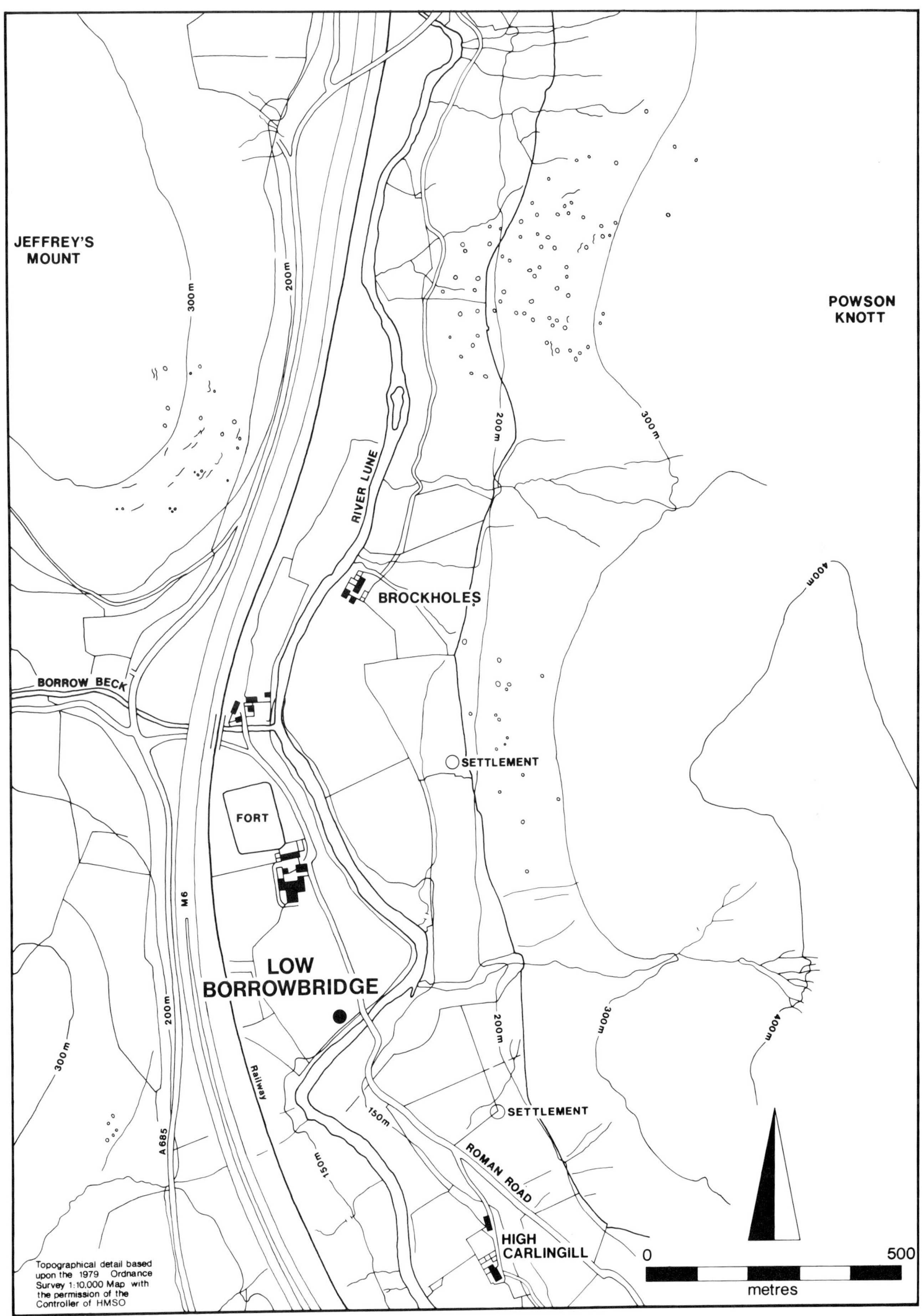

*Figure 5:2 Low Borrowbridge (**1137, 1139, 11318**), location plan*

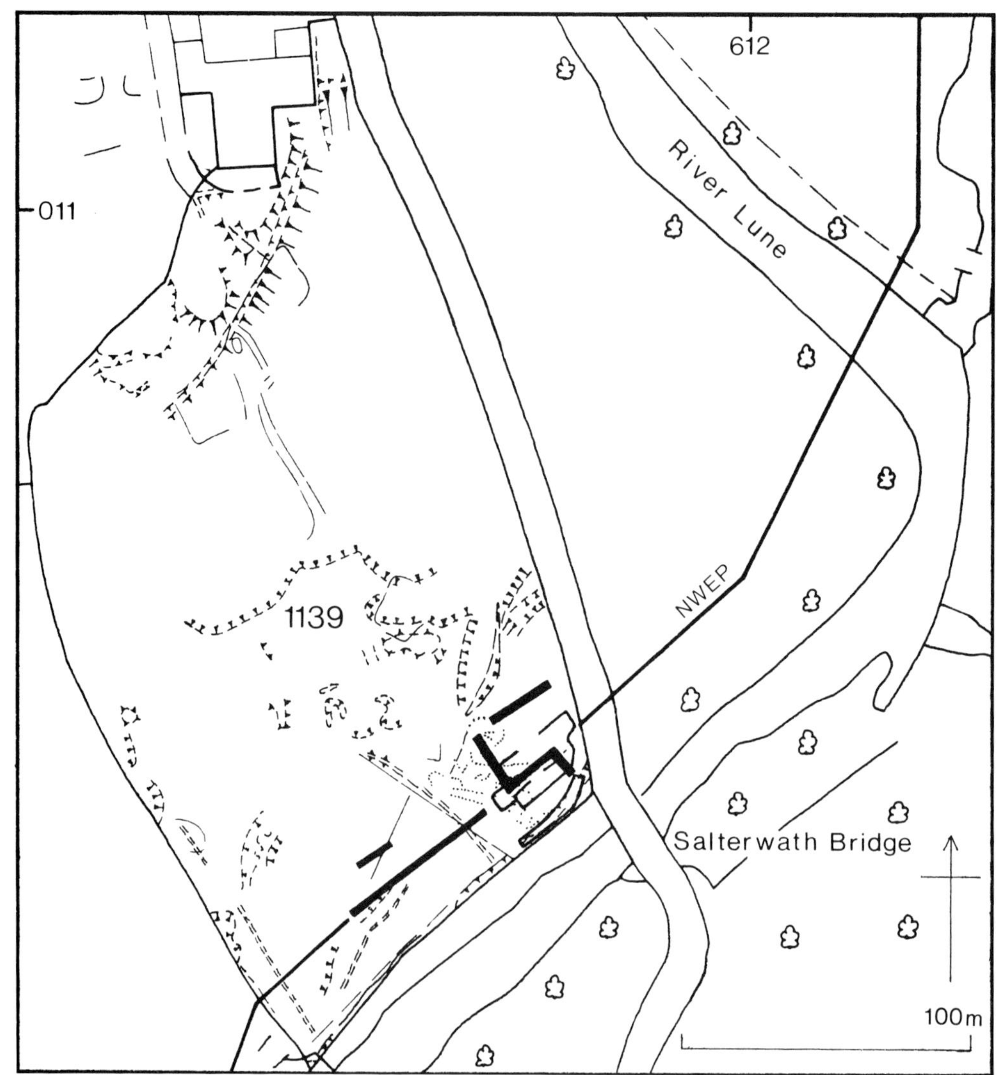

*Figure 5:3 Low Borrowbridge (**1139**), surveyed features and trial trench locations*

*Figure 5:4 Low Borrowbridge (**11318**), a cremation vessel revealed just below the freshly topsoiled surface in March 1992*

The Romans in the Lune Valley

David Shotter

The rural economy of the upper Lune Valley will have been encouraged and enhanced by the existence of the fort at Low Borrowbridge. Roman forts were intended to act as centres for 'police forces'; such a function must at first have been vital for security reasons, but in the long term will have continued to be necessary to ensure the stable development of a Romanised economy. Essential to these troops was an efficient system of communications; however, just as essential was a developing industrial and agricultural landscape to service their requirements. Whilst some manufacturing could be provided in larger centres such as Wilderspool (near

Warrington) and distributed through army depots, such as Walton-le-Dale (near Preston), much remained locally based, in the civilian settlement and in the broader hinterland (*territorium*) of each fort. Viewed from the other side, the presence of these well-paid troops was a stimulus to local people—manufacturers and farmers—to produce not just what was needed to provide for themselves and to pay their taxes, but also a realistic surplus that could be taken to the centres of population and sold for profit, or bartered. Over the period, therefore, during which Roman troops occupied this fort and others in the Lune Valley, there is likely to have been steady social and economic development in the area as a whole.

Fundamental to this development was the system of communication; whilst it is unlikely that the river at this point could itself form part of the system, it certainly did lower down the valley, and the valley itself dictated the nature of the man-made communications. From Lancaster, roads ran along either bank of the Lune, converging near Burrow-in-Lonsdale (Shotter and White 1990, 47-50; Shotter and White 1995) and joining the main arterial route from Chester and Ribchester, possibly at its crossing of the River Wenning (Shotter 1993, 22). Leading through Casterton and Barbon, its course is marked by considerable stretches of tracks and modern roads. Near Cowan Bridge, there is by the side of the Roman road the short stump of a cylindrical stone, which now does duty as a parish boundary marker, but which looks very like the remains of a Roman milestone (Charlesworth 1965). At Middleton another, this time well-preserved, milestone can be seen, though re-erected in 1836 some 200 yards to the east of its original position. The line of the road itself at this point appeared as a linear cropmark during the drought of 1992; it ran much closer to the river than the present position of the milestone would suggest. The significance of the milestone has been discussed frequently (Birley 1953); marking a distance of 53 miles, presumably from Carlisle, it has been proposed as an indicator of the southern boundary of the *civitas Carvetiorum* (Higham and Jones 1985, 12).

From Middleton, the road runs a little to the west of Sedbergh, and then is marked by a minor road, Howgill Lane, on the steep fellside, closely following the river and heading for the fort at Low Borrowbridge, crossing the river a short distance to the south of the fort. A small, square earthwork with rounded corners on Holme Fell (Shotter 1974, 51–2), and a circular one near Middleton Hall (Higham and Jones 1985, 51), could be elements in a system of watchtowers related to the road up the Lune Valley.

Beyond Low Borrowbridge fort, the line of the road has been the subject of much discussion (Allan 1985). It appears to continue on the western side of the river, diverging from it north-west of Tebay and making for the clear stretch of road running over Orton Low Moor. This road was briefly excavated at Sproatgill (**1091**, *see Chapter 2*) in 1991, and its foundations shown to have a central spine of heavy boulders, presumably to lend stability in such an exposed environment. The road from here runs towards the fort at Brougham and a junction with the road from York which crosses Stainmore.

A substantial collection of minor trackways led into the principal roads, and thus drew manufacturers and farmers more closely into the Romanised network. Such trackways may well continue to serve villages and farms, or to be used for moving stock between pastures. Their Roman origin, however, although often strongly suspected, is scarcely capable of proof.

There will have been a considerable amount of industry in the civilian settlements, as has been clearly demonstrated in the case of Manchester (Jones 1974). Many of the 'strip-houses' will have provided both home and business premises for potters, metalworkers, and people working in leather and cloth. Such people provided a variety of plates, dishes, religious objects, decorative metalwork, tools, clothes, and shoes—for all of which there would have been a constant and steady demand. Special items, such as samian ware imported from Gaul, will have been brought in by itinerant traders, and then sold in shops in the civilian settlements. At none of the civilian settlements outside the forts of the Lune Valley, however, have such activities as yet been positively recognised and located, although their products obviously feature in the site-finds.

The only industrial site which has been confirmed in the area of the Lune Valley is that at Quernmore, some three miles to the south-east of Lancaster (Jones and Shotter 1988, 84–93), where floor bricks, roofing tiles, and a wide range of pottery vessels were manufactured. Quernmore was not an isolated site and it is certain that other military industrial complexes await discovery in the Lune Valley. It is also likely that other forms of industry remained outside the civilian settlements; some metalworkers may have preferred their traditional ways and remained outside the new settlements, following an ancient trade but now providing for a new market. Further, the manufacture of items from leather and wool may also have been carried out at the farms themselves, and were not necessarily always based upon centralised settlements. It is unlikely, however, that such settlements could have long survived if their forts were demilitarised for any length of time.

The development of such communities with their wide range of needs will also have led to an 'industry' based upon the acquisition of raw materials; building stone for the fort at Low Borrowbridge may have been brought over a considerable distance, and there was a need for such commodities as iron, coal, limestone, potters' clay, and the gritstone required for the manufacture of querns. Likewise, the raw material for the salt industry may well have been acquired in the Lune estuary, and brought perhaps to Lancaster for processing.

Within the Lune Valley, as elsewhere, the majority of people will have remained what their families had long been, arable farmers on the valley floors and up to approximately 200m OD (Higham 1986, 117–149), and stock managers on the higher ground. Some undoubtedly continued to exploit nature by hunting deer and wild boar, trapping wildfowl and, to judge from the discovery of salmon bones at Lancaster, by fishing in the Lune and its tributaries. Already, in prehistory, a tribal élite had evolved which had progressed from a simple self sufficiency to the production of a saleable surplus, and signs of ploughing have been found beneath a number of Roman forts in the north. It is evident that in the North West, as elsewhere in Britain, some farmers became sufficiently wealthy to be able to take on certain functions of locally developed administration. Thus, we should not be trapped into believing in the north-western stereotype of a small rural population, pathetically struggling to stay alive. Before the Romans came, some were already prosperous and powerful; the opportunities offered by the occupation meant that more followed in their footsteps.

Woodland clearance was already under way in late prehistory, and the coming of the Romans with their extensive requirements for timber for building and for burning in such amenities as bathhouses must have greatly accelerated this process. A result of this was increased soil erosion at higher altitudes and enhanced soil fertility in the valley floors. There cannot, however, have been uncontrolled removal of woodland, since this would not only have diminished the supply of this particular raw material, but also upset the ecological balance of the valley, destroying, for example, the habitats of those wild animals which provided a source of livelihood for some. This presupposes the practice of some level of woodland management, which may, for example, have lain behind the forestry clearance noted in the fourth century in the hinterland of Lancaster (Oldfield and Statham 1964–5).

The land of the Lune Valley will have been divided into the *territoria* of each fort; if, indeed, devolved government came into the valley in the third century, the administration of these *territoria* would then become the jointly held responsibility of military and civilian authorities. Otherwise, the writ of the fort commanders would run unchallenged through the valley.

The boundaries of the fort *territoria* cannot easily be reconstructed although natural boundaries, such as sizeable streams, played a part. Milestones possibly provided boundary markers. At the time of occupation, each fort commander will have decided on the usage of the land in his *territorium*. Some, no doubt, was 'confiscated' for distribution to time-expired military veterans, for example *Julius Januarius*, a retired *decurio* from Lancaster, who was settled near Bolton-le-Sands (RIB 600; Collingwood and Wright 1965). This will probably have consisted mainly of the fertile land of the valley floors.

Some land may have been appropriated for the direct use of the garrisons themselves; there may have been a tendency for this to happen in the close vicinity of forts whose garrisons consisted wholly or partly of cavalry, for it will have been particularly convenient to have had supplies of fodder and bedding at hand. Analysis of the material recovered in 1973 from a timber-lined well, close to the east gate of the fort at Lancaster, emphasises the large-scale need for hay for horse fodder and bedding (Jones and Shotter 1988, 170–8). This may have been supplied locally, though the organisation by the army of bulk supplies remains a possibility (Manning 1975).

The bulk of the land organisation in each fort *territorium*, however, probably left existing farmers largely undisturbed, either as continuing owners or as tenants of Rome, if the land concerned had been formally appropriated. In general, the Roman authorities were pragmatists, believing firmly in the principle that local people knew best how to exploit local conditions.

Fieldwork to elucidate features of the rural landscape has proceeded patchily, although most attention has so far been given to the upper and middle reaches of the Lune Valley (Higham and Jones 1975, 1985; Higham 1979, 1980; Lowndes 1963, 1964; RCHM(E) 1936). The lower reaches (Howard-Davis 1983–4, 9–25), as the valley widens towards the estuary, have been subject to more long-term and extensive ploughing, which has caused severe damage to, even obliterated, such fragile sites. Thus, whilst a great density of sites is recorded in the area around Crosby Ravensworth and Crosby Garrett, between the headwaters of the Eden and the Lune, and again in the fells around Leck Beck and Eller Beck, only occasional sites are recorded in places such as Cantsfield (Shotter and White, 1990, 55), Arkholme, and Halton. This should not, therefore, be taken as a true reflection of the landscape of the valley in the Roman period.

Building materials also contribute to the question of site survival; in the valley itself, most sites consist of a nucleus of subcircular and subrectangular structures, built of timber and turf. From these nuclei radiate networks of the mostly small fields of the arable farmer. Above about 250m OD the sites themselves, which may differ little in type, are constructed mostly of stone, and are the centres of systems of the much larger fields required for stock ranching. All of these sites are notoriously difficult to date, as neither shape nor building material appears to have much relevance to the debate. Indeed, many such sites date back well beyond the Roman period, thus prompting the suggestion that for some of them the period of the Roman occupation may not have been much more than an interlude (Higham 1986, 182).

There is wide variation in size amongst recorded sites; many are essentially small farmsteads, presumably for a single family group, whilst others, such as Ewe Close, near Crosby Ravensworth, are so extensive that they have sometimes been thought of as villages rather than farms. The difference in size, however, may be no more than a reflection of the simple, but important, difference between success and failure.

Agricultural success in the North West appears to be confirmed by the establishment in the third century AD of the *civitas Carvetiorum*, for this presupposes the existence of people commanding sufficient wealth to perform the tasks in the community that were normally expected of *civitas* leaders. As we have seen, the *civitas* of the *Carvetii* may have extended as far south as the northern end of the Lune Valley. Of course, some of the larger (and more successful) farms may have belonged to discharged veterans of the Roman army who presumably enjoyed resources superior to those available to many of their local counterparts. Findspots of Roman coin hoards or even single coins, for example, the gold *solidus* of the emperor Valens (AD 364–78) (Shotter 1990, 82) which was found some 5km south of the fort at Low Borrowbridge, may point to a farm nearby which belonged to such a veteran.

Farmers of all kinds will, of course, have found success by catering for the markets that the Roman forts and their associated civilian settlements rep-resented. This will have meant not just grain crops and meat for human consumption, but animal fodder also. There were the by-products, too, such as leather and skins for clothes and tents. In the somewhat better climate that apparently prevailed in the second and third centuries, the area may have seen the provision of some specialist crops, such as vines.

The civilian settlements outside forts were usually small in overall extent, giving way rapidly to a 'suburbia' of small farms. Those farmers who lived in such close proximity to the main centres of population, for example at Low and High Carlingill, just south of the fort at Low Borrowbridge, obviously had the opportunity to 'study the market' and thus provide for it more precisely. Studies of the bones of ox, sheep, and pig from archaeological sites (Jones and Shotter 1988, 167–9; Jones 1975, 93–106) may point to the choice of an optimum age of slaughter for the meat trade; this, in turn, suggests the existence of arrangements between individual farmers and the fort authorities, or perhaps with individual traders within the civilian settlements.

Thus, although the picture of the rural population is far from perfect, enough survives to suggest that in time a relationship developed between forts, civilian settlements, and farmers that was not only harmonious, but mutually profitable too. Some, however, remained marginal to this success story, for every society has its underclass. Some may have ended up as slaves in the households of those whose status and wealth encouraged them to enjoy this symbol of their position; others may have been beggars in the streets of the civilian settlements; others still, perhaps, lived out a life of brigandage in hideaways such as Dog Hole cave on the Iron Age hillfort at Warton Crag, near Carnforth. This underclass was in its own way as much a symbol of the prosperity of the Roman occupation as those who profited from it in a more orderly and conventional fashion, and who, like *Aurelius Verulus* at Low Borrowbridge, were able to demonstrate that success by means of a tombstone (*see below*), which has preserved their record over nearly two thousand years.

The Roman fort at Low Borrowbridge

The Roman fort, usually known as Low Borrowbridge, which stands in the centre of the Lune gorge to the south of Tebay, presents something of a paradox. Visually, few Roman forts have better retained the integrity of their physical outlines: yet knowledge of the history and development of the site is notably inadequate (Birley 1947; Jones 1975, 164). Little excavation has taken place and, in contrast to most other Roman sites in the North West, few finds have been recorded. The rural setting of Low

Borrowbridge has both to an extent protected it and at the same time served to preserve its mystery.

The early antiquarians, such as Camden, Leland, and Horsley, appear not to have noticed the site at all; further, even its earliest notice, in the late eighteenth century, failed to recognise the site as of Roman origin (Birley 1947, 1–2). It was not until the early nineteenth century that this identification was made, and published in the *Westmorland Advertiser and Kendal Chronicle* of 19 December 1812. Nonetheless, it would appear from the name Borrow Beck that there remained a long-term recollection of the presence of a fortified site in the vicinity (*see Chapter 3*). A number of accounts appeared during the nineteenth century, which established some features of the site and recorded a small number of finds.

Features noted included the presence of two ditches on the fort's western side, a hypocaust inside the northern part of the fort, and a bridge abutment and stretch of road to the north at the crossing of Borrow Beck. At that time it was assumed that the site was *Alone* of *Iter X* of the Antonine Itinerary, and the objective of the first excavations, in 1883, was to recover inscribed stones which might throw conclusive light on the name of the site (Ferguson 1886; Shotter 1993, 105–9).

The 1883 excavations did not, however, produce inscriptions, although they did indicate some curious features of the site; for example, survey showed that the fort was in fact a parallelogram rather than a true rectangle, and observation suggested that there was no gateway in the southern rampart. The eastern gateway was recognised as a normal construction of two carriageways, and its western equivalent was assumed, probably wrongly, to be of similar type. Such lack of symmetry between side gateways can be paralleled, for example at Vindolanda. Similarly, Birley has cited Bainbridge as a parallel for the absence of a gateway in one wall, at least until very late in the occupation (Birley 1947, 11–12). This work also identified a building outside the fort's south-east corner, which is probably the bathhouse (Anstee 1975a). Further work, though unfortunately never published, was carried out in the 1930s on the area of the north gate and on the south-east angle. In the former area, it was shown that the north wall had undergone a late rebuilding which had obliterated the gateway, whilst the latter part of the site indicated a complex chronology (Hildyard and Gillam 1951, 42; Birley 1947, 9).

The fort itself is well sited, although some have thought that a stronger position could have been found a little further north, closer to Tebay. It is protected on the northern and eastern sides by the confluence of Borrow Beck with the River Lune. To the east and west of the fort, the fells rise sharply to 400m. Roads run northwards to Brougham and south to Burrow-in-Lonsdale, whilst to the west the fort is connected by road with both Watercrook and Ambleside. The size of the visible fort is a little less than three acres, which would offer sufficient accommodation for a *cohors quingenaria equitata* (a 500-strong infantry unit with a cavalry element); the presence of this type of unit is apparently confirmed by one of the two surviving tombstones from the cemetery south of the fort. This stone, which was broken up in order to construct a bridge across an unidentified beck, is said to have depicted a mounted soldier spearing a fallen enemy, and to have contained *XX* in its inscription, presumably part of the soldier's age or length of service.

There is no record of the existence of a civilian settlement, although the flat meadowland to the south of the fort has been regarded as a suitable situation. Further, the discovery of a cemetery 300m south of the fort (*see below*) lends weight to the suggestion that the civilian settlement lay in this field, between the cemetery and the fort's southern rampart. Various suggestions have placed the parade ground on meadowland either to the south or the north of the fort, though there is no certainty with regard to this.

Problems concerning the chronology and morphology of the fort remain considerable, though some progress was made as a result of further excavation in 1950 (Hildyard and Gillam 1951). There seems to be little doubt that activity continued at the site into the late fourth century and beyond; indeed, it was long ago noticed that the remoteness of the spot may well have encouraged the long-term survival of a sub-Roman (or semi-Romanised) group in what remained of the site. Events such as the removal of the north gate and the blocking of the north carriageway of the east gate (RCHM(E) 1936, 100) represent attempts to enhance the protection of the fort area, which are readily paralleled at other sites. Indeed, some such activity may also explain the apparent absence of a south gate. Late fourth century pottery was well represented in the excavations of 1950, especially at the south-east corner (Hildyard and Gillam 1951, 49). Although no sign was found there of an angle tower, disturbances in the area which were dated to the late Roman period were considered consistent with the insertion of a platform, now vanished, to accommodate an artillery piece.

Thus, although detail is sparing, occupation in the second half of the fourth century can be regarded

as certain, and connected with not insignificant al-
terations to the fabric of the fort. Excavations have
detected at least three phases of activity prior to
this, and have shown with little doubt that the visible remains do not represent the fort's earliest
phase. The presence of a ditch-like feature inside
the western rampart, and of postholes apparently
running beneath the fort wall at the south-east corner, suggests strongly that a presumably smaller
fort, perhaps broadly sharing a part of the southern
and eastern ramparts with its successor, predated
the visible structure. Pottery from this early level,
though not closely datable, clearly derives from the
Flavian period. It would appear natural, as the Lune
corridor represents the obvious route from Chester
to Carlisle, to assign the earliest fort at Low
Borrowbridge to a date at least as early as Agricola's
governorship, if not to that of Cerialis.

Since so little of the early fort has been examined, it
is difficult to determine how many phases of activity are represented; however, the layout of postholes
(Hildyard and Gillam 1951, 48, fig 2) is suggestive
of more than a single phase. In this case, it may be
appropriate to refer the reconstruction and enlarg-
ing of the fort to the Trajanic or Hadrianic periods.
It can be seen from the spacing of the gateways
along the eastern and western ramparts that the
fort faced towards the south unless, of course, it
had six gates and two more remain to be located in
the eastern and western ramparts. If the fort was
orientated towards the south, then the absence of a
south gate would appear perverse, particularly as a
section of probable Roman road has been excavated
west of the cemetery (*see below*). If indeed there was
no south gate, then the impressive eastern gate,
which had the closest access to the main north-south
route, may have been used as the fort's principal
entrance.

The visible fort has signs of two ditches on its southern, western, and northern flanks, although some
reports have claimed to identify as many as four on
the western side. It is, of course, perfectly possible,
as at the fort at Watercrook (Potter 1979, 151, plan),
that ditches might be combined with other obstacles, such as palisades and stone banks. No obvious
trace of extended defences remains on the eastern
side of the fort. The excavations of 1950 recognised
on the western side two phases of clay rampart
fronted by a stone wall, which appeared to be of a
single build with the earliest rampart, rather than,
as sometimes happens, predating it.

The pottery suggested that the first clay rampart
should be placed relatively early in the second century, certainly not later than the Hadrianic period.
The only indication of date for the second phase of

clay rampart was a little-worn *denarius* of Com-
modus (AD 180–192) beneath it. This might suggest
a Severan date for the refurbishment, although it
has been suggested that the structural quality of
the east gate points towards significant reconstruction in the late third century under the orders of
Constantius I. On present evidence it is impossible
to produce a more precise chronology, or to
tell whether, or when, the fort may have temporarily lost its garrison as troop dispositions were
reviewed.

The fort wall, which has been heavily robbed, was
evidently faced with good quality ashlar; some of
the surviving stones displayed diamond-broaching,
perhaps to prevent rainwater—a constant problem
here—from standing in the joints; similar stonework
was observed in 1975 in the bathhouse. Such stone
would have had to be imported from some distance,
the nearest source being Orton Low Moor or Shap.
Local slates and river boulders were used for the
wall core, which was bound together with a runny
mortar, as well as for foundations.

Little is known of internal buildings, although one
with a hypocaust, reported in the northern portion
of the fort, might represent either the commander's
house (*praetorium*) or a feature inserted into the
headquarters (*principia*). The general absence, however, of reported internal buildings may reflect the
fact that, because good quality ashlar was hard to
acquire, many of them may have been built of timber or at least have been half-timbered.

As has been noted, it has been generally assumed
that the civilian settlement was situated to the south,
and perhaps to the east, of the fort, possibly deriving advantage from close proximity to the main
road. The boggy state of the ground to the west
would appear to preclude settlement in that area.
The only extramural building about which there is
any information is the bathhouse, which is situated
off the fort's south-east corner. It appeared to have
been faced with sandstone blocks, which the excavator attributed to a desire to provide the building
with a good appearance (Anstee 1975a). Elements
of walls and floors, made of concrete with pounded
brick, have been identified, together with a furnace
area. Finds include fragments of box tiles which
carried the heated gases into the walls of the warm
and hot rooms. Although a complete plan of the
building could not be recovered, it has been estimated that it was a structure of impressive appearance, possibly with porched entrance-ways, and in
the region of 18m long on its north-south axis. It
appears also that the water required both for the
bathhouse and for the fort itself was channelled to
the site from Birk Knott, on the western side of the

valley, where a man-made aqueduct has been observed for nearly 600m, falling *c*80m at a constant gradient (Anstee 1975b).

Excavation of the Roman cemetery in 1991 and 1992

Nick Hair, Christine Howard-Davis

Phase summary

Phase 1

The earliest recorded activity occurred before the site was flooded around the mid third century AD. Seventeen ditched enclosures and two large oval pits within enclosures represent the earliest known activity. These appear to precede eight large pits, probably inhumations, which were cut into the enclosure ditches in the early to mid third century; six similar pits were cut into the natural gravels. A group of three cremation burials was also associated with this phase of cemetery use.

Phase 2

Flooding in the mid to late third century deposited river silt across much of the site, sealing many Phase 1 features. Between the mid third and fourth century, cremation was the dominant burial practice, and 71 cremation burials have been identified.

Phase 3

The excavated part of the cemetery fell out of use in the fourth century. There is no indication of any later activity other than agriculture.

The cemetery lay 300m south of the Roman fort (**1137**), in flat pasture land overlying the fluvio-glacial silts and gravels of the narrow valley floor. The excavated part of the cemetery covered an area more than 30m square, and while its extent to the north remained undefined by the excavations, to the south the River Lune formed a natural boundary (Fig 5:5). To the east, the limit of the cemetery coincided with Howgill Lane, reinforcing the supposition that this is on the line of the Roman road, and from here it extended westwards some 35m across the field. A number of features appeared in section at the northern limit of the excavations, demonstrating that in this direction the cemetery extended beyond the pipeline corridor, but although land to the east of Howgill Lane, and also to the west of the excavations, was examined closely, no associated features were observed outside the area shown on the plan.

In the summer of 1991 the site was excavated under rescue conditions, with severe constraints on time and access. The LUAU rapid response team was called out, initially for four days, and the excavation was eventually extended to a total time of seven weeks.

Topsoil was stripped, under close archaeological supervision, by the pipeline contractor using a large backhoe excavator. The cleared surfaces within the construction corridor were cleaned to remove residual topsoil and define archaeological features. Priority was initially accorded to the strip designated for the pipeline contractors' vehicular access and turning space, which was available for excavation only briefly before being covered with Terram matting and stone chippings.

The fills of many features, especially the enclosure ditches, were very similar to the natural subsoil, and the differences were best observed during preferential drying, when the features were visible as slightly darker stains contrasting with the more rapidly draining subsoil (Fig 5:6).

Each of the excavations, including the 1990 evaluation, was assigned a unique block of numbers, which were subsequently combined as a single sequence for contexts (*1–620*), and for objects (1001–2228, 5001–5156), input during post-excavation to a Delilah database. The results of all three excavations were combined in a single archive, and the finds catalogue is on microfiche (*see Appendix 2*).

Finds recovery and sampling

As Romano-British cremation cemeteries from the northern military zone are not generally well known (Philpott 1991, 37), and in the North West even less so, the finds retrieval and collection policy sought to maximise the potential for new data from the site within the constraints of rescue excavation. A policy of total collection was adopted for all finds categories, using hand recovery by stratigraphic unit rather than the routine sieving of archaeological deposits, except as a random check on recovery levels. With the exception of burnt bone, all finds locations were recorded three-dimensionally using a Zeiss Elta–4 total station, before removal from their soil matrix. This enabled the use of CAD software to facilitate the rapid production of distribution plots and the reconstruction of individual burial deposits without recourse to detailed planning on site.

The cremation burial pits were normally examined by half-section. Where they proved to contain intact funerary vessels these were lifted *en bloc*,

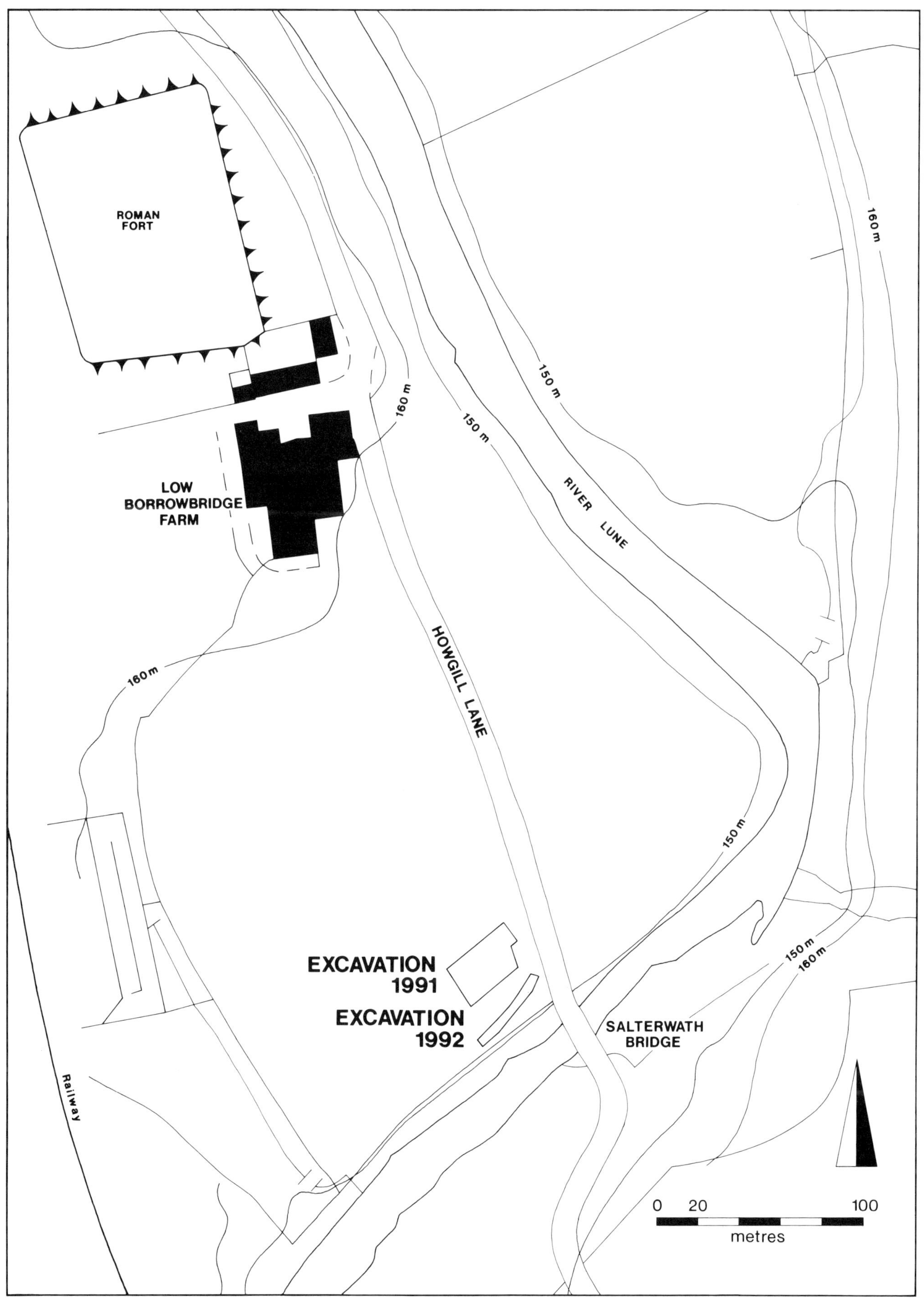

*Figure 5:5 Low Borrowbridge Roman cemetery (**11318**), outline location of excavations in 1991 and 1992*

*Figure 5:6 Low Borrowbridge (**11318**) enclosure ditches revealed by preferential drying*

together with their contents, wrapped in plaster of Paris bandage, and removed from the site for excavation under laboratory conditions at LUAU. The recovery of all cremated bone from the pits by sieving, whilst desirable, was impracticable, especially as many of the bone fragments were not only extremely small (5–10mm) and friable, but also evenly distributed throughout the fills. In consequence larger fragments (>10mm) were recovered by hand, and representative samples of each fill were retained for sieving.

Twenty-five intact, or almost intact, funerary vessels were removed *en bloc* for laboratory excavation. Initially the contents of these vessels were excavated and recorded in shallow spits (50mm) and the position of each fragment of bone or other material recorded in three dimensions with reference to the rim of the vessel, thus enabling a complete reconstruction of its contents. This proved to be a time-consuming procedure for little return in terms of additional data, and after a random sample of 20% of the vessels had been examined in this way the practice was abandoned, in favour of recovery of bone by sieving and the three-dimensional recording of other artefacts within the fill of the vessel. Comparison of results from the two batches

of excavated vessels suggest that little or no extra data were lost by this change of procedure.

Site stratigraphy

Severe truncation of the site by ploughing has resulted in a simplified vertical stratigraphy, with many of the features isolated from their neighbours; nevertheless, it was possible to determine three phases of activity. The first two phases relate to the use of the site as a cemetery during the Roman period, and it seems likely that the division between them is more physical—the result of a sudden flood—than chronological, and that in reality they represent a single unbroken period of cemetery development. Phase 3 represents the subsequent ploughing of the site for agricultural purposes. Considering the shallow soils of the valley bottom, the cremation burials are relatively undisturbed (*see* Herring and Howard-Davis 1992, for an indication of how far only two seasons of ploughing can spread the contents of a cremation vessel), suggesting that ploughing over the site has been infrequent.

The subsoil (*12*) comprised a substantial depth of natural fluvio-glacial gravels, extending over the entire site. In the northern and central areas it lay immediately below disturbed topsoil and many of the surviving archaeological features were cut directly into it. These gravels dipped towards the south, east, and west, and were covered, in these areas, by fairly substantial layers of silt (*14, 90*) and sand (*505*).

Silt 14 completely sealed the gravels in the eastern part of the site, and thin lenses of pea gravel (*251*), sand (*247, 263*), and iron panning (*219*) were recorded at the interface of the two layers. Silt *90* likewise sealed the gravels in the western part. Lenses of gravelly silty sand (*275*) were encountered in patches, between silt *90* and gravel subsoil *12*. To the south a layer of sand (*505*) sealed the gravel subsoil, and appeared to predate the cemetery. These silt layers sealed Enclosure N, six large pits (*252, 261, 278, 280, 284, 299*), and three cremation pits (*254, 294, 296*), clearly defining the first phase of funereal activity. The silts, up to 0.30m thick, were fine-grained and homogeneous, suggesting that they were probably deposited relatively rapidly, as a result of a single episode of river flooding, which may have left the northern and central parts of the site relatively dry. Part of the central gravel ridge (*12*) was sealed by silt *118* (identical to both *14* and *90*), which also clearly postdated Phase 1 activity.

The remainder of the features, mainly cremation burials, were cut into these silts. Several of the more disturbed cremation burials were first identified at the level of horizon *15*, but had clearly been damaged and spread by ploughing. Layers *41* and *504*, like *15*, were located directly above the natural subsoil, and were almost certainly formed as a result of plough action within the upper part of this deposit.

The entire site was sealed by a layer of topsoil (*1*) *c*0.25m deep. Clearly, disturbed horizon *15* and topsoil *1* represent a third phase of activity, probably beginning long after the abandonment of the cemetery, possibly as late as the nineteenth century.

The features and finds in context

Overall stratigraphic phasing appears to be of limited use in the interpretation of the cemetery. However, three discrete feature types—enclosures, large oval pits, and small round pits containing cremation burials—were identified within the cemetery and probably form a broad chronological succession (Figs 5:7, 5:8).

The earliest activity is represented by a shallow ditch (*35*) aligned north-south, towards the extreme southeast of the excavated area. It clearly preceded, and its fills were cut by, Enclosure B. A second short

north-south ditch (*172*) predates Enclosure F, in the centre of the excavated area. The fill of ditch *35* (*36*) produced pottery fragments of early to mid second century or later date, whilst that of ditch *172* (*173*) produced only a hobnail and a nail. Subsequent to the cutting of these two isolated ditches, the main activity was characterised by a neatly aligned series of 16 ditched rectilinear enclosures, oriented with respect to the cardinal points of the compass. One of these enclosures can be shown to predate the flood episode, although most lay in the central and northern areas, where the silt was absent.

Sixteen large, relatively deep, oval pits clearly postdated these enclosures, and usually respected their position and alignment. These approximated in size to inhumation graves, although they were devoid of bone, other than small quantities of presumably redeposited cremated bone, and few contained any artefacts which might be interpreted as grave goods. One (*155*) lay centrally within Enclosure H, suggesting a close link, and several appeared to be cut into the fills of the enclosure ditches, often at the corners, strongly suggesting use of a pre-existing plot.

Lastly there were 71 small subcircular pits, containing urned or unurned cremation burials and usually a dense concentration of burnt material, including bone. These were consistently stratigraphically later than the enclosures, often cut into the ditch fills or, in the western part of the site, cut into, rather than beneath, silt layer *90*. Their stratigraphic relationship with the oval pits was more ambiguous, although in most cases they were cut into the fills of these (*eg 85*); only one cremation (*294*) was cut by one of the oval pits.

In consequence, whilst it has been suggested that the flood, which appears to divide use of the cemetery into two clear phases, probably did not entirely disrupt its use, there is sufficient evidence to suggest that the three discrete feature types recognised at the site follow a chronological sequence. When considered alongside the flood episode, this can perhaps suggest a change of rite rather than a change of use.

The date range of pottery from the site suggests a limited period for the use of the cemetery, perhaps only a little more than a century. It is important to note, however, that none of the dating evidence derives from the rectilinear enclosures, only their subsequent ditch fills and later features. Since stratigraphic evidence places them early in the life of the cemetery, predating both the oval pits and the cremation burials, which date at the latest to the second and third centuries AD, it can be suggested

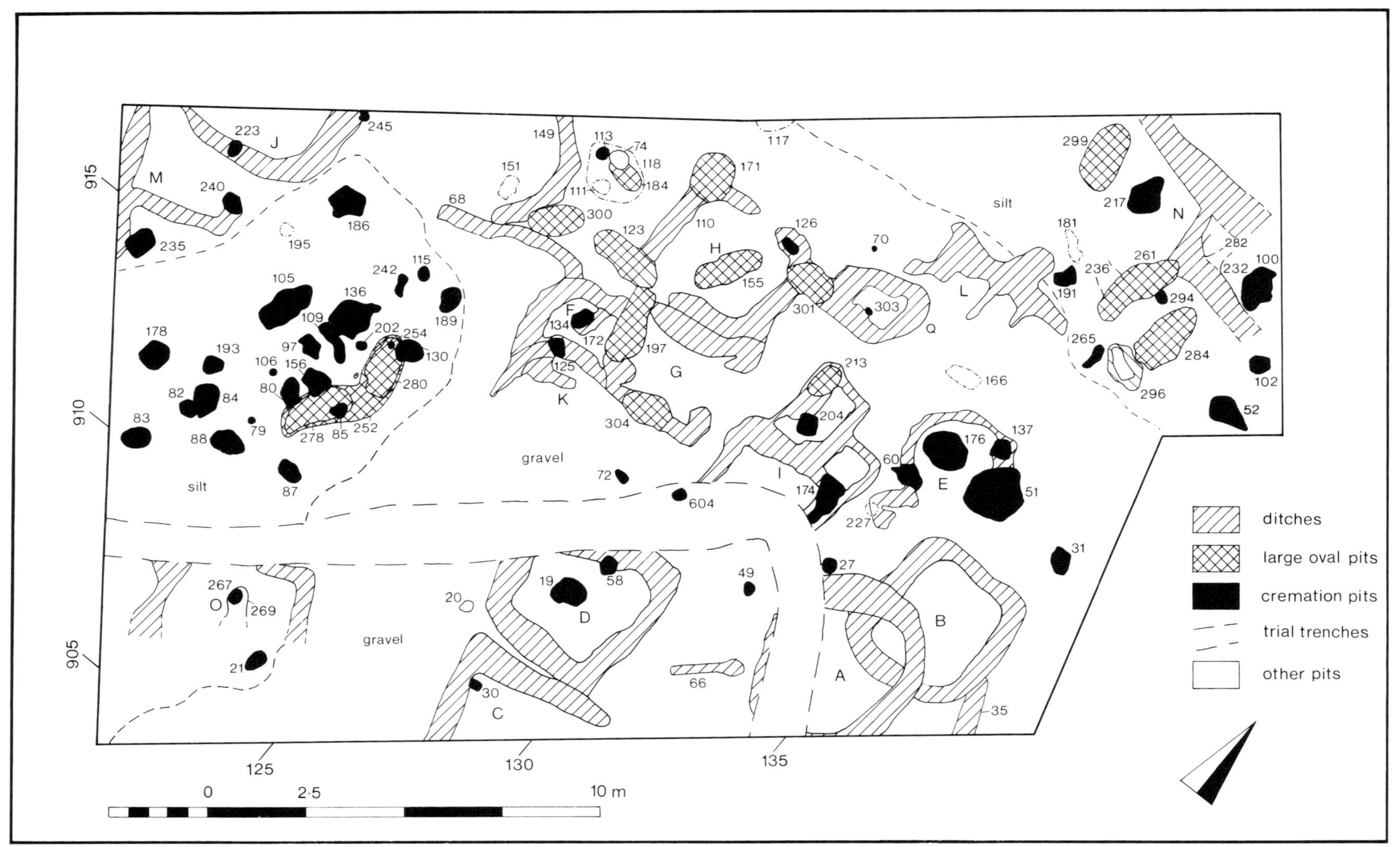

Figure 5:7 Low Borrowbridge (11318) 1991 excavations, features in plan

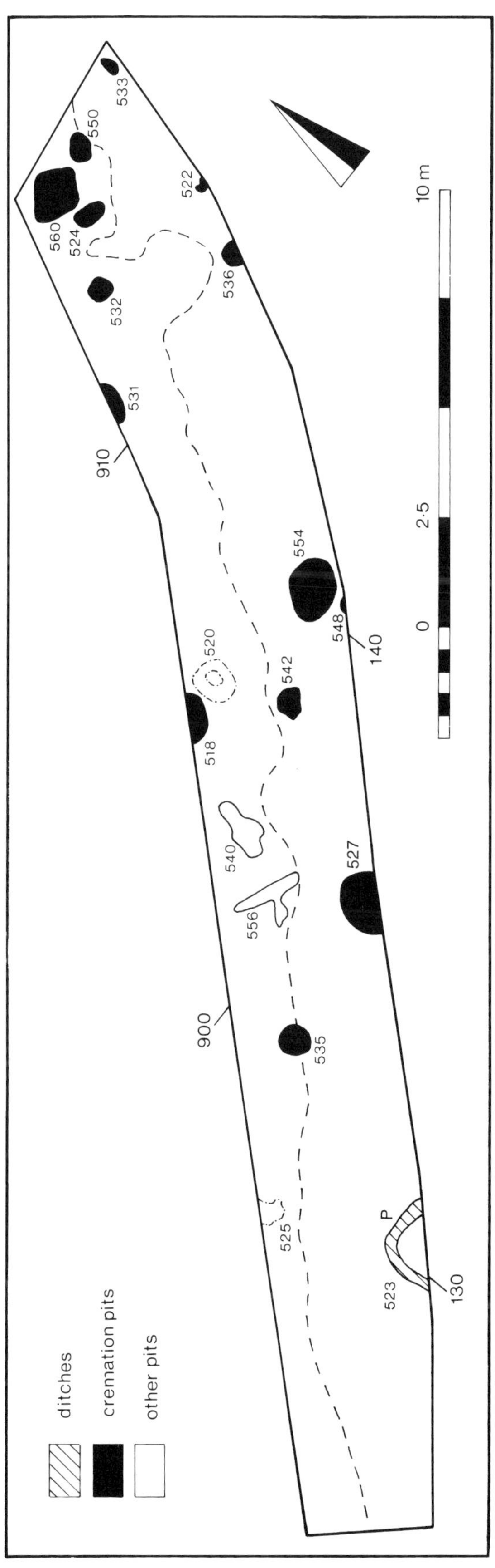

Figure 5:8 Low Borrowbridge (11318) 1992 excavations, features in plan

that the cemetery was first in use before the beginning of the third century. Absence of the latest pottery forms from the river silts might suggest a date early in the second half of the third century for the flood, with subsequent cremation burial continuing, unusually, into the early fourth century.

The enclosures

Ten more or less complete (A-D, F-J, Q) and a further six badly damaged (K-P) rectilinear ditched enclosures were recognised. In general they were square, with rounded corners, whilst one, Enclosure E, was effectively penannular. They appeared to be oriented towards the cardinal points, although it is possible that the orientation was dictated by the terrain. They were 1.50–4.50m wide externally, and were delineated by shallow, U-sectioned ditches 0.25–1.00m wide, and on average 0.25m deep, cut into the subsoil gravels (*12*). All were directly overlain by topsoil *1*, except for Enclosure N, which was sealed by silt *14*. The fill of these enclosure ditches was remarkably similar to the subsoil, which led to difficulties in recognising and interpreting stratigraphic relationships, as well as in differentiating between them and the chronologically later oval pits.

Only three enclosures (E, G, H) had obvious entrances, but they had no particular orientation or size. In most cases the ditches defined a simple central island, with no obviously associated burials except in enclosures E and H, which both surrounded large oval pits (*176, 155*). Enclosure I was more complex, comprising three linked cells, the two smaller enclosures possibly added subsequently. Enclosures L and N, whilst both badly truncated, may also have been more complex. Enclosures H and Q were physically linked by a later large oval pit (*301*) which obliterated any former relationship.

Three of the enclosures had been cut by later ones: Enclosure B by A, F by K, and G by H. In the latter case it is clear that the later enclosure was intended as an addition, rather than a replacement, strongly suggesting a period of continuity during which either the ditches themselves remained visible or knowledge of the plots remained. It is likely that the complex enclosures described above were created in the same way and similarly represent a slow, almost organic agglomeration of enclosures, added one by one as necessary; this perhaps implies family or other groups attaching special significance to a specific site within the cemetery.

There are no finds which might be regarded as stratigraphically contemporary with the creation or primary use of the enclosures. All finds derived from the ditch fills, and were presumably deposited as they were allowed to fill, or had been gradually backfilled. Small patches of burnt material were noted amongst the fills, suggesting perhaps that some material from pyres was incorporated, possibly as a means of disposal. The small, very dispersed amounts of cremated bone recovered from three of the fills might be more likely to indicate a careless attitude to the general disposal of pyre debris, than the presence of disturbed burials.

The finds, including some nails and hobnails but mostly pottery, range in date from the early second to the fourth centuries AD, implying a sustained level of disturbance and activity throughout the duration of the cemetery. Although inconclusive, those from the enclosure sealed by silt could all be placed before the mid third century; it must be noted, however, that one vessel type represented has a rather longer date range (AD 190–340). Most of the pottery appears to derive from prolonged general occupation of the vicinity of the fort, rather than being linked with funerary practice, and thus can serve only as a loose *terminus ante quem* for the ditch fills.

Enclosure E stands out as anomalous in shape, in the presence of a possible central burial, and in the relatively large amount of finds within the fill. The pottery from this enclosure probably dates to the third century, although the numerous nails and hobnails cannot be dated.

The following summary catalogue lists the enclosures and details their principal features. Unless otherwise stated the enclosures were cut directly into gravel layer *12*. Many enclosures were originally excavated as several elements, each of which was assigned a separate context number. This was rationalised during post-excavation, when a single context number was allocated to each enclosure, or isolated enclosure element.

Enclosures

Enclosure A (26) Subrectangular, externally c4.50 x 4.10m, internally 3.40 x c2.50m; overlay Enclosure B; west side largely obliterated by trial trenching (Trench 6), southern side largely beyond limit of 1991 excavation.

Enclosure B (33) Subrectangular, externally 3.90 x 3.60m, internally 2.80 x 2.40m; overlay linear ditch *35*, overlain by Enclosure A.

Enclosure C (54) Subrectangular, externally >4.10 x 4.10m, internally >3.10 x 3.10m; possible entrance at north-eastern corner suggested by absence of southern return and rounded end of northern ditch; almost certainly related to Enclosure D, directly to north, although no clear relationship demonstrated archaeologically; southern and eastern sides largely beyond limit of 1991 excavation.

Enclosure D (56) Subrectangular, externally 4.10 x 3.90m, internally 2.60 x 2.40m; almost certainly related to Enclosure C, directly to the south, although no clear relationship demonstrated archaeologically; location of a cremation (19) at its centre may be of significance; north-western corner removed by trial trenching (Trench 1).

Enclosure E (139) Penannular, external diameter 2.80m, internal diameter 1.60m; entrance, c1.10m wide, on south side where ditch formed rounded terminals; a large oval pit (176) lay slightly off-centre within enclosure.

Enclosure F (144) Subsquare, externally c2.90m, internally c2.30m; possible entrance at south-east corner, badly damaged by ploughing; appeared to be cut by Enclosure K, and by a large oval pit (197).

Enclosure G (153) Subrectangular, externally 3.70 x 3.00m, internally 2.70 x 1.70m; entrance, 1.15m wide, central in east side; south-western part truncated, presumably by ploughing.

Enclosure H (157) Subrectangular, externally 3.85 x 3.60m, internally 2.80 x 2.50m; entrance, 0.60m wide, central in north side; a large oval pit (155), aligned north-east to south-west, in centre of enclosure, may be of significance; connected to Enclosure Q by a large elongated pit (301).

Enclosure I (164) Complex enclosure comprising three adjoining subrectangular cells; the largest (to the south), externally 3.30 x >1.50m, internally 2.20 x >1.0m; southern half removed by trial trenching (Trench 1); two small subrectangular cells, joined back-to-back, incorporated northern ditch of large cell as their southern side; western cell externally 2.50 x 1.80m, internally 1.60 x 0.60m; eastern cell, externally 1.60 x 1.50m, internally 0.90 x 0.90m; fill throughout homogeneous, making it impossible to define relationships between cells, probably either contemporary or closely related.

Enclosure J (210) Subrectangular, externally >4.00m wide, internally, >3.30m; north and west sides beyond northern limit of 1991 excavation.

Enclosure K (146) Probably subrectangular; overlay south-west side of Enclosure F; north and west sides clearly visible, others destroyed by ploughing.

Enclosure L (161) Possible complex enclosure, comprising a shallow depression, 3.70 x 0.60m, aligned east-west, and three short ditches, c0.15m wide, projecting at 90° from its southern side; southern side destroyed by ploughing.

Enclosure M (221, 224) T-shaped ditch complex, comprising east-west ditch *221* (2.75m long), with short (1.10m) northern return at east end; western end joined north-south ditch *224* (4.0m long) at 90°.

Enclosure N (232, 229) Possibly subrectangular, externally >3.0 x >2.0m; east and north sides were destroyed; western end of south ditch (232) joined west ditch at 90°, forming a corner; west ditch of enclosure (229) contained an atypical concentration of finds, probably remnant of subsequent cremation burial rather than component of ditch fill; north end of west ditch branched at right angles to east and west, forming a T-shape, extending beyond north and east limits of excavation; enclosure sealed by silt *14*.

Enclosure O (276, 258, 269) Possibly subrectangular; truncated by contractor's running track to south, removed by trial trenching to north (Trench 1); north and east sides (276), west side (258), parallel but not joined; ditch 269, central to enclosure, may be of significance.

Enclosure P (523) Possibly subrectangular; only short length of north and west sides examined; cut sand layer 505; continued beyond southern limit of 1992 excavation.

Enclosure Q (305) Subrectangular, externally 2.40 x 1.90m, internally 1.20 x 1.00m; connected to Enclosure H by a large elongated pit (301).

The ditches

A further seven ditches were excavated (*66, 68, 149, 236, 282, 540, 556*). They were morphologically identical to those which formed the enclosures but did not appear to comprise elements of enclosures themselves. Two survived in reasonable condition (*68, 149*), whilst the others, especially *66, 540,* and *556,* were badly truncated, undoubtedly as a result of later agricultural activity. Many of them appeared to be closely related to the enclosures, although their stratigraphic association was ambiguous. Two (*236, 282*) were sealed by silt *14* and thus clearly belong in the first phase of activity. Although most produced few or no finds, their proximity to the enclosures and their physical similarity suggest that they are contemporary.

The large oval pits

Sixteen large, usually oval pits were recorded, all cut into the natural gravel subsoil (*12*). These, in contrast to the cremations, had a distinctly elongated shape, were generally larger and deeper, and contained little carbonised material. Where they cut extant features the similarity of the fills made differentiation extremely difficult.

The pits were divided according to their relationship with the preceding enclosures and ditches. Two lay within enclosures, eight cut into the corners or sides of enclosure ditch fills, and a further six apparently were not associated with them at all. Their shape, size (*c*1.20–2.00m long, 0.40–0.50m wide), and surviving depth (*c*0.40m) strongly suggest both crouched and extended inhumation graves.

Two pits (*155, 176*) were cut into the centres of Enclosures H and E respectively. Like the enclosure ditches, they were cut directly into the natural gravel subsoil (*12*). They were almost without doubt inhumation graves, although the very acidic soils have destroyed all traces of their occupants. Both contained within their fills a noticeable layer of medium and large water-worn cobbles, possibly intended as packing around or above the corpse, a phenomenon noted at both Cirencester and Winchester (McWhirr *et al* 1982, 92; Clarke 1979, 143). Limited evidence from the fill of Pit *155* suggests a date around the end of the second to the mid third century, probably contemporary with the enclosures.

A further seven putative graves (*123, 171, 197, 213, 261, 301, 304*) appeared to have been cut deliberately into the fills of the enclosure ditches, and an eighth (*300*) just cut ditch *149*. The fills of these pits were, with the exception of *123*, almost identical to the ditches, often making it difficult to determine a relationship between the two types of feature. With the exception of Pit *261*, which was sealed by silt *14*, all were sealed by topsoil. None of this group appeared to contain stone packing. Pit *261*, however, provided evidence of a substantial wooden box or coffin within the grave. On the whole there were few objects that could be described specifically as grave goods: Pit *301* contained a bead necklace, probably consisting of several strings of small beads, of grey shale and black jet, strung alternately with bright blue, green, black, and gold-in-glass, presumably a prized personal possession; Pit *304* contained an inverted, miniature Black Burnished ware 1 cooking jar of later third century date. Such miniature pottery vessels often seem to have been used in a votive context. Other finds, odd pottery vessel fragments, nails, and hobnails, are likely to be residual. The grave goods might suggest a later third century date for those two graves at least, whilst the location of Pit *261* beneath silt *14* probably indicates a slightly earlier date, perhaps mid third century.

The six remaining large oval pits (*184, 252, 278, 280, 284, 299*) were again cut into the natural subsoil. They had no obvious relationship with the enclosures, although on the whole they followed the same general alignment. Again it is likely that all were inhumation graves, despite the lack of skeletal material. All were sealed by silts *14, 90,* and *118*.

Two pits (*184, 252*) were lined with large stones, and Pit *284* may have contained a wooden box. Only Pit *252* appeared to have contained grave goods: a shattered Nene Valley ware beaker and numerous hobnails, probably representing the presence in the grave of several pairs of shoes. The latter appear to have been a common symbolic inclusion, representing, in Roman belief, the journey to the Underworld. It is likely that the displaced tombstone found close to Pit *284* commemorated its occupant, *Aelia Sentica*, aged 35, wife of *Aurelius Verulus* (*see below*). The implication of a Roman burial rite, drawn from the presence of shoes and a tombstone, must imply a degree of Romanisation amongst the third century inhabitants of Low Borrowbridge, even though *Aelia* and her husband are unlikely to have gained their citizenship until the very late second or early third centuries, probably after the emperor Caracalla's decree of AD 212, granting universal franchise. Pottery from Pits *252* and *299*, along with the epigraphic evidence, suggest a mid third century date for these features and, by extension, for the flood silts which covered them.

The stratigraphic evidence implies strongly that the pits are broadly contemporary, although those not covered by flood silts appear marginally later, perhaps confirming the suggestion that the cemetery continued in use. There is no doubt that they postdated the enclosures, and with one exception (Pit *261* appears to have cut Cremation *294*), they undoubtedly predated the cremations, since many of these were cut into their fills or into the silts which overlay them. Not only did cremation replace inhumation here, but it persisted at an unusually late date. This challenges the accepted position that the cremation rite dated largely to the first two centuries AD and was then gradually replaced by inhumation as Christianity, with its promise of bodily resurrection, gained a hold.

The following summary catalogue lists the large oval pits and details their principal features. Unless otherwise stated they were cut directly into gravel layer *12*.

Pits within enclosures

Pit 155, Fill 147 Large oval pit, central within Enclosure H, long axis aligned north-east to south-west; 1.80-x 0.60m, depth 0.35m. Gently sloping sides and rounded base; fill *147* incorporated a layer of medium and large cobbles.
Finds Five small fragments late second to early third century pottery; one nail fragment; 15.2g cremated bone.
Pit 176, Fills 177, 179 Large oval pit, slightly off-centre to east, opposite entrance, within Enclosure E, long axis aligned east-west; 1.01 x 0.73m, depth 0.30m; gently rounded sided and base; fill *177* incorporated a layer of medium and large cobbles.
Finds One small undated pottery fragment.

Pits cut into enclosure ditches

Pit 123, Fill 122 Large oval pit, cut through south-west corner of Enclosure H, long axis aligned east-west; 2.00 x 0.75m. depth 0.40m; steeply sloping sides and flat base.
Finds 7.6g cremated bone.
Pit 171, Fill 170 Large oval pit, cut through north-west corner of Enclosure H, long axis aligned east-west; 1.12 x 0.90m, depth 0.40m; steeply sloping sides and slightly rounded base.
Finds One fragment burnt bone, 0.1g.
Pit 197, Fill 198 Large oval pit, cut along line of west side of Enclosure G, aligned with ditch; 2.10 x 0.75m, depth 0.40m; steeply sloping sides and gently rounded base.
Finds One hobnail.
Pit 213, Fill 214 Irregular oval pit, cut through north-west corner of northernmost cell of Enclosure I, aligned with ditch; 1.30 x 0.80m, depth 0.30m; irregularly sloping sides and slightly rounded base.
Finds 15 small fragments undiagnostic pottery; one nail fragment.
Pit 261, Fill 262 Large irregular oval pit, cut extreme southern end ditch *229* (possible complex Enclosure N), and Cremation *294*; overlain by silt *14*, aligned north-south; 2.20 x 0.80m, depth 0.35m; steeply sloping sides and rounded base; imprint of sides and base of large decayed wooden container within fill.
Finds 31 fragments of third century vessels; one clenched iron nail.
Pit 300, Fill 271 Large oval pit, just cut south-eastern edge of ditch *149*, aligned north-east to south-west; 1.20 x 0.84m, depth 0.49m; steeply sloping sides and slightly rounded base.

Finds Two fragments of undated pottery; 12 nail fragments; nine hobnails.
Pit 301, Fill 302 Large oval pit, cut through north-east corner of Enclosure H and south-west corner of Enclosure Q, physically connecting the two, aligned east-west; 1.20 x 0.70m, depth 0.30m; steeply sloping sides and irregular base.
Finds 67 stone and glass beads from a single necklace, third or fourth century AD.
Pit 304, Fill 307 Large oval pit, cut along south side of Enclosure G, aligned with ditch; 1.20 x 0.75m, depth 0.40m; steep sides and gently rounded base.
Finds Complete miniature Black Burnished ware 1 cooking pot, late third century; two nail fragments.

Pits not associated with enclosures

Pit 184, Fill 185 Large subrectangular pit, sealed by silt lens *118*, long axis aligned east-west; 1.20 x 0.50m, depth 0.17m; steeply sloping sides and flat base, lined with medium and large rounded stones; no finds.
Pit 252, Fill 253 Very large, roughly oval pit, overlay Pits *278* and *280*, sealed by silt *90*, long axis aligned north-south; 3.10 x 1.80m, depth 0.30m; irregularly sloping sides and flat base, lined with large rounded stones.
Finds Nene Valley ware beaker, AD 220–270; Black Burnished ware 1 vessel fragment; one nail fragment; 197 hobnails, in clumps, representing several pairs of shoes.
Pit 278, Fill 279 Oval pit, underlay Pit *252*, long axis aligned north-east to south-west; 1.10 x 0.70m, depth 0.45m; steeply sloping sides and flat base; no finds.
Pit 280, Fill 281 Oval pit, underlay Pit *252*, long axis aligned north-south; 1.20 x 0.50m, depth 0.17m; steeply sloping sides and flat base, lined with medium and large rounded stones; no finds.
Pit 284, Fills 285, 286, 295 Large subrectangular pit, sealed by silt *14*, long axis aligned north-south, parallel to large oval Pit *261*; 2.00 x 0.90m, depth 0.35m; gently sloping sides and rounded base; imprint of sides of possible decayed large wooden container within fill; pit possibly associated with third century tombstone of *Aelia Sentica* found immediately to south.
Finds Nine nail fragments; small drip of melted lead.
Pit 299, Fill 298 Large subrectangular pit, sealed by silt *14*, aligned north-south; 1.50 x 0.80m, depth 0.30m; steeply sloping sides and flat base.
Finds Small fragments of undiagnostic pottery; one iron nail.

Cremation burials

Seventy-one, mainly small, pits were classified as cremation burials. Most were subcircular in plan, with shallow U-shaped profiles, and all contained some cremated bone and high concentrations of carbonised material. In contrast to the large oval pits, these had a distinctive dark appearance, and were generally smaller in size. It seems likely that most, if not all, of these burials had been badly disturbed by agricultural activity (Phase 3). Many contained substantially less bone than might be expected from a cremation, and many of the burial urns were shattered, or their tops had been removed by ploughing.

Most of the cremation pits lay directly below topsoil *1*, mainly cut into the natural gravels (*12*) or river silts (*14*, *90*). Three pits (*254*, *294*, *296*), however, were sealed by the river silts, clearly indicating that cremation was practised both before and after the site flooded (Phases 1 and 2).

Of the 71 pits containing cremation burials, at least 25 contained one or more pottery vessels; none, however, contained more than two. All had a distinctive black fill, often heavily flecked with charcoal and tiny fragments of burnt bone. Most produced odd hobnails and other nail fragments in small quantities, as well as small fragments of other pottery vessels, sometimes heavily burned.

Most pits were relatively small, ranging in diameter from 0.20m to an uncharacteristic 1.70m. Their depth varied from a very shallow 0.05m to 0.50m and the angle of their sides varied greatly from a shallow scoop to a deep vertical-sided pit. Most had irregular bases suggesting perhaps the use of a small-bladed tool for their excavation.

Cremation pits were identified over most of the site, although a particular concentration seemed to cut the river silts in the north-western area; these, and the pits to the south-east, appeared to fall outside the main concentration of rectilinear enclosures. Where the two types of feature overlapped, in the north, east, and extreme north-west of the excavated area, the cremation pits were usually cut into the infilled ditches, implying knowledge of the existing plots.

Only one of the pits (527) produced as much as a quarter of the amount of bone (498.9g) to be expected from an adult body (c2kg; see McKinley 1989, 1993b). Many produced very little indeed (<10g) and only 35 of the 71 pits produced sufficient quantities for valid analysis.

At least two of the burials contained cremated animal or bird bone. The inclusion of a token food offering or last meal was common practice in Roman burial. In these cases the meal was clearly burnt along with the corpse.

Some of the burials were placed in the pits without containers (unurned) whilst at least 25 were contained in ceramic vessels. In every case, quite normally for Roman cremation burials, the vessels were ordinary domestic types, often cooking pots. The sooting and slight burning noted on several vessels suggests that they had actually been used for cooking, and possibly old or slightly damaged vessels were reused for burial. This pragmatic approach appears quite normal amongst Roman burials (Philpott 1991, 30).

Two graves each contained an accessory vessel, one a fineware beaker (535), the other a miniature cooking pot (186). The inclusion of secondary vessels, often drinking vessels, was again a common practice in the Roman period. Three of the burials (134, 191, 548) contained Black Burnished ware 1 bowls or dishes, possibly used to contain the burial, but possibly as accessory vessels to unurned burials. The majority of the vessels (from Cremations 27, 51, 52, 58, 60, 82, 84, 87, 115, 156, 174, 186, 204, 303, 532) were Black Burnished ware 1 cooking pots of third century date, but four were narrow-necked Severn Valley jars, of late second to mid third century date (from Cremations 102, 527, 535, 542). The vessels stood upright in the graves, except one which was tilted and another which was inverted, probably as a result of later plough damage, but none appeared to have been covered to protect the contents. This, and the presence of bone around the pots, might suggest that the cremated remains were poured, or shovelled, into the pot as it stood in the grave (Wenham 1968). This would accord well with the notion of a token amount of burnt material deposited symbolically at the graveside, rather than a deliberate effort to dispose of the entire remains of the deceased.

Almost all the graves had evidence of pyre debris, often odd nails, presumably deriving from a bier or the pyre itself. There was also evidence for objects burnt on the pyre with the deceased. The most frequent objects were hobnails, small numbers of which were found, randomly dispersed, in many of the graves. This raises the possibility that the dead were cremated wearing shoes; alternatively the shoes may have been placed separately on the pyre. The presence of nailed shoes is no indicator of sex, since all heavy duty shoes were nailed.

In one or two graves that produced large numbers of hobnails, however, it might be suggested that several pairs of shoes were deposited separately in the graves as symbolic offerings, as may have been the case with the inhumation graves. Cremation 527 also produced a burnt fragment of a decorated bone plaque, probably part of a comb, and Cremation 536 included a burnt antler peg, presumably from a pyre offering. The presence in many of the graves of small fragments of burnt pottery might suggest that this too was sometimes burned with the deceased.

Some of the objects are likely to have been grave goods, placed within the burial unburned. Three of the burials (51, 217, 240) included brooches, possibly again from the clothes of the deceased, but equally likely as personal keepsakes from mourners. Evidence suggests that at least three of the graves may have contained small wooden boxes, two including iron hinges or hasps (*109, 178*), the other with plain copper alloy fittings (*536*). There were no objects of high intrinsic value.

Two burials (*303, 531*) included worn, low denomination coins, a symbolic payment for Charon, ferryman across the River Styx. Such offerings were extremely common in the Classical world. The symbolism and practice does not, however, appear to have been adopted widely in Roman Britain. This contrasts with the ready adoption of the practice of including shoes for the journey to Hades, another idea deriving from the Classical world, also seen at Low Borrowbridge. The presence of coins might therefore suggest individuals with a more ingrained knowledge or usage of Classical belief (Alcock 1980).

It is perhaps of note that the four Severn Valley vessels were grouped towards the south and east margins of the site. This might indicate a slight spatial differentiation within the cemetery, possibly an area in use at a specific time.

The following summary catalogue lists the cremation burials and details their principal features. Unless otherwise stated they were cut directly into gravel layer *12*. Small amounts of cremated bone were found in all the pits; larger fragments were hand collected, and an overall sample was retained for analysis from each fill.

Cremation burials

Cremation 19, fills 40, 44 Oval pit, central within Enclosure D; 0.63 x 0.33m, depth 0.25m; relatively steep sloping sides and rounded base.
Finds 13 fragments of Black Burnished ware 1 vessel, mid third century, perhaps the burial urn; fragments of fourth century Huntcliff ware from upper fill; five hobnails, one nail.
Cremation 21, fill 48 Subcircular pit, cut silt *41*; diameter 0.40m, depth 0.05m; gently sloping sides and a rounded base.
Finds One iron nail.
Cremation 27, fill 47, urn 413 Circular pit; diameter 0.30m, depth 0.12m; gently sloping sides and flat base.
Finds Upright base of a Black Burnished ware 1 cooking pot, probably used as a burial urn.
Cremation 30, fill 46 Subcircular pit, within Enclosure C, nicked internal edge of enclosure ditch; diameter 0.40m, depth 0.08m; gently sloping sides and rounded base.
Finds Two hobnails; two amber glass cylinder beads; 4.7g cremated bone: >infant.
Cremation 31, fills 23, 32 Oval pit; 0.55 x 0.42m, depth 0.35m; steeply sloping sides and rounded base.
Finds Two undiagnostic pottery fragments, possibly third century; 5.3g cremated bone: adult.
Cremation 49, fill 50 Irregular pit; possible stone packing; 0.32 x 0.29m, depth 0.17m; steeply sloping sides and rounded base; no finds.
Cremation 51, fill 18, urn 417 Irregular pit, cut eastern side of entrance to Enclosure E; diameter 1.50m, depth 0.13m; gently sloping sides and uneven undulating base; two distinct lenses of burnt material might suggest two burials.
Finds Upright Black Burnished ware 1 cooking pot used as

burial urn, set towards north-east of pit; third century pottery types; copper alloy knee brooch, third century, from fill *18*; six nail fragments; 24 hobnails; 73.7g cremated bone from fill *18*: subadult/adult; 0.7g cremated bone from fill *417*: immature individual—probably confirms double burial.
Cremation 52, fill 53, urn 419 Oval pit, cut silt *14*; 0.60 x 0.50m, depth 0.10m; gently sloping sides and rounded base.
Finds Upright Black Burnished ware 1 cooking pot, mid third century, used as burial urn, set towards west of pit; urn contained 60.9g cremated bone: adult.
Cremation 58, fill 59, urn 416 Subcircular pit, cut internal edge of Enclosure D; 0.45 x 0.42m, depth 0.12m; sloping sides and rounded base.
Finds Upright lower half of Black Burnished ware 1 cooking pot, early to mid second century or later, probably used as burial urn; nine sherds Black Burnished ware 1 cooking pot; four nails; unidentifiable fragment of iron; urn contained one hobnail.
Cremation 60, fill 61, urn 415 Subcircular pit, cut west side of entrance to Enclosure E; diameter 0.30m, depth 0.14m; steeply sloping sides and flat base.
Finds Upright lower half of Black Burnished ware 1 cooking pot, third century?, used as burial urn; burnt pottery fragments; urn contained 16.6g cremated bone: infant.
Cremation 70, fill 71 Subcircular pit; diameter 0.20m, depth 0.05m; gently rounded profile; no finds.
Cremation 72, fills 73, 133 Subcircular pit; diameter 0.35m, depth 0.28m; steeply sloping sides and flat base.
Finds 26 third century pottery fragments from upper fill.
Cremation 79, lens only Subrectangular lens, cut silt *15*; diameter 0.20m, depth 0.05m; gently rounded profile; no finds.
Cremation 80, fill 81 Oval pit, cut silt *15*; 1.05 x 0.66m, depth 0.25m; relatively steeply sloping sides and rounded base.
Finds One copper alloy nail fragment; nine nail fragments; 81g cremated bone: adult.
Cremation 82, fill 77, urn 411 Oval pit, cut silt layer *15*, probably cut by Cremation 84; 0.70 x 0.50m, depth 0.20m; almost vertical sides and slightly rounded base.
Finds Upright Black Burnished ware 1 cooking pot, used as burial urn; 21 Black Burnished ware 1 potsherds; fourth century Huntcliff ware pottery fragment; nail fragment; 189.8g cremated bone from urn; 8.3g cremated bone from fill *77*: young/mature female?
Cremation 83, fill 76 Subrectangular pit, cut silt *15*; 0.80 x 0.40m, depth 0.05m; gently sloping sides and flat base.
Finds 11 very small fragments Rhenish beaker, AD 220–240; 1g cremated bone: subadult/adult.
Cremation 84, fill 78, urn 409 Subcircular pit, cut silt *15*, probably cut Cremation 82; 0.80 x 0.70m, depth 0.20m; relatively steeply sloping sides and flat base.
Finds Upright Black Burnished ware 1 cooking pot, third century, used as burial urn, set to north of pit; urn contained one hobnail; 11.1g cremated bone from urn: older subadult/adult.
Cremation 85, fill 7 Subcircular pit, cut silt *15*; diameter 0.35m, depth 0.19m; almost vertical sides and slightly rounded base.
Finds Three sherds Black Burnished ware 1; nail fragment; hobnail.
Cremation 87, fill 86, urn 408 Subcircular pit, cut silt *15*; 0.50 x 0.40m, depth 0.20m; steeply sloping sides and rounded base.
Finds Upright Black Burnished ware 1 cooking pot, third century, used as burial urn; third century pottery fragments; one clenched copper alloy nail, two nail fragments, and one unidentified iron object from urn; 56.9g cremated bone from urn: older subadult; 2.1g cremated bone from fill.
Cremation 88, fill 89 Subcircular pit, cut silt *15*; 0.69 x 0.63m, depth 0.10m; gently sloping sides and uneven base; no finds.
Cremation 94, lens Irregular lens within silt *15*; diameter 1.20m, depth 0.10m.

Finds Third century pottery fragments; one nail fragment; 0.8g cremated bone: adult.

Cremation 97, lens Amorphous lens, on surface of silt *15*; diameter 0.50m, depth 0.05m; no finds.

Cremation 100, fills 98, 99 Subcircular pit, cut silt *14*; 1.02 x 0.90m, depth 0.40m; steeply sloping sides and rounded base.

Finds Eight small undiagnostic pottery fragments.

Cremation 102, fill 101, urn 406 Kidney-shaped pit, cut silt *14*; 0.59 x 0.50m, depth 0.22m; gently sloping sides and rounded base.

Finds Narrow-necked Severn Valley ware jar inverted over burial; urn contained two nail fragments; 3.9g cremated bone: subadult/adult and unidentified animal bone.

Cremation 105, fill 96, urn 418 Oval pit, cut silt *90*; 1.70 x 1.10mm, depth 0.25m; gently sloping sides and irregular base.

Finds Upright local grey ware cooking pot used as burial urn; undiagnostic pottery fragments; eight nail fragments; clump of three hobnails; urn contained one hobnail; 6.2g cremated bone from urn: subadult/adult.

Cremation 109, fill 8 Oval pit, cut silt *15*, probably cut by Cremation *136*; 1.20 x 0.25mm, depth 0.25m; steeply sloping sides and uneven base; contained fire-cracked stones.

Finds Two hobnails; five nail fragments; iron fittings for a hinged wooden box; 11.6g cremated bone: >infant.

Cremation 113, fill 114 Subcircular pit, cut silt *118*; diameter 0.60m, depth 0.20m; steeply sloping sides and rounded base; no finds.

Cremation 115, fill 116, urn 405 Subcircular pit, cut silt *90*; diameter 0.60m, depth 0.08m; steeply sloping sides and flat base.

Finds Almost complete Black Burnished ware 1 cooking pot, late third century, slightly tilted, used as burial urn; late third century pottery; urn contained seven nail fragments; 28.5g cremated bone from urn: infant.

Cremation 125, fill 95, urn 410 Oval pit, cut north side of Enclosure K; 0.55 x 0.35m, depth 0.14m; steeply sloping sides and flat base.

Finds Crushed handmade grey ware cooking pot, third century, used as burial urn; undiagnostic pottery fragments.

Cremation 126, fill 120 Subcircular pit, cut Enclosure H; diameter 0.20m, depth 0.10m; gently sloping sides and rounded base.

Finds 3.6g cremated bone .

Cremation 130, fill 131 Subcircular pit, cut silt *90*; diameter 1.20m, depth 0.50m; gently sloping sides and rounded base.

Finds Third century pottery fragments; one hobnail.

Cremation 134, fill 135, urn 401 Subcircular pit, cut ditch *172*; 0.80 x 0.75m, depth 0.20m; gently sloping sides and rounded base.

Finds Upright Black Burnished ware 1 bowl, mid to late second century, used as burial urn; urn contained one Black Burnished ware 1 sherd; three nail fragments; 31.7g cremated bone from urn: adult.

Cremation 136, fill 128 Irregular oval pit, cut silt *90*, probably cut Cremation *109*; 1.60 x 1.0m, depth 0.20m; gently sloping sides and almost flat base.

Finds 45 pottery fragments, mid third century; one nail fragment; 39 hobnails; one unidentifiable iron fragment; 160.1g cremated bone: adult.

Cremation 137, fill 138 Subcircular pit, cut inner north-eastern edge of Enclosure E; 0.50 x 0.37m, depth 0.15m; gently sloping sides and uneven base.

Finds Undiagnostic pottery fragments; 13 nail fragments; seven hobnails; two unidentifiable iron fragments.

Cremation 156, fill 129, urn 400 Subcircular pit, cut silt *90*; 0.30 x 0.25m, depth 0.25m; steeply sloping sides and irregular base.

Finds Upright Black Burnished ware 1 cooking pot, late third century, used as cremation vessel, containing eight fragments burnt pottery, presumably from pyre goods; 88.5g cremated bone from urn: older/mature adult female; 3.8g cremated bone from fill: subadult/adult.

Cremation 174, fill 175, urn 414 Subrectangular pit, cut Enclosure I; 1.15 x 0.45m, depth 0.60m; gently sloping sides and almost flat base.

Finds Base of upright Black Burnished ware 1 cooking pot, used as burial urn; 18 fragments undiagnostic pottery; 8g cremated bone from fill; 0.5g cremated bone from urn.

Cremation 178, fill 169 Subcircular pit, cut silt *90*; diameter 0.57m, depth 0.20m; relatively steep sloping sides and irregular base.

Finds 16 fragments early to mid second century or later pottery, some burnt; two hobnails; an iron staple or hasp, perhaps suggesting a wooden box; 2.1g cremated bone: subadult/adult.

Cremation 186, fill 187, urns 402,403 Irregular pit, cut silt *90*; 0.60 x 0.40m, depth 0.30m; steeply sloping sides and irregular base.

Finds Upright Black Burnished ware 1 cooking pot (*402*) used as burial urn, third century, burnt; secondary miniature Black Burnished ware 1 cooking pot (*403*), third century; early to mid second century or later pottery fragments; both vessels contained burnt Black Burnished ware 1 sherds; four nail fragments; five hobnails; four unidentified iron objects; burial urn *402* contained five nail fragments; secondary urn *403* contained one unidentified iron object; 211.7g cremated bone from urn: adult.

Cremation 189, fill 190 Subcircular pit, cut silt *90*; 0.60 x 0.52m, depth 0.18m; steeply sloping sides and flat base.

Finds One pottery fragment, early to mid second century or later; ten nail fragments; one hobnail; 116.2g cremated bone, probably unurned burial: adult.

Cremation 191, fills 6, 192, 196, 199 Oval pit; 0.45 x 0.35m, depth 0.20m; steeply sloping sides and almost flat base.

Finds Upright Black Burnished ware 1 dish, AD 190–340, used as burial urn, damaged by plough; ten nail fragments; >1g cremated bone .

Cremation 193, fill 194 Subcircular pit, cut silt *90*; diameter 0.56m, depth 0.20m; steeply sloping sides and an almost flat base.

Finds 0.7g cremated bone: infant.

Cremation 202, fill 203 Circular pit, cut silt *90*; diameter 0.25m, depth 0.05m; gently sloping sides and slightly rounded base.

Finds Two hobnails.

Cremation 204, fill 205, urn 407 Subcircular pit, cut internal edge of north-west cell of Enclosure I; diameter 0.40m, depth 0.10m; gently sloping sides and rounded base.

Finds Base of upright Black Burnished ware 1 cooking pot used as burial urn; two nail fragments; three hobnails.

Cremation 217, fills 218, 220 Subcircular pit, cut silt *14*; diameter 1.00m, depth 0.30m; gently sloping sides and almost flat base.

Finds Pottery fragments, early to mid second century or later; small fragment of the foot of a copper alloy bow brooch; seven nail fragments.

Cremation 223, fill 212 Subcircular pit, cut south side of Enclosure J; 0.62 x 0.39m, depth 0.14m; steeply sloping sides and flat base.

Finds Eight nail fragments; one hobnail; 54.5g cremated bone, suggests unurned cremation: young/mature adult.

Cremation 235, fill 234 Subcircular pit, nicked southern element of Enclosure M; diameter 0.50m, depth 0.20m; steeply sloping sides and almost flat base.

Finds Undiagnostic pottery fragments.

Cremation 240, fill 241 Subcircular pit, cut eastern side of Enclosure M; diameter 0.45m, depth 0.18m; relatively steep sloping sides and almost flat base.

Finds Pottery, early to mid second century or later; copper alloy crossbow brooch, third century; two nail fragments; 51 hobnails; 50.2g cremated bone, suggests unurned burial: adult.

Cremation 242, fill 243 Subrectangular pit, cut silt *90*; 0.40 x 0.30m, depth 0.30m; steeply sloping sides and rounded base.

Finds 121.4g cremated bone: older mature/older adult, suggests unurned burial.

Cremation 245, fill 246 Subcircular pit, cut east side of Enclosure J; diameter 0.50m, depth 0.20m; gently sloping sides and rounded base.

Finds Pottery fragments, early to mid second century or later; two hobnails; 26.8g cremated bone: subadult/adult.

Cremation 254, fill 255 Subcircular pit, cut large oval Pit 252, sealed by silt *90*; 0.28 x 0.26m, depth 0.08m; gently sloping sides and rounded base.

Finds Two small fragments pottery, early to mid second century or later; 0.3g cremated bone .

Cremation 256, lens Subcircular pit, cut silt *90*; diameter 0.20m, depth 0.10m; gently rounded profile.

Finds 10.1g cremated bone: adult.

Cremation 265, fill 266 Irregular elongated pit, cut silt *14*; 0.76 x 0.30m, depth 0.09m; gently sloping sides and rounded base; no finds.

Cremation 267, fill 268, urn 404 Subcircular pit, cut ditch *269*, central to Enclosure O; diameter 0.35m, depth 0.26m; steeply sloping sides and almost flat base.

Finds Base of upright grey ware cooking pot used as burial urn; undiagnostic pottery fragments; two nail fragments; urn contained one nail fragment; 68.1g cremated bone from urn: older mature/older adult.

Cremation 294, fill 274 Subcircular pit, cut by large oval Pit *261*, sealed by silt *14*; diameter 0.30m, depth 0.20m; steeply sloping sides and narrow irregular base; no finds.

Cremation 296, fill 297 Oval pit, sealed by silt *14*; 1.37 x 0.90m, depth 0.45m; almost vertical sides and flat base.

Finds Several Black Burnished ware 1 pottery fragments, mid third century, almost certainly a single vessel; 1g cremated bone: infant.

Cremation 303, fills 13, 124, urn 412 Subcircular pit, cut inside edge of Enclosure Q; diameter 0.40m, depth 0.10m; gently sloping sides and rounded base.

Finds Upright Black Burnished ware 1 cooking pot, used as burial urn; ten Black Burnished ware 1 fragments; undiagnostic pottery fragment; *sestertius* of Hadrian, AD 117–138, very worn, from urn; three nail fragments; light blue glass cuboid bead; 40.2g cremated bone from urn: infant.

Cremation 518, fill 519 Subcircular pit, cut gravel *508*; diameter 1.04m, depth 0.33m; relatively steep sloping sides and almost flat base.

Finds Six undiagnostic pottery fragments.

Cremation 522, fill 515 Irregular pit, cut sand *505*; diameter 0.45m, depth 0.21m; steeply sloping sides and flat base; half-sectioned only, at limit of 1992 excavation.

Finds 7.1g cremated bone: adult.

Cremation 524, fill 513 Oval pit, cut layer *504*; 0.70 x 0.30m, depth 0.10m; gently sloping sides and irregular base.

Finds Undiagnostic pottery fragment; seven nail fragments; one hobnail.

Cremation 527, fill 528, urn 421 Oval pit, cut sand *505*; 1.60 x >0.65m, depth 0.20m; near vertical sides and flat base; half-sectioned only, at limit of 1992 excavation.

Finds Upright narrow-necked Severn Valley ware jar used as burial urn, set on eastern side of pit; pyre goods: chicken bone, fragments of a decorated antler or rib bone plaque, possibly a composite comb; 498.9g cremated bone from urn: older mature/older adult male.

Cremation 531, fill 502 Subcircular pit, cut layer *504*; diameter 1.05m, depth 0.19m; gently sloping sides and rounded base; half-sectioned only, at limit of 1992 excavation.

Finds Sestertius of Trajan, AD 103–11, very worn; 20 hobnails; three nail fragments.

Cremation 532, fill 510, urn 530 Subcircular pit, cut gravel *508*; 0.43 x 0.38m, depth 0.09m; steeply sloping sides lined with medium and large stones, and almost flat base.

Finds Upright Black Burnished ware 1 cooking pot, mid third century, used as burial urn; third century pottery fragments.

Cremation 533, fill 514 Subcircular pit, cut sand *505*; 0.51 x 0.30m, depth 0.14m; irregular sloping sides and gently rounded base.

Finds Undiagnostic pottery fragment.

Cremation 535, fill 506, urn 539 Subcircular pit, cut sand *505*; diameter 0.75m, depth 0.32m; steeply sloping sides and almost flat base.

Finds Upright narrow-necked Severn Valley ware jar, late second or third century, used as burial urn; Nene Valley beaker, fourth century, secondary vessel; four nail fragments; two hobnails.

Cremation 536, fill 503 Subcircular pit, cut sand *505*; diameter 0.38m, depth 0.15m; steeply sloping sides and flat base; half-sectioned only, at limit of 1992 excavation.

Finds 78 sherds of a grey ware cooking pot; possible copper alloy casket furniture; ten nail fragments; three hobnails; burnt antler peg.

Cremation 542, fills 543, 551 Subcircular pit, cut gravel *508*; diameter 0.67m, depth 0.10m; irregular sloping sides and rounded base.

Finds Upright narrow-necked Severn Valley ware jar, late second or third century, used as a burial or accessory vessel; 47.9g cremated bone, not from urn: older mature/older adult, included horse or cow tooth enamel.

Cremation 548, fill 547 Subcircular pit, cut sand *505*; 0.35 x 0.25m, depth 0.05m; very gently sloping sides and rounded base; half-sectioned only, at limit of 1992 excavation.

Finds Damaged Black Burnished ware 1 dish, AD 190–340.

Cremation 550, fill 512 Subcircular pit, cut layer *504*; diameter 0.43m, depth 0.10m; steeply sloping sides and uneven base.

Finds Pottery fragments, mid third century; one nail fragment; seven hobnails.

Cremation 554, fill 549 Roughly circular pit, cut sand *505*; diameter 1.40m, depth 0.16m; steeply sloping sides and gently rounded base.

Finds Burnt pottery, third century; 21 hobnails; 13 nail fragments; 46.4g cremated bone, possible unurned burial: adult.

Cremation 560, fill 553 Irregular pit, cut sand *505*; 1.25 x 0.45m, depth 0.20m; steeply sloping sides and rounded base.

Finds A few fragments of Black Burnished ware 1, Black Burnished ware 2, Nene Valley ware, and local grey ware pottery; 37 hobnails; 21 nail fragments.

Cremation 604, fill 605 Circular pit, cut silty loam *602*; diameter 0.50m, depth 0.20m; steeply sloping sides and rounded base.

Finds Four sherds Black Burnished ware 1 pottery; four sherds undiagnostic pottery; 11 nail fragments; one iron ring; three unidentified iron objects.

Other pits

In addition to the 16 large oval inhumation pits, and 71 cremation burials, a number of other pits were excavated. They can be divided into two groups.

Five pits (*151, 166, 181, 227, 520*) appeared to have been backfilled with redeposited subsoil, which sometimes contained small amounts of burnt bone and carbonised material. Most were subcircular in plan, although two (*166, 181*) were oval, both with their long axis aligned east-west. They had steeply sloping sides and slightly rounded bases and measured 0.30–1.08m in length or diameter, and 0.09–0.35m in depth. They lay immediately beneath

topsoil or ploughsoil and were, with the exception
of *181*, which was cut into silt *14*, cut into the gravel
subsoil (*12*). It is possible that some of these were
also inhumation burials.

Seven pits (*20, 74, 106, 111, 117, 195, 525*) were identical in appearance to the cremation burials, but contained no cremated bone or pottery. All contained
concentrations of charcoal. They were clearly associated with the cremation cemetery, although their
exact function remains unclear. They perhaps represent truncated cremation burials, displaced by
later agricultural activity, or may alternatively represent the disposal of pyre debris.

The road

A cobbled surface, 35m west of the cemetery, 7m
wide and aligned north-south, was revealed in two
parallel trench sections 10m apart during the evaluation in August 1990, and examined in plan in
July 1991. The surface comprised small pebbles 0.04–
0.15m in diameter, the lowest of which were set into
natural silt layer *90*, and appeared to dip gently to
east and west, suggesting a deliberate camber.

By its nature and location, the surface was considered to be a road, possibly Roman, although there
was no associated dating evidence. The road ran
parallel to Howgill Lane, the supposed route of the
main Roman road, and may have been a secondary
road serving the extramural settlement (D Shotter
pers comm). On the other hand, the projection of
this fragment of road to north and south hints at an
alignment both with the unlocated south gate of the
fort and with Howgill Lane south-west of Salterwath
Bridge. Tumbled masonry on the north bank of the
Lune, west of the present bridge, may indicate the
site of a Roman bridge abutment (J Anstee pers
comm).

Howgill Lane is the more likely candidate for the
main Roman road, serving the east gate of the fort,
as it appears to define the eastern limit of the cemetery. Roman cemeteries were, by tradition, situated close to roads, outside areas of settlement. The
tombstone was located near this road, in a position
where passers-by might read the inscription, as was
customarily the intention (Reece 1977, 44). Nonetheless when, during construction in October 1991,
the narrow pipe trench provided a section across
Howgill Lane, no evidence for any earlier road surface was revealed, perhaps because the instability
of the sand and river gravels necessitated the bat-
tering of the trench sides, obscuring the section. The
tarmac of the modern road was observed to overlie
a deposit of white gravel which in turn overlay the
natural river gravels.

It is not impossible that the western road, and not
Howgill Lane, which is aligned with the later
Salterwath Bridge, represents the true course of the
main Roman route to the fort at Low Borrowbridge;
but it may equally have been a minor road or street
within the settlement outside the fort.

The finds

The Roman coarsewares

Louise Hird

The total weight of pottery is 20.134kg, made up of
2186 sherds, of which only six were of *amphorae* and
nine of *mortaria*. The pottery comprised, to a large
extent, traded wares, especially Black Burnished
ware 1 (Fabric 1) and Severn Valley ware (Fabric 3),
and to a lesser extent Nene Valley ware (Fabric 5),
Rhenish ware (Fabric 4), and Black Burnished ware
2 (Fabric 14) (Figs 5:9, 5:10). Together they made up
86–88% of the coarse pottery, calculated by weight
and sherd count (Table 5:1).

Black Burnished ware 1 (Fabric 1) accounts for 58%
by weight and 70% by sherd count of the pottery.
The vessels are almost entirely cooking pots (1: *44/*
1026; 2: *129/1262*; 3: *307/1240*), all of third century
date. There were two examples of a bowl (4: *135/*
1206) of later second century date, one example
(5: *534/2097*) of a bowl of late second or early third
century date, and three examples of dishes (6: *199/*
1526) of predominantly third century date. There
was a small amount of Black Burnished ware 2 (Fabric 14), including a dish of Gillam 313 (7: *37/1009*)
and one or two fragments of cooking pots. The dish
is the later type of Black Burnished ware 2 dish,
which has already been noted from previous excavations at Low Borrowbridge (Hildyard and Gillam
1951).

Three fairly complete vessels in Severn Valley ware
(Fabric 3) (8: *11/1008*; 9: *527/1854*; 10: *506/2109*,
2110, 2023) mean that the ware makes up over 22%
by weight but only about 9% by sherd count. The
types present are all likely to be third century in
date, although none of them are dated very closely
(Webster 1978). There are two vessels in Rhenish
ware (Fabric 4), both probably dating to the first
half of the third century (11: *231/1687*). The ware
as a whole makes up less than 1% by weight and
just over 2% by sherd count. Nene Valley colour-
coated ware (Fabric 5) is present at just over 3% by
weight and just over 5% by sherd count. There were
two beakers, one (12: *253/1779*) dating to the mid

Table 5:1 Coarse pottery

Fabric	Weight	Sherd count	% Weight	% Sherd count
1	11550	1524	57.83	70.19
2	65	2	0.32	0.09
3	4500	195	22.53	8.98
4	150	48	0.75	2.21
5	630	109	3.15	5.02
6	90	12	0.45	0.55
7	60	10	0.30	0.46
8	10	2	0.05	0.09
9	20	2	0.10	0.09
10	80	13	0.14	0.59
11	2115	163	10.59	7.50
12	605	80	3.03	3.68
14	95	11	0.47	0.50
Totals	**19970**	**2171**		

Amphorae

100	35	6		

Mortaria

50	95	8		
51	45	1		
Totals	**140**	**9**		

Fabric series

1 Black Burnished ware, Category 1 (Williams 1977)
2 Grey Crambeck ware: very pale grey fabric with lead grey surfaces (Evans 1989)
3 Severn Valley ware: fine-textured, slightly micaceous oxidised fabric, usually with a pale grey core (Webster 1976)
4 'Rhenish' ware: very hard, fine-textured, orange-grey-orange sandwiched fabric with glossy black slip (Greene 1978)
5 Nene Valley colour-coated ware: fairly hard, white or pink fabric with colour-coat of various colours from dark grey to orange-brown (Howe, Perrin, and Mackreth 1981)
6 Hard, rough, gritty and sandy very dark grey fabric with hackly fracture; sand is quartz; could well be handmade
7 Huntcliff ware: calcite-gritted, grey or greyish-black fabric with grit or voids, depending on soil conditions (Corder and Birley 1937)
8 Hard, sandy, creamy white fabric with occasional red grit inclusions
9 Sandy, orange fabric with cream slip, probably locally produced
10 Rather rough grey, grey-black fabric with voids (as for calcite grit) and large (2–3mm) quartz pebble inclusions
11 Unidentified grey wares, the products of several probably local sources
12 Unidentified oxidised wares, the products of several probably local sources
13 Not used
14 Black Burnished ware, Category 2 (Williams 1977)

Mortarium fabrics
50 Mancetter-Hartshill: white, 'pipeclay' fabric with mixed, red or grey trituration grit
51 Local? sandy, self-coloured, pinkish-orange fabric

Amphora fabrics
100 Very sandy, orange-grey, grey or buff fabric; usual fabric from South Spanish Peacock and Williams Class 25 (1988)
101 Fairly fine-textured, hard, buff fabric with sparse quartz sand and red particle inclusions, South Spanish?

third century; the other (13: *504, 506/2022, 2064, 2073, 2093, 2110*) is one of a handful of vessels from the excavations which has a fourth century date. There is also a fragment of a 'castor' box of Gillam 342 type, dated AD 180–320. Grey wares (Fabric 11), which are presumably of local manufacture, make up over 10% by weight and 7.5% by sherd count. There are two jars worthy of note (14: *268/1745, 1746*; 15: *503/2090, 2106, 2116, 2124*). There were six tiny sherds of *amphora*, all of South Spanish origin (Fabric 100). The excavations produced nine small sherds of *mortaria*, eight of which were of Mancetter-Hartshill manufacture (Fabric 50) and one of more local production (Fabric 51).

Most of the pottery is of third century date, although there is a small amount of fourth century material made up of Grey Crambeck ware (Fabric 2), less than 1% but including a bowl (16: *1000/1837*), and Huntcliff ware (Fabric 7), less than 1%. There is also one beaker in Nene Valley ware (13: *504, 506/2022, 2064, 2073, 2093, 2110*) of fourth century date.

As might be expected of vessels used in cremation pits, over 68% were cooking pots or jars and another almost 8% were narrow-necked jars (Table 5:2). Almost 6% were beakers, 3% dishes, and 2% bowls. The remaining vessel types, flagons, *amphorae*, and *mortaria* made up less than 1% each. Two bowls and at least one dish were, however, certainly used as cinerary vessels. The fragments of flagons, *amphorae*, and *mortaria* were so incomplete that they were certainly just background rubbish on the site.

Table 5:2 Vessel distribution by percentage
sherd count

Vessel	Sherd count	% Sherd count
Cooking pot/jar	1496	68.43
Narrow-necked jar	174	7.96
Flagon	2	0.09
Beaker	126	5.76
Bowl	46	2.10
Dish	71	3.25
Amphora	6	0.2
Mortarium	9	0.41
Others/uncertain	256	11.71

110

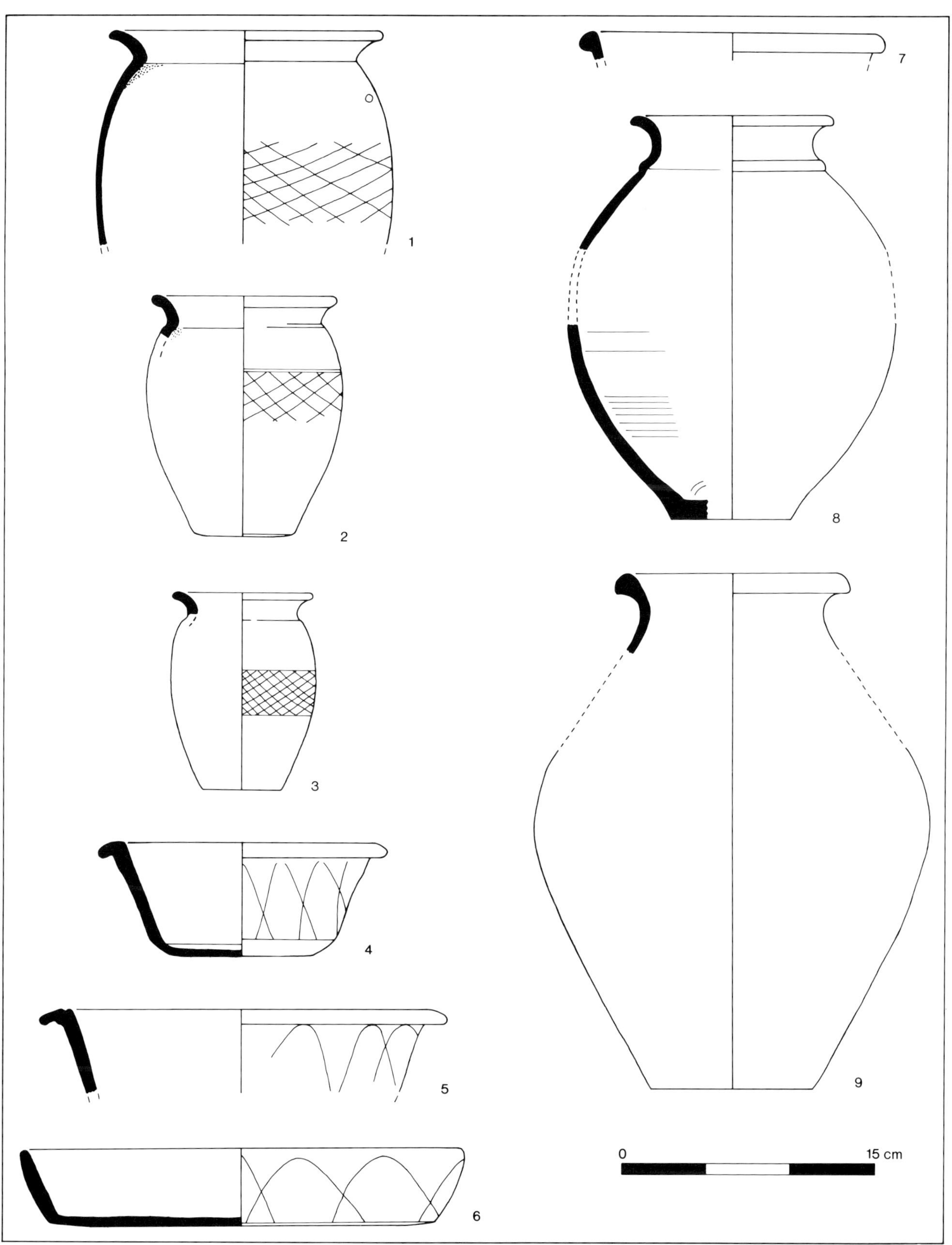

*Figure 5:9 Low Borrowbridge (**11318**), Roman pottery type series 1*

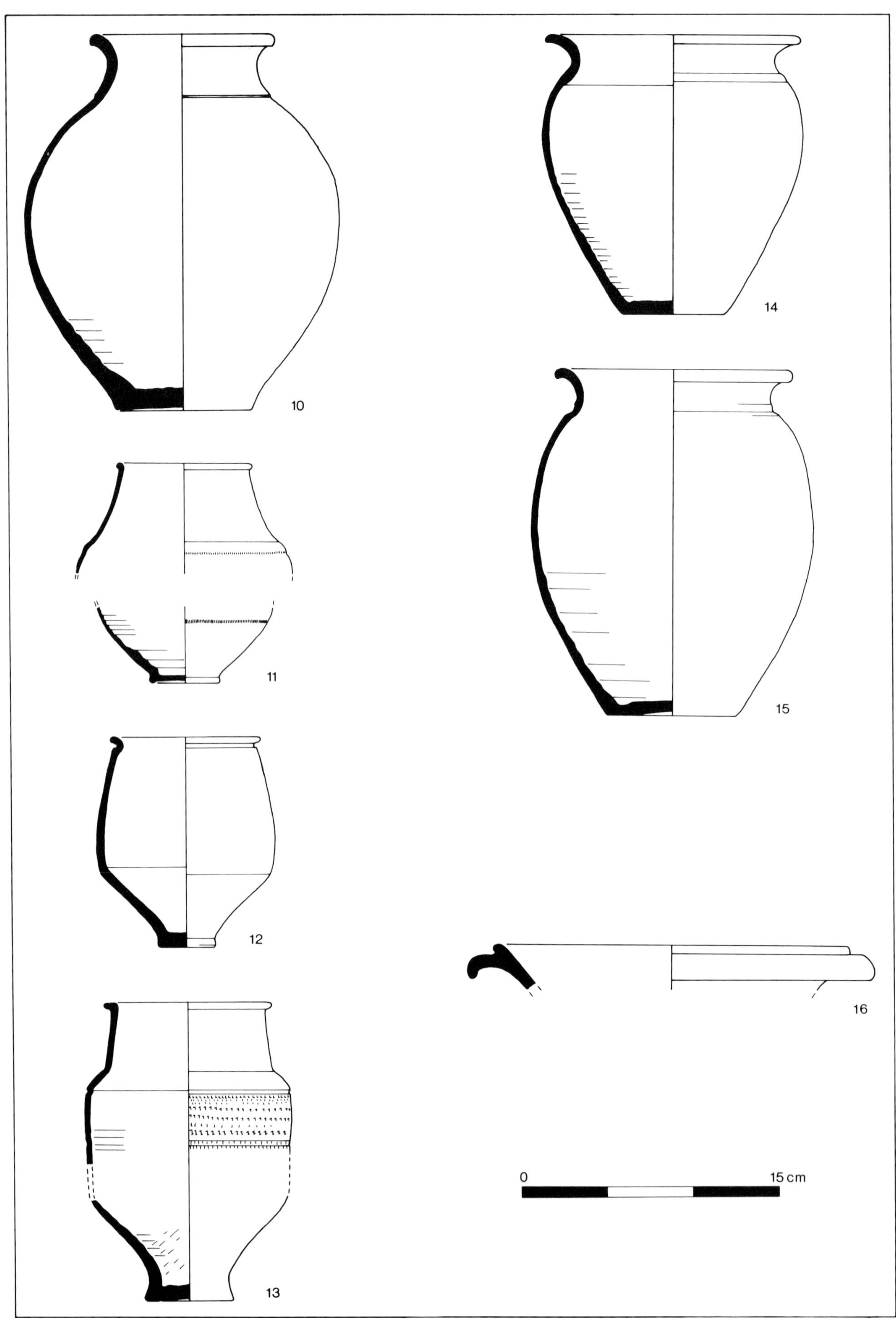

*Figure 5:10 Low Borrowbridge (**11318**), Roman pottery type series 2*

The Roman coins

David Shotter

Three Roman coins were found, all *aes* denominations and all badly corroded and exhibiting advanced degrees of wear.

Ae *As*, Trajan, AD 103–117,
very worn and fragmentary
LBB91, *1000/1830/1*

Ae *Sestertius*, Trajan, AD 103–111,
very worn and fragmentary
LBB92, *502/2004/1*

Ae *Sestertius*, Hadrian, AD 117–138,
very worn
LBB91, *13/1833/1*

The worn state of all of these coins would indicate that, despite their relatively early issue dates, all three were probably lost or deposited in the first half of the third century.

The *sestertii* of Trajan and Hadrian were recovered from cremation burials, and may therefore represent the fare given to the deceased to pay for his journey across the River Styx to the Underworld. The *as* of Trajan was recovered from an unstratified context.

The copper alloy

Christine Howard-Davis

Twenty-three fragments of copper alloy, probably representing eight objects, were recovered. All were fragmentary and in poor condition. With the exception of some small, undiagnostic fragments of sheet copper (1), which were derived from the disturbed upper surface of sand layer *505*, and a *ligula* or cosmetic spoon (2), from the subsoil surface, all the fine metalwork derived from cremation burials (Fig 5:11). It has not been possible to determine whether the objects were burnt on the pyre prior to deposition or deposited as grave goods, although either is likely, but the crumpled nature of 8 and 10 might suggest that the box to which they were attached was no longer complete on deposition.

The *ligula*, or cosmetic spoon (2), presumably originally derived from a burial, although it was recovered from a disturbed context. While it is a common Roman type, such objects are not often found in graves (Philpott 1991, 182). Its presence presumably implies the inclusion of a favoured possession in the burial, either the spoon itself or the perfume or cosmetics it is thought such spoons were used to dispense.

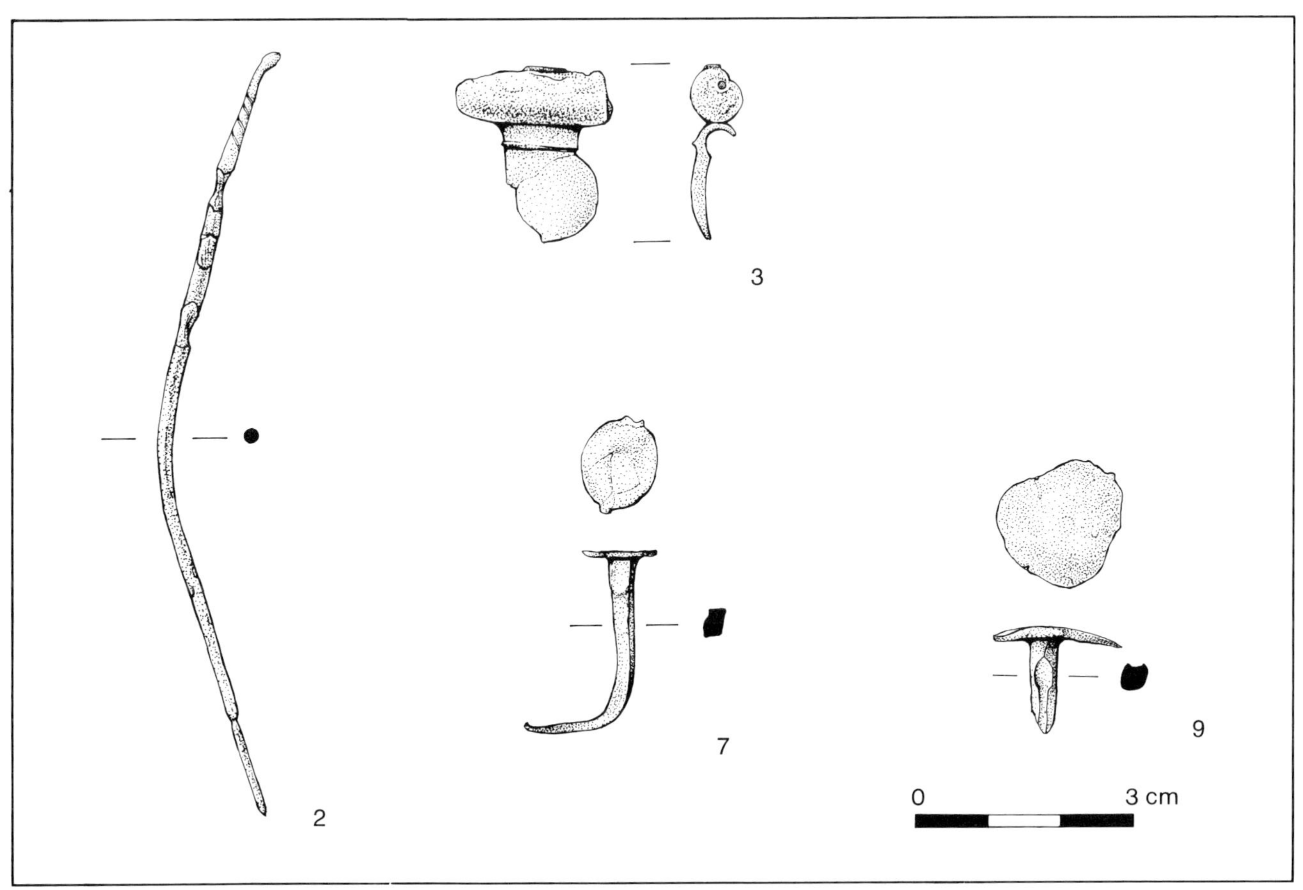

*Figure 5:11 Low Borrowbridge (**11318**), copper alloy*

There are fragments of three brooches (3–5), all presumably deposited in the course of cremation burials. Whilst it is impossible to identify 4 with confidence, 3 is a knee brooch and 5 a crossbow brooch, both common types with wide distributions from the late second century onwards. The deposition of personal objects within cremation burials is markedly less common in the north of England than elsewhere (Philpott 1991, 128, table 24), reflecting the general tendency in this area to furnish burials only sparsely, if at all. Brooches, however, are amongst the more frequently found items, and although in some contexts (especially temples) the deposition of brooches does hold a ritual significance (A Olivier pers comm), in this instance they do not appear to have done so.

It is widely accepted that corpses were dressed when cremated, and thus it is highly likely that a fastening device, such as a brooch, possibly a favourite, would be used amongst the clothing, and in consequence collected up with the ashes for burial. Alternatively it is possible that mourners may have added a small token of their own to the grave. It has been suggested that, as an object used for joining items, such deposition may have an opposite symbolism, representing relationships torn asunder by death (Olivier 1991, 401).

The remainder of the objects were either nails (6, 7, 9), sheet (8) or a combination of the two (10). No specific explanation can be given for the solitary nails from Cremations *80* (6) and *87* (7), although the fact that both were clenched implies that they had been used in joinery. The group of nails and sheet (8–10) from Cremation *536* are almost certainly the last remnant of a small box or casket. The fragments of crumpled sheet appear originally to have been carefully cut and squared, suggesting that they are casket furniture, possibly a lock plate,

nailed to the box. Caskets are a relatively common feature of cremation burials. There is no evidence from the grave to indicate whether the box contained the cremated bone or was a separate addition. There appears, however, to have been little or no bone from the grave which, along with the poor condition of the box furniture, might imply the latter.

The ironwork

Christine Howard-Davis

All the fragments of iron recovered were in very poor condition and all identification was made from X-ray (Fig 5:12). Almost all the group was made up of typically Roman hand-forged nails, of relatively small size, and conical-headed hobnails. Both are extremely common and effectively undatable types.

The nails are most likely to have been included in funeral biers, or in the construction of pyres, and to have become incorporated with the remains when they were collected after cremation. Many were clenched, clearly indicating their use in carpentry. One of the larger nails (331), however, from Cremation *240*, appears to bear mineralised wood impressions, implying that it was deposited whilst still lodged in a timber.

The presence of hobnails in most of the graves (*see above*) is likely to have resulted from the practice of cremating the deceased fully clad, including their shoes. The obvious large groups would suggest pairs of nailed shoes deliberately placed in the grave as a symbolic recollection of the journey to the Underworld.

Two fragments of hinge were recognised from layer *15* (91) and findspot *16* (436). Neither of these

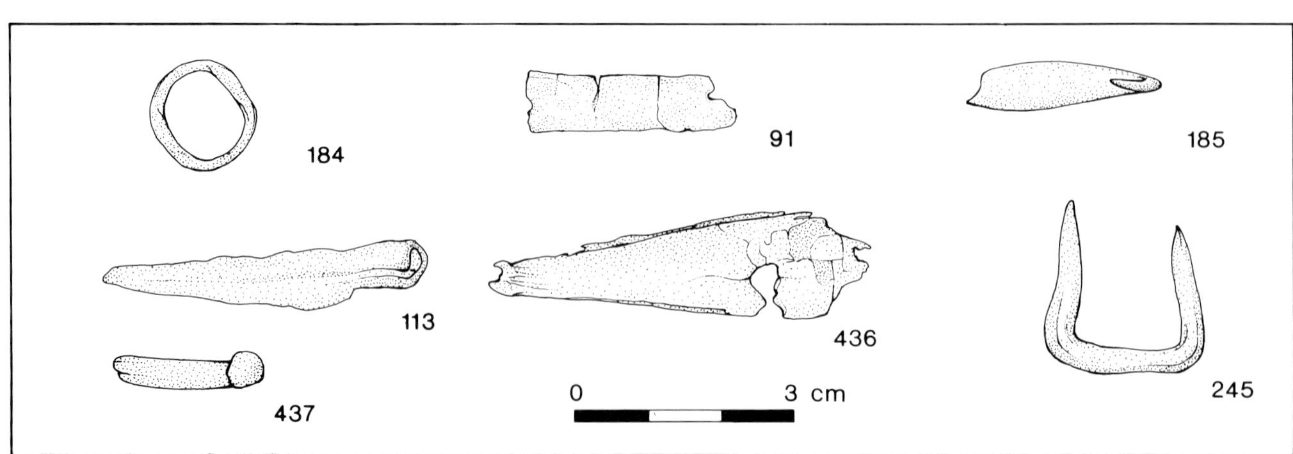

*Figure 5:12 Low Borrowbridge (**11318**), ironwork*

derives from burial contexts, but it is likely that both came from simple lidded wooden boxes, like that from the late grave at Burgh Castle (Johnson 1983, 74, fig 32.37), which may well have served as coffins.

Cremation *109* produced a fragmentary hook (185) and a small diameter ring (184), which may have served together as a simple catch. The fill (*169*) of Cremation *178* produced a staple or smallish carpenter's dog (245), used for joining timbers, again likely to derive from a box or coffin.

The lead

Christine Howard-Davis

A single small fragment of partially melted lead wire was recovered from Pit *284*. It presumably derives from pyre debris.

The bead necklace

Christine Howard-Davis

Seventy beads were recovered, 67 of them deriving from a single necklace; the remaining three were found within two cremation burials. The necklace was found in the fill of a possible inhumation burial (Pit *301*) and is likely to represent a small deposit of grave goods (Fig 5:13).

Most of the beads were loose when excavated, but a small number, cemented by iron panning, retained some evidence of the arrangement of the necklace. Impressions of three rows of beads were identified. It is possible that the rows represent nothing more than a single strand, looped round several times. However, the symmetrical arrangement might imply a three-strand (or more) necklace. The outer row was the best preserved, alternating black jet beads with small cuboid or globular beads of green and blue glass. The middle row appeared to be exclusively dark grey turned shale segmented beads, and the third, inner row included blue and gold-in-glass segmented beads.

The necklace comprised jet, shale, and glass beads in a range of forms. The use of jet and shale is regarded as typical of the third and fourth centuries. Raw jet was available at Whitby on the Yorkshire coast, which seems to have been the primary source during the Roman period, and jet beads of varying types are widely known. Those from Low Borrowbridge are relatively plain, turned cylinder beads. The Romans are known to have used shale derived from a number of sources, the best documented being the Kimmeridge oil shales of Dorset, although there is no doubt that the shales and cannel coals of the North East coalfields were also used. The shale beads (26–41) were probably all originally identical, around 8mm long, and turned to produce a row of four biconical segments. Although many are now broken, the uneven nature of the breaks suggests that the beads were not deliberately broken into segments, as was often the case with glass segmented beads.

Many of the glass beads are common types, small globular, cuboid, or biconical beads in blue and green glass, likewise dating mainly to the third century. There are, however, a number of unusual beads amongst the group. The gold-in-glass and white metal-in-glass segmented beads (14–25) are an uncommon type, although widely distributed. Guido has summarised the work of Boon, noting that segmented beads of this type are widely distributed though rare, and have appeared in contexts from the late second to the fourth centuries (they are most common around this time), reappearing again in the medieval period (Boon 1977; Guido 1978, 93). It is likely that they are imports and were probably made principally in Egypt and the Near East. This does not necessarily suggest that those from Low Borrowbridge were imported direct, but that they reached the settlement by a more roundabout trade. Neither Boon nor Guido mentions biconical beads, but there are two (19, 20) amongst the group.

Black glass beads are likewise uncommon; there are three (42–4) from the necklace. Two (43, 44) are rare types, especially 43, a black cylinder bead which can be paralleled at the fourth century cemetery of Lankhills, near Winchester (Clarke 1979). Bead 45, a blue biconical glass bead with a prominent red and white chevron, is another uncommon form, likely to have originated in North Africa or the eastern Mediterranean, and dating to the late third or fourth century.

There are two identical amber glass cylinder beads (68, 69) from Cremation *30*. They have not been burnt and thus derive from an object placed directly in the grave. Amber glass cylinder beads, like the black glass one mentioned above, are uncommon.

Finally, a single blue cuboid bead (70) similar to that from the necklace (63) was found in Cremation *303*.

The tombstone

David Shotter

The tombstone, which was found face down, is made from a sandstone block, and measures 0.94 x 0.39 x 0.17m (Fig 5:14). Although worked on the front and sides, the stone was left rough-

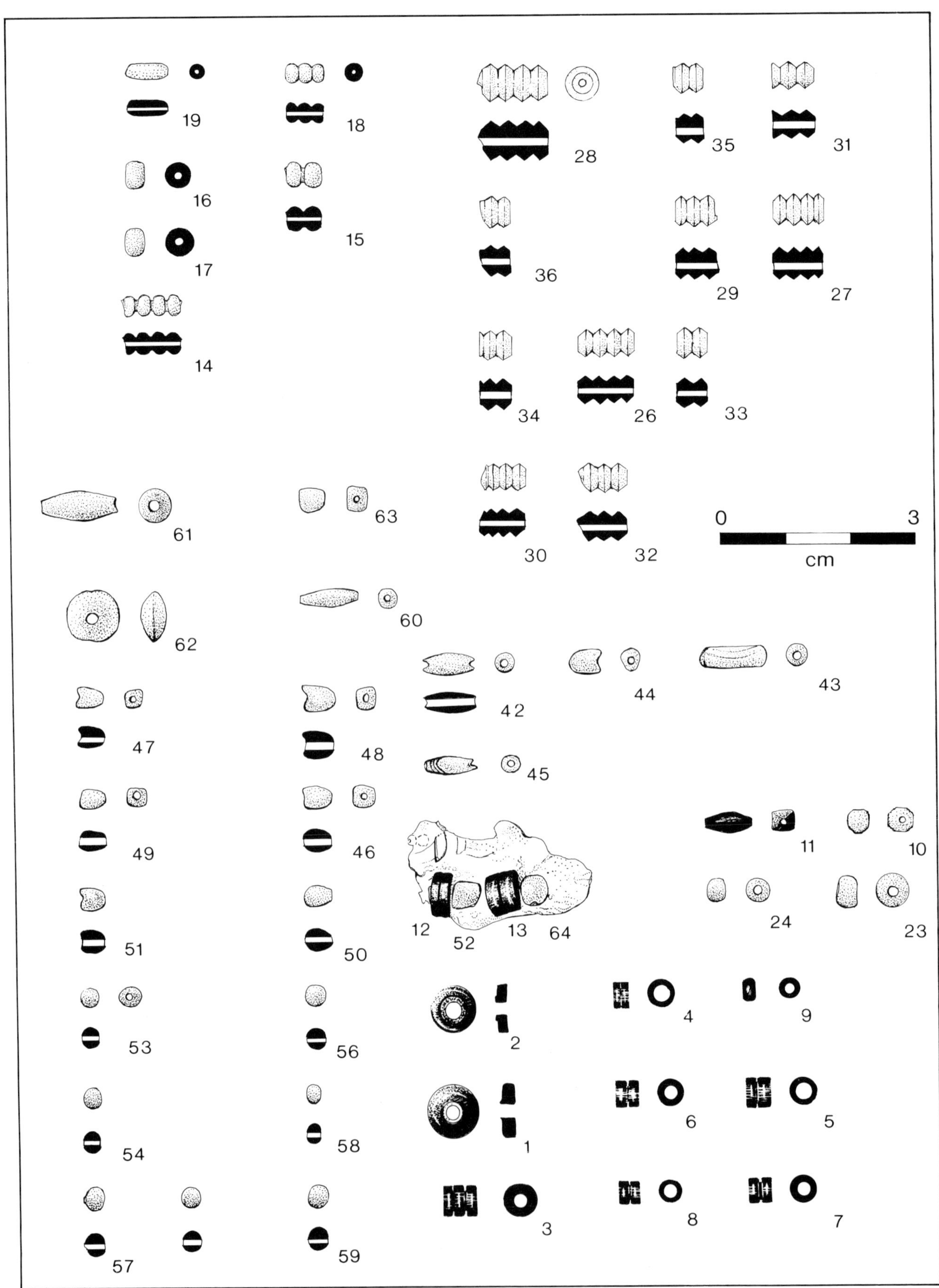

*Figure 5:13 Low Borrowbridge (**11318**), bead necklace*

116

*Figure 5:14 Low Borrowbridge (**11318**), tombstone of Aelia Sentica*

hewn on the back, indicating that it was placed in a position in which the back would not be seen: it may have been built into a wall or laid on the ground.

The tombstone consists of an inscribed panel, measuring 0.51 x 0.25m, beneath a stereotyped female bust contained within a panel which itself consists of three adjacent convex mouldings, creating the shape of a clover leaf. This should be taken as a variation of the gable-end of an *aedicula* tombstone.

The text is inscribed in letters of good quality: the eight lines are arranged in two groups of four, separated by a gap which balances that at the end of the inscription. The majority of lines consist of seven letters with an intermediate space, with the exception of line 4, in which the age of the deceased has to be crammed in to the detriment of the symmetry of the inscription.

The text:

D M
AELIA SE
NTICA VI
XITAN XXXV
AVREL VE
RVLVS CO
NIVGI KA
RISSI ME

*D(is) M(anibus)/Aelia Se/ntica Vi/xit an(nos) xxxv/
Aurel(ius) Ve/rulus Co/niugi Ka/rissime*

'To the Gods of the Underworld: *Aelia Sentica* lived for thirty-five years. *Aurelius Verulus* set up this stone for his dear wife.'

Similar sentiments are expressed in RIB 612 from Burrow-in-Lonsdale (Edwards 1971, 17–23).

Neither of these individuals is known from elsewhere, although the *cognomen Verulus* (diminutive of *Verus*) is not uncommon (Birley 1979, 76); nor is there any indication of the profession of *Verulus*, whether military or civilian. However, the ability to purchase a tombstone indicates a reasonable degree of family prosperity, perhaps matched by the ownership of a burial plot. The gentile names, *Aelius* and *Aurelius*, are relatively common, indicating enfranchisement in the period of the second and early third centuries. Indeed the *Constitutio Antoniniana*, Caracalla's decree of AD 212 granting universal enfranchisement, will have brought citizenship to many provincials, giving them Caracalla's family name of *Aurelius*.

This would suggest the likelihood of a third century date for the tombstone: so too would the use of the abbreviation, *D M*, for *Dis Manibus*. A further indication of such a date is the use of the gentile *nomen* (*Aurelius*) and *cognomen* (*Verulus*), omitting the *praenomen*. Similarly, if *Aurelius Verulus* was a soldier, then his ability to have and refer to a legal wife (*coniunx*) would suggest a date later than Septimius Severus' (AD 193–211) reforms of the army, which included a serving soldier's right to contract a legal marriage.

Only one other inscription has previously been recorded from the site (RIB 756; Collingwood and Wright 1965); this was apparently a cavalryman's tombstone, found approximately one mile south of the fort, near the line of the Roman road (Birley 1947, 9), not far from the cemetery.

The cremated human bone

Jacqueline I McKinley

The cremated bone from 65 contexts was examined. The assemblage included bone from 17 urned, and a further 21 probable unurned cremations. Material from the remainder of the contexts represented redeposited and unstratified bone.

The site had been badly damaged by ploughing, which had led to the truncation of many features, and in turn had disturbed many of the cremations, leading to a high background level of cremated bone, dispersed throughout most of the contexts over the site. In general bone was recovered by hand. Soil samples were taken from many of the pits but few of these were sieved.

The material from each context was passed through a stack of sieves of 10mm, 5mm, and 2mm mesh size. The weight of bone collected from each sieve, and maximum fragment sizes for skull and long bone, illustrates the degree of bone fragmentation. Identifiable bone was separated for further examination, divided into the following categories; skull, axial, upper and lower limb. The percentage of identifiable bone from each area can be used to illustrate any deliberate bias in the skeletal elements collected for burial (McKinley 1989; 1994a).

The age of immature individuals was assessed by the stages of tooth development and eruption (Van Beek 1983), ossification and epiphyseal bone fusion (Gray 1977, McMinn and Hutchings 1985). The age of adults was assessed from the stage of epiphyseal bone and cranial suture fusion (McMinn and Hutchings 1985, Webb *et al* 1985), and the general degree of degenerative changes to the bone. Ranges, rather than an absolute age in years, are used in view of the difficulties involved in the accurate

118

assessment of age for adults over 25–30 years (Table 5:3).

Table 5:3 The ranges adopted

	Years
Infant	0–4
Juvenile	5–12
Subadult	13–18
Adult	18+
Young adult	18–25
Mature adult	25–40
Older adult	40+

The sex of adults was determined by examination of the sexually dimorphic traits of the skeleton (Bass 1987), including maximum cranial vault thickness measure '1a' according to Gejvall (1981) (*see also* McKinley 1993a). Three levels of reliability have been used (*see microfiche table, pages 384–5*) although a more precise classification is not regarded as possible because of the paucity of information available in some cases, and the unclear or contradictory dimorphism encountered in others.

Fifty-one of the 65 contexts yielding bone contained identifiable fragments. Bone from the remaining contexts was all human, but allowed little other comment. Only contexts containing identifiable bone are included.

Full details of all the identified bone are presented in the archive report (*on microfiche, see Appendix 2*). The data include: variation in colour from the normal buff-white for individual bones; adhering substances, for example iron; detailed descriptions of pathological lesions; measurements other than those in the archive report; the presence of cremated animal bone; pyre goods recognised in the course of examination.

All the bone, from both urned and unurned burials, was in a good state of preservation. There was no evidence for bone erosion during burial. The bone was almost uniformly buff-white in colour, indicative of efficient cremation with full oxidation of the bone (Shipman *et al* 1984, McKinley 1989).

Only one of the 17 urned cremations (*156*), was apparently undisturbed, a further six were relatively complete although the cinerary vessels had been slightly damaged; all others were badly damaged by ploughing. All 17 of the contexts containing unurned cremations were truncated to some extent. The very small quantities of bone recovered from the majority of these contexts, <50g in most, and as little as 1g in two, would suggest they were either very severely truncated or that their status as buri-als is questionable. Ten of the unurned cremations fall into this latter category. Thirteen contexts contained redeposited bone, two were unstratified and one, which contained little or no cremated human bone, may represent a dump of pyre debris or, less likely, a pyre site.

Analysis of bone fragmentation was limited. The disturbed nature of the site has undoubtedly led to increased bone fragmentation and thus, with regard to the unurned cremations, comment on the present state of the bone can have little validity. Only Cremation *156*, which was undisturbed, can provide a reliable indicator of fragment size. In this case 72% of the bone was >10mm, and maximum fragment sizes were 43mm for skull and 55mm for long bone. From the other, relatively undisturbed urns the average percentage of bone fragments >10mm was 54.4%, with the average maximum fragment sizes being 29.4mm for skull and 42.4mm for long bone. It should be noted that many factors can affect the size of cremated bone fragments and all figures should be regarded as post-excavation fragment sizes only, not fragments at time of deposition (McKinley 1994b). Fragment size from these burials would not suggest any deliberate breakage of the bone prior to burial.

The quantity of bone which appears to have been recovered for burial after cremation was in general very small. The one undisturbed cremation (*156, 400*) contained only 92.3g of bone. This represents only 5.8% of the minimum total weight of bone expected from an adult cremation (McKinley 1989, 1994a), and even anticipating the maximum bone-to-dust loss in cremation (McKinley 1993b) the amount is still only *c*8%.

The greatest quantity of bone recovered was from Cremation *527* with 498.9g (maximum 31.2%) which is within the average expected range (McKinley 1989, 1993b, 1994a, 1994b). This was, however, a notable exception. The average weight of bone from the relatively undisturbed urned cremations (excluding the two containing infants) was 179.1g. Only 14 cremations had over 50g of bone, with only six of those being in excess of 100g.

Eighteen individuals were identified from the cremation burials, with a probable four more, though the latter were represented by <50g of bone (*ie c*3% of the minimum total weight of bone expected from an adult cremation—*see* McKinley 1989, 1993b). Nine other burials examined contained <12g of bone (*ie* <0.8% expected weight), which was considered insufficient to designate the presence of an individual burial. They are divided by age as shown in Table 5:4.

Table 5:4 Number of individuals in each age group

	No. of individuals
Infant	4
Older subadult	1
Subadult/adult	2 (including 1?)
Adult	8 (including 2?)
Young/mature adult	1
Mature adult	1
Older mature/older adult	5 (including 1?)

Only four of the cremations produced sufficient evidence to allow the sex of the individual to be ascertained; two probable and one possible female and one probable male were identified. All were mature or older adults.

The paucity of demographic information, resulting to a large extent from the small quantities of bone present in the cremations, precludes comment, especially since the full extent of the cemetery remains unknown. It can, however, be suggested that age and sex were not obvious factors affecting the mode of burial or its location within the cemetery.

Few pathological lesions were noted. Osteophytes and exostoses probably result from age-related wear and tear. The cysts are of unknown aetiology and may have resulted from a number of conditions.

Fragments of cremated animal bone were noted in one unurned and two urned cremations, as well as in one context likely to have contained redeposited material. Species included bird (domestic fowl), pig/sheep (identified by size), and horse/cattle (identified by tooth enamel). The presence of animal bone in cremation burials is not uncommon in the Romano-British period, and it was, for example, noted in up to 48% of the cremations from St Stephen's cemetery, St Albans (McKinley forthcoming). Domestic fowl and pig appear to be the most common species encountered.

Other pyre goods recovered from the cremations include a worked antler peg and fragments of a decorated antler/bone plaque. Fragments of iron nail were found adhering to bone in some burials; this is most likely to have occurred after burial, as a result of corrosion. The inclusion of valued objects on the pyre would emphasis the importance of the cremation ritual in the disposal of the dead.

The very small quantities of cremated bone apparently deposited as burials are a notable feature of the site. The cremation pits varied in depth between 0.05m and 0.45m with an average depth of 0.20m, the surviving depth reflecting the level of disturbance. It is thus likely that some bone, at least, was lost from a number of the pits as a result. If, however, the bone had been placed in the bottom of the pits, as appears to be the case in the majority of unurned cremation burials, most of the bone would have remained *in situ*. An extensive loss of bone through subsequent disturbance, as might be suggested by the quantities recovered from these pits, would imply that bone was mixed or scattered through the fill rather than a single homogeneous deposit. Bone from these fills was hand recovered rather than sieved, but it is unlikely that the loss caused by this method would have amounted to more than a few grams, since large amounts would not easily have been overlooked, even in difficult excavation conditions.

Complete recovery of bone from the pyre for burial appears to have been rare, if not unknown, during all periods of use of the ritual in Britain. Weights of bone from undisturbed single adult cremations from other sites have ranged from 117.2g to 3105.1g (McKinley 1994b). Why so much more of the remains of one individual should be collected for burial than another is unclear. It may be related to rite or status, or simply to the inclination of the collector. Whatever the reason, the fact remains that from the one undisturbed cremation at Low Borrowbridge *c*90% of the cremated human remains were not included in the burial. Even from pits with a remaining depth of 0.20-0.45m the maximum quantity of bone recovered was 160.1g, with most less than 100g.

Bone in the urned cremations had not been separated from other pyre debris prior to burial. A few charcoal flecks were noted in some urn fills, but were limited to the upper levels and had probably filtered in with other soil from the pit during burial. There is no evidence for the urns having been covered at the time of deposition.

All the pit fills included some quantity of pyre debris: charcoal, pyre goods, burnt stone, etc. Some cremated bone, usually only a few grams, was recovered from the pit fills of four urned cremations. In all but one of these (*156*) the bone may have been spill from damaged urns, and in Cremation *156* the small amount of bone within the pit fill may have been included with other pyre debris. The sides of one pit (*186*) may have been scorched, perhaps indicating the deposition of hot pyre debris. These features have been noted in other cremation burials including Romano-British, *eg* Baldock (Burleigh and Stevenson forthcoming). The presence of pyre debris, particularly hot deposits, would imply the close proximity of the pyre site to the place of burial.

Excavation at other Roman northern frontier zone

military sites has produced cremation burials with some similar characteristics to those noted at Low Borrowbridge, *ie* mostly unurned cremation burials in pits containing much pyre debris and small amounts of bone. At Petty Knowes, for instance (Charlton and Mitcheson 1984), the burials were undisturbed but all contained relatively small amounts of bone spread through the pit fills and mixed with other pyre debris.

Although the number of excavated sites in the North is not great, such emerging similarities might suggest a common rite. The paucity of bone presents interesting scope for speculation. Were these deposits, in the true sense of the word, burials? A burial, by implication, involves the deposition of human remains. When 80–90% or more of those remains are absent can a deposit still be termed a burial? There is no doubt that the deposits at Low Borrowbridge are associated with a ritual deposition of the dead, involving cremation.

It is likely that some bone may have been lost in post-depositional disturbance, but the small quantities of bone recovered from many of the pit fills, where it was mixed with other pyre debris, may reflect what was left on the pyre site after the bulk of the bone had been collected. These deposits may represent some form of memorial, the actual burial being elsewhere. If some of the individuals using the cemetery were non-indigenous military personnel, could not their remains have been returned to their place of origin?

The palaeoenvironmental evidence

Jacqueline P Huntley

Bulk soil samples of various volumes were submitted to the Biological Laboratory, Department of Archaeology at the University of Durham, for technical processing and subsequent assessment of any biological material in them. Given that the site was dry the samples were floated with the flots being collected over 500µ. A few of the samples were so small that they were simply wet sieved to 500µ. The residues were sorted to 2mm and notes made of their animal bone content.

All of the flots were examined under a binocular stereomicroscope at magnifications of up to x50 and notes made of their constituents and any seeds that were present (Table 5:5). The material sorted from the residues consisted of small fragments of burnt bone and fragments of iron and the occasional piece of pot, for all of which no further work is possible, since they are too comminuted for identification; they are not from small mammals. The flots were predominantly tiny (<20ml) and, not surprisingly, few seeds were present in any of them. The only species clearly attributable to human usage was the pea (*Pisum sativum*) from context *506*. The single grain of oats (*Avena*) may indicate food but may have been a seed from wild oats. A few weed seeds were recovered, mainly from docks (*Rumex* sp), although single occurrences of black bindweed (*Polygonum convolvulus*), buttercups (*Ranunculus repens* type), and small grasses (Gramineae) were recorded.

Charcoal fragments were present in most of the samples although always as tiny pieces only. Some were clearly from oak (*Quercus*) and others from a fine-grained ring-diffuse species such as alder (*Alnus*), hazel (*Corylus*), or birch (*Betula*). There was no obvious dominance of any species and the pieces were too fragmentary to make interpretations possible.

From the very limited evidence available, it is suggested that local wood was used for the funeral pyres.

Table   5:5 Details of samples processed and sorted

Cut	Fill	Sample	Volume processed (ml)	Residue material in >2mm fraction	Botanical comments
Enclosures					
56	57	1345	6800	Burnt bone	No seeds
139	140	1199	2300	Burnt bone, iron	One oat
161	160	1274	5200	Burnt/cremated bone, iron	Weed seeds
Large pits					
155	147	1255	6200	Burnt bone	Weed seeds
300	271	1738	4000	Burnt bone, iron	Weed seeds
Cremation pits					
87	86	1113	2100	Burnt bone, iron, pot	Weed seeds
134	135	1201	4700	Burnt bone, iron	One pea, one dock
535	506	2112	2000	Burnt bone, iron	No seeds

Nick Hair, Christine Howard-Davis

Discussion

The lack of horizontal stratigraphic relationships, together with the great similarity of many of the ditch and oval pit fills, has made detailed phasing of the site difficult. However, a number of conclusions can be drawn, and the sequence of three broad phases of activity on the site can be somewhat refined.

Phase 1

There is some indication that activity to the mid third century AD, before the site was flooded, can be subdivided. The ditched enclosures were the earliest significant features on the site. It is likely that the two large oval pits that lie within enclosures are contemporary with them.

All the enclosures except one were rectilinear, often almost square, and were aligned in rows along the cardinal points of the compass. Some contained possible entrances, although there was no common position. These enclosures almost certainly represent funerary monuments although, since they are badly damaged by ploughing, it is now impossible to determine their original appearance.

There appears to be a chronological succession, with three enclosures obviously preceding the others. It can be suggested, however, that some of the later ones were added to, rather than replaced, the original enclosures. Thus, whilst most enclosures were single cells, at least three appear to have had up to three conjoined cells.

The ditches, some straight, others curving, are likely to have been more or less contemporary with the enclosures. Their profiles and fills were identical, and several seem to have been joined, at one end, to extant enclosures. Occasionally they appear to have been cut by enclosure ditches, perhaps suggesting an element of renewal. There is no evidence to date the period of use of either the enclosures or the other ditches, but material from the fills suggests that they filled up over a period between the late second and mid third centuries AD. This range can be extended slightly for the enclosures not covered by silts.

It is difficult to assign a precise function to the enclosures, but it is likely that they served to define burial plots. Only two are directly associated with probable burials, but it can be suggested that if these ditches defined, and provided material for, small barrows, evidence for many of the inhumations would have been destroyed by ploughing. It is not impossible that the corpse was laid on the ground surface and the barrow constructed over it: extremely acid soils would then have destroyed all trace of the burial. The marked similarity of the ditch fills to the natural subsoil may indeed be accounted for if small, inherently unstable barrows, made largely of heaped gravel, had been allowed to collapse back into the surrounding ditches. The nature of the subsoil may have made this a fairly rapid phenomenon, effectively precluding the build-up of obvious silt lines within the fills.

The two probable burials (no skeletal material remains) associated with the enclosures are similar. Both contain a layer of cobbles within the fill which may have acted as packing or a cover for the corpse. Pottery from the fills, which can be assumed to have been deposited as the burial pits were backfilled, shortly after burial, suggests a date in the late second or early third century.

Square ditched burial enclosures are a well-known type, closely linked with some Iron Age groups in North East England (Stead 1991) and there is no doubt that in some of the large Iron Age cemeteries of northern England burial continued well into the Roman period. Other Romano-British cemeteries have produced enclosures, although these usually encompass a number of burials, for example Skeleton Green (Partridge 1981, 246) and Winchester (Clarke 1979). Stone built square mausoleums are also known, for example that at Skorden Brea, Corbridge (Gillam and Davies 1961), although they resemble the Low Borrowbridge enclosures in little but shape. Petty Knowes in Northumberland (Charlton and Mitcheson 1984), however, appears to provide a closer parallel, with rectilinear enclosures and small barrows associated with individual burials.

It is possible that the enclosures never contained barrows and simply delineated a special area. The widespread, low-level occurrence of cremated bone could, without too much speculation, be seen as the result of scattering, rather than formally burying, the remains of the deceased within a family plot. Whilst not easy to recognise, this practice has been suggested at Derby Racecourse, where the area within a walled enclosure appeared to have been scattered with charcoal and calcined bone from either disturbed or deliberately scattered cremations (Wheeler 1985, 231). In such a case the ditches could be suggested as bedding trenches for small hedges or similar, marking each plot. The acidic soil conditions, however, precluded palaeobotanic investigation of this possibility.

There is some indication of a chronological division between the ditched enclosures and the majority of the oval pits. Seven large pits appear to have been deliberately cut into the infilled ditches of enclosures, often across the corners; an eighth was cut into one of the other associated ditches. It is likely that all were inhumation graves, although the evidence was not conclusive. They were similar in size and shape to the two discussed above, although none contained obvious stone packing. One, however, appeared to have contained a large wooden box, perhaps used as a coffin. Two others contained small but significant artefact assemblages which could be interpreted as grave goods, a miniature Black Burnished ware 1 jar of late third century date, and a group of 67 beads from a single necklace, also of third century date or later. Most of these pits were located towards the centre of the site, and were sealed only by topsoil. One, however, to the east of the site, was sealed by river silts, implying that some, if not all, of these graves were constructed prior to the cemetery flooding. One grave lay near, and parallel to, one of the more isolated graves discussed below, which might suggest that the difference between them is spatial, rather than chronological.

An anomalous group of three cremations appeared to overlap the two subphases. All were beneath the silt; one was isolated, one was cut by a large pit, and the third cut a large pit, suggesting that all were roughly contemporary with Phase 1 activity, and represent slight overlapping of the two burial rites. In all other cases stratigraphic evidence indicates that the inhumation burials clearly preceded the cremations.

A further six large pits did not appear to be associated with enclosures but are also likely to be graves. One of these pits also appeared to contain evidence for a wooden box or coffin, whilst two others were lined with stones, like those located in the centres of the enclosures. In general these pits produced few artefacts, although one may have contained several pairs of nailed shoes as well as a Nene Valley ware beaker. A third century tombstone appeared to be associated with one of the pits, supporting the interpretation of these features as graves. All were covered by the flood silts, clearly indicating that they predated the flooding.

Phase 2

Evidence suggests that the site was badly flooded at some point around the mid to late third century, presumably on an occasion when the River Lune burst its banks. This resulted in the deposition of a substantial depth of river silt over the east and west margins of the site, sealing many of the Phase 1 features. Seemingly, after this episode, the excavated area of the site was used exclusively for cremation burials. The cremations can be divided broadly into two groups: those carefully cut into the upper fills of the enclosure ditches or within the enclosures, and a group which appears to have clustered towards the south-west of the site, away from the main concentration of enclosures. The cemetery is a mixture of urned and unurned burials and also a number of token, almost cenotaph deposits, closely resembling the burials but containing very little cremated bone.

It is questionable whether such deposits can be regarded as true burials, for they might simply represent the disposal of general pyre debris. At Low Borrowbridge, however, it is clear that equal care was taken, whether or not there was an appreciable amount of bone present. The pyre debris was placed in deliberately dug pits with as much care as the larger deposits of bone, probably suggesting more significance in the act of burial than in the body itself, and thereby implying that, however little of the individual was present, these were still intended as burials.

It is clear that the bodies were cremated at a communal site (*ustrina*), following the usual practice, rather than the substantially less common practice of firing the pyre directly over the grave (*bustum*) which appears occasionally in the northern military zone. At Low Borrowbridge the location of the crematorium was not determined, confirming that the cemetery was larger than its excavated extent. The general scatter of pyre debris encountered as small lenses of burnt material within fills (charcoal, odd fragments of burnt pottery, small amounts of bone), might suggest, however, that the burning place was relatively close by.

The cremation burials at Low Borrowbridge can be characterised by their lack of manifest wealth (although this may be illusory, since organic objects of value, burnt on the pyre, would leave no trace) and their apparent lack of concern with the disposal of the complete remains of the deceased. Since the burials contained so little bone, many pyre goods may also not have been collected for burial (McKinley 1994b).

These traits have been noted elsewhere in the North West, at Brough under Stainmore (Jones 1977), Brougham (Andrews *et al* forthcoming), and also at Trentholme Drive, York (Wenham 1968), where they were attributed to the low social status of the occupants. Philpott takes a broader view, suggesting that this apparently spartan, even casual, approach to the dead might rather reflect differing belief, placing 'little emphasis on the physical needs of the deceased in the grave' and probably reflecting the survival of Iron Age religious concepts (Philpott 1991, 47).

Philpott has noted a number of traits common to Romano-British cremation burials in the northern military zone, including a relatively large number of unurned cremations, occasional box or casket burials, the paucity and apparent poverty of grave goods, with few, if any, accessory vessels accompanying the cinerary urn and, importantly, the persistence of the cremation rite into the later third and fourth centuries (Philpott 1991, 47). Low Borrowbridge proves no exception to his observations, appearing as a typical rural cemetery.

Phase 3

It would appear that this part of the cemetery went out of use during the fourth century, since none of the cremation urns are significantly later in date, although fragments of Huntcliff ware (fourth century AD) were found within the fills of several features. Shotter has suggested that low-level occupation of the fort continued to a late date (*see above*), and there is increasing evidence from northern military sites for continuity of occupation long after the formal departure of the Roman army in the early fifth century (Wilmott forthcoming). In this case, it would seem that the later occupants of the fort disposed of their dead elsewhere. Otherwise the cemetery fell into neglect, was presumably forgotten, and the site remained untouched, and probably uncultivated, until a late date.

Conclusions

While the group of rectilinear enclosures from the first phase of activity on the site is almost without doubt of Roman date, the closest regional parallels are the Iron Age cemeteries of East Yorkshire, which date from the later centuries BC to the first century AD (Stead 1991). These are similar in layout, with ordered rows of square enclosures of roughly comparable size, often associated with a small number of round enclosures and even unenclosed graves. They also appear to have been orientated roughly north-south, and contained entrances. It must, however, be stressed that Iron Age cemeteries are not as yet known in the North West and therefore links must remain tenuous.

The cemeteries of East Yorkshire lie specifically within the Arras tradition and it is more than likely that the general similarities between them and the enclosures at Low Borrowbridge result, not from defined cultural affinities, but from the existence of a more general northern Iron Age rite. It is thus reasonable to suppose that the civilian inhabitants of Low Borrowbridge, many presumably of local origin, may well have adapted only slowly to the influence of Rome, incorporating it within, rather than abandoning, their traditional burial practice. Such continuity and admixture of native with Romanised traits is known elsewhere, for instance at Camelon, in Stirlingshire (Breeze *et al* 1976). General 'rural conservatism', the argument often advanced to account for the late survival of the Roman cremation rite in the North, is no less valid as an explanation of the persistence of an Iron Age rite, apparently late into the second century AD.

It is of note that in Arras cemeteries there is often evidence for secondary burials within the enclosure ditch fills, and even later reuse (Anglian burials). Such continued use of individual burial plots is clear at Low Borrowbridge, and appears to persist over a relatively extended period. This preference must indicate either that the graves were marked, or that their location was common knowledge. An obvious explanation would be the existence and exclusive ownership of family plots within the cemetery, and a strong wish to associate the deceased, even after many years, with the primary enclosures. There can be many reasons for this, including the acquisition of status by association, and the arrogation of historical significance, but perhaps family or tribal ties are the most likely (Dent 1983). It can be suggested that a deliberate act, associating even Romanised cremation burials with the earlier enclosures, represents the continuity of local family or tribal groupings well into the Roman period. Within this context the apparent cluster of cremations in the west of the site, away from the enclosures, is of interest. It might be suggested that they represent incomers, soldiers and their families or others attracted to the flourishing civilian settlement, who were without local tribal or family ties. Such newcomers might respect and use a traditional cemetery, especially if suitable land was at a premium, but would be encouraged to use vacant or defunct parts, rather than having access to extant family plots.

It is unlikely that Low Borrowbridge fort was ever much more than an outpost, at best a staging post between larger settlements, thus it is equally unlikely that the local impetus towards Romanisation was ever great. Perhaps the continuity of formalised burial sites, undoubtedly deriving from a native tradition, is a clear indication that even in the later third century, for many of the inhabitants of this part of the Lune gorge, ancestry and tradition were at least as important as the manifest assimilation of Romanised cultural attributes.

To date, relatively few Roman cemeteries have been excavated in the North West. Results from Low Borrowbridge have thus added significantly to the available body of data. Synthesis of the results, especially the succession of grave types has, in addition, contributed towards greater understanding not only of the immediate relationship between fort and local population, but also the vexed problem of Romanisation, or its failure, in the North West and the Northern military zone in general.

6

A POST-ROMAN SETTLEMENT AT FREMINGTON, NEAR BROUGHAM

Tove Oliver, Christine Howard-Davis, Rachel Newman

Following evaluation in 1990, a site on land at Fremington Farm near Brougham (NY 54702880–54772870) was partially excavated in 1991, in advance of pipeline construction. The Brougham area has been a focus of human activity since prehistory, and although fieldwalking and aerial survey revealed no surface evidence within the pipeline corridor, a prehistoric burial cist uncovered during sand quarrying in the nineteenth century (**1008**, Cumbria SMR 2865), if correctly located by the OS, lay directly on the route. A programme of evaluation was therefore instigated to test the archaeological potential here, but geophysical survey revealed only two faint linear anomalies. Two areas were then evaluated by narrow machine-cut trenches, on either side of the modern field boundary. The discovery of several features and finds, including simple handmade pottery and also vessel fragments of Roman date, indicated possible multiperiod remains of domestic, rather than funerary, activity.

In order to define and record this activity more fully, the site (**10014**) was further examined by open area excavation from May to August 1991. Several linear features were subsequently identified, and briefly investigated during pipeline construction, and a further area, some distance to the south, but containing a possible hearth stone, was examined by the rapid response team (**10015**).

Fremington Farm is situated 3km south-east of the medieval town of Penrith, and 1km south-east of the Roman fort and medieval castle at Brougham (Fig 6:1). The excavated site lay in two fields north-east of the farm, 160m south of the former Roman road, now superseded by the A66, near the Countess Pillar (**1005-6**). The general position, at the confluence of the Rivers Eamont and Lowther in the Eden Valley, is a natural meeting point for routes from Stainmore to the east, Ullswater and Keswick to the west, and from Carlisle south through the Lune Valley. Brougham, in consequence, was a major junction of Roman and later roads.

The site, on the western side of the Eden Valley, lies on mixed glacial deposits, manifest locally as sands and gravels, above Permian Penrith Sandstone. The broad fertile valley, at the foot of the Pennine outlier of Cross Fell, is characterised by well-drained, easily worked, sandy soils with good and diverse agricultural potential. Such light soils are, however, subject to an increased risk of wind and water erosion, particularly on valley slopes (Jarvis *et al* 1984), and much of the former arable land in this area is now under permanent pasture.

A Bronze Age burial cist, containing a contracted skeleton associated with a beaker and a food vessel (Cumbria SMR 2865), was discovered in *c*1870 by the farmer at Moorhouse Farm, in a field a short distance south-east of the farmhouse (Harkness 1873–6, 270; Harkness and Stalker 1880, 411–16). Another cist and cinerary urn had previously been discovered in 1869, during ploughing in the next field, itself adjoining the stockyard at Moorhouse Farm (Cumbria SMR 2866). The OS, perhaps mistakenly, mapped the cist at a point north-east of Fremington Farm, and consequently the Cumbria SMR located the find site at NY 54772873, which fell within the pipeline corridor.

These burials were not isolated occurrences: the Brougham area is well known for its wealth of archaeological monuments of prehistoric and Roman date (Fig 6:2). Antiquarian accounts indicate a focus of Romano-British settlement to the east of the fort which Stukeley, in 1725, distinguished from the fort itself when he observed that 'The high ground by the Countess pillar, where most of the inscriptions were found, seems to have been the site of the city', *ie* the civilian settlement outside the fort (Birley 1932, 127).

Rescue excavations on the north side of the A66, during road improvements in 1966–7, confirmed the location of a Roman cemetery, which produced more than 240 cremations and two inhumations (Ministry of Public Building and Works 1967, 12; 1968, 17).

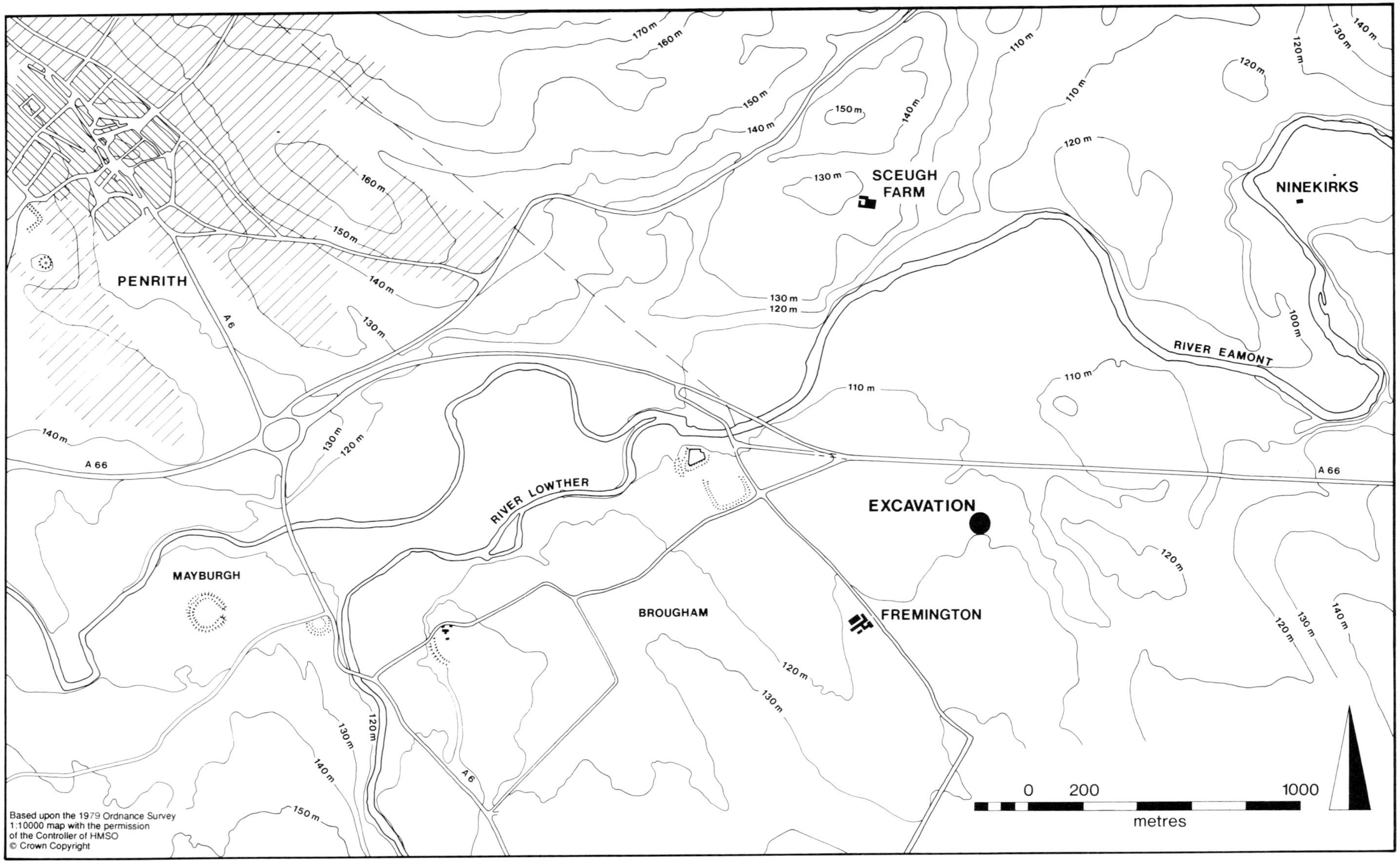

Figure 6:1 The Eamont Valley (1:20,000)

128

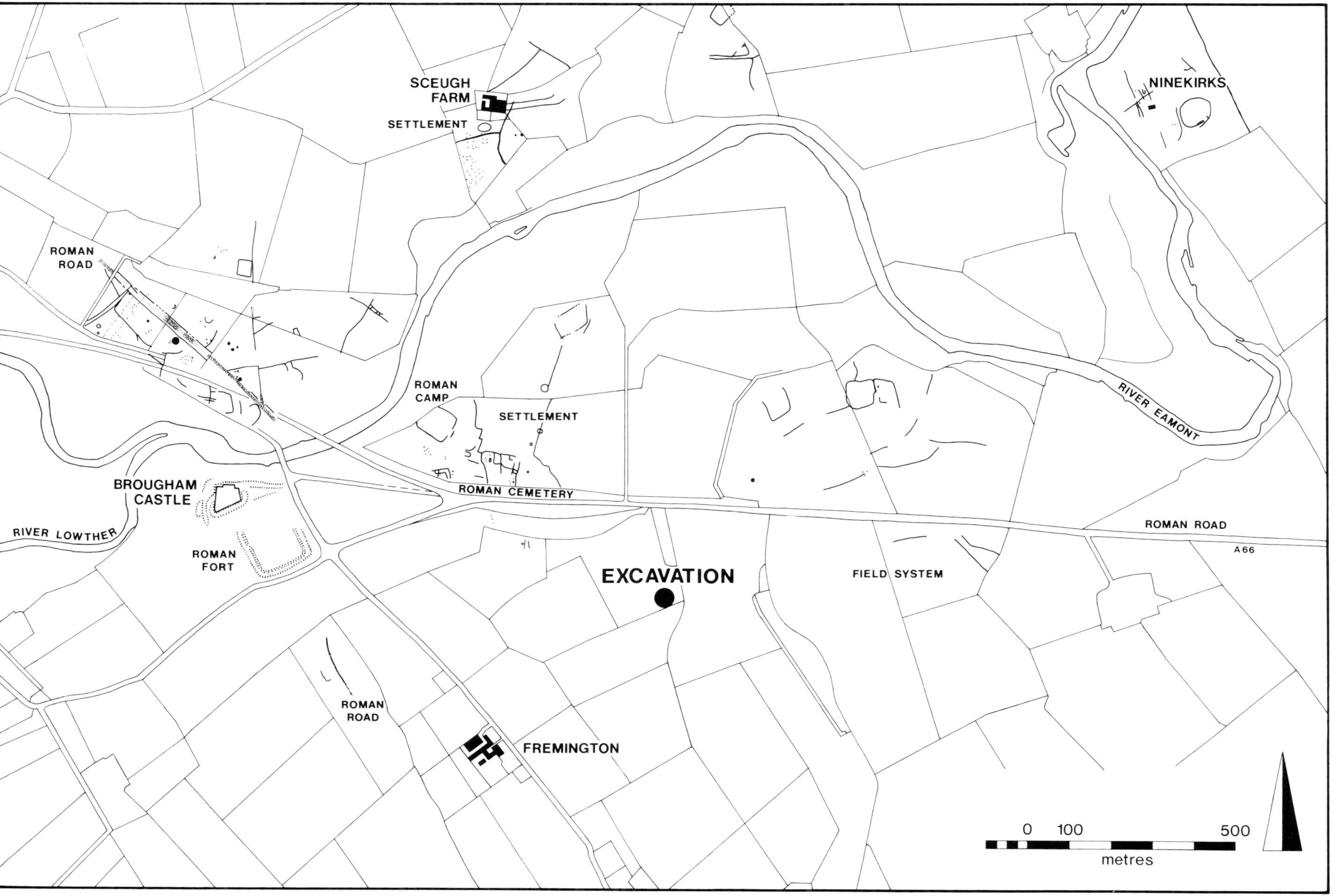

Figure 6:2 The Brougham area (1:12,500)

Intensive aerial photography in the early 1970s recorded cropmarks in the vicinity which appeared to demonstrate that extramural civilian settlement at Brougham was 'widely dispersed and thinly populated' (Higham and Jones 1975, 27), although little formal investigation has taken place to confirm this supposition.

The east-west Roman road remained a significant and well-used route throughout the medieval period and, indeed, it appears on the fourteenth century Gough map (Gough 1780). The north-south route is, however, less well-defined at Brougham. Margary considered that it would join Moor Lane at the bend by Moorhouse Farm, following the lane past Fremington Farm to Brougham, and passing east of the fort to the ford on the River Eamont (Margary 1957, 118). Traces of this route have now been identified from aerial photographs, together with a possible alignment extending south from the fort (Higham and Jones 1975, 26, fig 5).

As elsewhere in the North West, there has until now been little evidence for activity between the Roman occupation and the development of Penrith and construction of the castle at Brougham in the twelfth and thirteenth centuries. The Anglo-Saxon Chronicle, however, refers to a treaty in AD 926 between Athelstan, king of the English, and Constantine, king of Scots, amongst others, which took place *aet Aemotum* (Earle and Plummer 1892). Although there are several candidates for the precise location of this meeting, the site of the fort at Brougham must be a strong contender, and the River Eamont seems likely to have been a cultural and political boundary at this period.

Although high-status sites of the post-Roman period have been excavated in recent years at Carlisle (Keevil forthcoming), Birdoswald (Wilmott forthcoming), and Dacre (Newman and Leech forthcoming), all in North Cumbria, the discoveries at Fremington have provided the first investigation of a rural settlement site of this period in the region.

The paucity of excavated remains has until recently presented significant problems in the study of early medieval settlement in North West England. The site at Fremington in the Eamont Valley has revealed evidence for a rural community which appears to have centred on the seventh and eighth centuries AD. The structural evidence includes sunken structures, which are frequently identified in South and East England at this period (*grübenhäuser*), in addition to, arguably, a more vernacular ground-level post-built structure. These building types were associated with domestic activity, including evidence of textile and pottery production, the latter

suggested by a putative kiln, together with simple handmade pottery. The seemingly diverse evidence is thought to reflect traditional technology, perhaps deriving from the long-lived prehistoric tradition coexistent with Romano-British activity in the area, together with some influence derived ultimately from 'Anglian' sources. The geographical position of this settlement, close to an established communications network, would have predisposed this community to the absorption of ideas, and perhaps cultural exchange.

The 1991 excavation

Phase summary

Phase 1
Several irregular and ill-defined features in the southern area perhaps represent structural remains and associated features, probably of Roman date.

Phase 2
Early medieval occupation, probably dating to the seventh and eighth centuries AD. Structural evidence indicates four sunken-floored buildings, a surface-laid structure, and a kiln.

Phase 3
The decline and abandonment of the settlement, represented by accumulations of debris within the structures.

Phase 4
Later agricultural activity.

The excavation was divided into three areas, within the parameters defined by the pipeline corridor (Fig 6:3). Areas 1 and 2 were located on the brow of a broad plateau, at 120m OD, whilst Area 3, to their north, was on the gradual slope down towards the River Eamont. Areas 1 and 3 were located with the aim of identifying the northern and southern limits of occupation, while the central Area 2 would assess the apparently multiperiod nucleus of activity.

Finds recovery
All three areas were stripped by machine of turf, topsoil, and much of the ploughsoil. In general, the ploughsoil lay directly above the natural sand and

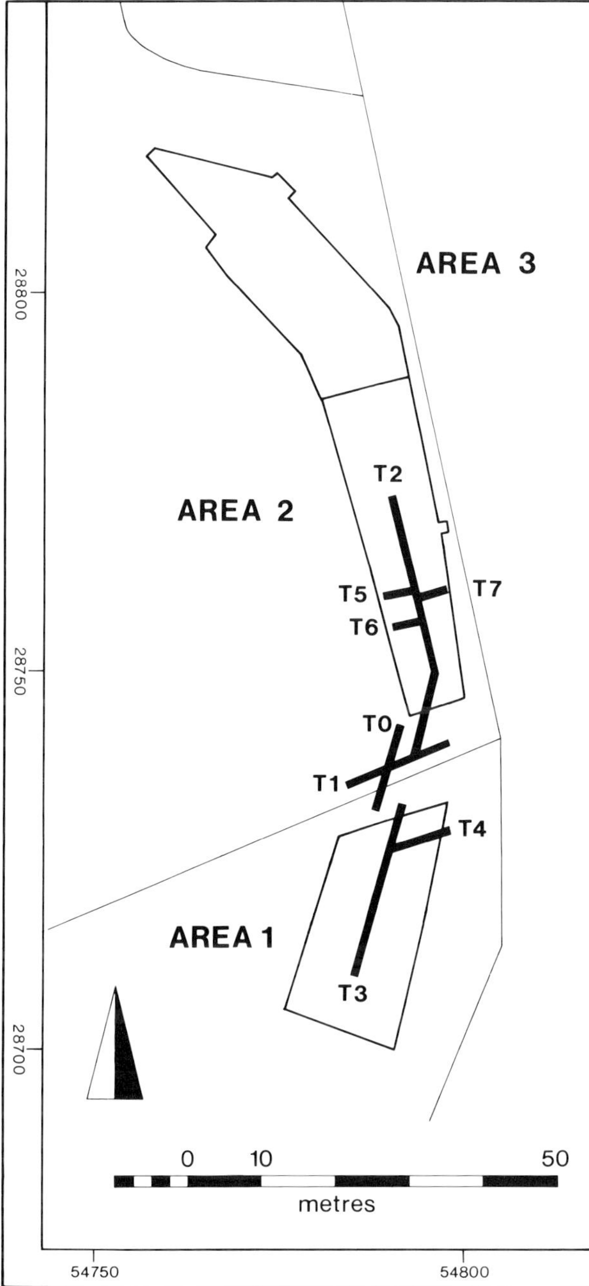

*Figure 6:3 Fremington (**1008, 10014**), location of excavations 1990–91 (1:1000)*

gravel, and consequently approximately the last 50mm was excavated manually. The interface was carefully cleaned, to enable the identification and plotting of any surviving features and concentrations of finds. Extensive post-depositional disturbance and truncation of archaeological deposits, mainly by medieval and modern ploughing, was immediately apparent, although concentrations of artefacts lay clustered within the ploughsoil directly above the major features. The three-dimensional recording of find scatters was therefore extremely important in the initial identification of the features. The differences between the ploughsoil and other deposits, especially those associated with the sunken structures, were very slight and often difficult to determine, although negative features and their fills tended to contrast well with the natural sand and gravel. This distinction could sometimes be enhanced by spraying.

Accurate three-dimensional recording of all finds, except those from the topsoil, continued in response to the problems associated with poorly defined features. This facilitated examination of the relationships between groups of finds from stratigraphically unrelated contexts, and evaluation of disturbed contexts and post-depositional processes.

Site stratigraphy and phasing

The glacial subsoil (*52*) was heterogeneous in character, consisting of coarse textured sand, varying in colour from pale yellow to dark orange-brown, and interspersed with irregular bands of gravel. It was highly disturbed, containing burrows and root hollows subsequently infilled with organic soil, which frequently formed small pockets across the site (M McHugh pers comm). These often resembled postholes or stakeholes, and it was not always clear at first whether this type of feature was natural or man-made. Unless otherwise stated, features cut directly into subsoil *52*.

Phase 1

The earliest activity was represented by several irregular linear features and two small pits, grouped within Area 1 (Fig 6:4). Four shallow, roughly parallel, linear features, with gently sloping sides and flat bases (*180*, each *c*3.40 x 0.53 x 0.05m), lay to the north of the main association of features; these were aligned west-north-west to east-south-east. They were roughly equidistant, approximately 1m apart, and were all filled by a loose orange or grey-brown loamy sand (*181*). At least one appeared to have been cut by Structure 2, to the north-west (Phase 2). Their similarity suggests that they were contemporary, and the most obvious interpretation is that they were associated with cultivation, perhaps cord rigg.

A group of features identified in the southern part of Area 1 included an oval pit (*97*, 1.1 x 0.55 x 0.25m) with irregular sides and base. The bright yellow and orange colouring of the natural sand on the southern side suggested scorching. The pit was filled by a loose dark grey-brown sandy loam (*90*), containing charcoal and burnt animal bone, perhaps representing fire debris. A shallow feature (*134*, 1.20 x 0.50m), 1.5m to the south-east, may be interpreted tentatively as the disturbed remains of a posthole.

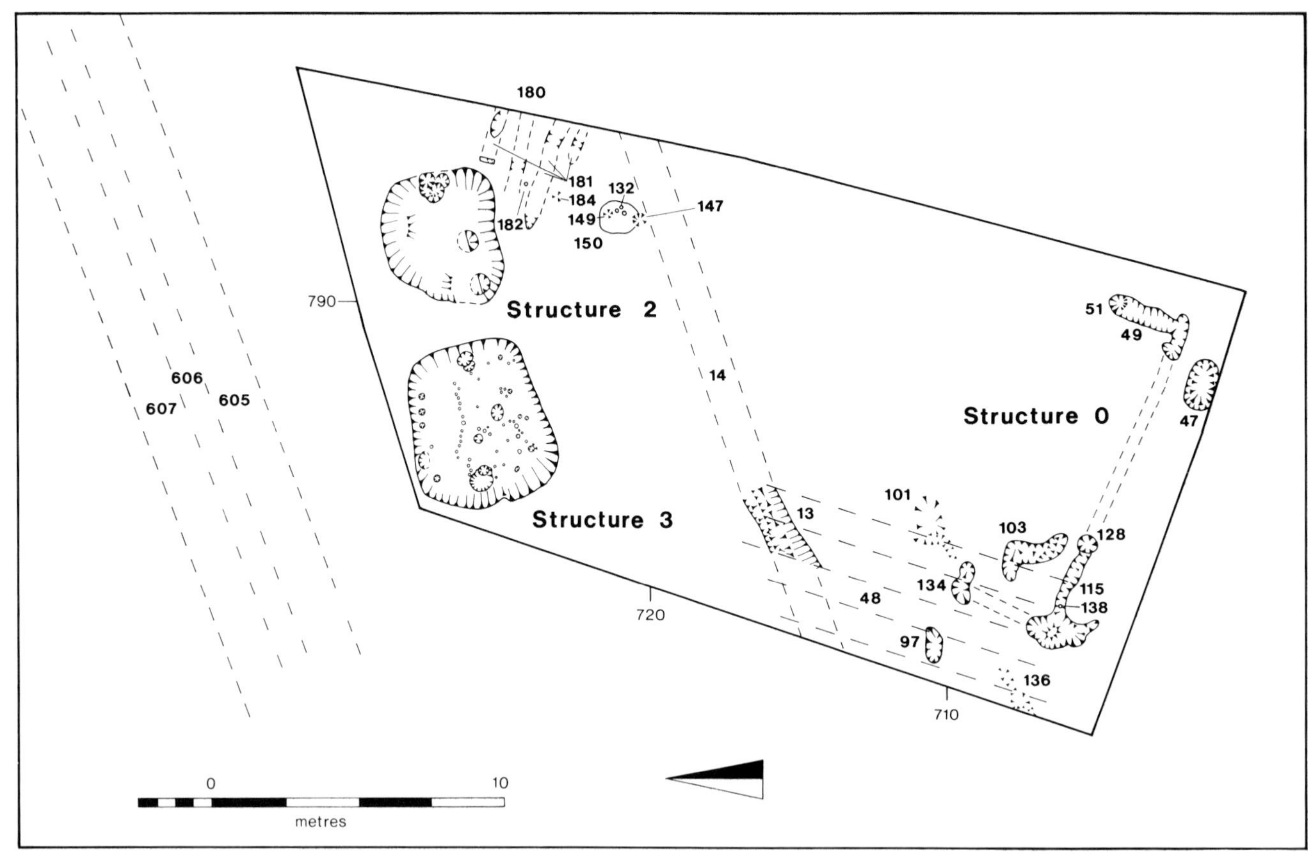

*Figure 6:4 Fremington (**10014**), Area 1, phases 1–4 (1:250)*

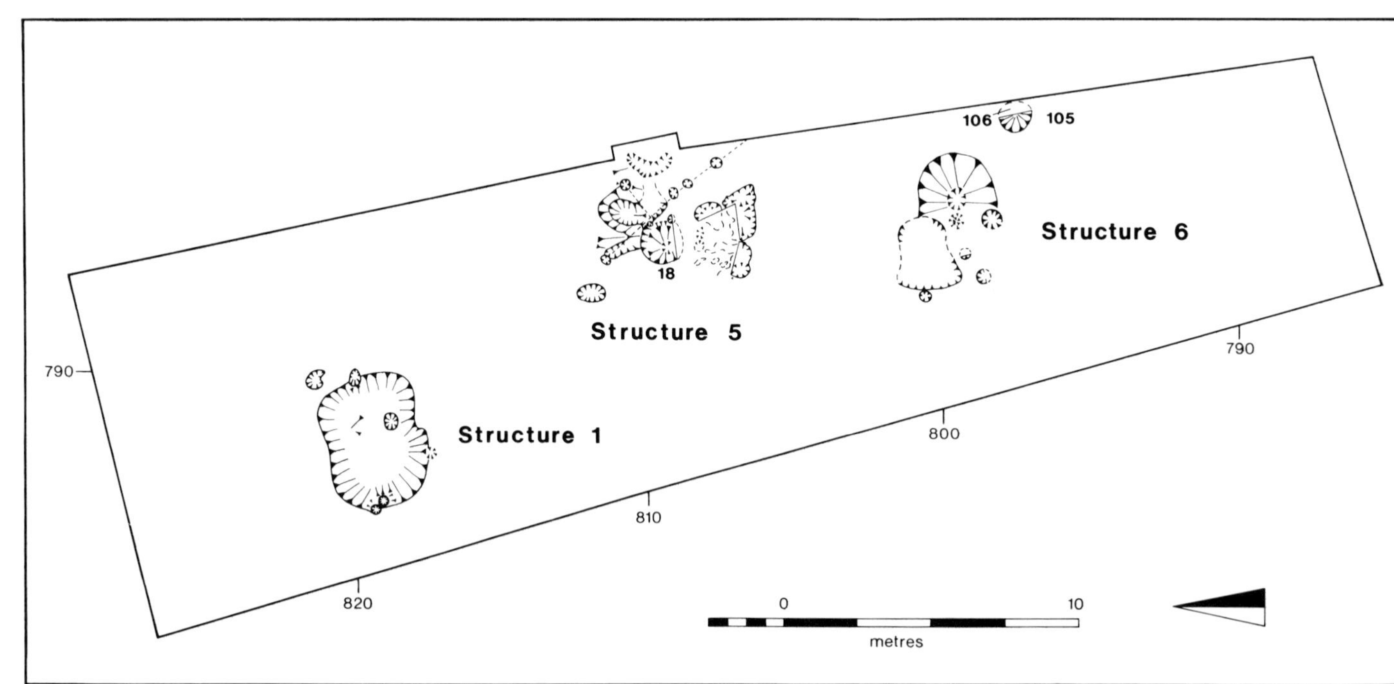

*Figure 6:5 Fremington (**10014**), Area 2, phases 1–4 (1:250)*

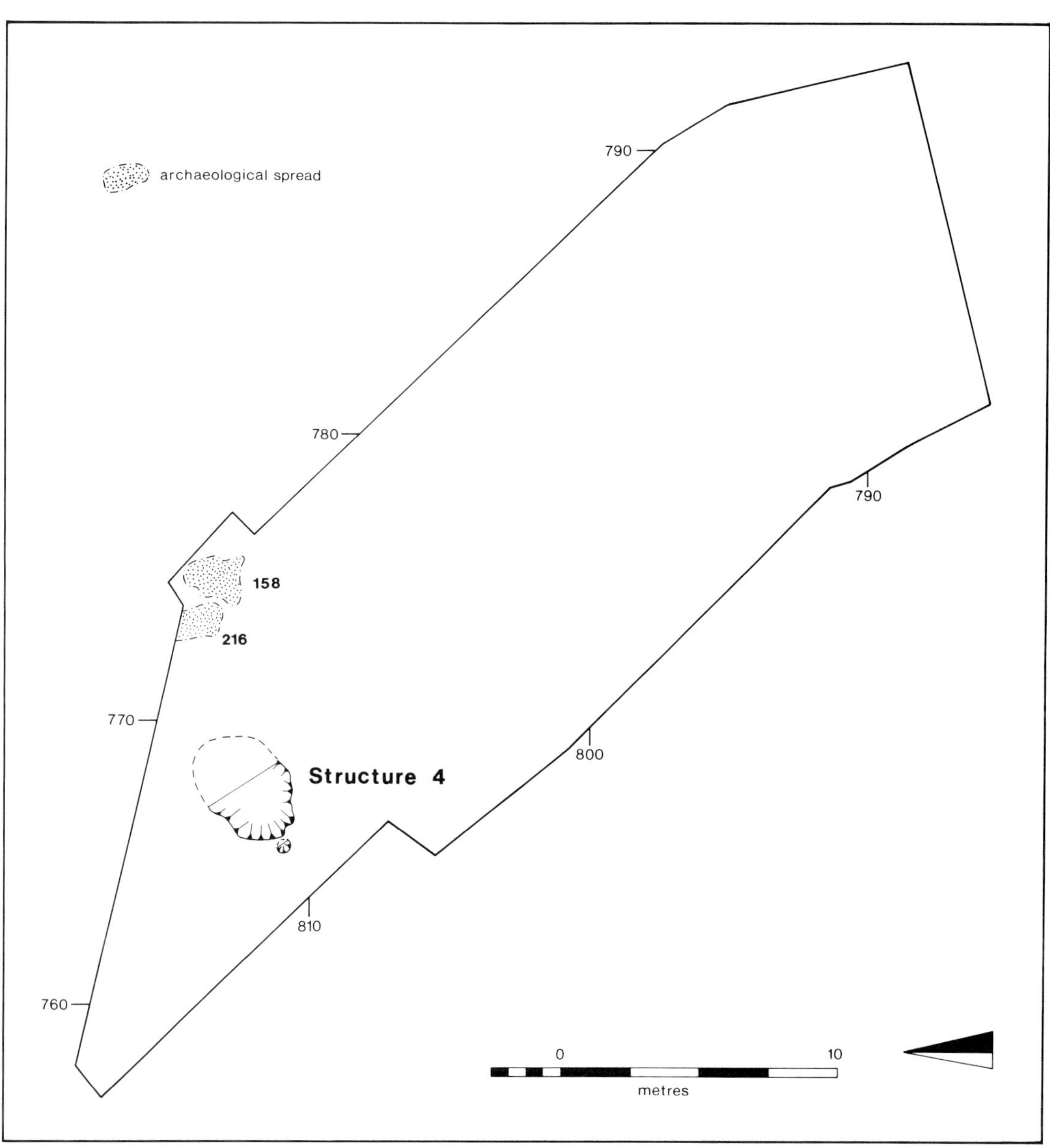

*Figure 6:6 Fremington (**10014**), Area 3, phases 1–4 (1:250)*

A curved linear feature (*103*, 2.3m long), with a well defined, steeply sloping, U-shaped profile, was oriented approximately north-west to south-east. Immediately to the south, another narrow, slightly curved, linear cut (*115*, 3.4m long overall) was oriented east-south-east to west-north-west. At the western end it broadened to form a circular hollow, and although there was no discernible variation of fill, the character changed markedly to a flat base and steeply sloping concave sides, and it encircled a small flat central mound. Stakehole *138*, lying in the base of *115*, perhaps defined a change of function between the two elements of this feature. Posthole *128*, containing broken rounded packing stones, was situated at the eastern end of *115*, although its precise stratigraphical relationship remained ill-defined. The fill of all the above features

was identical: a dark greyish-brown sandy loam containing charcoal. The clear definition, and the presence of burnt animal bone fragments, implies an anthropogenic origin.

At the eastern edge of Area 1, a very shallow feature, possibly a posthole (*51*), filled by a brown silty sand with gravel, was associated with a very shallow, narrow L-shaped cut (*49*). The principal arm (3m long) of the latter was aligned north-north-east, and the lesser (1.6m long) east-north-east. The irregularity of the sides, and the homogeneous fill of dark grey-brown silty sand (*10*), with rounded peagrits and pebbles, consistent with water-sorted material, suggest that it could have been an eaves-drip gully, associated with a rectangular structure. The westerly arm of *49* was closely aligned with

133

115, to the west, and it might be suggested that these features formed opposing ends of the southern wall of a rectangular structure, some 12m long (Structure 0). Posthole *134* could, perhaps, be seen to define a northerly return. This would suggest that feature *103* may represent disturbance of the interior, possibly associated with a tentative entrance marked by posthole *128*.

A small, shallow, oval pit (*47*, 1.60 x 0.80 x 0.30m), immediately to the south of *49*, appeared to share the same alignment. It was filled by a loose medium orange-brown loamy sand (*7*), the homogeneity of which possibly indicates a single, intentional backfilling. Bone representing part of a forelimb of a cow, and teeth possibly belonging to the same beast, were recovered from the fill of this pit, perhaps indicating the disposal of a single animal.

A few other features were identified in the same area as those described above but were considered to have been formed by natural processes. These included two irregular shallow cuts (*101*, *136*) and five small, shallow, subcircular features (*132*, *148*, *149*, *182*, *184*). It must be emphasised that these features were extremely elusive. Nevertheless, two discrete but potentially related entities can be defined: a large rectangular building (Structure 0), presumably of timber, in the extreme south of the excavated area and, to the north, stratigraphically unrelated, but on the same alignment, a small area of putative cord rigg (*180*). Dating is difficult, but it is clear that the cord rigg predates Structure 2 (Phase 2).

One notable feature of the finds from the site is the persistent occurrence of abraded Roman material within early medieval contexts. This, and the lack of post-Roman material from the area of Structure 0, as well as the presence of a single fourth century bead, might be used to argue a date towards the latter part of the Roman period for the building. A number of rectangular structures have been identified from parchmarks in aerial photographs, to the north-east and south of the fort at Brougham (Andrews *et al* forthcoming). These have been interpreted tentatively as strip-buildings of Roman date, and may be analogous to Structure 0. The possible association of building and cord rigg could suggest an agricultural function, reinforced by the presence of animal bone in several of the features. The presence amongst the finds of a quantity of East Gaulish samian and a small amount of vessel glass of relatively high quality might suggest a connection with the fort, rather than any native rural settlement, although the precise nature of this relationship cannot as yet be defined.

Phase 2

This phase defined the main period of activity within the excavated area, located on a different alignment to, and generally north of the features in Phase 1, and apparently quite separate from them (Figs 6:5, 6:6). A single stratigraphical interface defined their relationship. Four sunken-floored buildings (Structures 1–4), a surface-laid post-built structure (Structure 5) and a simple kiln (Structure 6), were recognised, as were two other irregular spreads of material near Structure 4. All the structures followed the same general alignment and were bounded to the south by a ditch, which maintained the alignment and separated the structures from the main group of Phase 1 features (Fig 6:4).

Structure 1

A wide and shallow subrectangular feature (*41*, 4.80 x 3.60 x 0.30m) cut into natural gravels (*52*) towards the north of Area 2 (Fig 6:7). It was oriented west-south-west to east-north-east, with gently sloping sides and a flat base. Whilst it had clearly been deliberately cut, the irregular and slightly stepped nature of a part of the south-east edge may suggest either wear, perhaps by repeated use as an entrance, or possibly collapse. There was a large posthole in the centre of each end (each *c*0.50m diameter, *c*0.50m deep); posthole *79* straddled the eastern side, whilst posthole *72* was set into the western edge. Both contained dark brown sandy loam, and rounded packing stones indicated that both posts were set towards the western edge of their post-setting. Their position and sizeable dimensions suggest that they contained the principal timbers of the superstructure. A conventional interpretation for this opposed two-post type ground plan has a basic ridge-pole construction over a sunken floor (West 1985, 14–15) (Fig 6:8).

The base of the structure was partially covered with a dark grey-brown sandy silty loam (*71*), intermixed with lenses of stony reddish-brown sand. This was up to 0.05m deep and followed the contours of the cut. The central area was compacted, suggesting a floor of beaten earth; a squared setting of angular, slightly fire-blackened sandstone flags (*62*, 1.10 x 1.00 x *c*0.08m) formed a hearth overlying *71* in the south-east corner of the structure. A few finds were recovered from the surface of floor *71*. All were domestic in nature and essentially Roman in date, although the two small fragments of pottery were abraded and undoubtedly residual. A spindle whorl (1) made from a decorated samian fragment cannot be dated with precision, since there is growing evidence for the reuse of Roman objects by early medieval communities, and a probable wool-comb tooth (Ironwork 1) is again undated, but its association

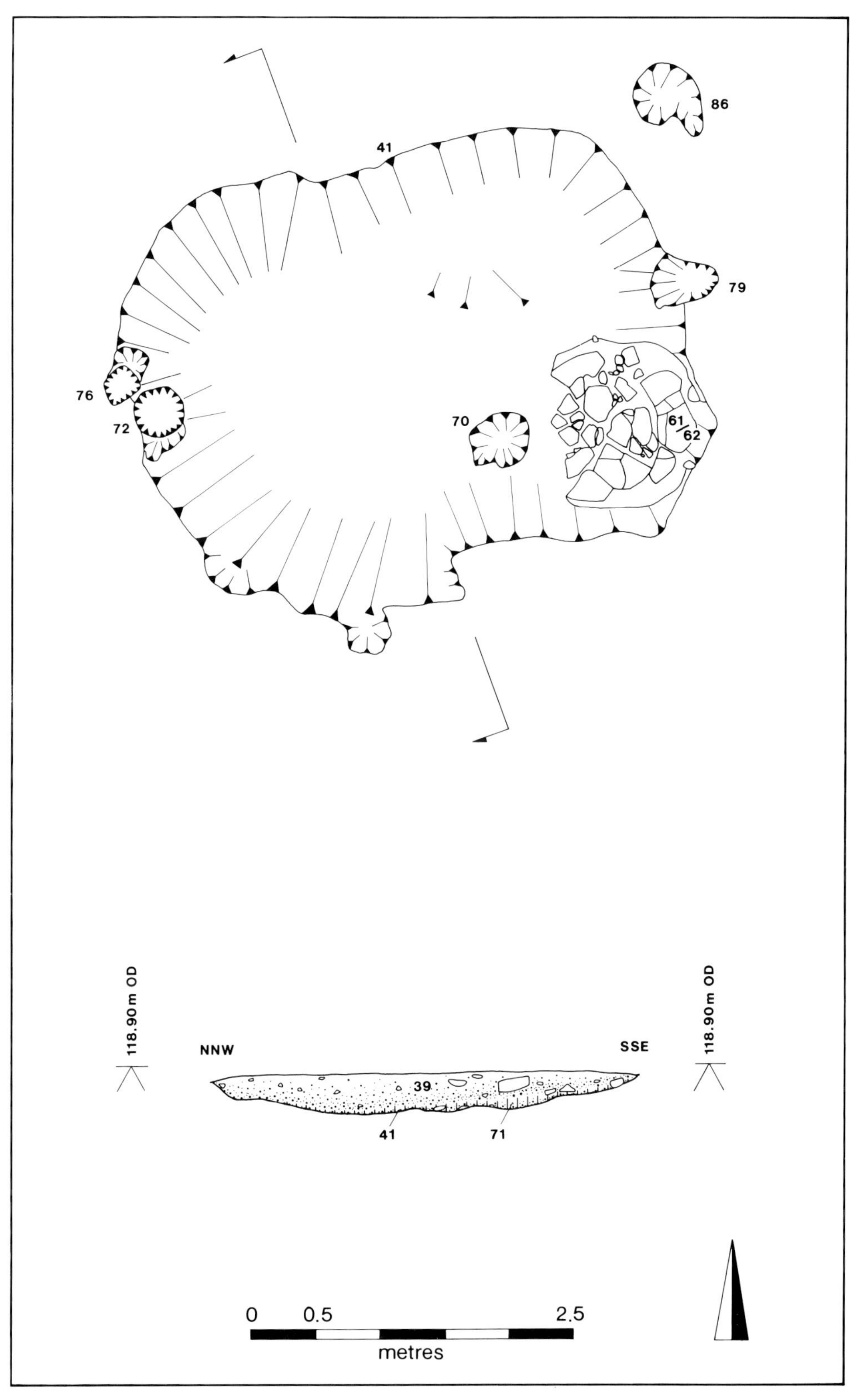

*Figure 6:7 Fremington (**10014**), Structure 1, plan and section WSW (1:50)*

*Figure 6:8 Fremington (**10014**), Structure 1*

with the spindle whorl might suggest the production of spun thread nearby.

Refurbishment of the superstructure was suggested by a small posthole (*76*) immediately to the north-west of posthole *72*. It was shallower and less well defined than *72*, but may represent a replacement or repair to the load-bearing post at this end of the structure. A second small, shallow, and irregular hollow (*86*) lay about 1m to the north-east of the cut for the structure. Its sloping profile suggests that it may have held a timber intended to shore the load-bearing post in posthole *79*.

Floor *71* was cut by a small subcircular feature (*70*, 0.50m diameter, 0.20m deep), less than 0.60m to the west of hearth *62*. It had straight, steep sides, a flat base, and was filled by a very dark grey-brown sandy silt loam. Although interpretation of this feature is inconclusive, its position makes it unlikely that it was a posthole, but rather a small, deliberately cut pit. A narrow band of very dark grey sandy loam (*15*), containing much burnt organic material, had accumulated over hearth *62*, and spread to the west over floor *71* and pit *70*. A brown sandy loam (*61*), stratigraphically contemporary with *15*, surrounded the rest of the hearth. Both these layers seem to represent accumulated material from the latest use of the hearth. Two small, abraded fragments of samian were recovered from accumulation *15*, and were presumably residual, although the lack of other finds suggests that the floor surface was otherwise kept clean.

Structure 2

Structure 2 (Fig 6:9) was formed by a large sub-rectangular cut (*87*, 4.60 x 4.00 x 0.50m) 48m to the south of Structure 1. This had gently sloping sides and a flat base. A large posthole (*107*, 0.57m diameter, 0.57m deep), cut into the sloping eastern edge

of this cut, contained a post, represented by a post-pipe, which had been set towards the western side; the lower part of the post-pipe was filled by a dark brown loamy sand containing angular packing stones. This post would have been a main structural support for the ridge-pole of the superstructure. Two large postholes were cut into the base of the structure; *229* (0.60m diameter, *c*0.09m deep) was positioned adjacent to the south-western side, and *217* (0.45m diameter, 0.36m deep) about 1m east-north-east. Posthole *229* was filled by a grey-brown loamy sand, and *217* by a loose brown loamy sand, with large stones and pebbles at the base. The stratigraphic evidence for both *229* and *217* suggests that they held timbers associated with the initial phase of construction. Unfortunately, any evidence there might have been for a timber support at the western end of the structure had been disturbed by trial trenching.

A thin, roughly rectangular, coarse, mortar-like layer (*212*, 1.10 x 0.70 x 0.02m) was situated close to the north-western side of the structure; its surface was scorched, suggesting use as a hearth, a type known from early medieval sites elsewhere (Horsman *et al* 1988). The siting, shape, and dimensions appeared comparable to hearth *62* in Structure 1. Its position implies that there was no deliberately laid floor, unlike Structure 1, and the lack of accumulated material suggests that the structure was kept scrupulously clean. Indeed, the only find, a small blue glass cabochon (Glass 27) of indeterminate date, was recovered from the base of posthole *217*.

A large post-pit (*213*, 0.68m diameter, 0.38m deep) cut the eastern edge of Structure 2 and the north-western edge of post-pit *107*. It was filled by a dark grey-brown loamy sand (*108*) with charcoal; two medium-sized sandstone blocks placed upright at the south-east edge, and rounded stones at the south and west edges, presumably acted as packing for a post (implying a post positioned to the north). It probably contained a replacement of the post in *107*. The extraction of the latter probably caused the collapse of the western edge of *107*. Further repair to Structure 2 is suggested by the presence of two other postholes (*219, 221*). Posthole *219* (0.40m diameter, 0.40m deep), to the west, cut *213* and was in turn cut by posthole *221* (0.46m diameter, 0.50m deep). Both were filled by a grey-brown loamy sand, and the latter also contained charcoal. The obvious refurbishment of the eastern end of the structure may account for the presence of postholes *219* and *221* to provide supplementary support for a somewhat unstable building. This instability may have been compounded here by the sandier nature of the subsoil, causing more rapid decay of the timbers.

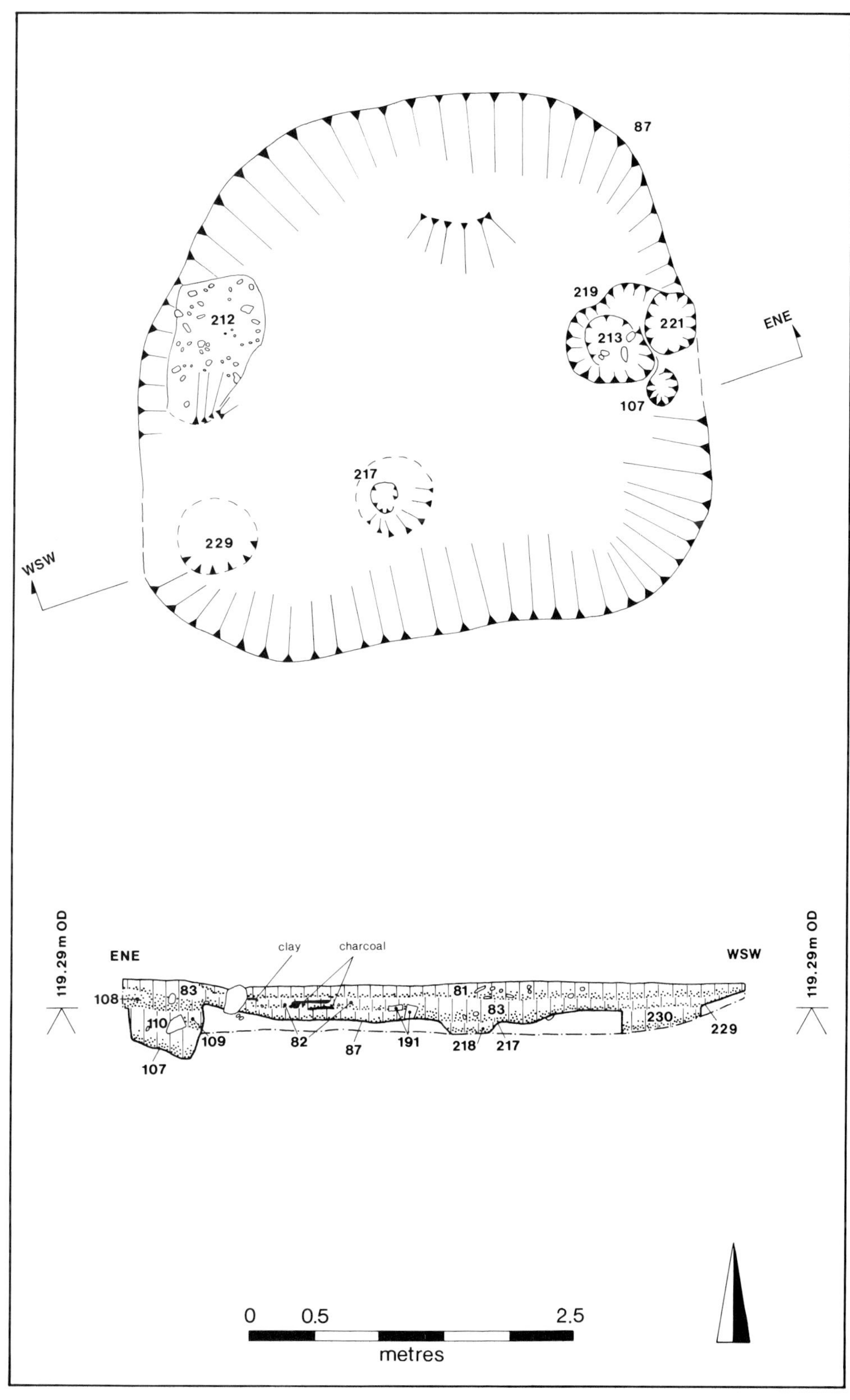

*Figure 6:9 Fremington (**10014**), Structure 2, plan and section NNW (1:50)*

137

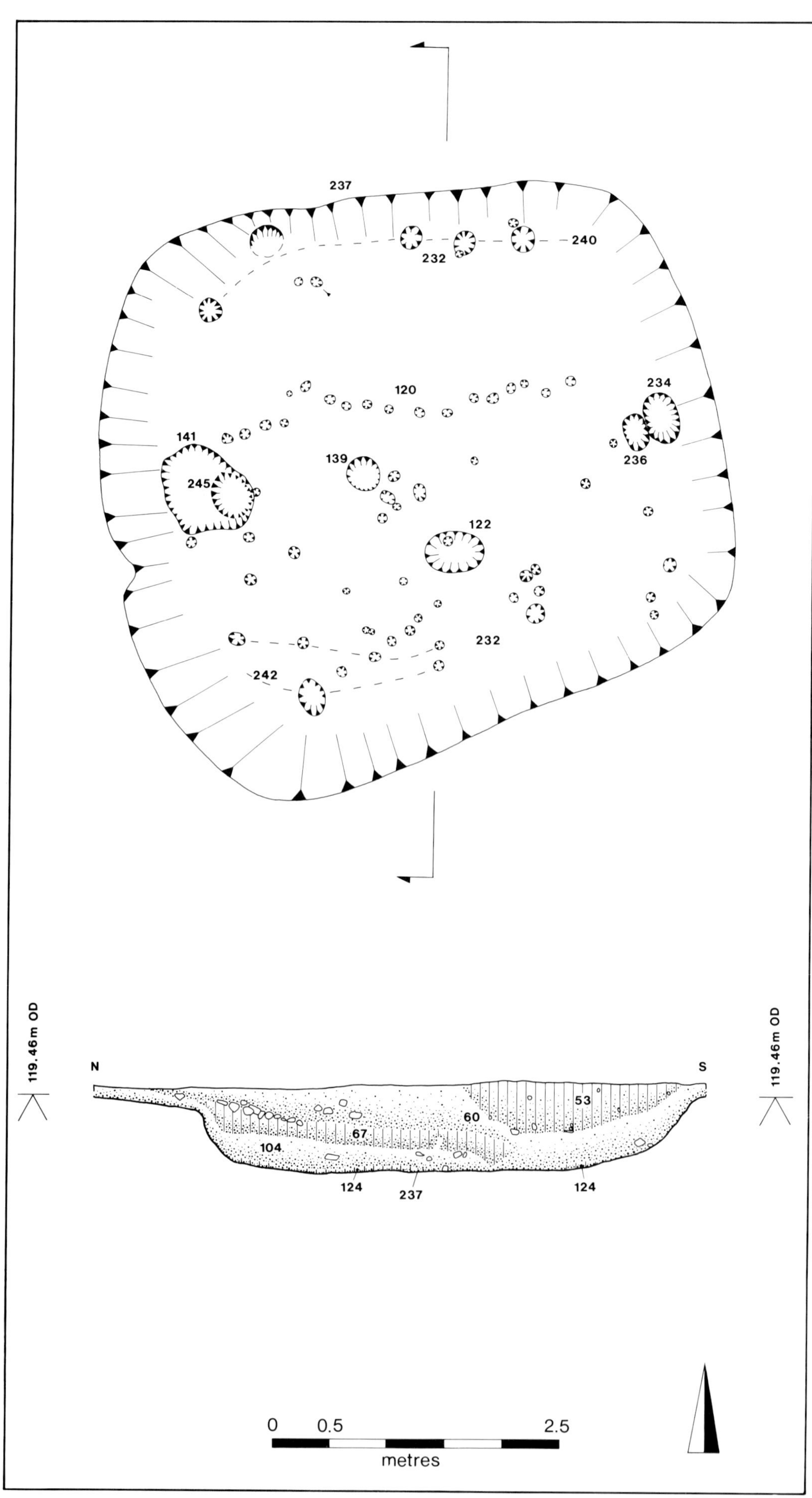

*Figure 6:10 Fremington (**10014**), Structure 3, plan and section W (1:50)*

Structure 3

The largest and best preserved of the sunken-floored buildings (Fig 6:10) was represented by a trap-ezoidal cut (*237*, 5.30 x 4.40 x 0.80m), on the same alignment as Structures 1 and 2. It lay only 7m west of Structure 2, and had steeply sloping sides and a flat base (4.70 x 3.70m). The main load-bearing timbers, represented by posthole *234* (0.32m diameter, 0.45m deep) to the east and posthole *141* (0.30m diameter, 0.50m deep) to the west, were set at the mid-point of the base at each end of the structure, unlike those in Structures 1 and 2, and cut into the sides. The fills of the two postholes varied; that of *234* was a grey-brown loamy sand (*233*), whilst that of *141* was looser and less sandy, and contained some small lumps of clay. A third posthole (*139*, 0.34m diameter, 0.20m deep) lay between the two, slightly off-centre. It was filled by a brown to dark brown loam with charcoal, and possible packing stones. A shallow oval cut (*122*, 0.52 x 38 x 0.14m), immediately to the south-east of posthole *139*, was also filled by a brown loam, within which was a large, flat, angular, sandstone slab, perhaps a padstone. The function of this feature remains unclear, although it may be related to posthole *139*.

The north and south sides of the structure were lined by a series of unevenly spaced postholes and stakeholes (*232*). The components of the northern line, five principal timbers and four stakeholes, were 0.12–0.24m in diameter, 0.12–0.18m deep, and 0.30–0.80m apart. Their counterparts along the southern edge, four small postholes and two pairs of stakeholes, were 0.12–0.18m in diameter, 0.09–0.25m deep, and apparently more symmetrically spaced (at 0.60–1.00m intervals). Whilst the northern alignment cut the base of the slope, the southern line was situated up to 0.17m in from the edge of the structure. All were filled by a medium to dark grey-brown loamy sand. A dark orange-brown soilmark (*240*) was seen as a fairly broad stain be-tween these alignments and the edge of the cut. It seemed to be organic in origin, and may have represented a timber lining to the cut, held in place by the posts. A possible interpretation here is of a plank-lined sunken-featured structure, although these tend to be an urban phenomenon (Horsman *et al* 1988, 101–2, fig 98). The timber lining may have had a range of functions, from simply retaining the sandy sides of the cut, to insulation against damp and cold. It may be of significance that this building, markedly different in construction from Structures 1 and 2, had no identifiable hearth. A thin compacted layer of dark brown loam (*124*, c0.05m deep) extended across the base of the building. This trampled accumulation contained small and medium stones and pebbles, as well as frequent concentrations of charcoal, and from its mixed nature is most convincingly interpreted as a floor surface.

At least 40 small stakeholes (*120*, c0.10m diameter, c0.12m deep) cut the base of the building. They did not become evident until *124* had been removed, but nonetheless it is likely that the stakes were in place during the build-up of the trampled surface. Approximately half of the stakeholes appeared to be part of an alignment, running east-west between the main internal timbers (*141*, *234*), effectively dividing the building in two. They were on average 0.20m apart and may have represented an insubstantial wattle partition (*for parallels, see* Murray 1983). The remainder were more randomly dispersed, but all were situated to the south of the suggested partition. In general, they formed no obvious pattern, but a short alignment seemed to be associated with a faint grey linear soilmark (*242*), perhaps also suggesting a partition. A single stakehole appeared to cut the northern edge of posthole *122*, implying that this, at least, was not primary activity. All were filled by a brown charcoal-flecked loam. They could have been temporary fixtures, and although the length of use cannot be determined, they had been removed before the accumulation of layer *124* ceased. Two additional postholes provided evidence for the refurbishment of the main load-bearing posts. Posthole *236* cut the western side of eastern structural posthole *234*. The fill was almost identical to that of its predecessor, a grey-brown loamy sand containing rounded stones and some charcoal. Similarly, posthole *245* cut the south-eastern side of the western structural posthole *141*, and had an almost identical fill to its predecessor. These two postholes may have been either replacements or repair to the standing structure.

As with Structure 1, the datable artefacts can all be ascribed to the Romano-British period. A single undiagnostic fragment of Romano-British pottery, again much abraded, derives from the fill of

*Figure 6:11 Fremington (**10014**), Structure 3*

possible posthole *122*. A number of artefacts came from compacted floor surface *124*, including a spindle whorl made from samian (Ceramic objects 3), several fragments of copper alloy (2, 3), none of which was closely datable and, of particular interest, a silver coin of early third century date (Julia Paula, AD 218–222). Elsewhere, Roman artefacts were deliberately collected and valued by early medieval communities (West 1985; White 1988), and the presence of this coin may therefore be deliberate rather than residual.

Structure 4

North of Structures 1–3, on a slight break in the north-facing slope within Area 3, was a small and much damaged sunken-floored structure (Fig 6:12) associated with several other features. The structure was represented by a shallow, suboval cut (*171*, *c*5.00 x 3.00 x 0.20m) with very gently sloping sides and an uneven base. Although isolated from all the other structures, its similar orientation might imply a causal relationship.

A single posthole (*167*, 0.40m diameter, 0.30m deep), with a central post-pipe (0.15m diameter), lay 0.12m to the west of cut *171*. It was filled by a dark brown sandy loam containing charcoal, and angular packing stones. One sizeable stone filled most of the hole, perhaps indicating deliberate removal of the post (during Phase 3?), although there had also been natural disturbance. Its close proximity to the western end of Structure 4, and the absence of postholes within the structure, may suggest that this posthole contained a load-bearing structural timber. No counterpart was identified at the other end of the structure, although this may be accounted for by the severe truncation of this part of the site.

Associated features

A roughly oval spread of brown loamy sand (*216*) was observed just to the east of Structure 4. It bore a generic resemblance to the fill of this structure and seems to have derived originally from disturbance to the natural sand subsoil (*52*). A second irregular spread of dark grey-brown sandy loam (*158*, 2.00 x 1.50 x 0.05m) was encountered slightly upslope, and less than 5m to the south-east, of Structure 4. Its nature suggests that it may have been an accumulation of debris from domestic fires, and it was noticeable that these spreads produced a greater number and range of finds than any of the sunken-floored structures. As well as the ubiquitous and probably residual fragments of Romano-British coarsewares and samian, there were also objects of early medieval date: two loomweight fragments (1, 2) and a turned mudstone spindle whorl (Worked

stone 4), closely paralleled at Dacre (Howard-Davis forthcoming) and Bryant's Gill (Philpott 1990, 55). There was also a small amount of heat-affected material, possibly industrial residues, and numerous fragments of burnt animal bone. This range of material, allied to the ashy nature of the deposits, may suggest the disposal of domestic rubbish. Several small fragments of a Roman glass vessel (Glass 5, 6) were present in spread *216*; this glass may be residual or, since it is markedly less abraded than the pottery, it may have been collected deliberately for recycling. The reuse of Roman glass at this late period is widely attested (Newman and Leech forthcoming).

Pit complex

Structure 5 (*see below*) appears to have been preceded by a period of largely uncharacterised disturbance, represented by pit complex *18* and isolated pit *58*. Complex *18* comprised four shallow interlinking subcircular or oval pits (all *c*1.50 x 0.80 x 0.20m). They each had moderately steeply sloping sides and slightly rounded bases which were mottled and apparently had been affected by heat. That the natural sands and gravels immediately beneath them had likewise been heat-affected is attested by the mottled grey-brown, pink, and orange colouring of the oxidised sand (*159, 162*). These pits may represent the last remnant of the hearth of an earlier building, suggesting that Structure 5 was a renewal. These features may, on the other hand, originate from another high temperature process, and indeed the close proximity and general morphological similarity of these pits to Structure 6 (*see below*), a simple kiln of indisputably early medieval date, suggests one obvious function.

Another small, regular, shallow, suboval pit (*58*), with a slightly rounded base and concave sides, lay immediately to the north-west of pit complex *18*, and may have been related to that complex.

Structure 5

Part of a post-built structure with internal hearth (Fig 6:13) was recognised to the south-east of Structure 1, at the extreme edge of the excavation. Although there was little or no stratigraphic evidence to link the components, they appeared to form a coherent whole, which comprised seven postholes. At least one of these, posthole *118*, clearly cut the pit complex described above.

Four of the post-settings formed a row (*118, 112, 130, 143*) aligned north-north-west to south-south-east. Of the remaining postholes, two (*77, 174*) lay slightly to the west of this line, between *118* and

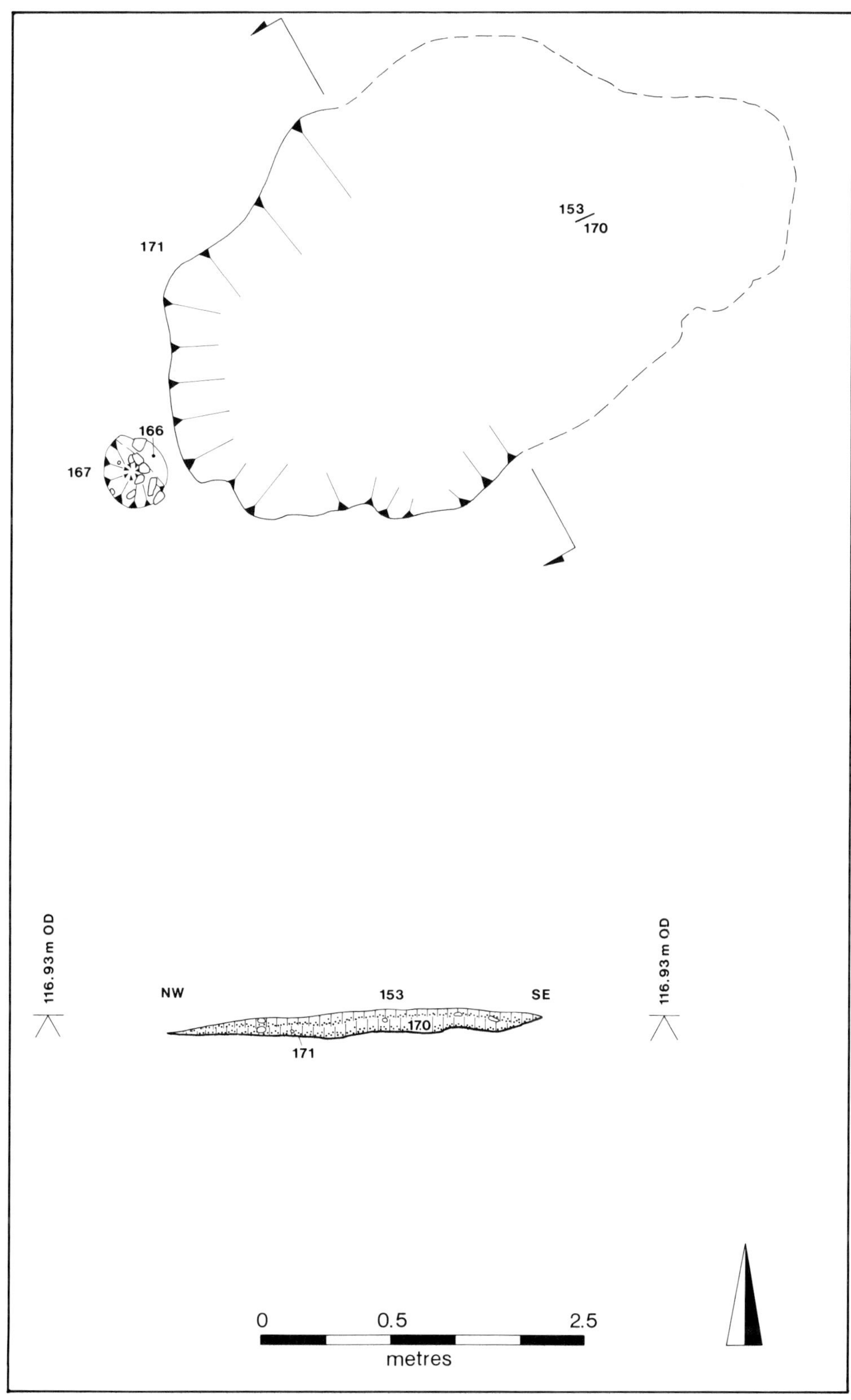

*Figure 6:12 Fremington (**10014**), Structure 4, plan and section SW (1:50)*

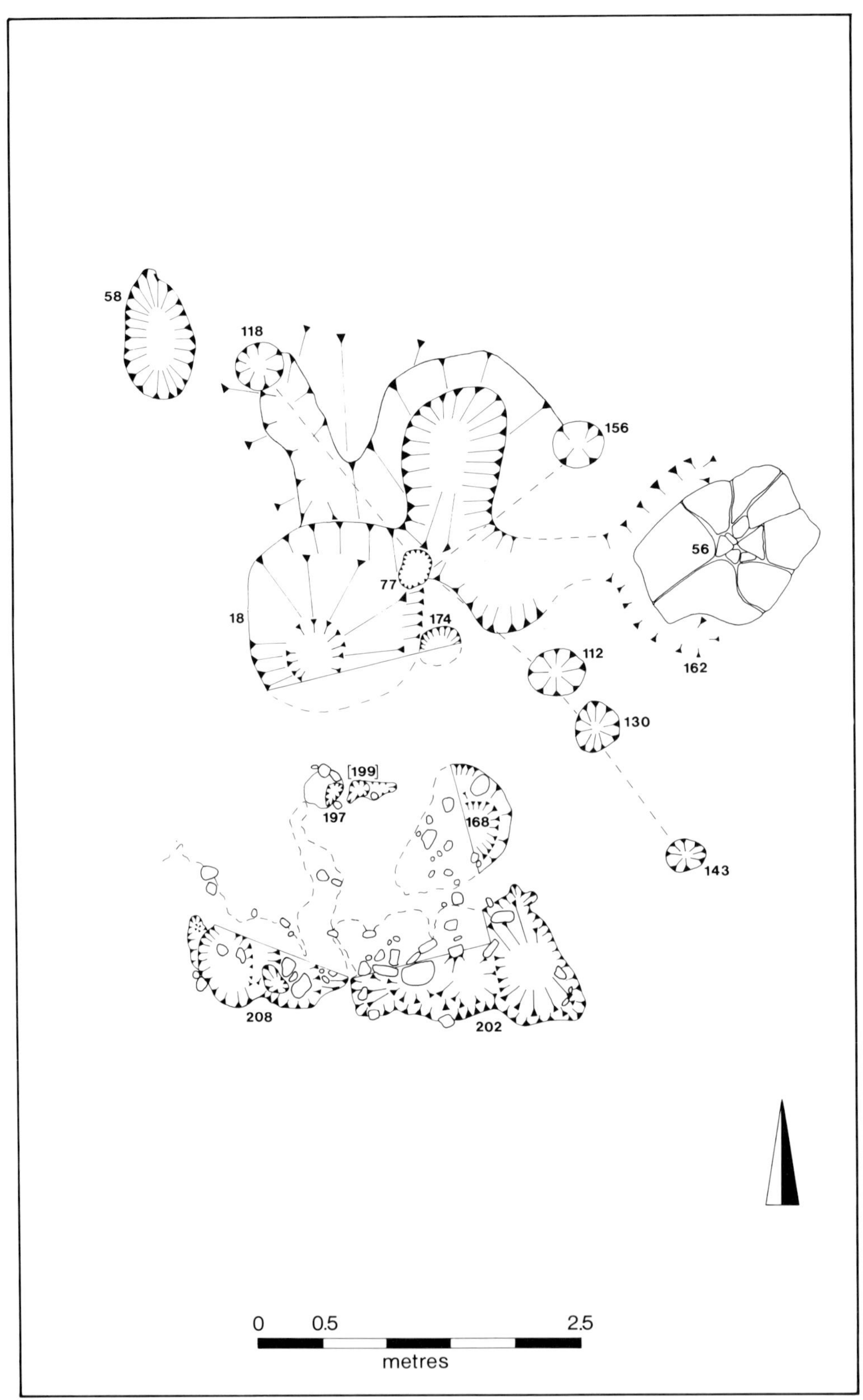

*Figure 6:13 Fremington (**10014**), Structure 5, plan (1:50)*

112, in an area of substantial disturbance, whilst the other (*156*) lay 1.2m to the north-east. All were filled by brown to grey-brown silty sand and some contained packing stones. Posthole *118* retained a rectangular setting of sandstone blocks which had apparently supported a boxed timber upright of scantling (0.20 x 0.30m). Posthole *112* (0.44m in diameter, 0.35m deep), 2.85m south-south-east of *118*, contained packing for a post approximately 0.15m in diameter. Posthole *130* (0.34m diameter, 0.20m

142

deep) was located 0.14m south-south-east of *112*, and the most southerly of the four postholes (*143*, 0.38m diameter, 0.25m deep) was a further 0.86m to the south; unlike the others it did not cut directly into the natural sand (*52*), but was separated by a thin ash deposit (*55*). The possibility that posthole *118*, probably a more substantial timber, may have required a more secure setting of packing stones than the haphazard arrangement of the others, may suggest that *118* was load-bearing, perhaps forming the corner of a structure, aligned at right angles to the sunken-floored structures, with the west wall formed by the main alignment of postholes. Although postholes *77* (0.24m diameter, 0.35m deep) and *174* (*c*0.28m diameter, 0.37m deep) were offset slightly to the west of the main alignment, they nevertheless appear to fill some of the gap between *118* and *112*, in a much disturbed area, and may represent a repair to the western wall of the structure.

Finally, posthole *156* (0.15m deep), offset to the east, was closely associated with the complex, resembling the main components of the structure in size, form, and filling. Its location, however, presents something of an interpretative problem, since it clearly does not form part of an eastward return from posthole *118*. As it lay at the eastern edge of the area of disturbance, it may have formed part of a complex internal entrance, the disturbance reflecting wear at this point. It seems more logical to suggest, however, that it represents the last remnants of an internal partition, since such divisions have commonly been identified in this type of structure (James *et al* 1984, 199).

A large sandstone hearth (*56*, 1.50 x 1.20 x 0.10m), less than a metre to the east of the wall formed by the posthole alignment, and to the south-west of posthole *156*, is a strong indication that the building extended beyond the excavated area to the east. A concentration of charcoal, numerous small fragments of burnt animal bone, and a small amount of industrial debris, lay immediately above and surrounding the hearth within the ploughsoil (Phase 4, *45*). This hearthstone sealed an area of mottled pink, orange, and brown coarse sand and gravel (*162*), containing traces of charcoal and ash on the surface, strongly implying that the hearth had been refurbished, and this, by extension, attests to the longevity of the structure. Directly adjacent to the hearthstone, and above *162*, was a fairly thin layer of light grey silt (*55*, 2.00 x 1.30 x 0.05m) with frequent charcoal flecks and a high proportion of ash, apparently representing debris from this hearth.

A further complex of pits lay immediately to the west of the building and appeared to be aligned with its western wall. Shallow, irregular, subcircular cut *197*, filled by grey-brown sand, may conceivably be natural in origin. However, three small irregular pits (*168, 202, 208*; each *c*1.50 x 1.00 x 0.36m), which may have suffered some natural disturbance, appeared man-made. All were filled by a stony grey-brown sandy loam, which contained relatively large fragments of charcoal. These features differed appreciably in character from pit complex *18*, and therefore may not be contemporary, although no clear interpretation of this amorphous complex can be offered. A small, very roughly rectangular feature (*199*), located close to this group, was filled by grey-brown sandy loam, and again may simply represent natural disturbance.

A bun-shaped loomweight (*3*) of undoubted early medieval date was recovered from this structure. It tends towards the later end of the range defined by Hurst (1959, 23–5), and is probably younger than other loomweights from the site. Such loomweights have elsewhere been interpreted as of eighth century date, for instance at Whitby (Peers and Radford 1943), and it must therefore provide a *terminus ante quem* for the construction of the building.

Structure 6

A further group of features (Fig 6:14) south-west of Structure 5 were partially exposed during the 1990 evaluation (Trenches 2, 5, 6, 7). The largest was a shallow subcircular pit (*64*, 2.40m diameter, 0.36m deep), filled by a loose reddish-brown sand (*92*), incorporating a great number of stones, many apparently fire-shattered, and frequent charcoal fragments. This material extended beyond the sides of the cut for pit *64*, apparently having been spread by subsequent ploughing (Phase 4). The top of *92* was defined by increased reddening of the matrix and a denser distribution of cracked stones. Set within this fill, towards the north of pit *64*, was a smaller subcircular pit (*163*, *c*2.10m diameter, *c*0.13m deep) whose edges were defined by an increased concentration of fire-cracked stone (*164*), particularly dense towards the base; it seems to have acted as a lining, above which was an arc of large rounded stones. The centre of pit *163* was filled by a loose mottled dark red-brown sand, distinguished from fill *92*, which surrounded it, by a higher stone and charcoal content. The sands into which both these features (*64, 163*) were cut had also been mottled orange, yellow, and red-brown by heat, and they were more intensely reddened within smaller pit *163*.

The shape, evidence of intense burning, and presence of substantial amounts of handmade pottery, led to the interpretation of these features as a simple kiln. It may be compared with a basic form found in the post-Roman period (Hurst 1981, 345, fig 7.32, Musty 1A), which consisted of a single flue and circular or oval firing chamber, with or without internal structures. Several aspects of the design appeared similar to those excavated at Purwell Farm, Cassington, Oxfordshire (Arthur and Jope 1962–3). Pit *163* may represent the firing chamber, lined with densely packed stone, the limit of which, to the south and east, was defined by the arc of large stones, perhaps the remnants of an internal structure (Swan 1984, 114). Such linings have been noted in kilns elsewhere (Arthur and Jope 1962–3), and small stones are known to have been used to line clamp kilns (Swan 1984, 114). A relatively large amount of handmade pottery, which appeared to be concentrated around the perimeter of the putative firing chamber, may have been wasters, cleared towards the edge of the chamber, or the remains of a layer of vessels arranged to facilitate stoking and draught circulation within the load (Swan 1984, 29–32, 114). The level of damage was such that there was no conclusive evidence for either a flue or an exhaust vent.

Four postholes (*226, 227, 507, 66*) at the southern and western perimeter of the pits seemed to be associated with each other. Posthole *227* (0.35m diameter, 0.12m deep), south of *163* and west of *64*, contained a large packing stone which probably retained a post set towards its southern side. Posthole *226* (0.30m diameter, 0.19m deep) lay 0.40m to the south-west. Another small posthole (*507*, 0.36m diameter, 0.20m deep) was situated on the south-west side of pit *163*. All the postholes were filled by a loose grey-brown sandy loam containing fire-shattered stone. Posthole *66* (0.60m diameter, 0.57m deep), considerably larger and deeper than the others, was filled by a loose mottled grey-brown silty sand, with a large upright angular sandstone block at the base, some rounded and several fire-shattered stones, suggesting that some of the material from the kiln had become incorporated in the fill. The post-pipe (*65*) identified towards the west of the cut was represented by a very loose, dark grey-brown, silty sand with frequent small charcoal fragments. The configuration of the post-settings around pit *163*, and the stratigraphic evidence, indicate that they may have formed part of a structure partially sheltering pits *64* and *163*. Fill *164*, like fill *92*, spread beyond the edge of pit *163* and thus sealed the posthole fills, suggesting that some of the stones at least, and the pottery, were incorporated as the posts were removed or decayed (Phase 3).

A small oval pit (*105*, 1.05 x 0.97 x 0.27m), with steep sides and curved base, was situated 1.50m to the south-west of pit *64*. It contained a loose dark brown loamy sand (*106*), which was mottled towards the edges and contained charcoal fragments. Its proximity to the kiln, and the similarity of the pottery within the fill, may suggest that the two features are related.

The identification of this group of features as a kiln was prompted by the presence of a large amount of crude pottery within the fills, comprising almost all the non-Roman pottery from the site. The vessels are of simple bucket-shaped form, handmade, in an unusually heavily gritted fabric. Many of the fragments are heavily sooted, even across breaks, which might lend weight to their identification as wasters, rather than discarded vessels in domestic use. The dating of such vessels is extremely difficult, as they clearly represent a long-lived native tradition. Small fragments were, however, found in association with more diagnostic early medieval objects elsewhere on the site, and dissimilarity to the local Romano-British pottery clearly sets them apart from the Romano-British activity on the site (Phase 1). Parallels are difficult but a single similar fragment is known from Dacre (Newman and Leech forthcoming) and the material bears a strong generic resemblance to 'native' fabric types from Yeavering (Hope-Taylor 1977). Several small fragments of Romano-British coarseware were also contained within the fills of Structure 6, but are likely to be residual.

Boundary ditch

The southern limit of the Phase 2 activity was apparently defined by a shallow ditch (*13*, *c*16.50 x 1.20 x 0.30m), which had a narrow yet regular U-shaped profile. The ditch followed a similar orientation to the principal features of the phase, from which it is inferred that it was a formal boundary to the settlement. A small oval pit (*150*, 1.60 x 1.50 x 0.14m), with irregular sides and a slightly rounded base, was located close to the northern side of ditch *13*. It contained no finds and its function remains uncertain, but although isolated from other features, it may best be considered within this phase of activity.

Phase 3

The decay of Structures 1–6, and the gradual infilling of boundary ditch *13*, form the main activity in this phase. This was represented by several fills in each sunken structure, which have been interpreted as abandonment and subsequent decay.

Structure 1

A brown sandy loam (*9*, 0.10m deep) filled the struc-

*Figure 6:14 Fremington (**10014**), Structure 6, plan and section WSW (1:50)*

145

ture (Fig 6:7), above occupation layers *71*, *15*, and *61*. A greyer sandy loam (*8*, *c*0.10m deep) lay above both this and hearth deposit *15*. Both these layers contained mixed debris which, coupled with their stratigraphical position, suggests that these were not living floors but infill following the primary abandonment of the structure.

The upper parts of postholes *72*, *76*, and *86* (*73*, *75*, and *85*, respectively) were all filled by dark grey-brown loam. These fills were similar to abandonment layer *39*, a dark brown silty sand (0.25m deep), which lay not only above them, but also above abandonment layers *8* and *9* and the fill of posthole *79* (*63*) and must, therefore, have been deposited after the disappearance of the structural framework. It was not possible to establish whether the posts rotted *in situ* or were deliberately removed. Layer *39* seemed, however, to derive in part from the decay of building materials, as it contained rounded stones and sandstone fragments, which might perhaps have come from the superstructure. The central part of *39* was compacted (*238*), indicating an element of trampling, perhaps associated with the use of the derelict building as a refuse dump.

Layer *9* contained only a single fragment of fourth century Crambeck ware, presumably residual, whilst *39* contained a wider range of material. This included part of a copper alloy annular brooch (Copper alloy 4), of fifth to seventh century date, part of a small iron knife probably of early medieval date (Ironwork 6), and a trapezoidal hone (Worked stone 1). The ceramic assemblage from *39* was mixed, and included both Romano-British coarse-wares, and a single fragment of handmade pottery identical to that from Structure 6.

Structure 2

The whole of the base of the structure (Fig 6:9) was covered by a dark greyish-brown loamy sand (*83*, *c*0.25m deep), which slumped noticeably towards the centre. It sealed hearth *212* and also postholes *107*, *213*, *217*, and *229*, which indicates that *83* post-dated the decomposition of the timber superstructure. It seems likely that this material represented the decay of the building, containing, as it did, domestic debris which probably reflected its final use as a dump.

A group of sandstone blocks and some rounded stones (*191*) lay on sand *83*, covering an area 0.90 x 3.94m. None of these stones displayed obvious signs of working, and it is possible that they were clearance debris from another part of the site. Some, however, formed a crude alignment, parallel to the edge of the structure, with a similar orienta-tion, perhaps suggesting a common origin towards the south-west edge. This may suggest that stones *191* were collapsed building material, perhaps from a drystone wall or stone footings, situated at the edge of the cut. The proportion of clay in the matrix could lend support to this theory, perhaps indicating daub.

The latest deposit within this building was a dark grey-brown loamy sand (*81*, *c*0.25m deep). A char-coal-rich lens (*82*, 0.08m deep), containing some clay and sandstone blocks, lay towards its base, above stone spread *191*. Both *81* and *82* were similar to fill *83* below, but contained more charcoal and clay. These again probably represent the casual infilling of the hollow.

Like Structure 1, all three fills produced objects of mixed Romano-British and early medieval dates. Domestic items included wool-comb teeth and a simple iron latch lifter (Ironwork 27). Although no Romano-British vessels were found, there was a fragment of handmade pottery, similar to that from Structure 6. Roman tile fragments from this phase of activity are likely to be residual.

Structure 3

A substantial layer of light orange-brown silty sand (*104*, *c*0.27m deep), containing stones and pebbles, charcoal, and small lumps of clay, sealed occupation layer *124* in the base of the structure (Phase 2) (Fig 6:10), covering the northern part, but it appeared to respect posthole *122*, implying that the timber was in place during its deposition. The stratigraphy, soil matrix, and general paucity of finds seem to indicate that *104* comprised re-deposited natural sand which had perhaps collapsed from the side of the feature. This is reinforced by the presence of a reciprocal hollow in the northern edge of the structure. Such instability may have hastened the abandonment of the building. A localised deposit of very dark sandy loam (*67*, *c*0.25m deep), containing substantial amounts of burnt material, including animal bone, as well as some large rounded stones, lay above sand *104*, and was coterminous with it. This may represent a dispersed hearth deposit.

An orange-brown silty sand (*60*, *c*0.39m deep), above *67* and *104*, was clearly a tipped layer, deposited from the northern edge of the structure. Like *67* it contained pebbles, charcoal, lumps of clay, and an unusually large number of finds, suggesting that it represented further decay of the structure. The similarity of these contexts, and cross-matches in the finds, indicates that they were closely associated and thus likely to have been relatively contemporary. The uppermost material (*53*, 1.90m diameter, 0.42m deep) lay towards the southern side of the structure, above *60*, which encircled it in plan. This dark grey-brown loam contained stones and pebbles, charcoal, and some clay and also produced a substantial amount of finds. As elsewhere, the remaining hollow was probably used as a casual dump for domestic refuse.

The abandonment layers of Structure 3 were notable for the numbers of finds within them, interpreted as the disposal of domestic rubbish. They included a large amount of fragmentary animal bone, often burnt, Roman and early medieval ceramics, iron nails, and a fragment of metalworking residue. Of particular interest was the group of four small iron knife blades from fill *53*. Whilst not easy to date, their form suggests a likely date at some point within the fifth to seventh centuries. A group of six loomweight fragments of early medieval type can be dated to the seventh to ninth centuries. In addition, fill *104* produced a small glass bead, most likely to be sixth or seventh century in date, which, when considered with the other early medieval material from the fills, implies a date around the seventh century for the deposition of the assemblage.

Structure 4

The base of Structure 4 (Fig 6:12) was filled with a brown sandy loam (*170*, 0.12m deep), which mainly comprised disturbed natural sand *52*. Above this, fill *153* (0.08m deep) was particularly rich in charcoal. These fills are likely to represent the deterioration of the structure. The few finds were characteristically mixed Roman and early medieval in date.

Structure 5

The elements of pit complex *18* (Fig 6:13) were filled with a dark grey-yellow-brown silty sand (*57*), its mottled colour perhaps implying that it was mixed with heat affected sand *159*. It contained fragments of sandstone, rounded pebbles and charcoal, especially concentrated around posthole *77*. Although fill *57* was superficially similar to those representing the deterioration of Structures 1–4, the fairly frequent occurrence of burnt materials could indicate that fill *57* contained debris accumulated during the final use of the building. Fill *46*, above *57*, was a loose dark grey-brown sandy silt with a range of pebbles and stones, including sandstone debris. It was slightly darker than the surrounding ploughsoil (*45*), extended beyond the limit of pit complex *18*, and was probably spread by later ploughing (during Phase 4). The numerous tiny fragments of burnt animal bone, particularly concentrated in the ploughsoil above hearthstone *56*, may relate to its use. Although few in number, the finds from these fills imply a date, range of activities, and depositional succession similar to those of Structures 1–4. The only quern-stone (Worked stone 7) from the site was associated with this phase of abandonment.

Structure 6

The upper levels of the kiln (*64, 163*) (Fig 6:14) were filled with a red-brown silty sand (*44*), only distinguishable from the ploughsoil by the presence of fire-cracked stones and a dense distribution of charcoal. A loose dark brown silty sand (*12*) containing some sandstone blocks, including one possible architectural fragment, lay above fill *164* and the fills of postholes *226* and *227* (Phase 2). Both of these were clearly deposited after the kiln fell out of use and would appear to have been disturbed subsequently by ploughing (Phase 4). Like the underlying kiln, fill *44* contained a substantial amount of early medieval pottery, again mixed with a small amount of Roman material, including a vessel fragment dated to the later second to mid third centuries which was clearly residual. Fill *12* contained a fairly typical mixture of domestic refuse, including an almost complete iron whittle-tang knife blade (Ironwork 3), like those from Structure 3, and probably of early medieval date.

Boundary ditch

This phase of decay also appears to encompass the gradual silting of ditch *13*, which was filled with a light orange-brown sand (*14*), presumably derived from the decay of the sides of the feature. The only find from this fill was a fragment of wavy-edged horseshoe (Ironwork 4), which can be broadly dated to the eighth to twelfth centuries, and provides a *terminus ante quem* for the duration of the settlement.

Phase 4

The final phase of activity encompasses the period between the abandonment of the area for settlement and the present. The activity relates exclusively to agricultural practices.

Phase 4A

Several shallow parallel ridges of compacted dark grey-brown sandy loam (*48*), aligned north-east to south-west (each 0.5m wide, 9m long, 0.10m high), were identified above ditch fill *14*, in the west of Area 1. These apparently represent narrow ridge and furrow (1m wide). Although their width was similar to cord rigg *180* (Phase 1), their orientation differed markedly and they were generally more regular.

Ploughsoil *45* covered most of the area excavated, with the exception of the south-east part of Area 1 and some of Area 2, where the fills of pit *47*, linear feature *49*, and Structure 1 were sealed only by topsoil *1*. It varied in depth from 0.10–0.30m, generally becoming deeper towards the north, presumably as a result of hillwash. The number and range of finds demonstrates the extent of disturbance and truncation of the site by ploughing.

Phase 4B

Three linear features (*605, 606, 607*) were identified in the vicinity of the modern fenceline separating Areas 1 and 2, presumably the linear anomalies noted in the geophysical survey. These represent recent boundaries postdating ploughsoil *45*. Topsoil *1* was a fine sandy loam. Plough furrows within it (*11*) in the south-western part of Area 1, cut ridge and furrow *48* on a different alignment. The topsoil varied from 0.10–0.25m in depth, again generally deepest over the northern part of the site. The distribution of finds within it, like that from ploughsoil *45*, reflects the truncation of earlier features. However, individual finds still clearly reflect the spatial distribution of underlying features.

<hr>

The finds

<hr>

The Roman pottery

Christine Howard-Davis (from identification by Sally Cottam and Louise Hird)

One hundred and eighteen fragments of Roman or Romano-British ceramic vessels were recovered (Fig 6:15). Of these, just under 50% (52 fragments) were from samian vessels; the remainder were coarsewares and *mortaria*. The fabric series for the coarsewares is identical to that for Low Borrowbridge (*see Chapter 5*). Neither the samian nor the coarseware assemblages are of great significance individually, and they are, therefore, discussed together with regard to the stratigraphic sequence and the problem of residuality on the site. The material spans a range from the second to the fourth centuries, with no particular date indicated. Most of the fragments are small, often badly abraded and damaged, adding weight to the suggestion that its presence on the site in contexts of Phases 2 and 3 is almost certainly residual.

Phase 1

The presence of a single fragment of fourth century Huntcliff ware (Fabric 7, CW1) in disturbed natural sand *200*, and other fourth century fragments as residual material in several Phase 3 contexts (*9, 67, 83*), perhaps points towards a fourth century *terminus ante quem* for Roman activity on the site.

Phase 2

Thirteen fragments, four samian (S1–4) and eight coarseware (CW2–10), were recovered from Phase 2 contexts, compared with 224 fragments of the crude handmade pottery tentatively assigned an early medieval date (*see below*). Within Structure 1, both ceramic fragments from loam *15* were samian (S1–2), the latter (Dr27) from the Lezoux potteries, dating to around the second quarter of the second century AD. The living floor (*71*) produced two further fragments (S3, CW2), neither closely datable. In Structure 3 two undiagnostic fragments of coarseware (CW5–6) were recovered from posthole fill *123*, and floor *124* above it. Spread *158*, closely associated with Structure 4, produced three fragments of coarseware (CW7–9) and a single small undiagnostic fragment of samian (S4). From Structure 6, kiln fill *92* produced a single Black Burnished ware 1 rim (CW3), of late second to early third century date, amidst 158 fragments of handmade vessels, and fill *504*, of pit *163*, produced a single *mortarium* rim (CW10). Pit fill *106*, slightly to the east of Structure 6, produced a single fragment of Romano-British coarseware (CW4) amidst numerous fragments of handmade pottery. The paucity of Romano-British pottery associated with the living floors of sunken structures and other contemporary features, compared with the amount of handmade pottery of later date, suggests strongly that it is residual.

Phase 3

Seventy-one fragments, 32 samian (S5–36) and 39 coarseware (CW11–37), were recovered from Phase 3 contexts, compared with 43 fragments of the later, handmade fabric. Within Structure 1 abandonment fill *9* produced a single fragment of coarseware (CW11), assigned a fourth century date. Fill *39*, also an abandonment fill, produced seven fragments: five coarseware (CW13–17) and two samian (S5, 6). None were closely datable, but it is perhaps of note that both fragments of samian were from Dr37 bowls, a long-lived and widely produced form. The abandonment of Structure 2 (fills *81, 83, 84, 89*), produced a single fragment of coarseware (CW38) and nine of samian (S22–23, 30–36), the former providing a possible fourth century date. The fragments of East Gaulish wares (S30, 32, 35) suggest a late second to mid third century date. Similarly, the

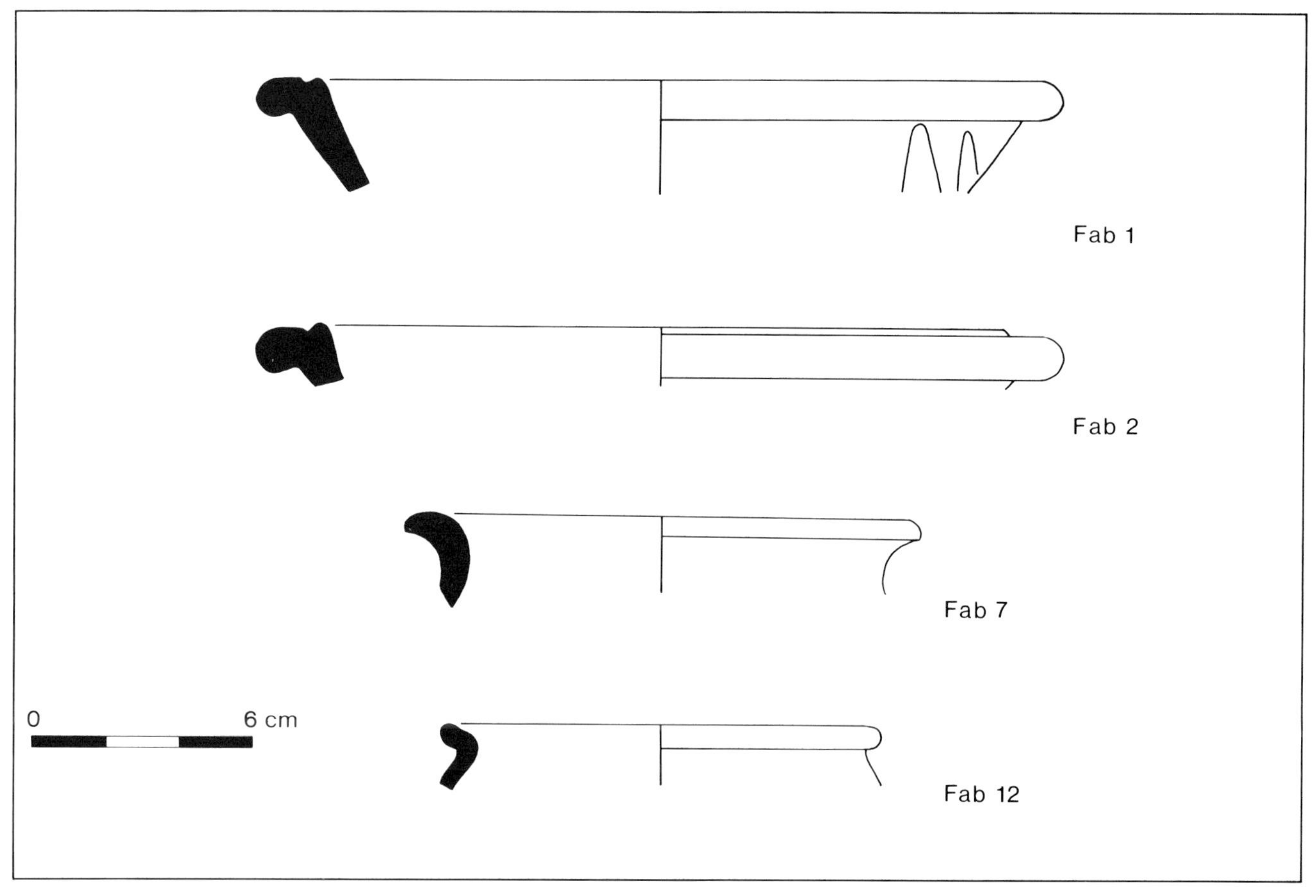

*Figure 6:15 Fremington (**10014**), Roman pottery type series*

decline of Structure 3 (*53, 60, 67, 68*) produced 25 fragments of coarseware (CW22–37) and 15 of samian (S7–21), the former providing dates of the late second century or later (CW23) and AD 300–370 (CW36), the latter including vessels from the Lezoux kilns and from East Gaul. Two of the East Gaulish fragments show signs of repair (S7, 9). From Structure 4, fill *153* produced a single fragment of coarseware (CW39). Finally the decay of the kiln (Structure 6) produced coarseware fragments from fills *12* and *44* (CW12, 18–21), with CW19 assigned a late second to mid third century date.

More than half of these contexts also produced fragments of the early medieval handmade ware. It is clear therefore that all are somewhat mixed, and it could be argued that the Roman pottery from them is entirely residual. It has, however, been noted elsewhere, for example at West Stow (West 1985, 82), that an unusually high proportion of samian on a site of probably early medieval date (here almost 50% of the assemblage) can be seen as suggesting the deliberate collection of samian, and other red ceramic types, by early medieval groups. Such activity is likely at Fremington, not only the collection of pottery, but also of glass (for recycling) and precious metal (the *denarius* from floor surface *124*,

Structure 3). This phenomenon has been discussed at length elsewhere with regard to grave goods (White 1988) and was undoubtedly also a widespread practice in settlements.

Phase 4

A further 27 fragments of Roman pottery were recovered from Phase 4 contexts: 15 coarseware (CW40–53) and 12 samian (S37–48). Whilst worthy of note, the highly disturbed nature of these contexts renders the material of little significance. A further six fragments (CW54–55, S49–52) came from evaluation trench backfills or were unstratified.

The early medieval ceramics

Christine Howard-Davis

Two hundred and eighty-seven fragments of crude handmade vessels were recovered (Figs 6:16, 6:17). The majority (225 fragments, 78%) derived from Phase 2 contexts, mainly kiln fill *92*. A further 41 were from Phase 3 contexts, only five from Phase 4, and another 16 derived from unstratified backfill contexts. At least five vessels were represented, and two forms can be recognised: a small, almost

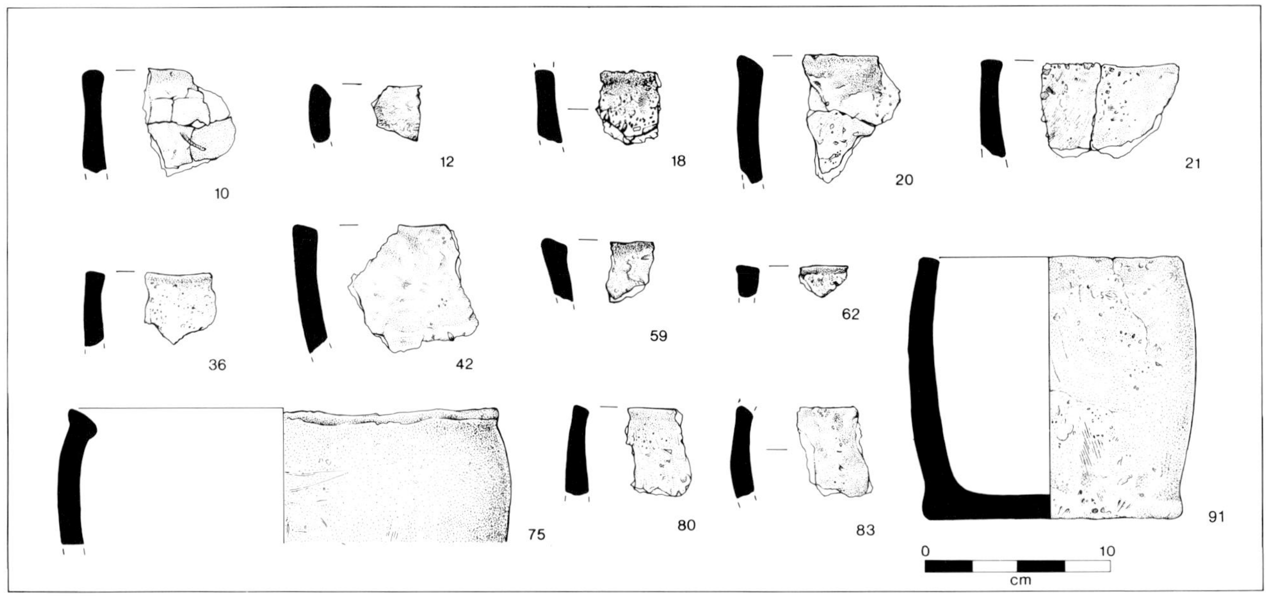

*Figure 6:16 Fremington (**10014**), early medieval pottery 1*

straight-sided, bucket-shaped vessel with plain upright rim and flat base (*see* 91 for a complete profile) and a larger jar with slightly inturned, thickened rim (*see* 75– no complete profile was recovered). Both are very thick-walled, *c*12–15mm. Some of the rim fragments suggested a third, open form, presumably a bowl, but the fragments were consistently too small for this to be established with confidence.

Visual examination of the fabric suggested that the group was remarkably homogeneous, with only a few fragments representing potentially differing fabrics. The main fabric (*see below* HM1) is extremely coarse and has masked the manner in which the pots were formed; however, it is likely that they were coiled, and certainly the base was formed separately as several of the vessels have broken across this join (*see* 203). The vessels appear originally to have had smoothed external surfaces, although the very large inclusions protruded on both sides, but secondary burning has badly damaged the surface of many of the fragments recovered. A slight alignment of the inclusions in several of the fragments might possibly suggest the use of a turntable for finishing, or might result from the method of construction.

A consistent but not universal feature of the fragments is the heavy sooting of the internal walls (but not the base, which is sometimes reddened and burnt) and, less frequently, the rim and upper external wall. This suggests that some of the vessels might have been used as fire covers, inverted over a heat source. On occasion, however, the sooting continues over breaks, implying that the soot was deposited after the vessel was broken. The presence of many of these fragments within a putative kiln strongly suggests that they might be abandoned waster vessels, not removed from the kiln; Arthur and Jope (1962–3, 9) have noted the difficulties of distinguishing wasters from other vessels when vessels are fired at low temperatures. Such an interpretation would also account for the secondary burning which appears to have damaged the surfaces of some of the vessels.

Such handmade vessels are difficult to date. They appear to derive from a long-lived native tradition rather than being intrusive early medieval types. Handmade vessels of this type are often difficult to differentiate from Iron Age material (Long 1988, IA Type 1). Iron Age activity is extremely poorly represented in the North West and in consequence there are few local parallels. There is, however, nothing else from the site to suggest a phase of pre-Roman activity and an Iron Age date can be discounted with reasonable confidence. Diagnostically early medieval artefacts have been identified, although predominantly in the abandonment phase of the structures (Phase 3); this has implied a *terminus ante quem* of the seventh to eighth centuries for the main activity on the site. It would seem reasonable to assign a similar date to the pottery. It has proved difficult to provide parallels, except for a single similar fragment from hillwash at Dacre (Newman and Leech forthcoming). The material certainly bears little resemblance to the assemblages from Jarrow and Monkwearmouth (S Mills pers comm), York (A Mainmann pers comm), or further south

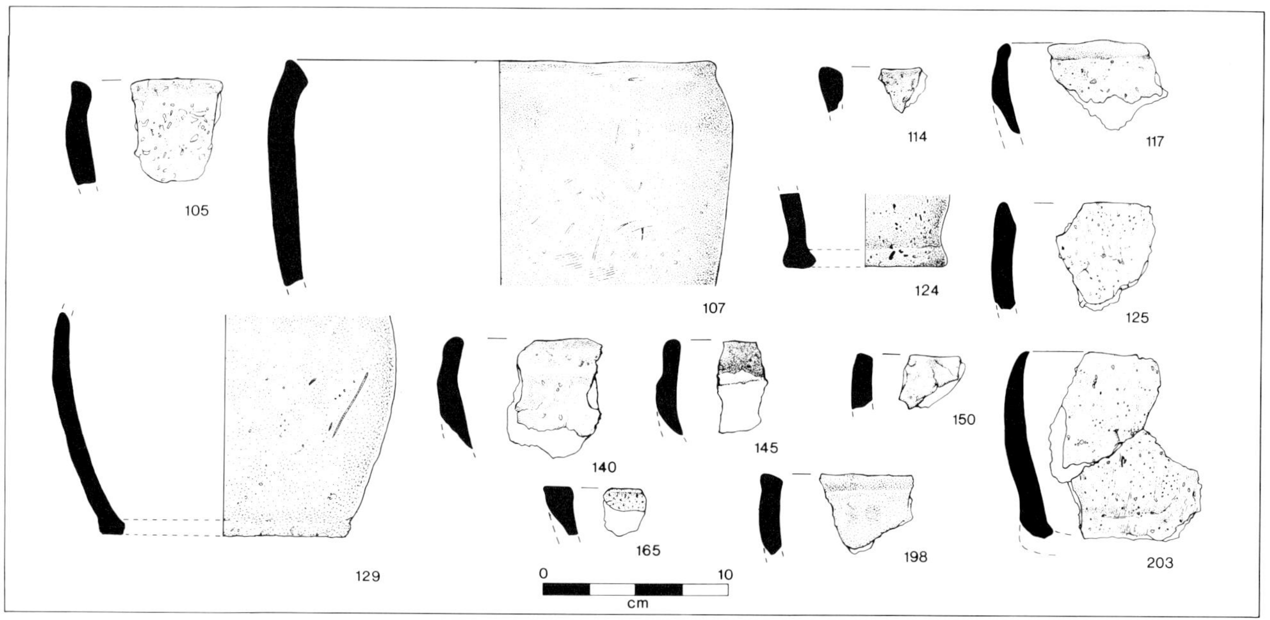

*Figure 6:17 Fremington (**10014**), early medieval pottery 2*

(H Hamerow pers comm). The closest related wares appear to be amongst the 'native' fabrics recorded at Yeavering (Hope-Taylor 1977, Class 1(A)) where, like many others, its resemblance to Iron Age antecedents is noted; others (McCarthy 1979, 153) have also noted parallels. The incidence of grass/chaff tempers and grass-marking (HM4) is often linked with early to middle Saxon pottery types (McCarthy 1979, 155, fabric 52).

Fabric series

Handmade fabric HM1 (2–9, 11–47, 49–63, 65–101, 103–114, 116–120, 122–150, 152–164, 166–186, 190–211)
Soft, with a harsh texture internally, many protruding inclusions, and a rough exterior, probably smoothed, and hackly to laminated fracture. Abundant, ill-sorted inclusions and possibly sparse grass/chaff voids. All inclusions are very coarse (up to c5mm), very angular, and of low sphericity. Limestone and an unidentified pale opaque pink mineral comprise the majority of the temper. The exterior surfaces are smoothed. Dark grey core and light pinkish buff margins and surfaces. Colour varies over the surface of vessels.

Handmade fabric HM2 (48, 64, 102, 121, 151, 165, 208)
Soft, with a slightly rough texture and hackly. Abundant, very coarse, well-sorted inclusions (up to c2mm), very angular, and of low sphericity. Both surfaces are smoothed. Salmon pink core and internal surface, variable brownish external surface.

Handmade fabric HM3 (1, 115, 187, 188, 189)
Hard, with a relatively smooth texture and irregular fracture. Generally abundant, ill-sorted, medium inclusions, but with occasional very coarse (up to 3mm) fragments. The smaller inclusions are quartz and the larger probably limestone. Both surfaces are smoothed, with some grass-marking, and the abundant quartz gives a twinkly effect. Dark grey except for the exterior surface which is brown. Colour varies over the surface of vessels. Includes a single, atypical fragment of a globular bodied vessel (188).

Handmade fabric HM4 (10) grass-marked
Medium, with a harsh texture, many protruding inclusions, and a laminated fracture. Abundant, ill-sorted inclusions and moderate grass/chaff voids. All inclusions are very coarse (up to c3mm), very angular, and of low sphericity. Limestone forms the majority of the temper. Both surfaces are smoothed and grass-marked. Dark grey throughout. Represented by a single rim fragment.

The medieval and post-medieval ceramics
Christine Howard-Davis

Sixteen fragments of later vessels were recovered. All derive from Phase 4 contexts, or were unstratified. Two (1–2) are probably of medieval date, whilst the remainder (3–16) are post-medieval. The most likely mechanism of deposition is agricultural practice, incidental to manuring or nightsoiling. They are of little significance to the interpretation of the site.

Ceramic objects
Christine Howard-Davis

Apart from vessels, only two categories of ceramic artefact were noted, spindle whorls cut from re-used vessel fragments, and loomweights. The spindle whorls are difficult to date but must be Roman or later, whilst the loomweights are exclusively early medieval in date.

Spindle whorls

Two ceramic spindle whorls (Fig 6:18) were recovered, as well as three stone examples (*see below*,

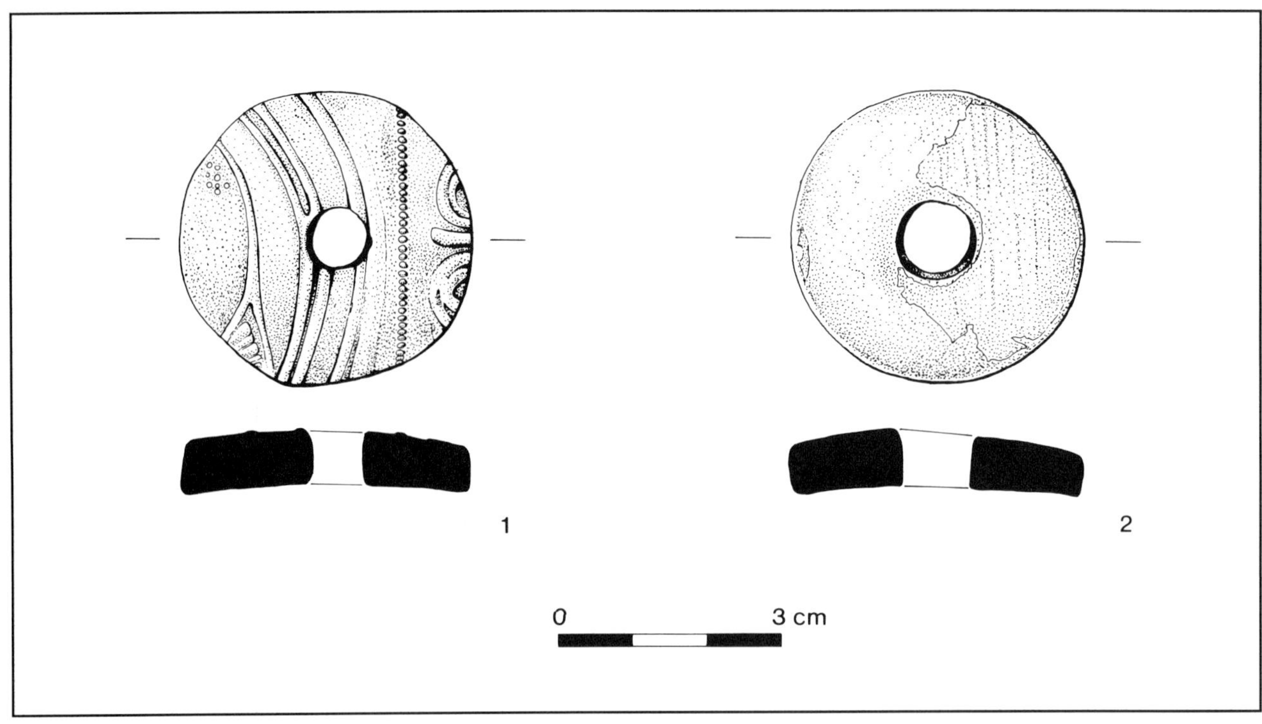

*Figure 6:18 Fremington (**10014**), spindle whorls*

Worked stone). Both derive from floor surfaces (Phase 2, Structures 1 and 3, *71* and *124*) and both are ground from fragments of samian vessels, one decorated (1), one plain (2). Such whorls are common finds on Roman sites, but also occur on sites of early medieval date, whether reused, made from deliberately collected samian fragments, or residual, is often unclear.

Loomweights

One complete, and thirteen fragmentary loomweights were recovered from ten contexts (Figs 6:19, 6:20, 6:21). All (with the exception of 13) were clearly handmade in a fine, slightly sandy fabric which incorporates some small flakes of mica, and occasional organic inclusions. This is very similar to HM2 (*see above*, Early medieval ceramics). Most, where their form can be determined, appear to be intermediate between the annular (early) and bun-shaped (late) types. The typology of loomweights developed by Hurst (1959, 23–5) appears to have grown somewhat subjective in the definition and dating of this type, but most of the examples at Fremington appear to fall within the appropriate size and shape ranges, veering, perhaps, towards the later, bun-shaped type in most cases. One, 13, may tend towards the annular form, and is definitely in a very different fabric, similarly 12 appears to be closer to the annular form, although in the common fabric. The only complete example (3)

from the site, however, would seem to be of the bun-shaped variety.

Similar intermediate examples from Yeavering (Hope-Taylor 1977, L1–4) are dated to the seventh to ninth centuries, but further south and on the Continent they are regarded as somewhat earlier (fifth century on). A date around the seventh or eighth century would accord well with the dating of other material from the site. Bun-shaped loomweights from Dacre (Quartermaine forthcoming) have been assigned an eighth to tenth century date, as have those from Whitby (Peers and Radford 1943).

The presence of loomweights, spindle whorls, wool-comb teeth, and a possible tenterhook suggests some textile production, probably at a small-scale domestic level. Most stratified examples derive from the abandonment levels of sunken structures on the site, suggesting that these buildings are likely to have been used for spinning and weaving.

Brick or tile

Christine Howard-Davis

Eleven small fragments (1–9) of brick or tile were recovered. Of these ten are too small for further identification, and the eleventh (6) is a small edge fragment of a typical Roman *tegula*. The majority derived from abandonment levels (Phase 3) and, like the Roman vessel fragments from these fills, is likely

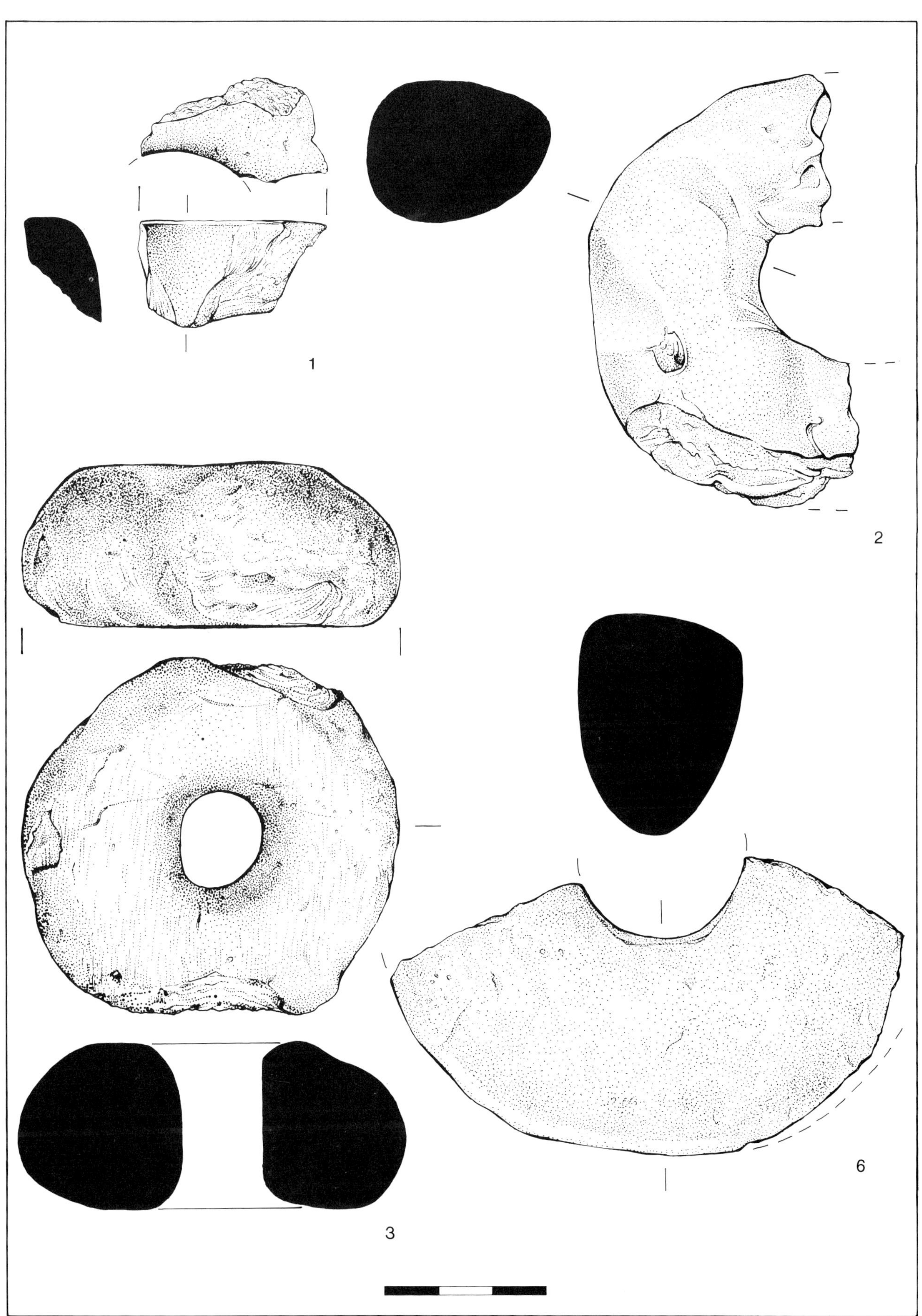

*Figure 6:19 Fremington (**10014**), loomweights 1*

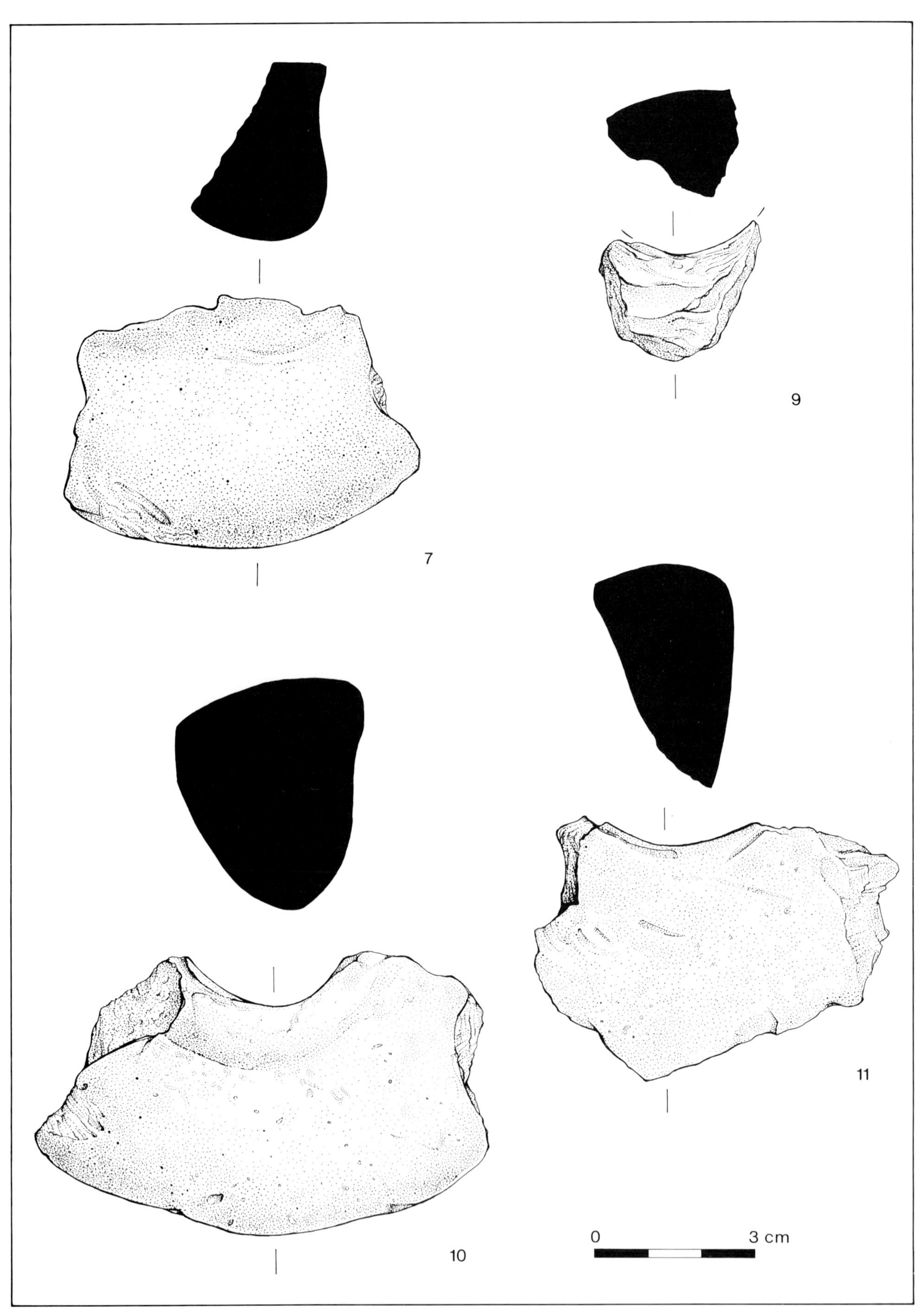

*Figure 6:20 Fremington (**10014**), loomweights 2*

154

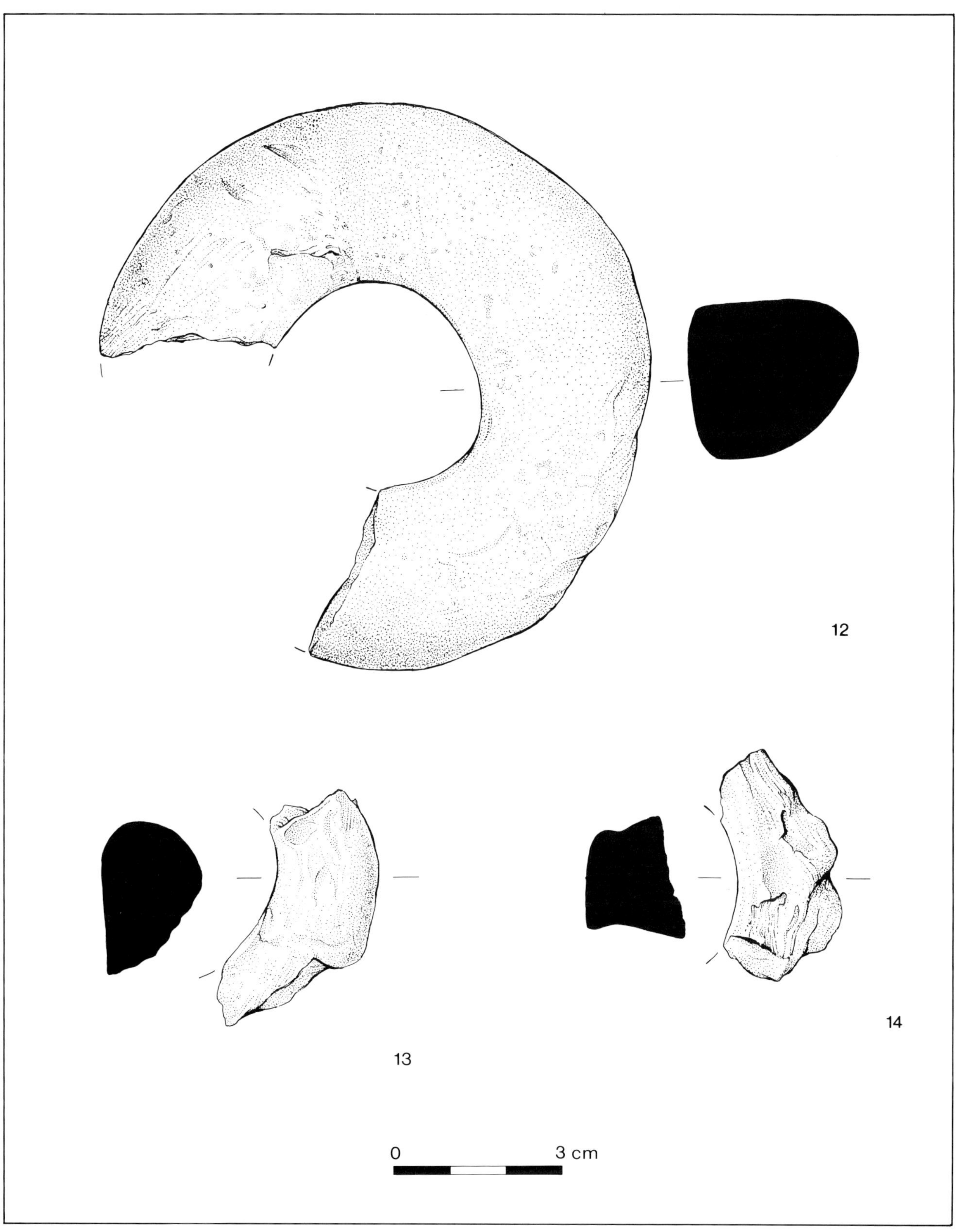

*Figure 6:21 Fremington (**10014**), loomweights 3*

to be residual. The amount recovered is too small to bear any implication on the nature of buildings on the site.

Burnt clay

Christine Howard-Davis

Only eight small fragments of burnt clay were recovered. Four (1–4), all probably daub, derive from Phase 2 contexts, but they are too small to add to the interpretation of the site. A single fragment (5) of fired clay might derive from a hearth or kiln structure, but again, it is too small to add significant information.

The silver coin

David Shotter

A single silver coin was recovered, a *denarius* of early third century date.

Ae *Denarius*, Julia Paula, AD 218–222
(RIC (Elagabalus) 214 LW)
fragmentary, but little worn
(MANAM 1226)
BRE91, Phase 2, *124/1489/1*

The copper alloy

Christine Howard-Davis

Six objects of copper alloy were recovered, of which two can be identified with confidence, the other four being poorly preserved or incomplete (Fig 6:22).

Phase 2

Three objects (1–3) derive from floor *124* (Structure 3), although they are all difficult to date. Plain rings like 1 are a very common type on sites of Roman and/or later date and they are simple functional objects which can be used in numerous activities, especially as components of harness, clothing, and furnishing. Object 2, a small, poorly preserved disc, is quite likely to be a coin. Interestingly, the only other coin, a third century *denarius*, derives from the same context, *124*, the primary occupation layer of Structure 3. Although fragment 3 is difficult to identify, its appearance would suggest a date of manufacture during the Roman rather than the early medieval period. The early date suggested by these and other finds from this structure is perplexing but, given that the site produced a relatively large number of Romano-British artefacts, it is perhaps possible to suggest that those from the structures (normally regarded as early medieval in date) are for the most part residual, deriving from prior Romano-British occupation of the site and its environs (Phase 1?).

Phase 3

Object 4 is likewise difficult to identify. It appears to bear a simple bead and reel decoration and narrows sharply at one end, perhaps forming a notch to accommodate a pin. Thus it is possible to suggest, albeit tentatively, that 4 is a small fragment of an annular brooch of early medieval type. Such brooches are comparatively common in eastern England and a parallel may be drawn with brooch G23 in the cemetery at Sewerby (Hirst 1985). Hirst notes an apparent connection between such brooches and areas of Anglian influence, and suggests that they derive from the Romano-British tradition: 'The annular brooches are just one element in the metalworking repertoire of the Anglo-Saxon that displays its Romano-British background in form and style' (Hirst 1985, 55). A precise date cannot be given to the plainer forms of annular brooch, but they have a general date range of fifth to seventh century. A date at the more recent end of this range would

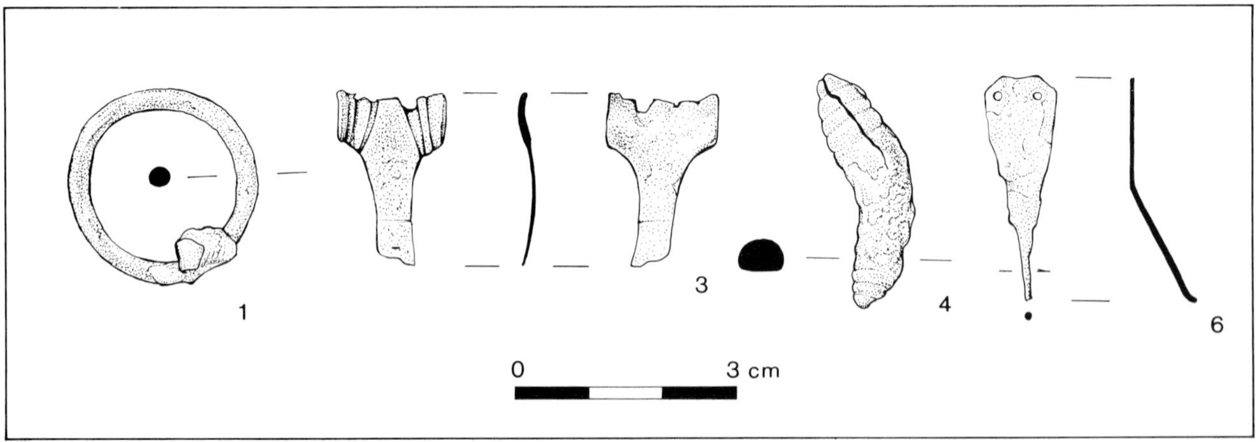

*Figure 6:22 Fremington (**10014**), copper alloy*

accord well with that of other early medieval material from the site, especially the loomweights, and its derivation from the abandonment fill (*39*) of Structure 1 might add weight to such a date.

Phase 4

Object 5 is very poorly preserved. It appears to be a decorative enamelled stud of fairly typical Romano-British type. Such objects are very common on northern military sites although seldom precisely datable. This example derives from ploughsoil and thus must remain undated. Object 6, a garment hook, is a typically early medieval type. It is a very plain example and the triangular attachment plate suggests an eighth century or later date (Tweddle forthcoming). This example derives from topsoil, and thus no more precise date can be offered, although a date in the earlier part of its range would seem more likely.

The ironwork

Christine Howard-Davis

Forty-seven fragments or objects were recovered from 21 contexts; 25% derive from abandonment layer *53* in Structure 3 (Fig 6:23). All are in a poor state of preservation, although their form is seldom completely obscured by corrosion products. All have undergone X-radiography. Approximately 50% of the objects (21) can be identified as nails with square-sectioned shafts and, where it can be determined, flat, round heads. Such nails are a common and long-lived type; none are large enough to have been used to join major timbers and so were presumably used to fix either small structural elements or wooden objects such as boxes or furniture. There is a single round-sectioned nail (31) which, deriving from topsoil, is probably modern. The limited range of artefact types comprises small blades (six), horseshoes (two), wool-comb teeth (four), latch-lifters (two), a hinge, and a large ring. All would fit comfortably within a small-scale rural domestic context. Three of the objects can be assigned a modern date (horseshoe 33, hinge 32, large ring 34). Many iron artefact types are long-lived and therefore difficult to date, and the material from Fremington is no exception; thus the date-ranges assigned to particular types must, of necessity, be long and often equivocal.

Knife blades

Six blades (3, 6, 9–11, 14) were recovered, all from abandonment contexts (Phase 3, *12* (Structure 6), *39* (Structure 1), and *53* (Structure 3)); three are almost complete (3, 9, 11). Five are of similar form, small (125mm long), narrow whittle tang knives with straight blades and slightly angled backs, the tang set more or less centrally (3, 6, 9, 11, 14). They resemble a common and long-lived Roman type (Manning 1986, type 14), but could as easily be placed amongst the group of early medieval and later blades from Lurk Lane, Beverley (Goodall 1991, fig 103), or examples from the cemetery at Portway, Andover (Cook and Dacre 1985), dated to the sixth to seventh centuries. Likewise, they bear a strong similarity to Evison's types 3 and 4 from the Buckland Cemetery, Dover (Evison 1987, 113), assigned a seventh century date on Continental parallels. The problem of residuality at Fremington must always leave room for dispute in the dating of common and undiagnostic objects. The presence, however, of other early medieval objects in abandonment layer *53* (Structure 3) might lend weight to the later date range for the blades. The sixth blade (10) is incomplete, but apparently has a short, triangular blade, reminiscent of an arrowhead. It is more likely, however, that it is a small blade or, perhaps, part of a spoon bit gouge.

Horseshoes

Two horseshoes (4, 33) were noted, one (33, from topsoil) is very large and almost without doubt recent, probably lost by a draught animal used in ploughing. The other (4), deriving from the fill of ditch *13* (Phase 3, *14*), is a small shoe of pre-Conquest or early post-Conquest date, displaying a typical wavy edge. Goodall suggests an eleventh to thirteenth century date range for this type (Goodall 1991) which, since it derives from the latest phase of activity, might provide a loose *terminus ante quem* for occupation on the site.

Textile-working equipment

Fragments of four possible wool-comb teeth were found (1, 15, 28, 42). They clearly fall into two types, one represented by a narrow strip with rectangular section, the shaft bent at right-angles (15, 28, both from the abandonment of Structure 3, Phase 3, *53*), the other a slender, round-sectioned pin with flattened, spatulate head, possibly bent at an obtuse angle midway along the shaft (1, 42, from Phases 2 and 4 respectively). The former is probably a Roman type (Manning 1986), whilst the latter resembles a pre-Conquest example from Lurk Lane (Goodall 1991, fig 102, no 303) but, again, such objects have so wide a date-range as to be effectively undatable. Object 21, from abandonment layer *60* (Structure 3, Phase 3), is a slender round or D-sectioned bar with a well defined barb at one end. It can be identified as a tenterhook, used in the production of cloth, although it could be a fish-hook, given the proximity of the River Eamont.

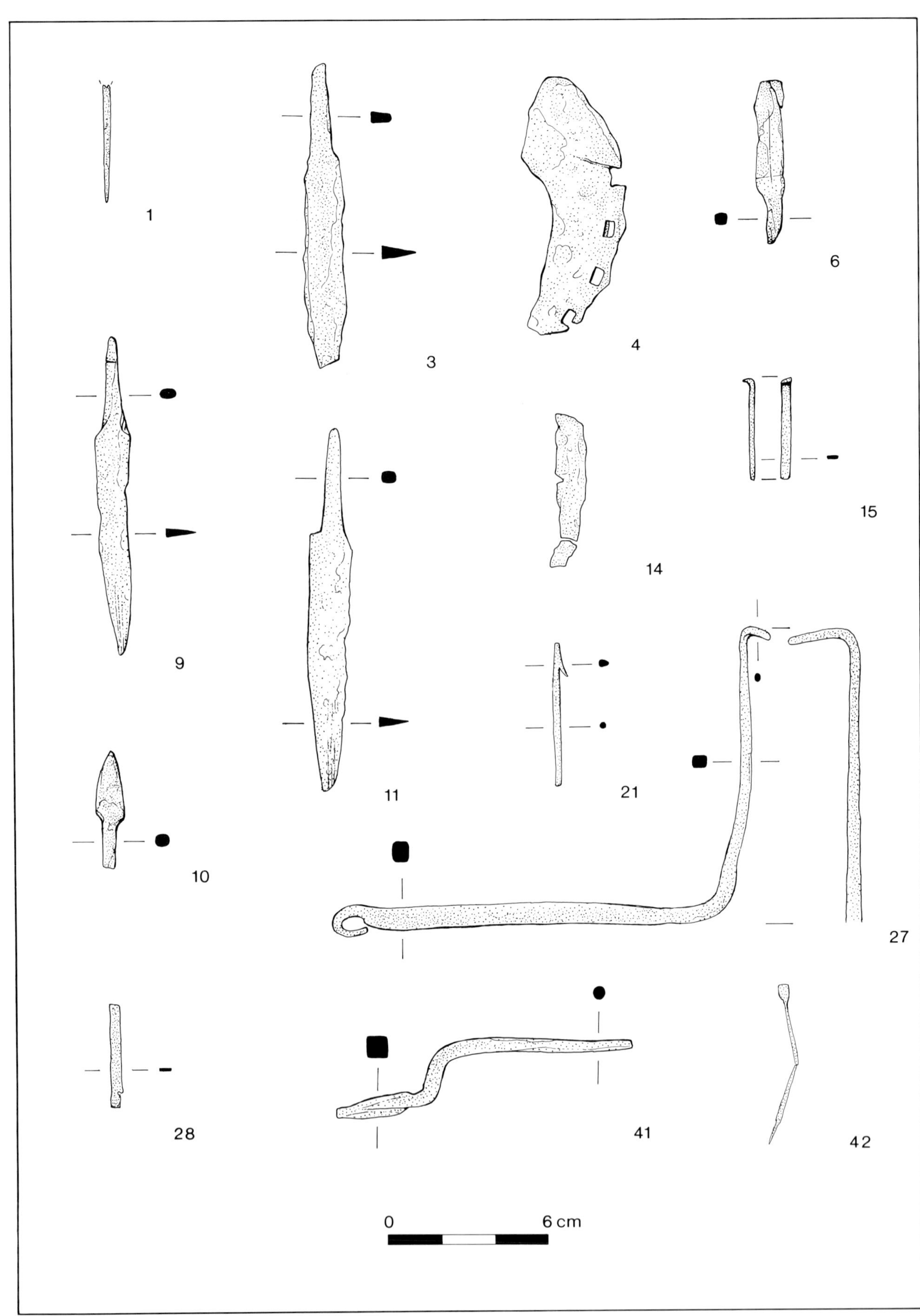

*Figure 6:23 Fremington (**10014**), ironwork*

Latch-lifters

Two latch-lifters (27, 41), one complete, were recognised. These too are hard to date, but the form of the best preserved one (27) appears to be a variant of a common Roman type. The use of such objects as substitute 'girdle hangers' is frequently encountered in Anglo-Saxon burials, suggesting that they were deliberately collected.

Miscellanea

One leaf of a substantial drop hinge (32) and a large ring or hoop (34) both appear to be modern. A further three fragments, probably sheet (7, 30, 40), and two bar-like objects, possibly nails (20, 29) cannot be further identified.

The glass

Christine Howard-Davis

A total of 37 fragments or objects of glass was recovered from 13 contexts (Fig 6:24). All were small, though largely unabraded. Four (18, 20, 23), all effectively unstratified, were fragments of dark olive-green vessel glass, which can be dated to the eighteenth century or later, and a fifth fragment (8) may also be post-medieval in date. A further 26 fragments can be identified as vessel glass, all most likely to be Romano-British in origin, with a date range centring on the third century AD. None of the vessel glass can be attributed an early medieval date. There are three fragments of probable matte-glossy window glass (24–26), which has a first to third century AD range. Finally, there are two beads (28, 29) and a small oval of dark blue glass (27), which can be tentatively identified as an imitation gemstone or inlay.

Vessel glass

Of the 26 fragments of Romano-British vessel glass recovered, more than 60% (15 fragments) are small, well-preserved fragments of natural dark blue-green glass. Six (3, 7, 9, 10, 17, 21) can be identified as fragments of square or rectangular mould-blown bottles, Isings 50 (1957), a common and robust form of first to third century date. There are three fragments of small bottles (1, 11, 15), possibly unguent bottles or bath-flask types, but all are too small for confident identification. Four of the remaining five fragments of blue-green glass probably derive from small cups; 16 is a small fragment of a delicate jug handle (Price and Cottam forthcoming), 4 and 12

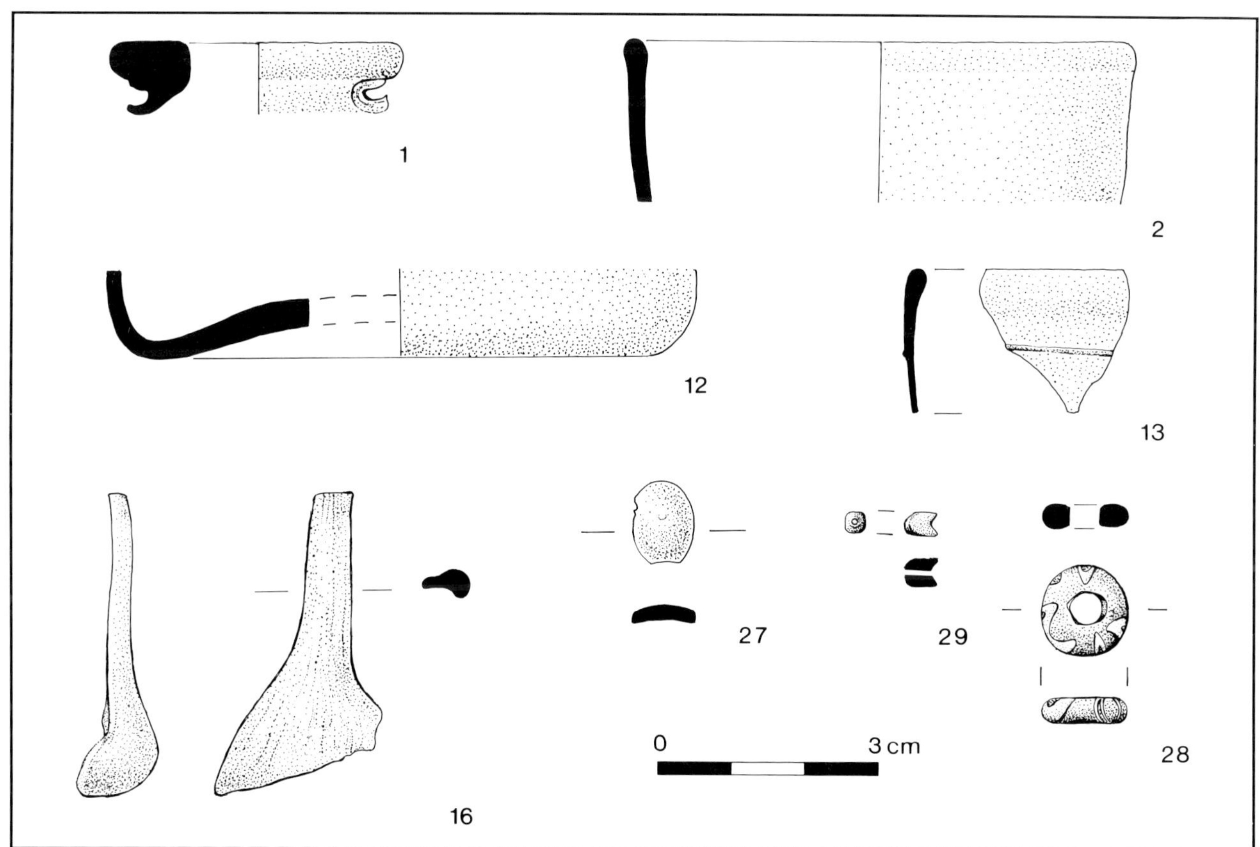

*Figure 6:24 Fremington (**10014**), glass*

are parts of bases of small blown vessels and 2 is a fragment of fire-rounded rim, probably a small cylindrical cup, Isings 85, of second to third century date. The fifth fragment (22) is undiagnostic. There are two fragments (13, 14) of colourless vessels, 13 is part of the fire-rounded rim of a small cup with a single self-coloured horizontal trail below the rim, possibly Isings 85; 14 is shattered and cannot be further identified. Object 19, in a greenish, slightly bubbly metal, is a base fragment of a blown vessel (the pontil mark remains) with indented base, possibly Isings 96, of third to fourth century date. The remaining nine fragments of pale greenish glass (5, 6) appear to derive from a single vessel; the fragments are too small to identify the form with confidence but the asymmetrical, fire-rounded rim, and fragments of a strap handle, suggest a jug.

Window glass

There are two fragments which can, with confidence, be identified as typical natural blue-green, matte-glossy window glass of first to third century type (24, 25), and a third (26) in natural greenish glass, which is most likely to be window glass, but might be an undiagnostic fragment of angular mould-blown bottle. Whilst none of the vessel or window glass fragments appear to be early medieval in origin, it is not uncommon to encounter glass of Romano-British date in later contexts. It is commonly accepted that early medieval groups sought out Roman glass for recycling, especially for bead production. The proximity of the site to the Roman fort at Brougham and, closer still, the Roman cemetery alongside the main road, would suggest such a process at this site. Examination of the industrial debris also offers the slight suggestion of glass-working. Evidence for bead-making, associated with a small amount of Roman and early medieval vessel glass, at the monastic site of Dacre (Howard-Davis and Quartermaine forthcoming), at a slightly later date, would tend to confirm the collection of Roman glass by the later occupants of the site.

Beads and a cabochon

Two beads were recovered from the site. One (29) is a small cuboid bead in dark blue translucent glass, Guido type 7 (1976), a common form dated to the later third and fourth century. The second (28) is a small poorly-made annular bead in bubbly, translucent, turquoise metal with a white marvered wave, Guido type 5. Guido assigns this particular form a very long date range, from the later prehistoric period to the late seventh century AD and beyond. It is tempting, due to the presence of other early medieval material on the site, to place this bead at the later end of its range. Object 27 is a small glass cabochon in streaky blue. It is oval, apparently deliberately cut or ground into shape. Glass imitation gemstones are commonly encountered set in rings during the later Roman period, but two similar objects were excavated at Whitby (Peers and Radford 1943, fig 22.8; Webster and Backhouse 1992, fig 107, 1 (i), (ii)) and were there interpreted as insets for pendant jewellery or furniture inlay, assigned a seventh century date.

Industrial residues

Christine Howard-Davis

Very little industrial debris was recovered, a total of 1.265kg from 14 contexts: 225g from Phase 2, 915g from Phase 3, and 135g from Phase 4. Few contexts produced more than 50g, many substantially less. Most of the material is small vesicular globules of a light, white material which has not been identified. Only three contexts produced relatively large amounts, in each case representing a single large fragment. A shattered stone (1) which had been subject to high enough temperatures to melt its surface, or was covered with glass, perhaps suggesting glass-working on the site, was found in *106*, associated with the kiln (Structure 6, Phase 2). A second partially vitrified stone (15, Phase 4, *54*) might add weight to this identification, but was effectively unstratified. A large fragment of metalworking residue (7), possibly associated with primary rather than secondary iron production, came from abandonment fill *53* (Structure 3, Phase 3), and a lump of possible forging slag (10) was also associated with this phase of activity (Phase 3, *82*). Although only a small quantity, possible hammerscale (11) was also found in Phase 3 activity (Structure 4, *153*). Whilst the evidence is insubstantial, there is sufficient to suggest some ironworking, definitely secondary working (routine blacksmithing) and possibly iron production, although there is no evidence for this on the site.

The worked stone

Christine Howard-Davis

Nine fragments of worked flint were recovered (22–30). Their prehistoric origin makes them irrelevant to the interpretation of the site. Otherwise, there were seven stone artefacts, three of which were whetstones or *ad hoc* sharpening stones (1–3), three spindle whorls (4–6), and part of the upper stone of a rotary quern (7). A further 13 fragments of stone were possibly construction material (9–21).

Whetstones

All three whetstones derive from Phase 3, and, like many stone artefacts, they are difficult to date

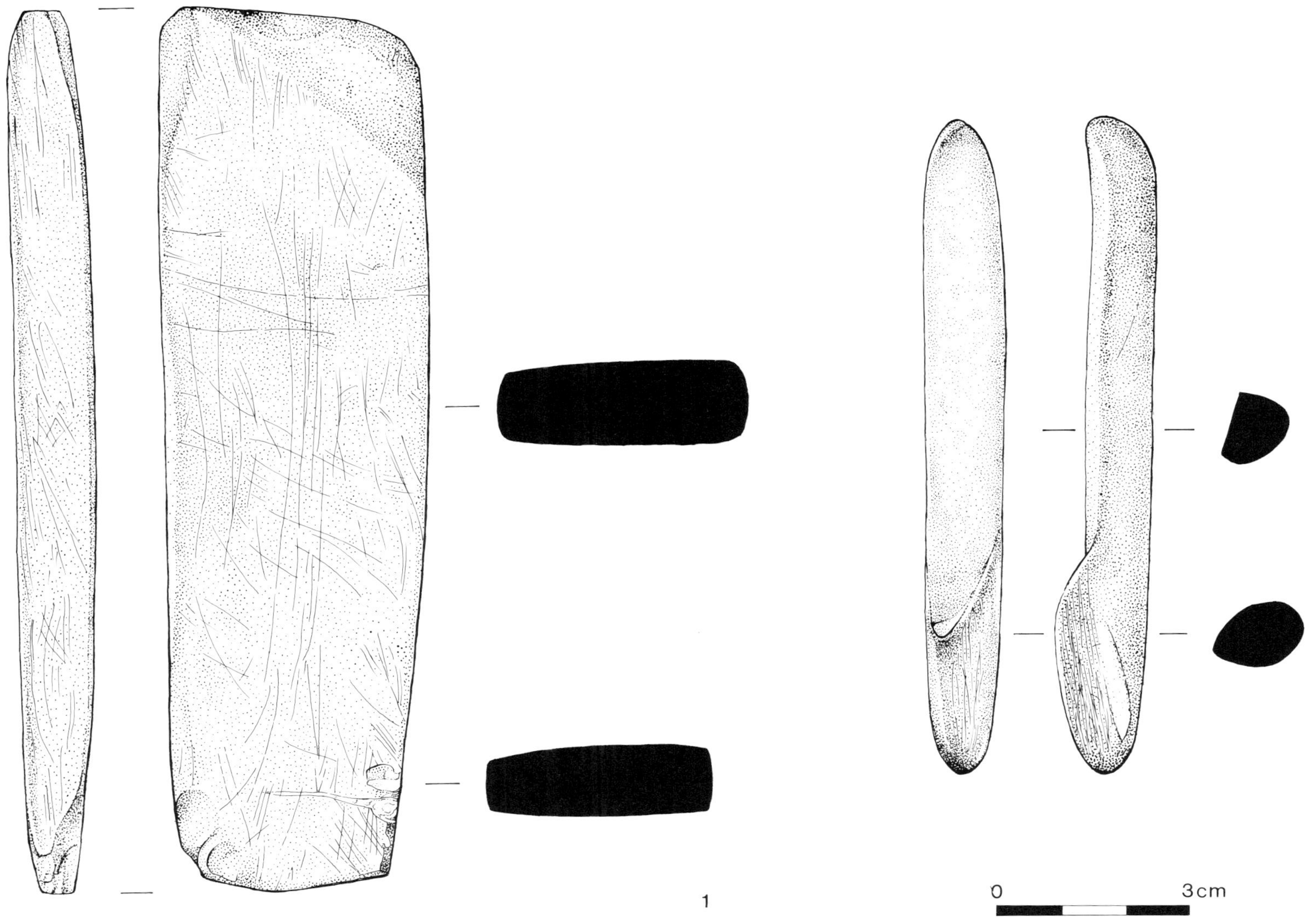

Figure 6:25 Fremington (**10014**), *whetstones*

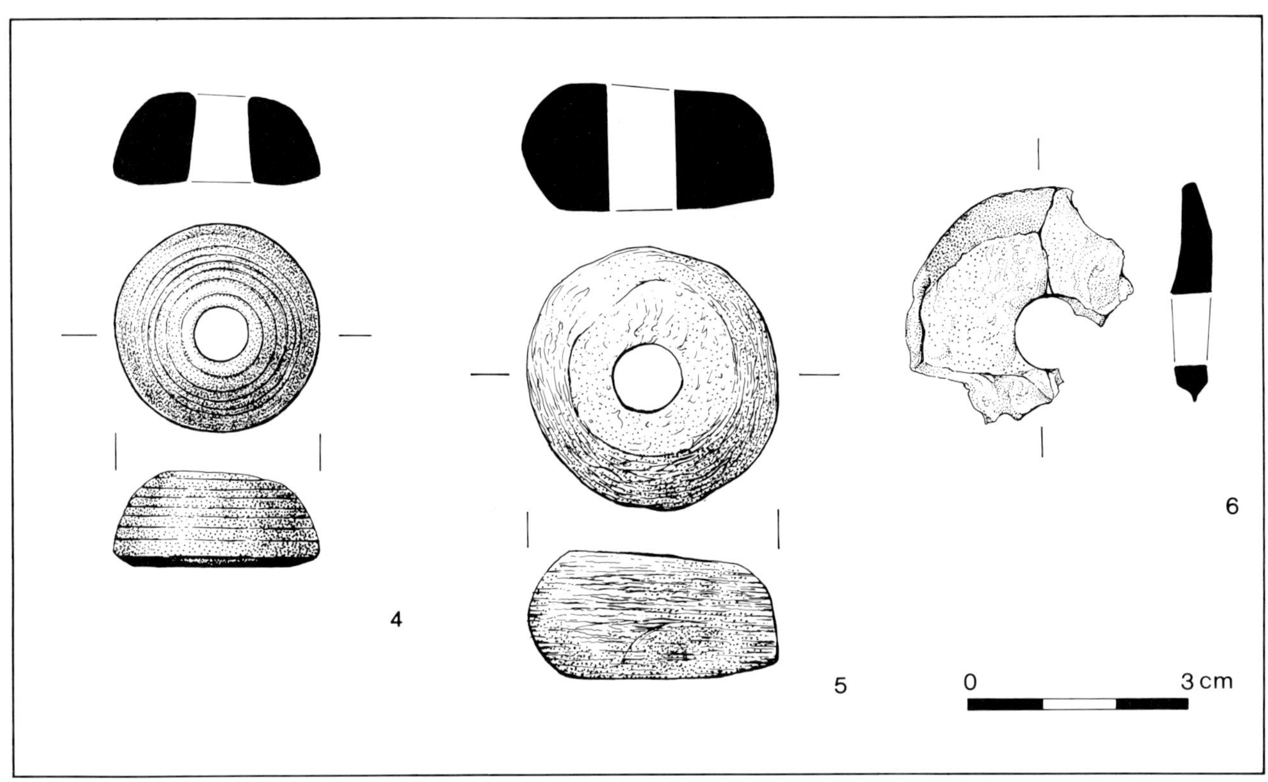

*Figure 6:26 Fremington (**10014**), stone spindle whorls*

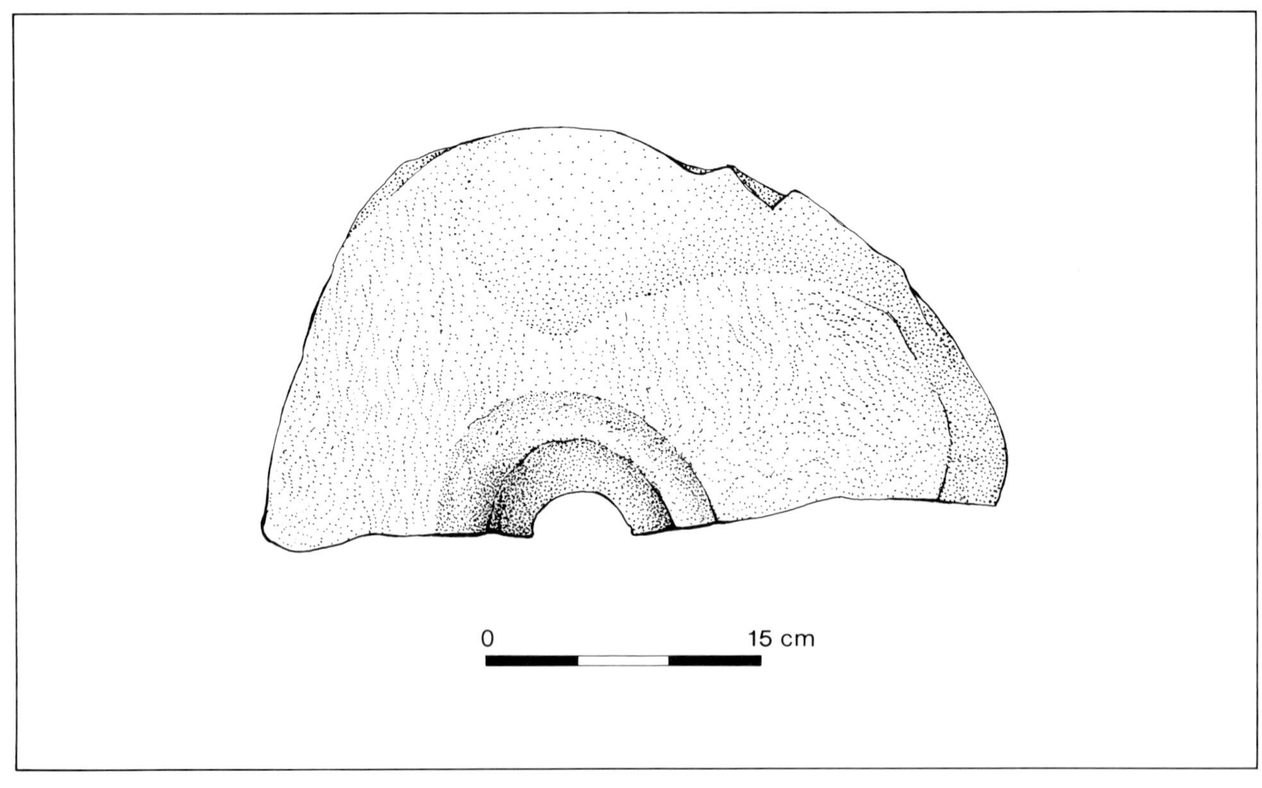

*Figure 6:27 Fremington (**10014**), quern stone*

(Fig 6:25). During the early medieval period there appears to have been an extensive and long-lived trade in suitable stone (Moore and Oakley 1979, 282–3), but two (2, 3) of the three from this site appear to demonstrate the *ad hoc* use of suitably sized fragments of local stone, in one case water-worn, for sharpening. The third (1) is a well made trapezoidal whetstone of deep green fine-grained rock. All three bear wear-patterns typical of use for sharpening blades (groups of parallel scratches) and their most obvious use would be for sharpening small blades, such as those found on the site (*see above*, The Ironwork).

Spindle whorls

The three stone spindle whorls all appear to be of early medieval type (Fig 6:26). One (5), of shale, is poorly preserved but appears to be of flattened biconical form. It can be paralleled by examples in jet from Dacre (Howard-Davis forthcoming) and shale from Portchester (Cunliffe 1975, 81, fig 141). The remaining two examples (4, 6) are turned conical (beehive) whorls. The former is a complete example in mudstone, whilst the latter is only a small fragment, possibly Lakeland tuff. Such objects are common finds on early medieval sites; very similar examples can be cited from Dacre (Howard-Davis forthcoming) and the farmstead at Bryant's Gill, Kentmere (Philpott 1990, 55), as well as numerous examples from York, Beverley, and Whitby.

Millstone

A single quern fragment (7) (Fig 6:27) appears to represent just less than half of the upper stone of a rotary quern, with a raised beaded rim around the central hopper. The grinding surface was very badly worn, suggesting that the stone had been discarded, but bore traces of pecking. The renovation of worn grinding surfaces by pecking has been discussed elsewhere and may possibly suggest an early medieval date for the stone, since Roman examples are usually grooved. A loose comparison may be drawn with the reused millstone from Dacre (Howard-Davis forthcoming).

Miscellanea

A single small, bead-like object (8) could be a small cylindrical stone bead, but is most likely to be a fragment of fossil crinoid.

Building material

There was little to indicate the use of stone (9–21) as a general building material on the site, at any phase. The local Penrith red sandstone tends to break naturally into rectangular blocks, leading to difficulty in the recognition of deliberately shaped or dressed building stone. Sandstone appears to have been used for hearth slabs (*see* 9) but for little else, despite the proximity of large amounts of dressed stone in the ruins of the nearby Roman fort.

Plaster or mortar

Christine Howard-Davis

Of the three small fragments of plaster or mortar, two (1, 2) are probably fragments of burnt lime mortar, possibly deriving from a mortar hearth (as in Structure 2), although recovered from the kiln (Phase 2, *92*, Phase 3, *84*). The other (3) is clearly modern and derives from topsoil.

The decorated bone

Christine Howard-Davis

The nature of the soils at Fremington has resulted in extremely poor preservation of bone, the only exception being heavily calcined, burnt bone. A single small fragment of burnt bone, from late material (Phase 4, *54*) is decorated with engraved parallel lines and paired ring-and-dot motifs (Fig 6:28). The most likely identification for the fragment is as part of the riveted side plate of a double-sided composite bone comb. Such combs were common in the late Roman and early medieval periods, declining in popularity in the seventh century, when they were gradually replaced by the single-sided composite comb (MacGregor 1985, 82–95, gives terminology and chronology).

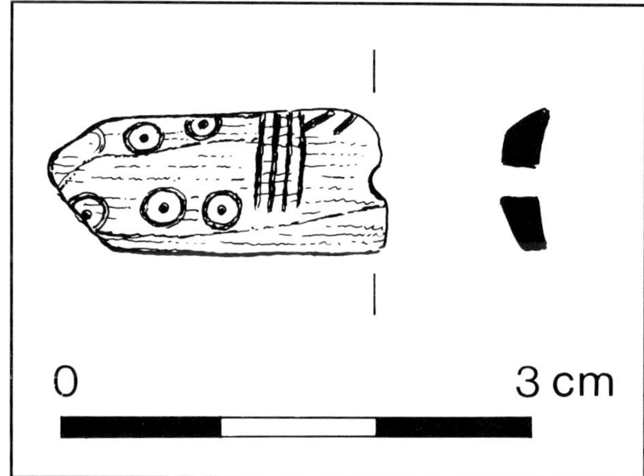

*Figure 6:28 Fremington (**10014**), bone comb*

The animal bone

Deirdre Winstanley

In general the bone was fragmentary and only moderately preserved, which may reflect soil conditions on the site. The preponderance of cattle teeth, both whole and fragmentary, is interesting. Although the numbers are small, they suggest the selective butchery of the carcasses; whether for the extraction of the tongue and other head meats, or for the extraction of the teeth and their enamel for other purposes, is unclear. The fragments (1158) from pit fill 7 (Phase 1) are therefore rather unusual in that they may well represent part of the forelimb of an individual beast. It is not possible to assign the teeth to the same animal positively, although this should not be ruled out altogether. The burnt bone was largely unidentifiable, due to the extremely fragmentary nature of the assemblage (*see Appendix 2*).

The palaeoenvironmental evidence

Jacqueline P Huntley

Bulk soil samples of various volumes, taken during excavation, were submitted to the Biological Laboratory, Department of Archaeology, at the University of Durham, for technical processing and subsequent assessment of any biological material in them. Given that the site was dry the samples were floated, with the flots being collected over 500μ. A few of the samples were so small that they were simply wet sieved to 500μ. The residues were sorted to 2mm and notes made of their animal bone content.

All of the flots were examined under a binocular stereomicroscope at magnifications of up to x50 and notes made of their constituents and any seeds that were present (Table 6:1). The material sorted from the residues consisted almost entirely of small fragments of burnt bone, which was too comminuted for identification, although they probably originated from large mammals, presumably domesticated species. The flots were predominantly tiny (*c*20ml) and, not surprisingly, few seeds were present in any of them. Oats (*Avena* sp) were the most commonly recovered cereal grain, with hulled barley (*Hordeum* sp), wheat (*Triticum* sp), and rye (*Secale cereale*) grains also present. Both barley and rye chaff was present. Although this was only in extremely small amounts it does tentatively suggest locally grown crops, since the species thresh easily and cleaned grain is more economical to transport long distances. The barley was, at least in part, derived from six-row *Hordeum vulgare* as some of the grains had twisted embryos characteristic of the lateral grains of this species. This is the species most abundant in the region until the late medieval period, and therefore does not give further help with refining the dating of the site. A variety of weed seeds was recovered and these all suggest cultivation on sandy to nutrient-rich, damper soils. Nothing is unusual about the weed assemblage.

The most interesting record for these samples is the presence of fucoid *thallus* fragments: these derive from the brown seaweeds. They are most like some of the *Fucus* spp but identification is uncertain since the pieces are small. Seaweeds are found around the Cumbrian coast on rocky shores and historically, in Scotland, they were collected and used in the making of cultivation beds – the inappropriately named lazy beds. The nutrients they contain make a rich soil when they eventually rot down; in addition, if they are mixed with a very sandy soil they will improve its water-retaining qualities as well as nutrient status. Seaweeds have been recovered from several archaeological sites of the Norse period within midden deposits; they have also been used in the manufacture of potash and, for this, are burnt in special kiln pits.

Table 6:1 Details of samples processed and sorted

Context	Sample	Volume processed	Residue material in c2mm fraction	Botanical comments
009	1135	1600	No finds	Oat awn
015	1145	1400	Burnt bone	Oats, barley
028	1147	1500	No finds	Oats, barley
057	1329	2200	Burnt bone, ind waste/slag	Oats, indet, barley
061	1148	1400	No finds	Wheat, legume
067	1255	4750	Burnt bone, 1 frag glass	Oats, barley, weeds
082	1472	800	No finds	Barley
082	1467	1700	One frag brick/tile	Oats, wheat, barley, chaff, seaweed
083	1483	1000	One frag glass	No seeds
114	1369	1800	One tiny frag burnt bone	Wheat
124	1367	2000	No finds	Oats, barley, weeds
162	1410	500	No finds	Oats, barley, indet, weeds

Discussion

An exhaustive examination of the settlement at Fremington was never intended, as only part of the site was disturbed by pipeline construction, although it demonstrably continued beyond the pipeline corridor; its full extent has therefore not been established.

The shallow and disturbed nature of the site caused a number of problems in the understanding and interpretation of the archaeological sequence, and two closely related factors have dominated the analytical process. Later disturbance severely truncated the stratigraphic record, leading to a virtual obliteration of relationships between most of the elements of the site, in effect leaving intact only the vertical relationships within individual features. Secondly, the level of Roman activity in the area has meant that the likelihood of residual Roman artefacts in subsequent phases is unusually high. Coupled with this is the lack of a clearly identifiable cultural assemblage in the North West which could be dated to the fifth to ninth centuries AD. Detailed analysis, however, has enabled two clear phases of settlement to be recognised at the site, dating broadly to the Roman and early medieval periods, followed by a long period of limited agricultural use.

The first settlement

Phase 1 activity in the southern part of the site proved elusive and difficult to characterise during excavation. Its situation at the top of a north-facing slope had led to increased erosion, drastically reducing the depth of the surviving features to as little, in some cases, as a few centimetres. Indeed, the only dating evidence for this phase was derived from the overlying ploughsoil, where increased concentrations of finds echoed the underlying features. It was, however, possible to identify a large rectangular structure (Structure 0), represented by shallow and discontinuous slots, the western end of which was defined by two irregular postholes. Another well defined posthole, about one third of the way along the south wall of the building, marks the position of either an entrance or a structural component. The close proximity of a pit containing articulated animal bone to the south-east corner of the building may be of significance. Evidence of possible cord rigg cultivation, to the north, has been associated with this structure on the basis of its similar alignment. Although insubstantial, the evidence suggests an agricultural character for this phase and perhaps also for the building. The articulated bone

from pit *47* represents a single bovid, and wheat was recognised in palaeoenvironmental samples from pit *97* to the west.

Structure 0 aligns with putative Roman strip-buildings recognised from aerial photographs in the fields between this site and the Roman fort to the west, and its size and shape are in keeping with those of extramural settlements in the North West, rather than the circular structures associated with the rural Romano-British tradition. Such an interpretation accords well with the suggestion (Higham and Jones 1975, 26–7) of a dispersed civilian settlement at Brougham, and strengthens the attribution of Phase 1 to the Roman period.

The second settlement

The activity attributed to Phase 2 was much easier to define and interpret, and can be assigned with confidence to the early medieval period. The group of structures and associated activity can be separated from that of Phase 1, both spatially and culturally, since it lay to the north of the Phase 1 structure, and one of the three building forms represented, a sunken-floored building, has long been associated with Anglo-Saxon settlement. The other types of structure identified were a post-built hall and a kiln.

Four sunken-floored buildings, in varying condition, followed a similar alignment, shared with ditch *13* which appears to define the southern limit of the contemporary settlement. Structures 2 and 3 lay close to this boundary, Structure 1 was *c*46m north of it, and Structure 4 was a further 30m to the north. There is no evidence, within the limits of the excavation, for a firm northern boundary to the settlement; the Roman road, on the line of the present A66, seems the furthest reasonable extent. All four buildings had in common a simple ground plan: a shallow subrectangular pit with single opposed postholes at the centres of the gables. This two-post plan is common in eastern and southern England, in particular at West Stow (West 1985) and Mucking (Jones 1979, 53–9; Hamerow 1993), and is normally regarded as the earliest structure of this type. They are less common, however, in the North and, to date, have not been identified elsewhere in Cumbria. In England, two distinct periods of use have been defined; in rural contexts they appear to be confined to the fifth to seventh centuries, but they become a common feature in urban contexts in the ninth to eleventh centuries.

Such buildings are thought to have had a relatively light thatched timber superstructure, carried on a simple ridge-pole laid between the two gable uprights. The roof would either be carried to ground level or supported on low walls, and the living floor may have been either at the base of the hollow, or suspended at ground level (*see* West 1985 for reconstruction). The evidence from Fremington can add little to a discussion on roof structure, but two distinct forms of below-ground construction were recognised. Structures 1, 2, and 4 were extremely plain, with the hollow apparently unlined, and an internal floor surface formed only by trampled earth. The floors of Structures 1 and 2 contained hearths, although whether the fires were for personal comfort or an industrial process cannot be determined. Structure 3, however, appeared to have a deliberately constructed plank lining, surviving only as a stain, retained by a row of small stakes (alignment *132*). Internal retaining walls can be paralleled elsewhere (Horsman *et al* 1988, 78–9; Hall 1982, 238–40), although substantial post-and-plank walls appear to be a feature of the later, urban, sunken-floored tradition. At Fremington, such extra provision might in fact suggest a different function, rather than a later date. It could be suggested that the lining of Structure 3 served to improve the internal conditions, perhaps to accommodate a sedentary task such as weaving, but no hearth was identified. The presence in Structure 3 of possible internal partitions seems to remove the possibility of a suspended floor, but reinforces the idea of a different function.

These structures appear to have been well maintained. The renewal of posts during the lifetime of the buildings, indicated by recut or supplementary postholes, implies a certain longevity. It is also evident that during this period the inside of the buildings must have been kept scrupulously clean since the occupation horizons are thin and almost devoid of finds. Nonetheless, the floor surface of Structure 3 yielded a number of finds, most of them Roman. These were either objects, notably glass, perhaps collected for recycling, or were of value, in particular a silver coin of early third century date. This cleanliness is in contrast to the apparently rapid buildup of domestic rubbish in the subsequent phase.

The spatial constraints of the excavation meant that little of Structure 5 was recorded. It seems, however, to have been a post-built hall, superficially consistent with the tradition of rectangular vernacular buildings which apparently spanned the Roman to medieval periods (James *et al* 1984). Such halls are frequently found in association with sunken-floored buildings on other sites in England, and do not necessarily denote differential status. Attention has been drawn to the uniformity between ground plans of these structures in the early medieval period, and it is now widely held that they may not have been introduced exclusively by the Germanic Settlement, but continued a tradition which grew out of Roman preference (Dixon 1982; James *et al* 1984, 205; Hodges 1989, 34–5). Similarities between buildings of this type include size, simple ratios (often 2:1) between the dimensions, a lack of internal structural supports, and partitions at one end (James *et al* 1984, 186–7, 203). Structure 5 was at least 3.6m wide and 5.2m long, dimensions comparable with contemporary structures elsewhere in England, where the majority of rectangular halls ranged from 4–5m in width, but with a greater variation in length, from 6–10m (James *et al* 1984; Horsman *et al* 1988, 66–7). There seems to have been a substantial partition close to its northern end. Reconstruction of the building was not possible, since the surface-laid elements had been disturbed by subsequent activity, but the building resembled others of its type excavated elsewhere, and reconstructed experimentally, in particular at West Stow (West 1985). These halls, when found in a close relationship with sunken-floored buildings, are often interpreted as dwelling and outbuilding. At Fremington, Structure 5 lay only a short distance east of Structure 1, respecting the same general alignment, and is likely to have been contemporary. Like the sunken-floored structures, this hall seems to have been in use for some time, and was well maintained, demonstrating some refurbishment including renewal of the hearthstone. It, too, may have been kept clean, as little occupation material was identified and the interior was devoid of finds, although this may be a result of later truncation.

Structure 6 has been interpreted as a kiln, although the level of disturbance was such that its exact form proved hard to establish. It is clear, however, that it was of simple type, either a clamp, or a single-chambered sunken kiln. There is no evidence for a deliberate internal structure, such as a raised floor, which would suggest the use of more complex technology. Only a few small fragments of fired clay remained of the superstructure, implying that it had been swept away, either in the course of recovering vessels after firing, or as a result of later disturbance. No fragments of kiln material were found in the disturbed ploughsoil above, and it may therefore be inferred that the material could have been deliberately removed from the site of the kiln as an adjunct to its operation. Some, if not all, of the vessel fragments found within the kiln, and adjacent shallow features, were very probably wasters, as at Purwell Farm (Arthur and Jope 1962-3), and some of them show signs of secondary burning, indicating, albeit tentatively, multiple use of the kiln site. The kiln at Purwell Farm was situated close to an apparent dwelling, similar in context to that at Fremington. Arthur and Jope (1962-3) have used this juxtaposition to suggest that pottery making was an entirely domestic occupation in the rural context. There the kiln was dated to the early Saxon period and, while the activity at Fremington cannot be dated so early, on such a moderately low-status rural site this simple technology could have continued in domestic use throughout the pre-Conquest period. The nature of the pottery clearly reflects a persistent indigenous tradition, originating in the prehistoric period, its simplicity needing no more than a basic clamp kiln for successful production. In consequence it is difficult to date independently, but its coincidence with elements of the Phase 2 settlement, which has been dated on other grounds to the middle Saxon period, suggests a similar date range.

Abandonment and decay

Phase 3, in direct contrast to the preceding activity, is marked by a substantial accumulation of material within the buildings, presumably the result of abandonment and decay. Structures 1–4 and 6 were filled by deep, mixed rubbish deposits, quite unlike the extremely shallow occupation horizons of Phase 2. Ploughing has removed almost all evidence of this phase in Structure 5. It seems likely that after abandonment the buildings fell into a gradual decline. There is slight evidence to suggest that timbers may have been removed on an *ad hoc* basis for use elsewhere, but in general the buildings appear to have decayed naturally. During this process they, or their ruins, would seem to have served as convenient domestic rubbish tips. Such irregular use would account for the number of fills, tipped and interleaving, identified within each of the sunken structures, which must represent both the dumping of rubbish and the piecemeal collapse of the building. Structure 3, in particular, provides evidence for a localised collapse of one side of the hollow.

As a consequence of the process outlined above the majority of the finds from the site derive from Phase 3 fills. They are somewhat mixed, with both Roman and early medieval artefacts present. The Roman element can perhaps be discounted as residual, deriving both from disturbed Phase 1 contexts to the south and the collection of Roman material for reuse. The early medieval material undoubtedly accumulated as this part of the settlement was abandoned, and therefore must provide a *terminus ante quem* for the buildings. The range of finds from the structures suggests an end date around the seventh to eighth century or slightly later. However, the finds from the fill of boundary ditch *13* suggest a later date, showing that the ditch fill accumulated rather more slowly and implying

that the abandonment of this part of the site was not contemporary with that of the entire settlement, which may have continued into at least the late pre-Conquest period.

Latest use

The centuries following the abandonment of the settlement have left remarkably little trace in the archaeological record, and the area seems to have been used exclusively for agricultural purposes. Evidence for ploughing was identified, although the relatively shallow accumulation of ploughsoil suggests that this was intermittent, consistent with the long-term use of the land as pasture.

Dating and residuality

The Roman material is in general unexceptional, with coarsewares dating from the second to fourth century AD. There is a surprisingly large amount of samian ware for a rural site, originating from both Central (Lezoux) and East Gaulish factories; various mechanisms have been suggested to account for its presence. The date range of this pottery is well corroborated by the glass, which likewise dates from the second to fourth century AD. It is difficult to assign a date to much of the ironwork, in particular the whittle tang blades, but contextual evidence suggests that they are more likely to be early medieval than Roman. Much of the Roman material derived from highly disturbed ploughsoil and topsoil contexts; it is fragmentary and abraded, suggesting either that it has been exposed for a long period and damaged by trampling, or that it has moved around within the soil. It is therefore clear that the Romano-British finds assemblage from the site can be regarded as largely residual.

Although the early medieval material cannot be dated with precision, as is the case with all Cumbrian sites at present, the general trend points to a seventh to eighth century date. The ceramic assemblage is of significance, for whilst the loomweights are clearly of early medieval type, and can be easily paralleled at numerous sites in the North, the vessels are in simple, handmade fabrics which were probably made on site and are not paralleled in any quantity elsewhere. The vessels do not correspond in fabric or form to any from York (A Mainmann pers comm), East Anglia (H Hamerow pers comm), or the monastic sites at Monkwearmouth, Jarrow, and Whitby (S Mills pers comm), and are clearly in the long-lived, very simple tradition of local prehistoric types. There appears to be sufficient evidence from the site, however, especially in view of the presence of a putative kiln, to suggest that the vessels from Fremington are of early medieval date.

Early medieval ironwork is also difficult to date and cannot be used to refine stratigraphic sequences, although the group of six small knife blades is probably of seventh or eighth century date. Fine metalwork was scarce, and only a possible annular brooch and a garment tag were recovered. There was also a single glass bead of possible seventh century date.

With the major exception of the ceramic material from the kiln, most of the early medieval material derives, like many of the Romano-British objects, from contexts associated with the demise of the settlement, and thus could also be described as residual. This material was, however, generally represented by larger fragments than the Romano-British material and thus had probably not travelled as far in the soil. The distinct concentrations of material in the ploughsoil and topsoil over the buried structures perhaps implies that the site was not disturbed frequently until more recent times, although ploughing has now seriously truncated the archaeological stratigraphy.

The nature of the settlement

Consideration of both the structural and finds evidence would suggest that Fremington was a small-scale, moderately low-status, rural settlement throughout its existence. Its origins are likely to have been associated with the Roman occupation of the area, but it is clear that settlement continued, perhaps sporadically, throughout the early medieval period, ending by the early post-Conquest period. As is characteristic of the region, there is no indisputably fifth or sixth century material but, without doubt, the settlement was in existence shortly after, perhaps slightly earlier than other sites known from the region, with the possible exception of Bryant's Gill (Dickinson 1985). As such, it begins to fill the gap between the early post-Roman occupation at Birdoswald on Hadrian's Wall (Wilmott forthcoming) and the well-attested monastic activity at Dacre, only 9km south-west of Fremington (Newman and Leech forthcoming).

Domestic buildings on the site have been divided into two groups: the hall-type, and sunken-floored structures. Current interpretation of hall-type structures is as living space, but the precise function of sunken-floored structures has long been a matter of dispute. There seems little doubt that at times this type of building was used as domestic accommodation, but the increasing recognition of hall-type structures in association with them has led to the suggestion that they were frequently more likely to be outbuildings, intended to house small-scale industrial processes such as weaving. Space allocation was obviously more fluid in the early post-Roman period than was the case in later urban contexts, where there is evidence for a rather more rigid delineation of functions. Evidence from Fremington suggests the use, at least, of Structure 3 for domestic textile production since, although spindle whorls, loomweights, and wool-comb teeth were found throughout the site, there was a notable concentration in that particular structure (Phase 3, *67, 60, 53*).

There is no reason to believe that the presence of a kiln on the site implies anything other than domestic production of pottery for use by the community. It need not imply the presence of specialist potters and indeed domestic-scale potting appears to be a characteristic of early medieval rural settlement.

The domestic economy

Apart from the textile production and potting mentioned above, very small amounts of industrial debris hint at blacksmithing and possibly glassworking, again for domestic purposes. It is certain, however, that a rural community such as Fremington would have relied principally upon agriculture. The local soils are of comparatively good quality for the region (Jarvis *et al* 1984; Higham 1986) and, although limited, the botanical remains include a variety of weed seeds which suggest sandy to nutrient-rich and damp soils during the period which spanned the occupation and initial decline of the settlement. The presence of brown seaweed (*Fucus* sp) within the decomposition material of Structure 2 may indicate one method used to supplement these soils, since manuring with seaweed improves both the water-retaining qualities and the nutrient levels of very sandy soils. Alternative explanations for the presence of seaweed include the manufacture of potash or the transport of sea salt; although there is no additional evidence to support either of these suggestions, some deliberate act must account for the import of seaweed to a site some 50km from the sea.

The evidence appears to suggest a mixed economy, since analysis of the botanical remains indicated that oats (*Avena* sp), hulled barley (*Hordeum* sp), wheat (*Triticum* sp), and rye (*Secale cereale*) were present on the site. The presence of barley and rye chaff, although only in extremely small amounts, suggests locally grown crops rather than threshed grain brought in from elsewhere. The domestic processing of grain is confirmed by the presence of a rotary quern (Worked stone 7) associated with Structure 5 (Phase 3, *43*). Soil conditions were not conducive to the survival of bone, but the small assemblage established the presence of the usual range of domesticated species (cattle, sheep, and possibly pig). The recognition of domestic fowl (*Gallus*) amongst the many very small fragments of burnt bone might imply their consumption.

Post-Roman settlement in the North West

Sunken-floored structures, or *grübenhäuser*, are without doubt of Continental origin (Rahtz 1981, 55–6), where they appear over a wide area in the late Roman period. In Britain, the earliest sunken structures are normally found in the south and east of England in rural contexts, where they are accepted as early Saxon in date. Although most closely linked with areas of early Anglo-Saxon settlement, the construction plan seems to have been readily adopted by indigenous communities and became widespread. The type persisted for much of the pre-Conquest period, although from the ninth century onwards it is found primarily in urban contexts and by then had undoubtedly changed somewhat in function.

In Cumbria, until the excavations at Fremington, there has been no evidence for any such structures. The closest parallels are from Manchester, where four large subrectangular features (ranging in size up to 6.4 x 3 x 1m) cut features of fourth century date (Holdsworth 1983; Tanner 1986). Although these may be attributed to the post-Roman period, their specific dating and function are open to question, and the lack of major structural members forming a classic ridge-pole construction is not typical of sunken buildings in Britain (Walker 1986). Other examples from Chester and York are clearly later in date and from a proto-urban or urban environment (Hall 1984; Mason 1985). Apart from the site at Fremington, the only comparable open rural settlement in North West England is Bryant's Gill in Kentmere, which can be dated to the eighth century, but this appears to have been significantly different in character, not least because it was largely constructed in stone (Dickinson 1985).

The site at Fremington should not be viewed in isolation: an early Christian site has been suggested at Ninekirks, only 3km to the north-east (Simpson 1958; Bouch 1955), where aerial photographic evidence has identified a large enclosure. At Dacre, activity seems to have commenced in the fifth or sixth century, although the religious settlement flourished from the eighth to eleventh centuries (Newman and Leech forthcoming). The widespread distribution of both Anglian and Scandinavian influenced stone sculpture illustrates an intensification of settlement in the later period, and at Carlisle and Penrith proto-urban activity appears

to have originated before the twelfth century.

At present, it is difficult to define the precise chronological relationship between Roman and early medieval settlement in the region. In some places, especially the Roman fort at Birdoswald (Wilmott forthcoming), it has been suggested that occupation continued unbroken. In contrast, at Fremington it would seem more satisfactory to propose a gradual shift in settlement within a limited area, rather than continued occupation of specific buildings. However, a continued knowledge and exploitation of local Roman material can be inferred from the presence of demonstrably early medieval living floors, which have produced an exclusively Romano-British assemblage. This is paralleled at West Stow, in Suffolk, where the amount of late Romano-British material in Anglo-Saxon contexts was interpreted as the result of salvaging material from a nearby Romano-British site (West 1985, 167–8). In addition, it is now widely accepted that early medieval groups not only sought, but valued, certain Roman artefacts, for example samian ware and copper alloy keys. Likewise, there is no doubt that much early medieval glass recycled Roman fragments (White 1988).

Conclusions

The excavations at Fremington have contributed significantly to an understanding of the early medieval settlement of the North West, despite the natural limitations of rescue archaeology. It has been possible for the first time to demonstrate conclusively the existence of sunken-floored structures within a post-Roman rural settlement in Cumbria. Analysis of the site has highlighted the persistence of indigenous tradition, characterised by the manufacture of simple handmade pottery, alongside the adoption of ostensibly imported practices, such as the use of sunken-floored structures. This implies that whilst it is not impossible that some Anglian settlement may have occurred at the site, the presence of sunken-floored structures can no longer be regarded as conclusive proof of immigration. It is likely that the location of the settlement, on a long-established communications and trading route, would have created a climate where new ideas and stimuli were readily adopted by the indigenous population. This accords well with a growing academic recognition of the inherent demographic stability of rural areas, in other words that change tends to occur through assimilation rather than invasion.

7

A FARMSTEAD AT POWSONS, NEAR TEBAY

The deserted farmstead at Powsons (Fig 7:1; **1132, 1133,** NY 61380237–61360225) was first located during the rapid field scan in March 1990, when it was recognised as a complex of features which, considered together, indicated a settlement. There were no standing structures, other than decayed field walls, nor was there any previous record of the site in the Cumbria SMR. Most of the features were directly on the pipeline route, and although this was subsequently revised to run slightly lower down the slope, the constraints of the topography meant that several features still could not be avoided. A range of techniques was therefore used to determine the nature of the earthworks observed during fieldwalking. Aerial photography, topographical survey, trial trenching, and eventually area excavation were used to record field boundaries, trackways, sheepfolds, and the most significant feature, a subrectangular stone building. The survey and excavation demonstrated the former existence of a small farmstead, and documentary research provided dating evidence for its use during the sixteenth to nineteenth centuries.

The topographical and historical setting

Powson Knott (374m) is a minor summit on the north–south ridge of Tebay Fell, at the narrowest part of the Lune gorge, opposite Jeffrey's Mount (378m). The valley side descends steeply as far as the intake wall, and a gentler gradient then coincides with the enclosed fields. The west-facing slope of Powson Knott features an eroding rock outcrop (at 300m OD) which has created a boulder field extending over a broad area of the lower slopes leading down to the River Lune, and this has affected landuse. The intake wall, built around the turn of the nineteenth century, arrested any further boulder runs onto the fields on the shelf above the final drop to the river, and also altered the drainage pattern. Although the boulders have been freely quarried to build field walls, sheepfolds, and farm

buildings, much surface stone remains to confuse the eye and obscure the man-made features. As the stone was too abundant to clear from the site completely, there has been very little scope for ploughing and drainage, in sharp contrast to the adjoining field to the north (**11315**) in which narrow ridge and furrow, representing late improved pasture, and the pattern of artificial drainage, are visible on aerial photographs.

The high annual rainfall in the Lune gorge has contributed to gullying of the upper slopes, and the thin soils overlying the rocky fellside, often saturated with rainwater, are affected by hillwash and occasional landslips. The narrow parallel gullies running off the fell to the north, and the deep ravine of Dry Gill to the south, contrast with the boulder-strewn fields of Powsons. These are crossed by two minor streams, rising from the spring-line just below the intake wall, and converging below the modern trackway which crosses the site from north to south. Water has evidently been channelled across the slope from the more northerly spring, to bring water to stock enclosures alongside the northern field boundary. The wall and enclosures are all now redundant and the water has formed a deep boggy hollow beside this decayed wall.

Only a few stunted trees survive at Powsons, although the stony part of the neighbouring field to the south has a higher density of trees, and all the indications are that the lower slopes of the Lune gorge were tree-clad until well into the medieval period (*see Chapter 3*). The physical setting of the deserted settlement is thus rugged and not conducive to arable cultivation, although faint ploughmarks may indicate cultivation of small plots (*see below: Site stratigraphy, Area 2, Phase 2B*).

The structural remains at Powsons include a well-defined subrectangular stone feature, perhaps a hut, on the boulder field above the intake wall. At the north end of the site, below the intake wall but outside the pipeline corridor, is a complex of subcircular structures, of which the most complete is described

171

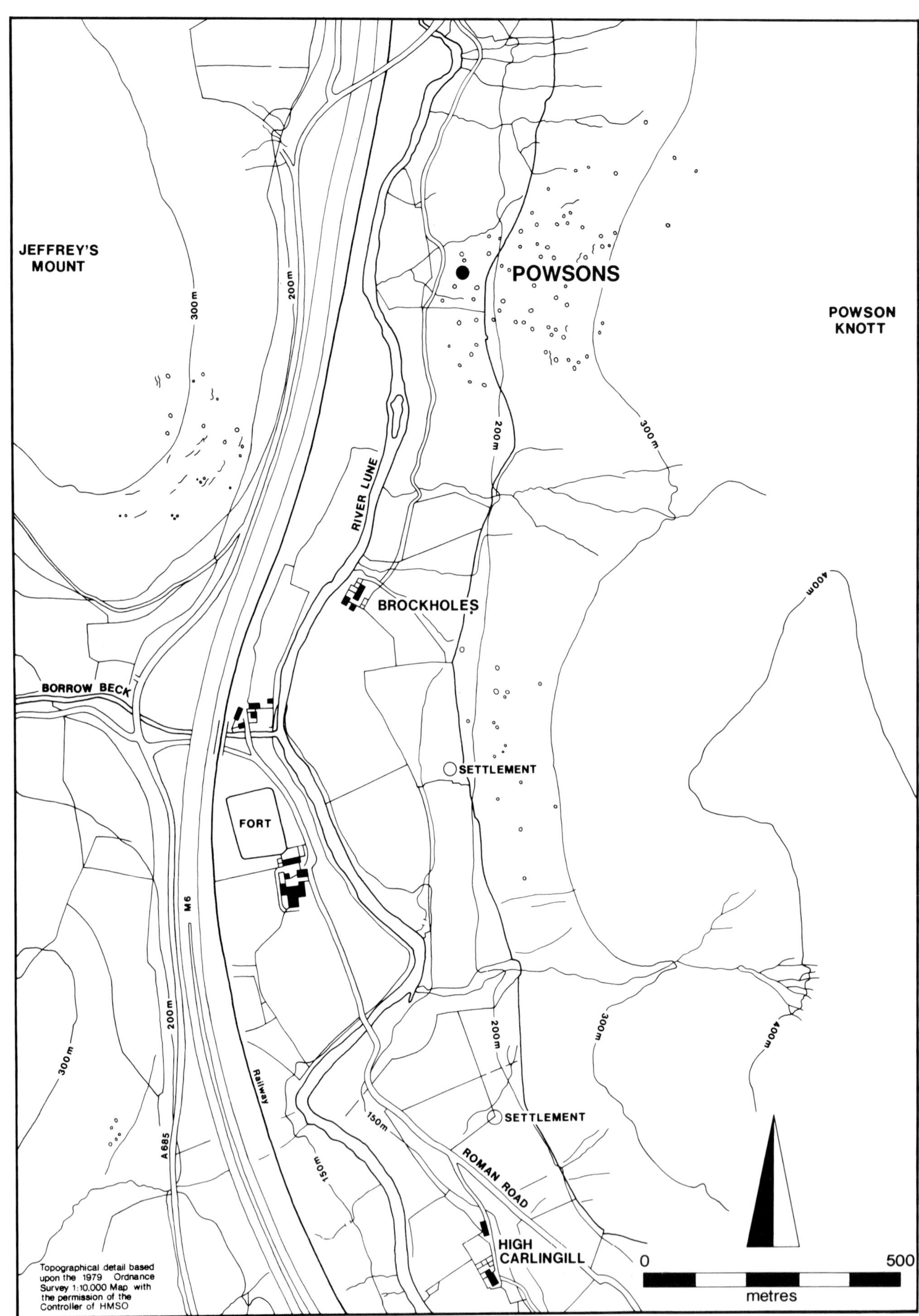

Figure 7:1 Powsons (**1132**), *location plan*

as a sheepfold on the OS 1st edn 25" map (OS 1858) (Fig 7:6). Fragments of another building, also dubbed a sheepfold by the OS, abut the rocky outcrop immediately adjacent to the upper side of the intake wall. The site of a barn and shippon, now vanished, is distinguishable as a building platform to the south of the modern trackway, while two earlier trackways link the site with a high-level track traversing the flank of Powson Knott. Among the trees and boulders to the south of the modern field boundary are several decayed stone walls and possible enclosures (**1133**). With the exception of one of the former trackways, all these features lay outside the pipeline corridor.

The settlement lies midway between Lune's Bridge and Brockholes farms, approximately 650m from each. The earliest known dwellings in the vicinity are supposedly Romano-British settlements (**1136, 1138**, SMR 1958), thought to be associated with the fort at Low Borrowbridge (**1137**). Within the enclosed fields, 350m south-east of Brockholes, are the partially excavated earthworks of a subrectangular settlement (**1136**, SMR 3525), represented by an embanked enclosure *c*15m square, with an internal platform and other stone structures, and additional external earthworks (Anstee 1986). On the evidence of pottery from the site, the suggested date for its primary occupation is AD 130–90, underlining its contemporaneity with the fort on the opposite side of the valley. Some 700m further down the valley, between Salterwath Bridge and High Carlingill, again below the intake wall and overlain by the present field system, substantial earthworks of a subcircular enclosed settlement associated with trackways (Fig 3:4; SMR 1958) occupy a site on the same contour as Powsons. This site, which was not investigated by LUAU as it lay outside the pipeline corridor, is morphologically similar to other sites throughout Cumbria and North Lancashire (*eg* Sealford near Kirkby Lonsdale; Clare 1981a, 30; 1981b, 47, fig 8a) which are thought to be farms associated with the Roman occupation. Powsons, however, does not in any way resemble these.

Powsons, although well within the sphere of influence of the Roman fort (**1137**), was probably beyond the limit of Anglian influence in the valley and is also unlikely to have been permanently settled in the Viking period (*see Chapter 3*). No mention of Powsons has yet been found in the documentary resource before the mid sixteenth century, and there is no place name evidence for a shieling here. It lies on the opposite side of the valley to the main through route, although the track from Lune's Bridge to Brockholes now bisects the site. Whereas the parishes of Orton, to the north, and Sedbergh, to the south, have documentary and earthwork evidence for a fair number of shieling sites, none have hitherto been identified north of Carlingill and south of Tebay in the Lune gorge (*see Chapter 3: Shielings*). The valley may have remained as woodland until long after the Norman Conquest (Cundill 1976, 308) and any shielings in clearings on the lower ground probably developed into permanent farms, most of which are still occupied. Powsons, whose fields drop steeply to the river, had very little meadow land on the alluvial floodplain, was less advantageously situated than the larger farms at Brockholes and Low Borrowbridge, and consequently failed by the early nineteenth century.

The tenants of Brockholes and Powsons

Powsons seems to have been a satellite settlement of Brockholes from the mid sixteenth to mid nineteenth centuries, and was bracketed with this larger farm in the manorial records (D/Lons/L, Wharton Box 1). The first known tenant was Hugh Powson, who paid 13s 4d rent in 1560 (Fig 7:2), and surely must represent the family which gave its name to Powson Knott, on the flank of which the settlement lies. In 1595, Christopher Powson was admitted tenant 'of the moytie of a Tenemente of the yearlie rente of 6s 10d, laite in the tenure or occupacion of Issabell Powson his mother deceased by vertue of a dede from James Powson his brother'. This rent is almost exactly half that of Powsons 35 years earlier, and it seems likely that the farm had been divided by this time between the descendants of Hugh Powson. No further mention has been found of the Powson family in Tebay after the mid seventeenth century, although they continued to thrive in Orton, where George Powson of Raisbeck had eight children baptised between 1656 and 1672 (WPR/9/2). Richard Powson, a farmer and weaver of Street, died in 1754 leaving an estate worth £178 (Turnbull 1984, 38), and a branch of the family also gave its name to another Powson Knott in Orton parish (WPR/9/Z10–11). The Powsons were also fairly numerous until the eighteenth century as relatively prosperous yeoman farmers in both Kirkby Stephen and Ravenstonedale (WQ/SR). Having bestowed their name, the Powsons moved on, and by the mid eighteenth century their tenement in the Lune gorge had passed into the hands of the Branthwaite family.

The neighbouring farm of Brockholes was tenanted over a period of at least a century by the Gowthropps, between 1560, when the tenant was William Gowthropp (D\Lons\L, Wharton Box 1), and 1668, at which time Leonard Gowthropp lived there (WPR/9/2). Other residents, however, were John Branthwaite, in 1655, and George Overend in 1662 (WPR/9/2), and although they were listed in the

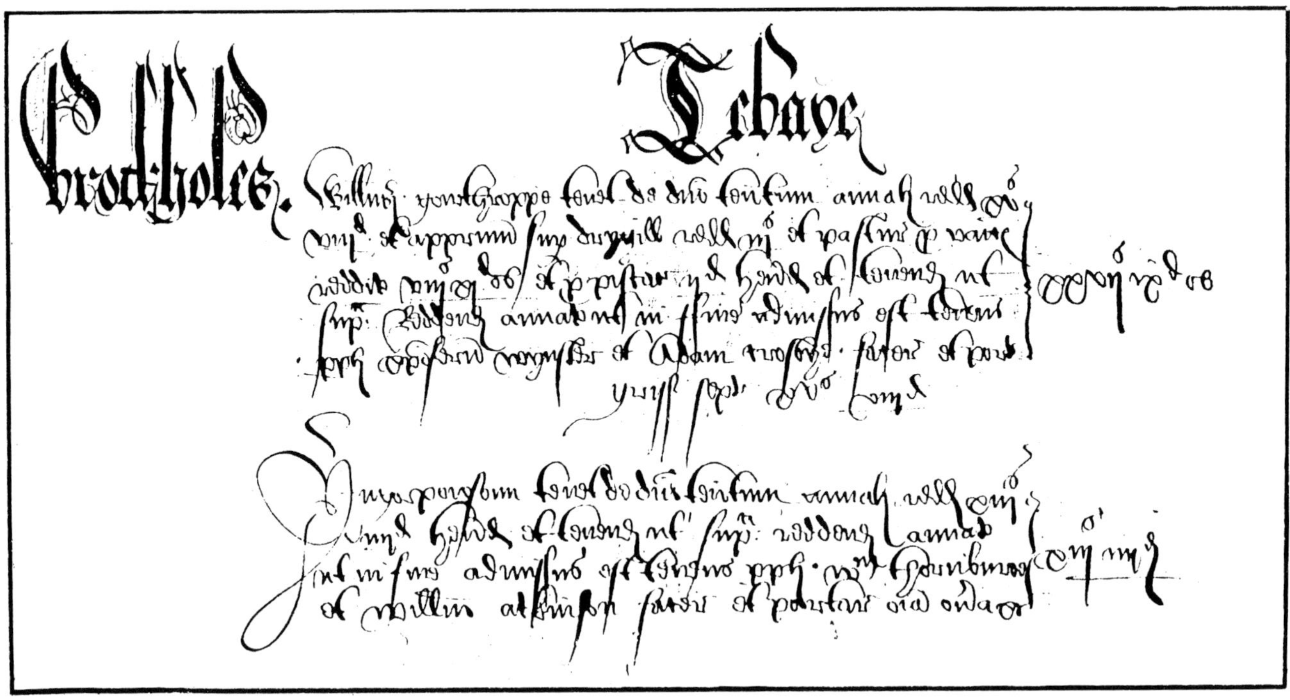

*Figure 7:2 Survey of Lord Wharton's estates in Westmorland, 1560 (D/Lons/L, Wharton Box 1), extract for Brockholes and Powsons (**1132**)*

parish register under Brockholes, they may actually have lived at Powsons. In 1560 there were also Gowthropps at Tebay and Redgill, but by 1841 they, like the Powson family, had vanished from the township (WDRC/8/110), and a complete lack of entries in the *Cumbria Phone Book* (1994) suggests that neither Gowthropp nor Powson has survived as a local name to the present day.

Brockholes farm commanded a basic annual rent of 15s 8d in 1560, and had in addition an improved parcel of land at Dry Gill, a ravine which perhaps then marked the farm's northern boundary, separating it from the Powsons tenement. The rent for this enclosure from the waste was 3s, and a further 8s 11½d was paid for cow pasture rights, and 2d for fisheries, totalling 27s 9½d (D/Lons/L, Wharton Box 1). The annual rent for Hugh Powson's adjoining tenement was 13s 4d, equivalent to one mark in the older currency, possibly an indication that the farm was an earlier, medieval foundation for which records have not yet been located. In sharp contrast to Brockholes, there were no additional enclosures or rights, suggesting that Powsons was not then, or indeed at any time in the next three centuries, expanding and prospering. When these farm rents are compared with those for Tebay as a whole, it becomes apparent that in the mid sixteenth century Brockholes paid the fifth highest rent in the manor. The rents ranged fairly evenly from 35s down to 6d, with Powsons, at 13s 4d, representing approximately the average (*see Chapter 3*).

The Branthwaite family was at its most powerful in the eighteenth century, owning several of the largest farms, and providing householders to act as commissioners and bailiffs on behalf of Tebay's manor court. In the late 1750s, Edward Branthwaite held a tenement whose customary rent was £2 2s 11d. After his death his heir, Michael, surrendered one part of the tenancy to another Edward, and the other part to William Branthwaite, who by 1778 tenanted both the holdings, with separate rents of 13s 8d and £1 11s 10d. The manor court was at this time held at William's house at Low Borrowbridge farm (as distinct from the nearby inn), and while he was described at his death in 1796 as a yeoman, his kinsman Edward Branthwaite of High Carlingill was already styled a gentleman in 1778 (D/Lons/L, Wharton Box 1). Before William Branthwaite died, he directed his trustees to manage 'the Estates called Brockholes and Powsons', until his son Michael should attain his majority, and to apply 'the rents and profits thereof to his Education and maintenance', paying him any surplus at the age of 21. William also had three daughters, who were provided for out of his Bybeck estate in Orton. Nanny, the eldest, would in addition inherit Brockholes and Powsons if her brother died without issue (WQ/SR). Michael Branthwaite therefore inherited these two tenancies, while James Branthwaite was admitted tenant of William's holdings at Low Borrowbridge. In the event, Michael only survived his father by six years, and his sister Nanny in due course succeeded to the inheritance. As William had lived at Low Borrowbridge, and his children were under age when he died, it is reasonable to infer that Brockholes and Powsons were subtenanted.

This was a difficult period, for the deaths of her father and brother in quick succession imposed a heavy burden of entry fines on Nanny Branthwaite at the change of tenancy, and on top of this the death of the Earl of Lonsdale, then lord of the manor, entailed payment of more fines. At this time, and for many years previously, the customary rents had remained unchanged, and by this means the tenements can sometimes be identified even where they are not named. The entry fines, however, had been steadily increased by succeeding lords of the manor since the days of Thomas, Lord Wharton, whose survey of 1560 was the starting point for a reassessment and raising of fines (*see Chapter 3: Rents and gressoms*). Thus by 1796, while the customary rent of Brockholes was still £1 11s 10d, and that of Powsons 13s 8d (little changed from the rent of 1560), their respective fines were £12 14s 8d and £5 9s 4d (D/Lons/L, Wharton Box 1).

Whether or not Nanny Branthwaite ever actually lived at Brockholes is unclear, but not long after she took on these tenancies in 1802, she married Francis Brown, a spirit merchant of Kendal, and in 1804 the couple surrendered the tenancy, 'she the said Nanny having been first secretly examined apart from her Husband by the said Lord and freely and voluntarily consenting', whereupon Joseph Swainson, a gentleman of Kendal, was admitted tenant, and the property went out of the Branthwaite family. In 1825, Joseph Swainson's eldest son John Fell Swainson inherited Brockholes and Powsons, but survived his father by only three years, and his daughter Ann Elizabeth was admitted tenant in 1828. At her death in 1847, the estate passed to her sister Agnes, a spinster of Kendal. Agnes disposed of the tenancy less than three weeks later to 'Roger Natters of No 10 New Square, Lincoln's Inn in the County of Middlesex Esquire'. At this transaction, it appears that the rent for Powsons had been reduced to 12s, presumably in recognition of the reduced acreage and decay of the property, while the Brockholes rent remained unchanged (D/Lons/L, Wharton Box 1).

These changes of tenancy recorded by the manor court were by the nineteenth century tantamount to sales of freehold property, for the occupiers, certainly by the 1840s, were not the landowners recorded in these transactions. Clearly there is more to the tenure of Brockholes and Powsons than this explains, however, as in 1841 (WDRC/8/110) and in 1856 (WQ/R/DP/83) Francis Brown was still named as the landowner, and Robert Yeates as the occupier, with no mention of Ann Elizabeth Swainson or Roger Natters. The two farms were by then considered as one, all the fields belonging to Powsons being listed under Brockholes, and the consolidated holding totalled 106 acres. As the tithe map does not show a dwelling house at Powsons, and the apportionment does not list any buildings at all (WDRC/8/110), this is fairly conclusive evidence that the premises were by then unoccupied. Roger Natters of Lincoln's Inn probably never saw Brockholes or indeed Powsons, and it is highly unlikely that the Swainsons had been resident. What seems certain is that the farms were no longer in the hands of local people. By the time Brockholes and Powsons were inherited by Nanny Branthwaite, this family had prospered and moved away from being simply yeoman farmers in Tebay. In 1869, John MacMillan Dunlop of Holehird, Windermere, Esquire, succeeded Roger Natters, and the two tenancies were finally enfranchised. This fundamental change released the tenants from the burden of entry fines and customary rents, marking the end of this relic of feudalism.

The difficulties inherent in attempting to assign a date for the abandonment of the dwelling at Powsons are compounded by the fact that while the tenancy continued to be entered, bracketed with Brockholes, in the court books and rentals at least until the 1860s, there is no dwelling house shown on any maps after 1770. Similar problems, though of an earlier date, were encountered in research into deserted farmhouses at Miterdale in West Cumbria, where a continuous process saw the gradual amalgamation of six farms into one over the two centuries between 1623 and 1821 (Winchester 1979, 154). Farmhouses might be deserted when their lands were bought or were rented by neighbouring farms, or alternatively the dwellings might continue in use for a time after the amalgamation.

The cartographic record

The only reliable map to name Powsons is Jeffreys' map of Westmorland (1770) (Fig 7:3), the first accurate county survey, with remarkable detail for its 1^2 scale. All the settlements in the Lune gorge south of Woodend are named: Roundthwaite, Low Borrowbridge, Carlingill, Brockholes, and Powsons, although individual buildings are not represented. While the others were relatively large and prosperous farms, Powsons was perhaps a stagnating smaller farm, and Brockholes expanded at its expense. Jeffreys' map does not show individual field boundaries, and so cannot be used to assist in dating the intake wall along the eastern fellside; nor does it show minor roads or trackways. It is surprising to find Powsons shown on the small-scale map in Pigot's directory (1829), where an arbitrary selection gives Powsons, Roundthwaite, and Carlin-

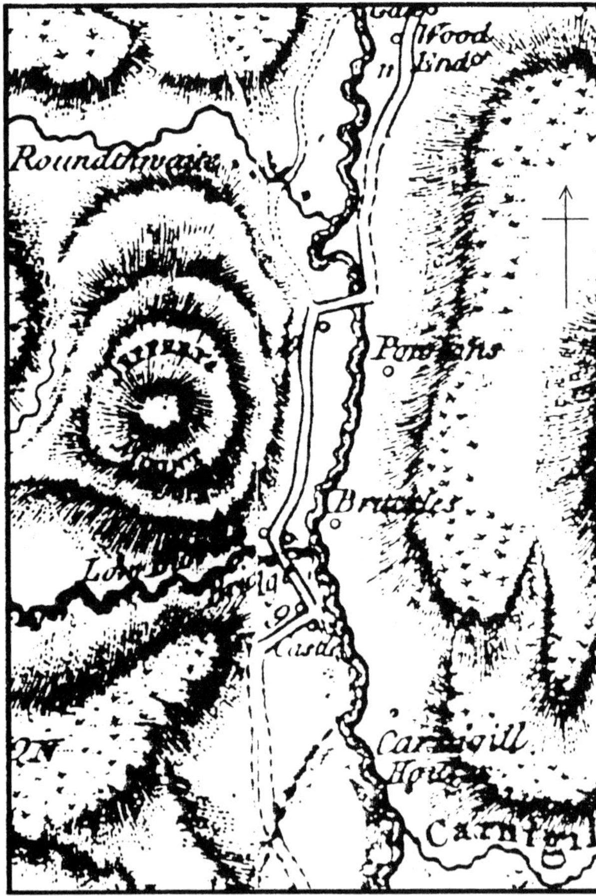

Figure 7:3 Jeffreys' map of Westmorland, 1770, extract showing 'Bruckles' (Brockholes) and Powsons (1132)

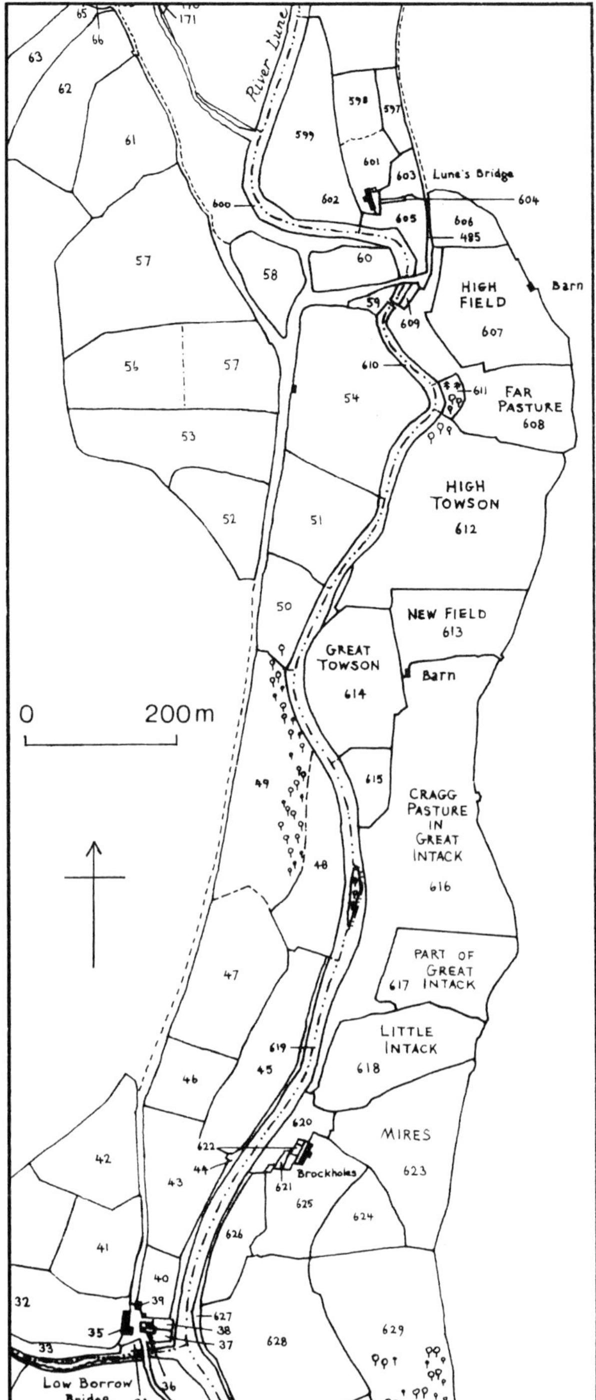

Figure 7:4 Tebay tithe map, 1841 (WDRC/8/110), extract showing Brockholes and Powsons (1132)

gill as the only settlements in the Lune gorge. This is all the more puzzling, since none of the nineteenth century trade directories contain a listing for Powsons. Greenwood's county map (1824), although still at 1″ scale, brings more accurate detail and shows, not every field boundary, but the main enclosure or intake walls separating the farmland from the commons. The intake wall from Lune's Bridge along the fellside to Carlingill is clearly indicated, and is unchanged since that date. On this map, Brockholes is marked but not named, while Powsons is not shown at all; this is significant, as the cartographer evidently intended at least to depict every farm, if not to name each one. The map shows even a small field barn, now a ruin, beside Howgill Lane at Carlingill, but of Powsons there is no trace.

The tithe map of 1841, together with the apportionment (WDRC/8/110), includes the Powsons fields under the single heading of Brockholes. Three of the northernmost fields are named High, Great, and Little Towson, which must be a misspelling of Powson (Fig 7:4). These may have been the only fields belonging to Powsons, the fellside to the east perhaps remaining unenclosed until the farm had

been absorbed into the Brockholes holding; indeed, the 'intack' field names suggest late enclosure, and the site of the Powsons farmstead is described as 'Cragg pasture in great intack'. The field named Little Intack is in the appropriate location for the enclosure above Dry Gill, listed as part of the Brockholes holding in 1560 (D/Lons/L, Wharton Box 1). Enclosure of the 'Great intack' could then have been achieved by completing the link in the fellside intake boundary by building a wall from the corner of the Powsons fields to the corner of the Dry Gill enclosure wall. That this wall is later than other sections seems likely, as it cuts across the earthworks of two trackways leading from Powsons onto the fell, and apparently across the footings of a stone structure which partly survives above the wall. The metalled trackway leads to a recess housing a walled-up gateway, demonstrating that when the intake wall was built, the track was still used for access to the fell (Fig 7:7). Similar provision was not made, however, for the narrow hollowed track leading more directly from Powsons, which rises steeply to join the high-level Brockholes to White Combs track. The two trackways at Powsons are not shown on any maps; only the high-level track was surveyed by the OS (OS 1858).

The descriptions of the two holdings in the Tebay manor court book remained essentially unchanged from the 1770s until 1869. Brockholes comprised a 'Messuage and Tenement with several closes Inclosures and Parcels of Land', while Powsons was merely a 'Messuage and Tenement' (D/Lons/L, Wharton Box 1). By the 1840s, if not much earlier, there was no longer a dwelling at Powsons, only a barn, probably used by the Brockholes farmer. Nonetheless, the structure abutting the intake wall is shown as a roofed building on the proposed Ingleton to Tebay Railway plan of 1856 (WQ/R/ DP/83) (Fig 7:5), although it is designated a sheepfold only two years later on the OS 1st edn 25″ map (OS 1858) (Fig 7:6). The farm buildings at Brockholes, as described in the book of reference accompanying the proposed railway plan, consisted of a calf house, barn, shippons, piggery, two outhouses, two goose houses, and three walled garden plots, all around the dwelling house and farmyard (WQ/ R/DP/83). By contrast, the same plan shows only a single building at Powsons, described as a barn and shippon. None of the maps, however, show any type of building at the location of the one excavated in 1990–91 (*see below*). The proposed Ingleton to Tebay Branch Railway, had it been built, would have dramatically altered the landscape between Brockholes and Powsons, but the junction with the Lancaster and Carlisle Railway was instead effected further south at Lowgill (OS 1858) (Fig 2:22).

The 'New Field' of the tithe map seems to have been carved out of the rough pasture known as High Towson. The New Field's northern boundary has subsequently been removed, but is visible as a regular linear bank, in association with faint ridge and furrow (**11315**). The field is noticeably boulder-free, and is probably a late improved pasture, perhaps contemporary with the improved drainage of the field, achieved by diverting the stream from a spring

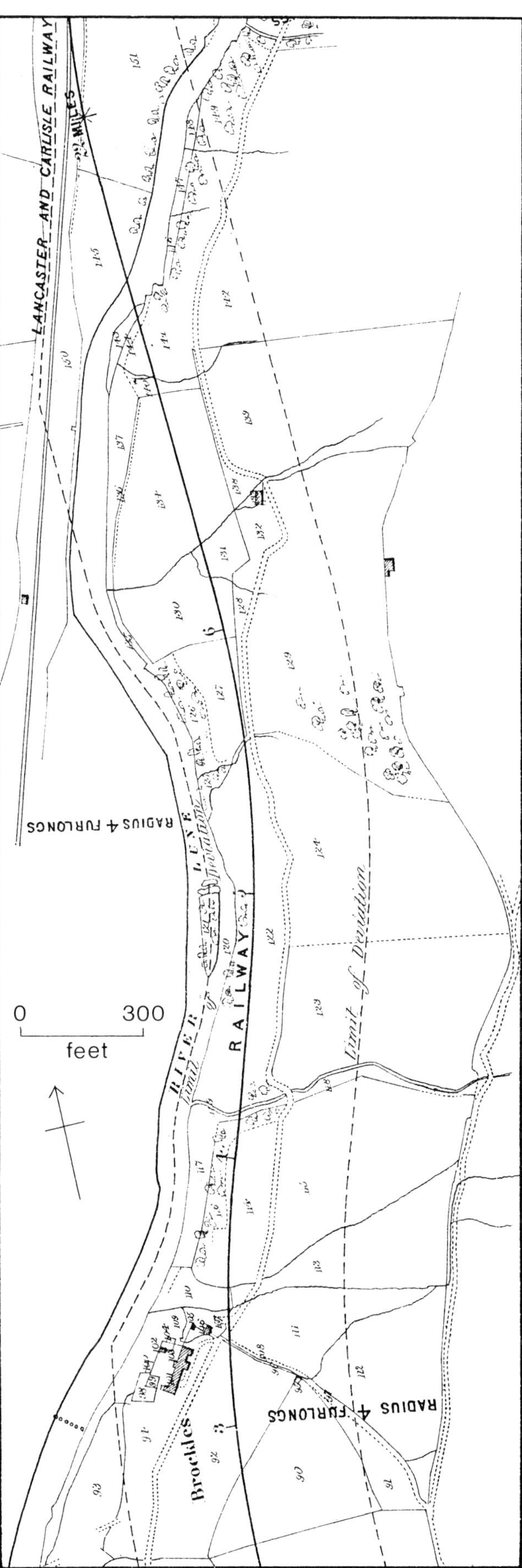

*Figure 7:5 North Western Railway map, proposed Ingleton to Tebay Branch, 1856 (WQ/R/DP/83), extract showing Brockholes and Powsons (**1132**)*

at the top of the field to run along the slope and down alongside the northern boundary wall at Powsons. The barn is shown on the maps surveyed between 1841 and 1858 but, together with the sheepfolds, is no longer represented on the OS revised series of 1899 and 1920, and so these structures can be presumed to have fallen out of use during the second half of the nineteenth century. Slightly to the south of the barn, the track shown on the OS maps makes a sharp turn away from the alignment with the metalled track heading up the fell. Great Towson had recently been reduced in size by the rerouteing of the River Lune in connection with railway construction. This slight decrease in acreage may explain why the rent was reduced from 13s 8d to 12s at the change of tenancy in 1847 (D/Lons/L, Wharton Box 1).

Of the various structures shown on tithe, railway, and OS maps, none could be construed as a recent dwelling, and either of the platforms observed outside the pipeline corridor could be the site of the farmhouse, but there are no upstanding ruins to confirm such a building. The house may have fallen into ruin when the last tenant left, or it may have been converted to barn or byre once the farm was consolidated with the Brockholes holding.

Topographical survey

Detailed topographical survey plots of the earthworks (Figs 2:20, 7:7) complemented the maps and aerial photographs to provide a composite picture of the site. The features, not necessarily contemporaneous, all appear to have been associated with farming. The combination of trackways, platforms, sheepfolds, turf-fast structural walls, and decayed field walls indicates a farmstead and field system predating the land divisions shown on maps from the 1820s onwards. Few of the features actually lay within the final pipeline corridor, which was only 20m wide. At the north-eastern limit of the field, a group of subcircular stone structures is clearer on aerial photographs (Fig 7:8) than on the ground, where only one of the circles was visible for the purposes of survey. Whether these structures are of prehistoric date or associated with the medieval farmstead, or are disused sheepfolds as designated on the OS 1st edn maps, remains unknown. The pipeline route was amended here to pass downslope of the features, owing to the steep gradient and rocky outcrops, and as a result this complex of huts or folds remained unaffected, well outside the revised corridor.

The significant remaining features within the corridor were a turf-fast subrectangular stone structure,

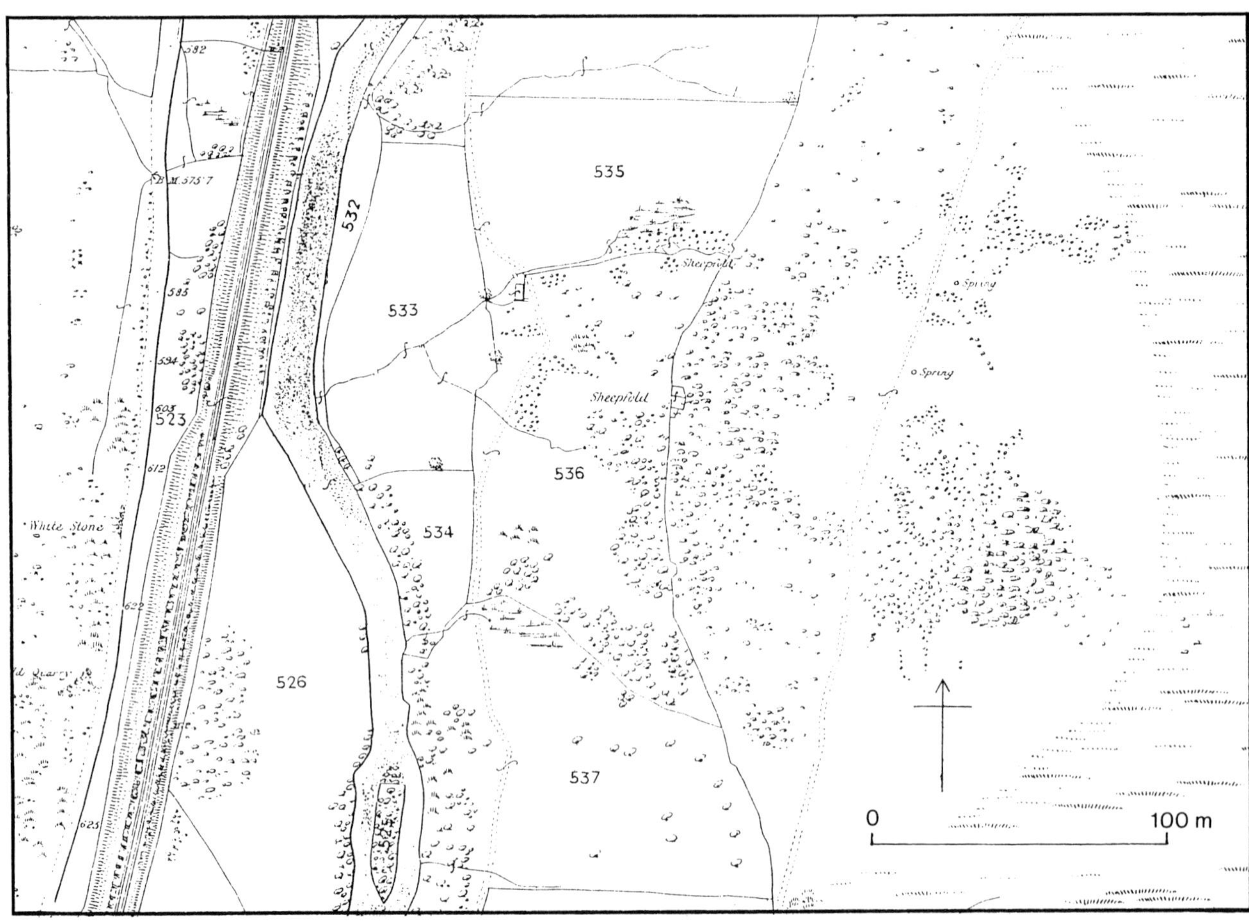

*Figure 7:6 Powsons (**1132**), OS 1st edn 25" map, 1858, extract*

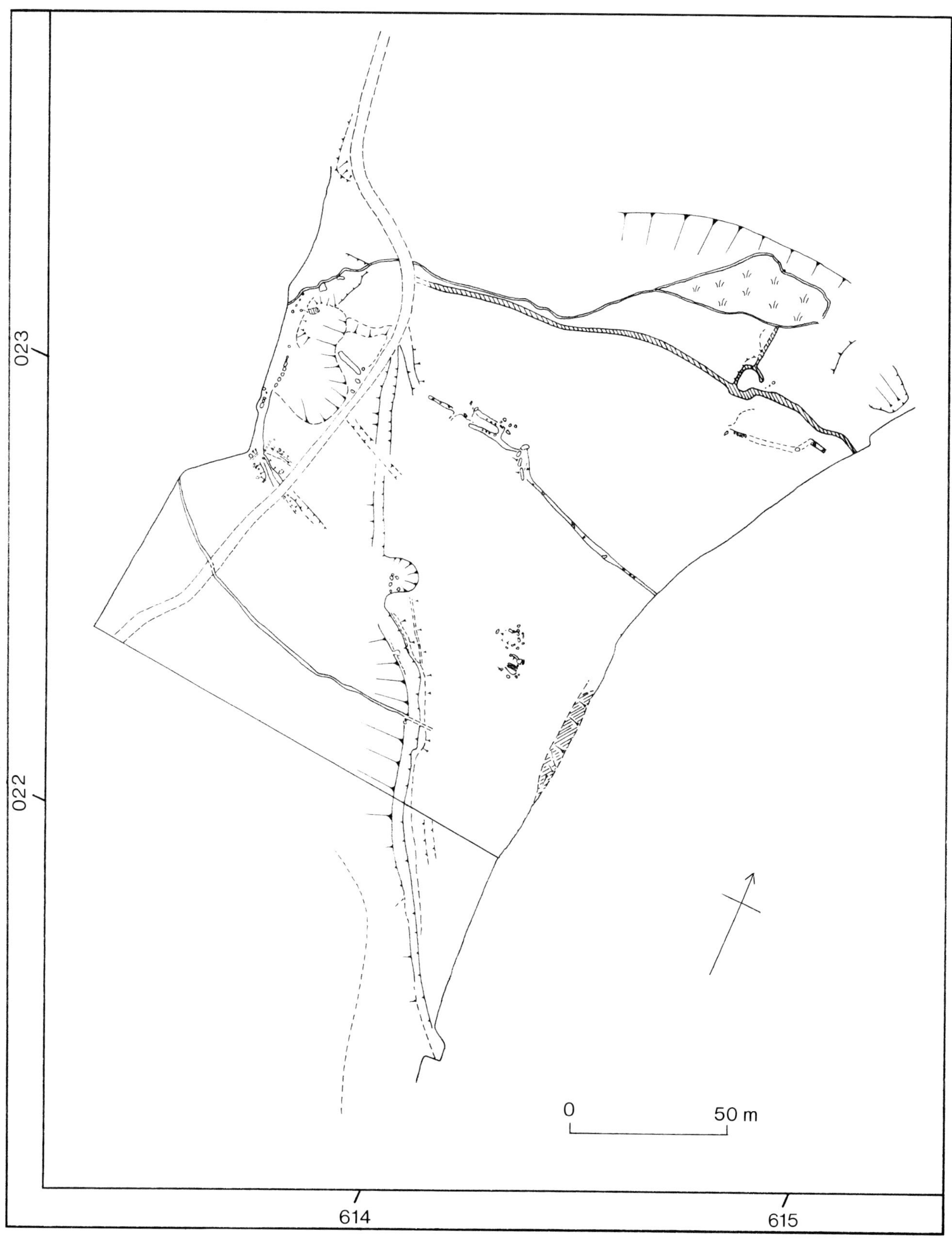

*Figure 7:7 Powsons (**1132**), surveyed features, 1990*

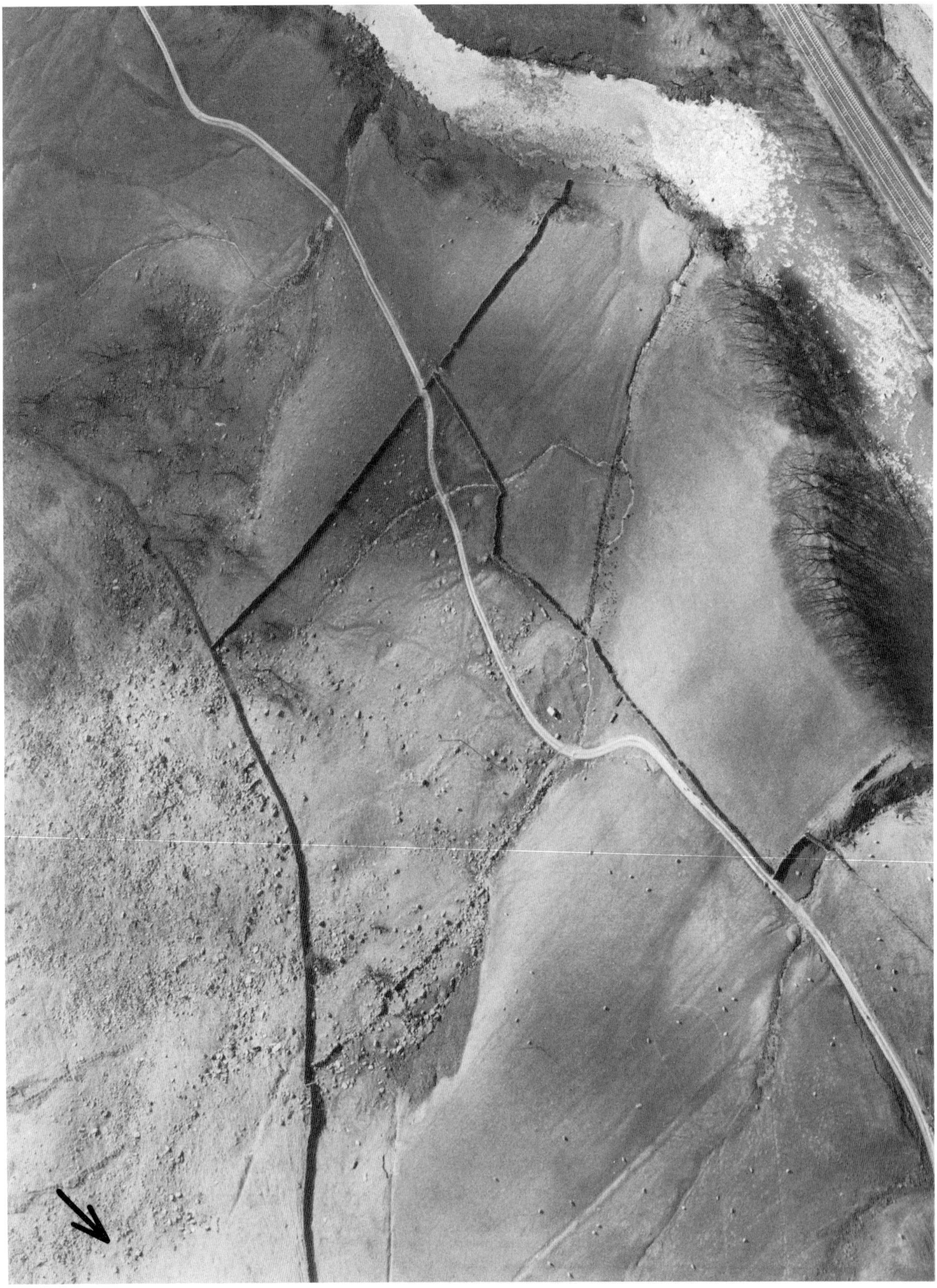

*Figure 7:8 Powsons (**1132**), aerial photograph, looking south-east*

the metalled trackway, a natural or quarried hollow, and two redundant field walls. The area of settlement affected was nonetheless 200m in length, and trial trenching was programmed in 1990 to determine the optimum locations for open area excavation. The trenches established the nature of the building and trackway, and enabled the selection of three areas to examine the subrectangular structure, the trackway and hollow, and the northern field wall. These were further investigated the following year by an excavation lasting seven weeks.

Excavations in 1990 and 1991

Nick Hair, Rachel Newman

In August 1990, six machine-cut trial trenches were excavated to examine all the features noted within the pipeline corridor. These included the subrectangular structure, the trackway, a large semicircular depression, and a field boundary. The evaluation revealed that the structure survived to a depth of 0.45m below the present ground surface, and that considerable care had been taken in its construction. The trackway appeared to be metalled, but without substantial foundations, and a large infilled ditch was found directly below the semicircular depression. None of the features produced any artefacts or dating evidence, but the evaluation raised questions which indicated a need for further excavation. In May and June 1991, excavation focused on the features sectioned in the evaluation, together with the derelict northern field boundary.

The three areas investigated within the pipeline corridor were situated in steeply sloping pasture land just below the open fell, at 185m OD. Area 1 (17 x 15m) was positioned in the south of the site to examine the trackway and a possibly natural hollow; Area 2 (24 x 25m), in the centre of the site, incorporated the subrectangular structure and its associated field wall; while Area 3 (10 x 4m) examined the northern field boundary. The topsoil was stripped from the three areas using a mechanical excavator fitted with a 0.90m wide bucket. The ground surface was then cleaned manually to remove residual topsoil and to expose and define the underlying stratigraphy. Features were recorded and removed manually. Each season of excavation was assigned a unique block of numbers for contexts and object records. In 1990 the contexts were allocated numbers 101–107, and in 1991 1–34, while artefacts were numbered from 1001–1034, and recorded three-dimensionally using triangulation combined with levelling. Records were input onsite to a Delilah database.

Phase summary

Separate phasing for each of the three areas excavated was inevitable in view of the lack of continuous stratigraphy across the site. Nonetheless, each area displays a similar three-phase progression, the earliest phase representing natural features, followed by the construction of a trackway, field boundaries, and a stone building, and finally the abandonment and decay of all the structures.

Area 1

Phase 1 The earliest features are a stream bed and bowl-shaped depression, both apparently natural.
Phase 2 A trackway was constructed and in use.
Phase 3 The trackway and associated gully fell into disrepair.

Area 2

Phase 1 The earliest activity was mainly natural, with some quarrying evident.
Phase 2 A rectangular stone structure was built and later modified, together with a possible yard and a field boundary, and the site was cleared and cultivated.
Phase 2A The stone building was constructed.
Phase 2B The west end of the structure was modified by the construction of a wall.
Phase 3 The site was abandoned and decayed.

Area 3

Phase 1 A natural gully contained an intermittent watercourse.
Phase 2 A drystone wall was built, predating the modern farm track and field system.
Phase 3 The wall fell out of use and decayed.

Site stratigraphy

A broadly similar stratigraphic sequence was identified in all three areas excavated. The natural subsoil everywhere consisted of stony cream clay (3) sealed by a 0.30m deep accumulation of orange-brown silty clay (2). This contained charcoal flecks indicating that, unlike natural subsoil 3, it may have been affected by human activity, although it produced no artefacts. It perhaps represents a stagno-podsol, an ancient leached topsoil horizon. Topsoil 1, on average 0.20m deep, sealed this layer and all of the archaeological features identified.

Area 1, phase 1

A possible stream bed (23) and bowl-shaped depression (28) were the earliest features, both apparently natural (Fig 7:9). In the centre of the excavation, accumulation 2 dipped steeply into a large semicircular bowl-shaped depression (*28*), 7m in diameter and at least 2m deep. Superficially, this feature bore a resemblance to a small quarry, but proved on excavation to be a natural feature, probably formed by water action in association with a spring. Depression *28* lay immediately upslope from, and appeared to be associated with, an infilled linear hollow (*23*) orientated east-west, the uppermost extent of which cut accumulation 2, as well as natural subsoil 3, and therefore presumably formed somewhat later. The linear hollow (*23*) had steeply sloping sides and a gently rounded, almost flat base; it was at least 9m in length, its width tapered westwards from 5m to 3m in the space of *c*7m, and it was on average 1m deep. It is likely that this again was formed by fluvial action, perhaps by water seeping from depression *28*, in time forming a stream bed. The colour and slightly loamy organic nature of its primary fill (*25*) suggest that this may have been deposited by natural silting. Its upper fill (*24*) (0.65m deep) consisted almost entirely of subangular and subrectangular stones, ranging from 0.05m to 0.70m in diameter. These stones, however, appeared largely unsorted, perhaps indicating that they had not been deposited by fluvial action, but accumu-

lated in the hollow over a long period of time, simply tumbling down the fellside into it. Neither depression *28* nor stream bed *23* produced any evidence, in the form of artefacts, to suggest associated human activity.

Area 1, phase 2

A metalled surface, 0.08m deep, of peagrits and small rounded stones clearly formed a trackway (*16*) (Fig 7:10), terraced into the hillside, which it crossed at an oblique angle from north-west to south-east. The metalling had been bedded onto accumulation 2, but also sealed the upper fill (*24*) of stream bed 23. A shallow U-shaped gully (*14*) (4 x 0.40 x 0.12m) formed in part the north side of the trackway, before diverging to the north, and was visible as a slight earthwork continuing upslope beyond the excavation. This perhaps channelled water running from the fellside away from the track. No evidence of wear was identified on the metalled surface. This, and the insubstantial nature of the metalling, suggest that the track was not designed for heavy usage or vehicles, but probably functioned as a route to the open fell grazings. The trackway must pre-

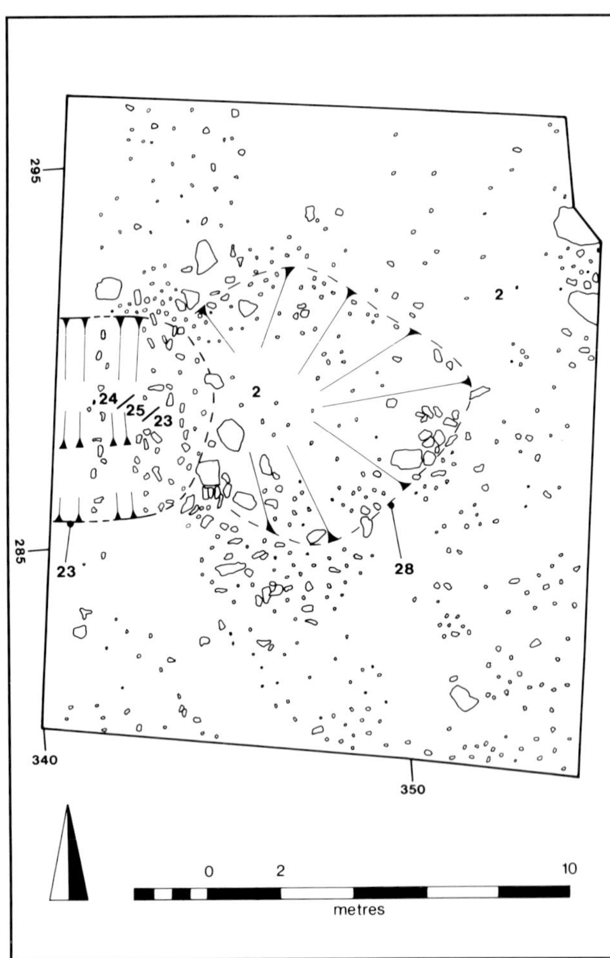

*Figure 7:9 Powsons (**1132**), Area 1, phase 1*

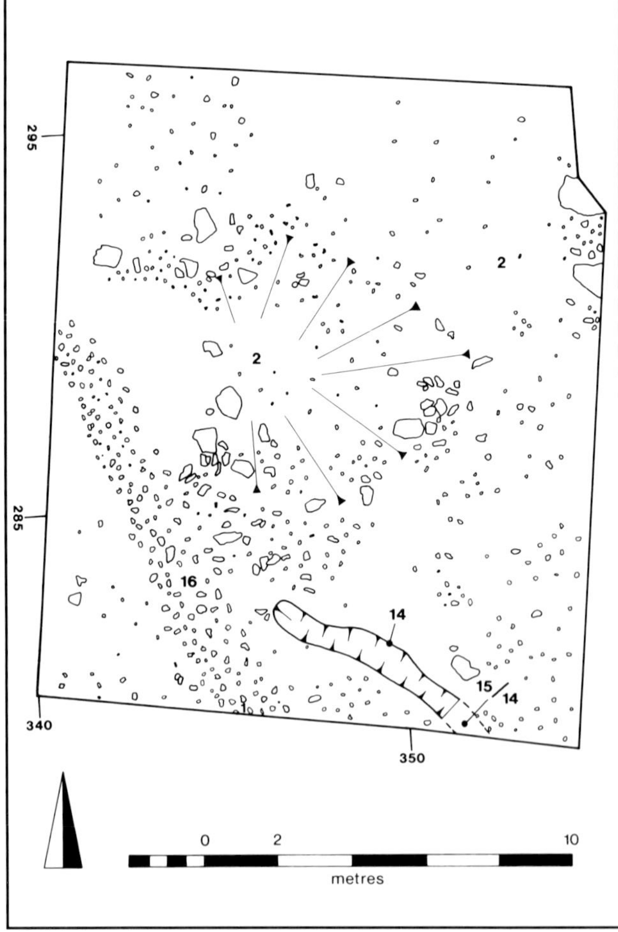

*Figure 7:10 Powsons (**1132**), Area 1, phase 2*

date the existing fellside boundary wall, as this makes provision for access to the fell via a recess and blocked gateway. Again, no finds were associated with these features to aid their absolute dating; however, despite the fact that they cannot be firmly related to the structure identified in Area 2 (*see below*), it is likely that they are both elements in a contemporary landscape.

Area 1, phase 3

Gully *14* silted up and the track became overgrown with weeds and grasses which encouraged the development of topsoil *1*. Trackway *16* must have fallen into disuse after the building of the intake wall, at the turn of the nineteenth century, but prior to the construction of the present southern field boundary, which overlies it, in the second half of the century (OS 1858, 1899).

Area 2, phase 1

The earliest activity may have been largely a result of natural processes, although some quarrying is evident. The sequence of natural clay subsoil (*3*) sealed by a disturbed accumulation (*2*) lay beneath the archaeological deposits identified in this area. A dense spread of stones (*26*) (15 x 9m) in the northeast ranged widely in diameter from 0.10m to 1.40m. This spread clearly derived originally from the effect of weathering on the upper fellside outcrops, causing large stones to frost shatter and tumble down the hillside, gathering on a slight flattening of the slope. No archaeological features were found in the spread, although two abraded fragments of samian were retrieved from the topsoil which had formed amongst the stones. These appear to be residual and their presence can be attributed to Roman activity, either military or civilian, in the vicinity.

A large outcrop of rock (*32*) lay in the centre of the excavation. Small deep circular holes, *c*0.05m in diameter, appear to have been drilled at *c*0.40m intervals along a horizontal fault line on its west face. The regular spacing and shape of these holes suggest shotholes associated with quarrying, although elsewhere on Powson Knott isolated boulders and outcrops display similar markings which appear to be natural. Another stone spread (*27*), in the centre of the site slightly north-west of outcrop *32*, was similar in form to stone spread *26*, comprising a dense scatter of subangular stones, ranging from 0.20m to 0.80m in diameter. This was probably formed by the same natural processes as *26*, although it may have been enhanced by other factors, such as the decay of wall *7* (*see Area 2, Phase 3*) and the debris left from the possible quarrying of outcrop *32*.

Area 2, phase 2

The main event in this area was the construction of a subrectangular stone building (*10*). Two periods of building activity were associated with this, in addition to a possible yard and a field boundary wall (*7*). There is evidence for the clearance and possible cultivation of the site.

Area 2, phase 2A

A stone building (*10*) had been constructed on a slight westerly slope below outcrop *32* (Fig 7:11). Its long axis was aligned approximately east-west and it was almost rectangular in plan, although its width gradually increased towards the west (8.50 x 4–4.80m). In its original form it seems to have extended beyond the excavated area, although its western end had subsequently been modified (*see below*). Three walls (*9*, *11*, *12*) of the original structure were identified, of which the foundations and lowest courses survived. Each wall was built of irregularly shaped stones, roughly coursed, which followed the contours of the slope. All were of drystone construction, with neatly arranged facing stones and a sparse core of small rubble, and all were bonded to each other. Of the side walls, that to the south (*9*) was 8.30m long and 0.70m thick, whereas the original north wall (*11*), of the same thickness, was only identified over a length of 6.40m, due to the effect of subsequent modifications to the west end of the building. A slight foundation trench (*18*) was identified at the western end of wall *9*, although elsewhere in the structure the foundations were embedded in the top of accumulation *2*. Some very large, apparently earthfast stones were incorporated in the base. The east wall (*12*) was 4m long and 0.80m wide, the internal junction with wall *9* being formed by a large erratic earthfast boulder. An entrance, 0.80m wide, was located in the centre; a large flat stone formed the threshold. Little evidence of occupation was associated with the original phase of construction, and no finds were recovered to aid dating.

Area 2, phase 2B

The west end of the structure seems to have been modified by the construction of wall *13* (4.80 x 0.80m) (Fig 7:12). It was built in an identical fashion to the other walls and survived in places up to three rough courses high. This wall was apparently constructed directly on top of a localised layer of brown silty loam (*34*), which may have been deliberately dumped here to provide a level platform for the revised west end of the structure. This material lay directly on accumulation *2* and bore a resemblance to humic topsoil. There was some evidence for a blocked entrance, 0.75m wide, at the south-west

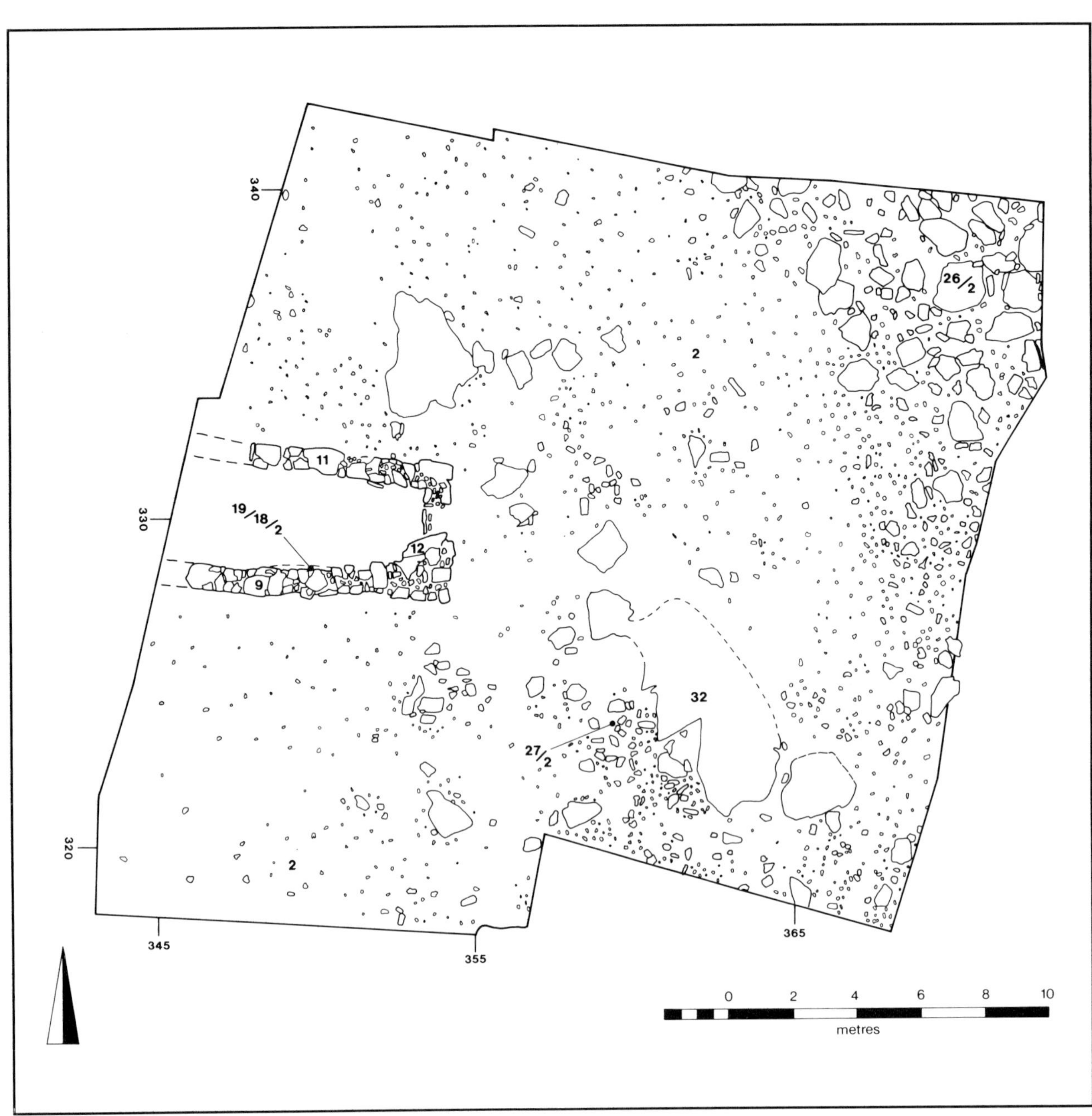

*Figure 7:11 Powsons (**1132**), Area 2, phase 2A*

corner of the modified structure. This was faced with neatly aligned stones, and had been blocked using quite distinct material (subangular stones 0.05–0.25m in diameter). The southern edge of this entrance was formed from the internal face of wall 9. The modified western end of the structure was filled by a stone platform (17) (3.00 x 1.20m), constructed of irregularly shaped subangular stones (c0.50 x 0.30 x 0.15m–c0.15 x 0.10 x 0.05m). These stones, like wall 13, lay directly above apparent levelling dump 34, and nowhere was the platform more than two stones deep. Its surface was uneven and formed of haphazardly laid stones, although its eastern edge was clearly defined by neatly aligned stone blocks. Parts of the platform were bonded into the lower

courses of wall 13, indicating that the two were contemporary.

In the centre of platform 17, a further area of flat angular stones (30) was identified, the north and south extents of which formed two slightly raised ridges. The platform covered an area 1.20m square; its southern edge was flush with the northern face of the blocked entrance in wall 13. By analogy with similar platforms found elsewhere (*eg* Coggins *et al* 1983), stone spread 30 may represent a fire setting, although there was no associated evidence of burning. It is more likely that it supported a partition or windbreak between the entrance and platform 17, perhaps separating different uses of the two parts

184

*Figure 7:12 Powsons (**1132**), Area 2, phase 2B*

of the building. The prevailing wind from the south-west would create a draught through the doorway, which was subsequently blocked, perhaps for this reason. The floor surface of the entrance was formed by a continuation of platform *17* to the south of area *30*.

Another possible blocked entrance was revealed at the interface between walls *11* and *13*, at the north-west corner of the building. The internal face of wall *13* provided the west side of this aperture, which had neat jambs, and the east side was formed by wall *11*. Thus the entrance had been created at the time the structure was modified, and was closely associated with platform *17*. It was 1.00m wide and

had been blocked by roughly arranged large angular stones up to 0.30m in length, creating a ragged internal face. The lowest course of wall *13* appeared to return eastwards and continue up to the eastern edge of the entrance, forming a sill or perhaps a step.

A few irregularly shaped stone slabs (*33*) (no larger than c0.50 x 0.25 x 0.05m), to the east of platform *17*, were all that remained of any internal flooring. These slabs and the platform were sealed by an organic clay loam (*6*) which covered part of the interior of the structure and also the area to the north as far as wall *7* (*see below*). This accumulation layer (*6*) was 0.08m thick and lay directly below topsoil *1*. Its or-

185

ganic nature and association with the structure suggest that it was an occupation layer, although it produced no artefacts. An area partially enclosed by stone tumble and rocky outcrops, defined to the east by an insubstantial line of stones (*31*), may represent a yard associated with the structure, perhaps a small stockyard or a sheltered annex to the building at its main, eastern entrance.

A substantial but poorly coursed drystone wall (*7*) dog-legged down the fellside and over the top of outcrop *32*, to butt against the south-east corner of the building, incorporating this pre-existing structure within its length. This wall (*7*) survived to a maximum height of *c*0.40m and consisted of neatly aligned stones enclosing a rubble core, varying between 1.25m and 1.40m in width. The wall continued to the east of the excavation as a small bank and line of turf-fast boulders extending up to the fellside intake wall, although it was not visible east of this boundary on the open fell; it was also identified to the west of the building (*10*), continuing downslope as a fragmentary bank. The dilapidated condition of wall *7* indicates that it did not relate to the present field system, although it was clearly a field boundary which was in use during or after the occupation of the building. Neither the wall (*7*) nor the building (*10*) is shown on the tithe map of 1841 (WDRC/8/110), and it is clear that both predate this map.

The area surrounding the structure was notably stone-free and seems to have been deliberately cleared, presumably in association with the occupation. A series of parallel ploughmarks (*20*) was tentatively identified cutting into accumulation 2 in the south-west of the area, orientated in a general north-south direction. These were no more than 2.50m long, and had a maximum width of 0.20m and depth of 0.05m. They contained a silty clay (*21*) which was devoid of artefacts.

Area 2, phase 3

A narrow spread of stone (*5*), almost certainly wall tumble, extended out as far as 1.50m around the building (Fig 7:13). The stones were scattered in a random fashion, but deposited quite equally both inside and outside the building. Only a small quantity of tumble was identified, relative to the amount of stone such a structure would require, which might suggest that much of the material had been removed and reused elsewhere. It is possible, though unlikely, that the walls were originally constructed with a stone base and a timber superstructure. The complete lack of any evidence for roofing material is unsurprising, as timbers would be recycled, and

materials such as turf or heather would not survive within the archaeological record.

Another spread of stone tumble (*8*), consisting of subangular stones 0.05–0.30m in diameter, was found approximately 1.50m to either side of wall *7*, but mainly to the north. Here again, relatively small quantities of tumble were recorded, suggesting that the majority of the suitable stone which originally made up wall *7* had been collected for reuse elsewhere.

The area appears to have been neglected, allowing the growth of weeds and grasses which encouraged the development of topsoil *1*. This extended across the whole of Area 2 and contained the majority of the finds, most of which can be regarded as residual.

Area 3, phase 1

The natural subsoil (*3*) was more clayey and plastic here than in the other areas excavated, as it lay within a gently sloping natural gully containing an intermittent watercourse. This gully was probably cut by fluvio-glacial action. The ubiquitous accumulation 2 extended above this, although it was no more than 0.10m deep and in places had been completely eroded away. A stone spread (*29*) was concentrated in the north of the gully, probably originally formed by stones from the fellside rolling into the gully. The stones were subangular in form, ranging from 0.10m to 0.70m in diameter, and were densely packed together.

Area 3, phase 2

A drystone wall (*22*) partially utilised stone spread *29* for its foundations, and incorporated some very large erratic and quarried boulders. Wall *22* was 0.90m thick, uncoursed, and orientated east-west. It was recorded in places standing up to 1.00m high, but also included many collapsed sections. It did not continue east of the present intake wall but extended downslope, following the watercourse, as far as the modern farm track. The tithe map (WDRC/8/110) shows both wall *22* and the intake wall, and wall *22* thus survived to a later date than the other excavated field boundaries, although it obviously predates the modern farm track and field system.

Area 3, phase 3

Wall *22* fell out of use and topsoil *1* was allowed to develop over its tumble, the wall eventually decaying to its present dilapidated state.

*Figure 7:13 Powsons (**1132**), Area 2, phase 3*

The finds

Christine Howard-Davis

Very few finds were recovered, as might be expected from a small rural site. Most derive from the topsoil (*1*), thus limiting the stratigraphic relevance of the assemblage. Two objects derive from stratified contexts: a small iron object from gully *14* in Area 1, and a block of possibly worked stone from the west wall (*13*) of structure *10*; neither of these can be assigned a close date. The artefact assemblage from the topsoil is varied, containing objects with a very wide date range. The presence of such a variety of material in topsoil, especially in hillwash, is usu-

ally interpreted as indicative of human activity in the area, but not necessarily at the excavated site. Three flint artefacts, all from the topsoil, derive from probable Bronze Age activity. Such activity is well attested for the nearby limestone uplands (Cherry and Cherry 1987) where worked flint artefacts are a common find. The small assemblage of nine fragments of pottery includes, from stone spread *26* in Area 2, two very small and abraded fragments of samian ware, an imported fineware in widespread use during the first three centuries of the Roman occupation. The remainder of the pottery is undiagnostic, but likely to be of post-medieval date. The only metal artefacts were a worn but identifiable Roman *dupondius*, and six badly corroded iron objects, the size and shape of which suggest that they were nails. The presence within the topsoil of a small

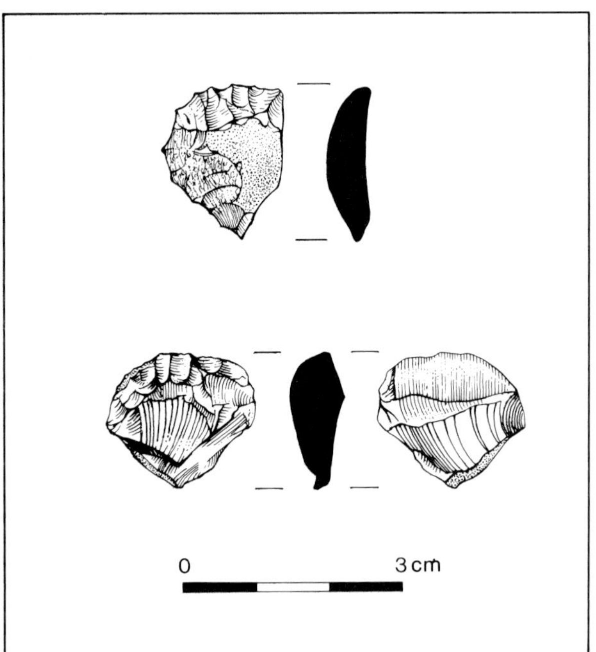

Figure 7:14 Powsons (11316), Bronze Age flint scrapers

amount of debris from some industrial process suggests industrial activity in the environs, although it is quite possible for such material to be imported for purposes such as road make-up.

The Roman coin

David Shotter

A well preserved but extremely worn Roman copper alloy coin was recovered from the topsoil (1).

Cu *Dupondius*, Marcus Aurelius, AD 161–80, very worn
PK91, 1/1006/1

Discussion

The most significant feature recorded during the excavations at Powsons was the stone building. The site, on a gentle slope in marginal pasture, has long been uninhabited, but still has a good water supply, from springs which give rise to two streams flowing to the north and south of the building. The upper section of the northern stream appears to have been deliberately diverted southwards around the hillside to flow into a nearby marshy area, probably to allow improvement of the land to the north, but incidentally or deliberately providing a water supply for livestock. It is likely that the building is contemporary with the trackway excavated in Area 1, which presumably functioned as an access route, both from Lune's Bridge to Powsons, and from the farmstead to the upper fellside.

Rectangular stone buildings of similar dimensions to the one at Powsons are a relatively common feature in northern upland landscapes, although they range widely in date. There are prehistoric precedents, but the earliest dated rectangular dwellings in the Pennine and Lakeland uplands, other than in a military or quasi-military Roman context, have been ascribed to the early medieval period, from the eighth century onwards. Such sites have been excavated at Gauber High Pasture near Ribblehead (King 1978), Simy Folds in Teesdale (Coggins *et al* 1983), and Bryant's Gill at Kentmere (Dickinson 1985).

Extensive fieldwork in North East Perthshire (RCAHMS 1990) and the northern Pennines (Ramm *et al* 1970) has identified many shieling huts, the structures inhabited principally during summer transhumance. Of closer relevance are the foundations of apparently similar huts recorded by Cleasby (1991) in the western Howgills south of Carlingill, only 3km from Powsons. Such sites are generally attributed to the centuries following the Norman Conquest, when expanding populations led to more intensive use of the marginal lands. For two centuries after the disastrous years of the mid fourteenth century the economy and the population dwindled, until improvements in agricultural techniques, coupled with renewed economic and population growth during the sixteenth to eighteenth centuries, led to the creation of permanent farmsteads on the waste, in some cases overlying the earlier shieling huts.

The Powsons building is likely to have originated either as a herdsman's hut in the post-Conquest period, when much of the surrounding area was still unreclaimed woodland and waste, or in the early post-medieval period, as a component of a small permanent farmstead. In comparison to the increasing study of shieling sites, there has to date been little examination of such small marginal farmsteads.

The building at Powsons does not bear a close resemblance to the few early medieval longhouses excavated in the region, since these are generally up to 10m longer, and tend to have somewhat irregular ground plans, with bowed sides and rounded corners. They also have substantially more robust drystone walls than the Powsons structure, and are usually found in the context of a small complex of buildings, including not only dwellings but storehouses and workshops, grouped around a central enclosed yard (*eg* Ribblehead; King 1978). The

188

only marked similarity with early medieval buildings is the platform at the west end of the Powsons structure. Platforms have been identified at the western ends of two of the long buildings at Simy Folds (Coggins *et al* 1983, 68; Site 1, building 1, Site 2, building 1), and these appear to have incorporated hearths. In the Powsons building, however, there was no firm evidence for a hearth, perhaps because the interior has been thoroughly cleared since its abandonment. The neat eastern edge of the platform at Powsons implies an internal partition, perhaps dividing a living area from stalls for animals; the raised area of stones may have incorporated a windbreak, forming a passage adjacent to the possible western door.

In terms of size and shape, and its relative isolation, Powsons resembles more closely a shieling hut than an earlier medieval building. From the evidence of around 100 examples, the shieling huts of the northern Pennines exhibit considerable variation in their dimensions, but the majority are 6.09–9.75m long and 3.04–4.87m wide (Ramm *et al* 1970, 9). The Powsons building, which was 8.50m long and tapered from 4.80m to 4.00m wide, falls comfortably within these parameters, but other than in overall size and shape, and drystone construction, it is dissimilar to the huts recorded in the northern Pennines (Ramm *et al* 1970, 11, 37, plans). The most striking difference is that, of the three entrances (pertaining probably to different phases of use) noted in the Powsons structure, two are in the gable walls, including what appears to have been the original doorway in the east end. This doorway, which showed no sign of having been blocked at any stage, faced into the slope and was thus sheltered from the prevailing south-westerly winds, while a rock outcrop and a yard or annex provided additional protection. Only half a dozen huts of the many examples in the northern Pennines survey area have an end entrance, but Ramm noted a regional variation in the peripheral areas, where a further five huts (at Ousby, Gosforth, and Buttermere in Cumberland, and Bampton and Patterdale in Westmorland) have such an entrance (Ramm *et al* 1970, 10, inventories).

Shielings were located on marginal land, often grouped together in small communities, but the hut sites identified in the western Howgills generally occur singly, with only one large group (*see Chapter 3*; Cleasby 1991). The shieling huts tend to be located near a confluence of streams on the west-facing lower slopes between 180–260m OD, and these are common factors with the Powsons building. Unlike Powsons, however, these huts appear to have rounded corners (partly as a result of tumble) and a single entrance in the centre of one of the long sides. Two of the hut foundations, recently surveyed by LUAU at Crosdale in the western Howgills (Krupa 1994), are located on the west-facing slope above the present intake wall, at 232m and 260m OD respectively, and measure *c*8 x 11m overall. Both these huts, together with a network of associated boundary banks, have been preserved as a result of the retreat of agriculture from marginal pastures, lying just above the modern enclosed fields. Powsons, on the other hand, lies within a field which has probably been enclosed since the late eighteenth century, and the later boundaries overlie and obscure the layout. The most likely reason for the lack of tumble from any of the buildings at Powsons is that the stone was reused to build the intake wall itself.

One of the few locally recorded medieval farmhouses, at Cow Green, near Crosby Ravensworth, had an entrance in the end wall, and measured 10.97 x 6.7m externally, plus an annexe (Collingwood 1933, 210–12, fig 5). The method of construction was quite different to that of the Powsons building, however, with far more massive walls using orthostats, although this would be expected in limestone areas as a variation in building technique to accommodate the less workable stone. The very limited amount of published work on later medieval farmhouses in the region provides little comparative material, but end entrances are not generally found among vernacular buildings of the early post-medieval period (Brunskill 1974, 1978). These houses are typically multi-celled structures of larger dimensions and greater sophistication than the Powsons building.

The lack of artefacts in direct association with the Powsons building is unsurprising, as excavations within the region have demonstrated a relatively aceramic culture in rural areas throughout the medieval period and until the eighteenth century, when cheap pottery became available. Until then organic materials, such as wood and leather, were generally used, and these rarely survive in the archaeological record; what is more, the site had obviously been cleared over a period after it fell into disuse. On the other hand, a small assemblage of artefacts has usually been found in association with early medieval structures. Two excavated shielings in Bewcastle (northern Cumbria) also produced a small assemblage, including fragments of late seventeenth century clay pipe; it was suggested by the excavator that this demonstrated that these structures belonged to the latter end of the sequence identified in the fieldwork (Ramm *et al* 1970, 19). The only shieling that to date has yielded a significant number of artefacts was constructed of puddled clay, again in Bewcastle; this produced early fourteenth century pottery and displayed evidence of a possible oven within its associated enclosure (Richardson 1979, 22–7). This might imply more permanent occupation than was the case elsewhere.

The evidence of clearance at Powsons indicates not only the use of surface stone for construction of the dwelling, but also some attempt at cultivation, as evinced by the slight remains of ploughmarks. This may suggest a rather more permanent occupation than simply transhumance, and the evidence taken as a whole may lead to the conclusion that the sixteenth century and later settlement listed in the manorial records superseded or continued an earlier settlement. The building may be the farmhouse occupied by Hugh Powson in 1560, perhaps in later centuries housing cattle and cowherd, until it was replaced by the nearby barn and shippon shown on mid nineteenth century maps.

Conclusions

The Powsons building may thus have been a shieling hut, a small farmhouse, or even a cattle byre, or any permutation of these. The deficiency in dating evidence means that few firm conclusions can be drawn from upland sites of this nature, and while Powsons is quite unlike recorded early medieval buildings in the region, except perhaps for the end entrance and platform at the opposite end, neither is it entirely typical of shieling huts in the same valley nor similar to medieval or early post-medieval farmhouses. As the other structures in this complex were unaffected by pipeline construction, it is not possible to interpret conclusively the excavated building in the context of the farmstead as a whole, or to establish a sequence of buildings, and their use, on the site.

Without further comparative and documentary study the Powsons building will remain an enigma, but two phases of use were established by the excavations, and manorial and parish records confirm the existence of a farmstead here from the sixteenth to the nineteenth century. The evidence accumulated from topographical survey, excavation, photography, and documentary research, as well as independent fieldwork (by J K Lambert) throughout the western Howgills, suggests that a shieling, probably of twelfth or thirteenth century origin, was adapted for use as a permanent farmstead, in accordance with the trend throughout the northern uplands in the later medieval period. Throughout its post-medieval history, Powsons was dominated by the neighbouring and much larger farm at Brockholes. In the period of consolidation of farms in the late eighteenth or early nineteenth century, it was absorbed by Brockholes and lost its identity, with only the fields named in the tithe award indicating its former extent. Gradually Powsons faded from memory, until it was rediscovered during field-walking in advance of the NWEP.

CONCLUSIONS

The foregoing chapters demonstrate that a project such as the NWEP can generate a wealth of new information, even though it is geared entirely to a construction programme within a long narrow corridor. The success of the project can and should be judged on the avoidance of sites wherever possible, so preserving the archaeological heritage. This confirms the importance of LUAU's involvement at the planning stage, when effort was directed to identifying and limiting the impact on areas of known archaeological potential.

The four major excavations described above (*Chapters 4–7*) were inevitable, because Hadrian's Wall had to be crossed, because of severe topographical constraints in the Lune gorge and, in the case of Fremington, because there was no prior indication of the site's existence and the density of known archaeology in the vicinity made rerouteing difficult. The close communication between developer and archaeological contractor in the initial stages of the project meant that resources could be concentrated on the handful of sites and areas where avoidance was impossible, thereby achieving a suitably high level of analysis and interpretation in those areas.

Consequently, the survival of the *vallum* associated with Hadrian's Wall has been demonstrated to the east of Brunstock Park, near Carlisle, where previously its exact location was unknown; an early medieval settlement at Fremington, near Brougham, which is to date unique in the North West, was identified and analysed; the hitherto unknown Roman cemetery adjacent to the fort at Low Borrowbridge was subject to intensive excavation and analysis; and a medieval farmstead at Powsons was discovered, recorded, and documented from the sixteenth century. Furthermore, prompted by the close proximity of the latter two sites in the Lune gorge near Tebay, an exploratory study has been made of settlement in the valley (*Chapter 3*). As research here was hampered by the lack of published historical material, two key documents, a sixteenth century manorial survey and the nineteenth cen-

tury tithe map and apportionment, were transcribed, translated, or traced, as appropriate, and these will be of value in any future landscape studies of the area.

The methodology of the phased approach is, of course, now standard for landscape evaluations on any scale, but this was new in the North West in 1988 when, with the arrival of contract archaeology, LUAU introduced phased archaeological assessments. Shell Chemicals UK Ltd was the first developer of a major linear project in the North to take full responsibility for its environmental and archaeological implications, and the relatively generous provisions of the NWEP's environmental budget enabled LUAU to refine fieldwork and excavation methodologies and recording systems in order to deal with the abundance of archaeological data in an efficient and pragmatic fashion.

Archaeological practices have been transformed since the late 1980s, and methods which are accepted as the norm today were then untested in the North. The phased approach was a new concept, and there was genuine debate as to the need for some of the techniques used, in particular topographical survey, which in the event proved the most apposite of all, especially in upland contexts. Our experience with other techniques demonstrated, in particular, that geophysical survey could feasibly be employed over very circumscribed areas of high potential, and the results did confirm features, especially in association with Hadrian's Wall. Trial excavation allowed the rapid testing of presumed subsurface features, but whilst it produced positive results at a few sites, repeatedly cropmarks on the alluvial floodplains had no subsoil existence. This may be a result of intensive ploughing or, in some cases, attributable to a geological origin. Equally, in upland areas, visible earthworks did not have any corresponding subsoil existence; again this may be determined by the nature of the soils or the underlying rock. In the upland and non-arable areas, once sites had been recognised through the rapid field scan (spot location of sites is now routinely achieved via the GPS satellite system), detailed topographical survey by Zeiss total station was particularly useful for extensive sites such as field systems, and proved to be the most effective and economical means of recording sites which did not warrant intensive excavation.

The progression from archive searches to field-walking and aerial survey located the vast majority of sites, and their number was then only augmented by means of the watching brief during construction. This was inevitably conducted under less than optimum conditions for archaeological observation, when the disturbance caused by machine removal of topsoil often confused or destroyed elements just below the modern ground surface.

This transect of North West England, within which the NWEP took shape, vividly confirms perceived differences in the survival of archaeological evidence between upland and lowland, and rural and urban landscapes. The clustering of sites in the identified areas of high potential reflects the original assessment, which was initially informed by the county SMRs, and the judgement made in the early stages of the project, regarding the higher concentration and survival of earthwork sites in upland areas only marginally affected by agricultural and industrial activity, has been sustained. Nearly all the areas regarded as being particularly sensitive were in Cumbria, where there has generally been less subsequent disturbance of the landscape than in Lancashire, Merseyside, or Cheshire. Pipeline reroutes, and the narrowing of the corridor to a final 20m width fenced off for construction, meant that most areas of high archaeological potential were avoided. The scale of the project made it necessary, from the outset, to direct the resources towards the sites which, by unremitting processes of selection, were deemed to have the greatest potential, and this is reflected in the flexible levels of recording adopted. The accurate primary records and survey data of every site, regardless of its importance, are contained in the archive and collated in the comprehensive gazetteer generated by the project (*on microfiche, see Appendix* 2), which has contributed several hundred sites to the county SMRs. The most encouraging result of all this work is that a great deal of interest has been focused on the characteristics of archaeology in the North West, with new insights provoked by the discoveries described in this volume.

APPENDIX 1

Summary gazetteer

Site no	Site name	NGR	Site type
Cumbria			
771	North British Railway	NY 37597030	Disused railway
773	Scaurbank	NY 38126939	Ridge and furrow
774	Scaurbank Wood	NY 38506939	Field boundary
781	Longtownmoor	NY 38956895	Find scatter
782	Ladyseat Wood	NY 39056845	Field boundary
791	Barrockstown	NY 39786477	Ridge and furrow
792	Barrockstown	NY 39806465	Findspot
793	Barrockstown	NY 39856497	Find scatter
801	Barrockstown	NY 39886445	Ridge and furrow
802	Down By Rigg	NY 40056393	Field boundary
803	Barrockstown	NY 39956417	Find scatter
811	Knells	NY 40976202	Wetland
821	Knells Park	NY 41946059	Field boundary, mound
822	High Moor Plantation	NY 42136048	Ridge and furrow
823	Moss Plantation	NY 42446030	Field boundary
824	Old Grove	NY 42855941	Trackway
825	Hadrian's Wall	NY 42675928	Roman wall
827	Old Grove	NY 42825918	Pit, findspot
831	Stanegate	NY 43035895	Roman road
832	Park Broom	NY 43055878	Field boundary
833	Park Broom	NY 43085873	Ridge and furrow
835	Scotby Holmes	NY 43895753	Findspot
836	Park Broom	NY 42965903	Ditch
841	Pow Maughan	NY 44095676	Flint
842	Pow Maughan Bridge	NY 44185628	Seal
844	Hortside	NY 44195612	Trackway, lynchet
846	Hill Head House	NY 44235595	Find scatter, wall
851	Scotby Shield	NY 45255374	Field boundary
852	Wetheral	NY 45575329	Chapel
853	Scotby Shield	NY 45015420	Ditch
854	Beck Bridge	NY 45755297	Hearth
855	Beck Bridge	NY 45635320	Hearth
861	Oak Tree Farm	NY 45805270	Charcoal spread
862	Wetheral Shield	NY 46105190	Findspot
871	Wrayside	NY 47175152	Charcoal spread
872	Oakville	NY 47505105	Charcoal spread
873	Oakville	NY 47695060	Findspot
9101	Stand End	NY 47304845	Ditch
912	Tarn Wadling	NY 48704458	Drained tarn
913	Tarn Wadling	NY 48814440	Stone building
914	Tarn Wadling	NY 48834435	Boathouse
915	Tarn Wadling	NY 48784440	Find scatter
916	Blaze Fell	NY 48654398	Charcoal spread
9201	Aiketgate	NY 47944647	Ridge and furrow
9202	Aiketgate	NY 47854705	Pit, ploughmark
921	Old Town	NY 48584390	Flint
923	Old Town	NY 48504370	Cropmark
924	Blackrack Beck	NY 48864254	Cropmark
932	Castle Rigg	NY 49814094	Boundary stone
934	Lazonby Fell	NY 50134030	Settlement, trackway, field boundary
935	Whinny bank	NY 50004048	Sculptured stone

Site no	Site name	NGR	Site type
936	Whinny bank	NY 50004048	Stone
938	Lazonby Fell	NY 50004054	Esker, trackway, ridge and furrow
939	Lazonby Fell	NY 50254000	Bank
9310	Low Plains	NY 49914060	Cairn
941	Tarn Plantation	NY 50274000	Cairnfield, urn
943	Lazonby Fell	NY 50003900	Axe
944	Lazonby Fell	NY 50003900	Arrowhead
948	Tarn Plantation	NY 50703900	Trackway
949	Tarn Plantation	NY 50733900	Cairn
9410	Scarfoot	NY 50743842	Bank, ditch
952	West Brownrigg	NY 51083707	Bank, ditch
953	Burnt Wood	NY 51123633	Trackway, bank, cairn
961	Fox Wood	NY 51993473	Ridge and furrow
962	Bowscar	NY 52203440	Ridge and furrow
981	Drovergate Plantation	NY 53773183	Pond
982	Lady Plantation	NY 53803138	Sheepwash
983	Hyde Park	NY 53833162	Charcoal spread
991	Roundthorn Farm	NY 53773108	Hollow
992	Hackmoor	NY 53773098	Trackway
993	Mounteden	NY 53823078	Lynchet
998	Sceugh Farm	NY 54553000	Settlement
999	Brougham	NY 54502965	Dyke, enclosure
9910	Carleton Hill Farm	NY 54133049	Findspot
1004	Brougham	NY 54602900	Roman cemetery
1005	Countess Pillar	NY 54612896	Pillar
1006	Countess Pillar	NY 54612896	Tombstone, alms table, altar
1008	Fremington	NY 54782873	Cist
10013	Brougham	NY 54652895	Find scatter
10014	Fremington	NY 54752882	Settlement
10015	Fremington	NY 54762866	Hearth
1011	Low Dykes	NY 54562643	Ditch
1013	Railway Cottages	NY 54602620	Findspot
1014	Clifton Dykes	NY 54532604	Field boundary
1015	Eden Valley Railway	NY 54532610	Disused railway
1018	Clifton	NY 54732571	Ridge and furrow, bank
10110	Howe Carl	NY 54772528	Ditch
1022	Hackthorpe	NY 54932381	Field system, trackway
1025	Hackthorpe	NY 55072311	Field system, bank
1026	Oaklands	NY 55072287	Trackway, field boundary, bank
1027	Oaklands	NY 55082271	Trackway, field boundary, platform
10210	Town Head	NY 55142213	Bank, ditch, ridge and furrow
10211	Great Strickland	NY 55332214	Field system, trackway
10213	Town Head	NY 55202313	Lynchet
1031	Great Strickland	NY 55402198	Stone building
1034	Sheriff Park	NY 55602128	Field boundary, ridge and furrow
1035	Sheriff Park	NY 55772104	Lynchet, ridge and furrow
1036	Thrimby Mill Plantation	NY 55902082	Ridge and furrow
1037	Thrimby Mill	NY 56042012	Field system, bank, ditch
10311	Thrimby	NY 55542151	Field system, trackway, mound, platform
10312	Thrimby	NY 55972054	Findspot
10313	Thrimby	NY 55942069	Findspot
1041	Little Strickland	NY 56091981	Enclosure, ridge and furrow
1043	Little Strickland	NY 56151945	Field system
1044	Capple Rigg	NY 56361905	Field boundary
1045	Towcett	NY 56701850	Field boundary, cairn
1046	Gunnerkeld	NY 56681850	Hand axe
1047	Towcett	NY 56851814	Field boundary
10411	Gunnerwell	NY 56901785	Ridge and furrow
1052	High Keverigg	NY 57531676	Mound
1056	High Keverigg	NY 57471685	Enclosure, mound, trackway, bank

Site no	Site name	NGR	Site type
1057	High Keverigg	NY 57461686	Enclosure
1058	Gunnerkeld	NY 57101752	Findspot
1059	Gunnerkeld	NY 57011768	Findspot
1061	Hardendale	NY 57901557	Field boundary
1062	Hardendale	NY 57901540	Stone building
1063	Hardendale	NY 57941535	Ridge and furrow, field boundary
1064	Hardendale	NY 57981507	Bank
1065	Hardendale	NY 57971492	Field system
1067	Hardendale	NY 57831465	Field boundary
1068	Hardendale	NY 57801460	Field system, farmstead
1069	Hardendale Nab	NY 57711404	Field boundary, ridge and furrow
10610	Hardendale	NY 57891569	Enclosure, pit, field boundary
10611	The Nab	NY 57891378	Findspot
10612	The Nab	NY 57671434	Findspot
1081	Crosby Ravensworth Fell	NY 58991134	Bank
1083	Crosby Ravensworth Fell	NY 59301022	Enclosure
1084	Crosby Ravensworth Fell	NY 58711139	Enclosure
1085	Crosby Ravensworth Fell	NY 58731100	Findspot
1091	Sproatgill	NY 60240807	Roman road
1092	Crosby Ravensworth Fell	NY 59700930	Findspot
1093	Crosby Ravensworth Fell	NY 59640950	Findspot
1094	Sproatgill	NY 60300780	Findspot
1101	Old Tebay	NY 61470594	Ridge and furrow
1112	Tebay	NY 62250535	Ridge and furrow
1113	High Beck Lane	NY 62300512	Hollow way
1115	Tebay	NY 62220497	Field system, bank
1116	Tebay	NY 62260480	Settlement
1117	Tebay	NY 62230482	Field boundary
1118	Tebay	NY 62240470	Field boundary
1121	Tebay	NY 62060369	Ridge and furrow, bank, ditch
1122	Tebay	NY 62070346	Trackway
1123	Tebay Gill	NY 61900290	Banks
1131	Powsons	NY 61400242	Field boundary
1132	Powsons	NY 61320233	Building, trackway, enclosure, field boundary
1133	Powsons	NY 61340215	Walls, banks, trackways
1134	Powsons	NY 61300193	Field boundary
1135	Powsons	NY 61250161	Field boundary
1138	Low Borrowbridge	NY 61260125	Bank, ditch
1139	Low Borrowbridge	NY 61050100	*Vicus*, platform, bank, ridge and furrow
11315	Powsons	NY 61450253	Field boundary, ridge and furrow
11316	Powsons	NY 61320233	Findspot
11317	Low Borrowbridge	NY 61170098	Findspot
11318	Low Borrowbridge	NY 61130092	Roman cemetery
1142	Salterwath Bridge	NY 61130056	Trackway, field boundary
1144	High Carlingill	NY 61320023	Watercourse, gully
1145	High Carlingill	SD 61889956	Enclosure, pit
1146	High Carlingill	NY 61170050	Bank, enclosure
1151	Low Park	SD 62509812	Findspot
1161	Lowgill	SD 62399700	Field boundary, trackway
1162	London and NW Railway	SD 61729670	Disused railway
1167	Lowgill	SD 61289629	Field boundary
1183	Drybeck Moss	SD 60299277	Wetland
1184	Killington New Park	SD 60009200	Enclosure
1188	Killington New Park	SD 59889107	Mound
1191	Old Scotch Road	SD 59899070	Drove road
1192	Mutton Hall	SD 59509000	Ploughmark
1208	Black Essett Plantation	SD 58478877	Field boundary, enclosure
1223	Cocklet Wood	SD 56088603	Lynchet, bank
1241	Hollins Farm	SD 54548263	Ridge and furrow
1242	Hollins Farm	SD 54348241	Lynchet, bank, trackway

Site no	Site name	NGR	Site type
1243	Dove House Farm	SD 54288210	Field boundary, platform, ridge and furrow
1246	Dove House Farm	SD 53978184	Conduit
12413	Farleton	SD 53728103	Lynchet, ridge and furrow
12501	Marsden Farm	SD 53618087	Limekiln, trackway
12502	Farleton	SD 53518070	Limekiln, trackway
12503	Farleton	SD 53508047	Field boundary, charcoal pitstead, trackway
12504	Farleton Fell	SD 53658005	Charcoal pitstead, trackway
12601	Holme Park	SD 53487923	Wall, enclosure
1263	Curwen Hall	SD 53147815	Mound
1264	Sexton Hagg	SD 53287804	Wall
1265	Clawthorpe	SD 53527770	Shrunken village
1271	Burton in Kendal	SD 53767699	Boundary stone
1273	Burton in Kendal	SD 53587657	Field system, bank, trackway
1275	Dalton Park	SD 53277576	Field system, trackway
1276	Dalton Lane	SD 53347590	Boundary stone

Lancashire

Site no	Site name	NGR	Site type
1282	White Beck	SD 52817435	Enclosure, ditch, trackway
1283	Priest Hutton	SD 52677418	Ridge and furrow
1284	Priest Hutton	SD 52587399	Ridge and furrow, lynchet
1287	Priest Hutton	SD 52907470	Enclosure
1288	Tewitfield	SD 52297342	Brick building, findspot
1293	Sander's Farm	SD 52347325	Ridge and furrow
1299	Manor Farm	SD 52397290	Ring bank
12910	Lancaster Canal	SD 52327370	Canal
12913	Capernwray	SD 52867204	Lynchet
12919	Capernwray	SD 52837187	Ridge and furrow
12920	Manor Farm	SD 52427285	Ridge and furrow
1302	Kellet Lane Bridge	SD 52207113	Settlement
1305	Over Kellet	SD 51467016	Field system, trackway, mound
1311	Over Kellet	SD 51696985	Field boundary, ridge and furrow
1313	Over Kellet	SD 51806973	Field system, platform
1314	Slacks Wood	SD 51956954	Field boundary
1316	Kit Bill Wood	SD 51986917	Stone wall, cairn
1318	Birkland Barrow	SD 52106898	Ridge and furrow
13110	Birkland Barrow	SD 52166882	Boundary stone
1322	Intack Farm	SD 52236806	Bank, mound
1323	Green Hill Lane	SD 52386763	Ridge and furrow, trackway, field boundary
1325	Green Hill Lane	SD 52346761	Bellpit
1331	Scargill Woods	SD 51766705	Field boundary
1341	Oakenhead Pond	SD 51346552	Ridge and furrow, pond
1342	Halton Green West	SD 51306540	Ridge and furrow, trackway, field boundary
1343	Little NW Railway	SD 51506473	Disused railway
1347	North Park Plantation	SD 51546461	Ridge and furrow
1353	Knots Wood	SD 50356267	Ridge and furrow, trackway
1354	Stanley Farm	SD 50176259	Ridge and furrow
1356	Lancaster Moor	SD 50076246	Ridge and furrow
1361	Lancaster Moor	SD 50056215	Trackway, hollow way
13701	Langthwaite Reservoir	SD 49695981	Ridge and furrow, field boundary
13702	Middle Langthwaite	SD 49545948	Stone building
13703	Middle Langthwaite	SD 49505940	Ridge and furrow
13704	Croftlands House	SD 49315887	Mound
13705	Blea Tarn	SD 49255876	Dugout canoe
13706	Blea Tarn Reservoir	SD 49125834	Trackway, field boundary
13707	Langthwaite Reservoir	SD 49505951	Burned area
13708	Scotforth	SD 49485958	Trackway
13801	Eastrigg	SD 49335706	Settlement, field system, trackway
13804	Barrow Greaves	SD 49404674	Ridge and furrow, findspot
13805	Higher Kit Brow	SD 49435666	Ridge and furrow, field boundary, findspot

Site no	Site name	NGR	Site type
1393	Lane House	SD 48385446	Trackway, hollow way
1394	Quarry Wood	SD 48285437	Lynchet, field boundary
1395	Quarry Wood	SD 48305420	Lynchet, trackway
13910	Keepers Lodge	SD 48125422	Lynchet
13912	Lancaster Canal	SD 48195425	Canal
13913	Ellel Grange	SD 48095420	Field system
13914	Pennine Farm	SD 48805468	Field boundary
13915	Normanton House	SD 48805516	Trackway
13916	Whitley Beck	SD 49365550	Field boundary
13917	Quarry Wood	SD 48235430	Trackway, field boundary
1401	Home Farm	SD 47975415	Field system, ditch, pond, mound
1402	Flat Wood	SD 47595398	Trackway, lynchet
1403	Batty Hill	SD 46685319	Ridge and furrow
1406	Hill House	SD 46355305	Ridge and furrow
1414	Marsh Houses	SD 45855160	Cropmark
1415	River Cocker	SD 45915128	Linear feature
1416	Hosty Beck	SD 45975275	Find scatter
1421	Crimbles	SD 45985066	Deserted medieval village
1422	Middle Crimbles	SD 46035022	Field boundary, hollow way, pond, platform
1423	Hardhead	SD 46344913	Field system
1441	Garstang–Knott End Railway	SD 46224599	Disused railway
1445	Nateby Lodge	SD 46254399	Field boundary, enclosure
1446	Nook Farm	SD 46374450	Wetland
1451	Watson's Wood	SD 46314360	Field boundary
1461	Hall Lane	SD 46904090	Findspot
1471	St Michael's on Wyre	SD 46604040	Field boundary, enclosure
1481	Plane Tree Farm	SD 46573983	Field system
1482	Inskip	SD 46703810	Ridge and furrow
1483	Inskip	SD 46693801	Ridge and furrow, hollow way
1484	Inskip	SD 46693792	Ridge and furrow
1485	Inskip	SD 46683784	Ridge and furrow
1486	Layton's Farm	SD 46673766	Ridge and furrow
1492	Carr House Green	SD 46583740	Ridge and furrow
1493	Higham Side	SD 46133676	Ridge and furrow
1501	Locking Stoops	SD 45823500	Field boundary
1503	Stanley Grange	SD 45703404	Field boundary, ridge and furrow
1521	Newton with Clifton	SD 45263205	Ridge and furrow
1522	Newton with Clifton	SD 45653076	Field system
1523	Newton with Clifton	SD 45613139	Ridge and furrow, field boundary
1532	Clifton Marsh	SD 45952910	Bank
1551	Hall Pool Bridge	SD 46212579	Ridge and furrow
1561	West Lancashire Railway	SD 46042321	Disused railway
1562	Much Hoole	SD 46012289	Field boundary
1563	Much Hoole	SD 46022309	Field system
1564	Much Hoole	SD 46032329	Field boundary
1565	Much Hoole	SD 46012276	Pit
1601	Hall Green	SD 47341763	Sand island, findspot
1611	Marsh Moss	SD 47091535	Bog oak
1621	Bleak Hall Farm	SD 46501230	Cropmark
1622	Bleak Hall Farm	SD 46401190	Ditch
1631	Leeds and Liverpool Canal	SD 46261090	Canal
1633	Ring O' Bells	SD 46251080	Field boundary, enclosure
1651	East Lancashire Railway	SD 44600756	Disused railway

Merseyside

Site no	Site name	NGR	Site type
1751	Startham Hall	SJ 52989884	Ruined building
1752	Shoots Delph	SJ 51579897	Trackway
1771	Arch Lane	SJ 55519886	Tunnel
1791	New Hall	SJ 56709833	Moated site

Site no	Site name	NGR	Site type
1792	Haydock	SJ 57429821	Disused railway
1801	Lodge Lane	SJ 57969734	Roman road
1811	Haydock	SJ 56809600	Disused railway
1812	Newton-le-Willows	SJ 56659590	Pond
1813	Hall Farm	SJ 56489578	Field boundary
1814	Hall Farm	SJ 56429574	Field boundary, bank, pond
1821	Newton Common	SJ 56319567	Racetrack stand
1822	Penkford Street	SJ 55939505	Canal
1832	Wheatacre Farm	SJ 55699258	Wall
1842	Further Mear Hey	SJ 54529008	Moated site

Cheshire

Site no	Site name	NGR	Site type
1871	Fiddler's Ferry	SJ 55608662	Waterlogged deposits
1872	St Helens Canal New Cut	SJ 55848630	Canal
1881	Manchester Ship Canal	SJ 55778457	Canal
1882	Bridgewater Canal	SJ 57598348	Canal
1895	Daresbury Hall	SJ 58208230	Wall
1901	Newton Bank	SJ 57598159	Lynchet
1902	Newton Bank	SJ 57578148	Find scatter
1923	Trent and Mersey Canal	SJ 58047816	Canal
1928	Longacre Wood	SJ 58047822	Findspot
1932	Bird's Wood	SJ 56377849	Ditch, findspot
1933	Aston Lane	SJ 55537888	Findspot
1942	Sutton Hall	SJ 54707870	Bank, trackway, ridge and furrow
1943	Sutton Hall	SJ 54507850	Ridge and furrow
1944	Sutton Hall	SJ 54757870	Linear feature
1945	Beckett's Wood	SJ 54657868	Pit, findspot
1951	Weaver Navigation	SJ 53767876	Canal
1957	Beckett's Wood	SJ 54177857	Brick kiln
1958	Beckett's Wood	SJ 55037895	Findspot
1959	Sutton Bridge	SJ 53407885	Cess pit
1971	Frodsham Marsh	SJ 49007865	Spearhead
1981	Frodsham Score	SJ 48457825	Findspot
1994	Holme Farm	SJ 45727727	Platform
1995	Ince Marshes	SJ 46007735	Axe

APPENDIX 2

BIBLIOGRAPHY

Maps and manuscripts

Ordnance Survey
Cumberland, 1st edn 6″, 1859–65
Westmorland, 1st edn 6″, 25, 1856–9; 1st rev edn 6″, 1896–9; 2nd rev edn 6″, 1910–13; National Grid edn 6″, 1956
Lancashire, 1st edn 6″, 1841–54
Cheshire, 1st edn 6″, 1872, 1st rev edn 6″, 1899, 2nd rev edn 6″, 1910
Old Series 1″, Sheet 98 (Kendal), 1864–5 (1970 facsimile edn, Newton Abbot)
Roman Britain, 3rd edn, 1956, Southampton
Hadrians Wall 1″, 1st edn, 1964, Southampton
Hadrian's Wall, 1:2500 plan, NY4259–4359, 1973

Cumbria Record Office (Carlisle)

J Hodskinson and T Donald, 1802 1″ map of Cumberland, 2 edn
D/LONS/L Wharton manors, Box 1: Survey of Wharton manors in Westmorland, 1560, Rentals and court books, 1587–1849
D/LONS/L5/3 Plan of the Manors of Grayrigg, Lambrigg, and Docker, surveyed 1764–5

Cumbria Record Office (Kendal)

T Jeffreys, 1″ map of Westmorland, 1770
C and J Greenwood, 1″ map of Westmorland, 1824
T Hodgson, 1″ map of Westmorland, 1828
WQ/R/C/5, Grayrigg tithe map, 1835
WDRC/8/110, Tebay tithe map and apportionment, 1841
WQ/R/DP/15, Caledonian Railway map, 1842
WQ/R/DP/45, Lancaster and Carlisle Railway map, 1844
WQ/R/DP/79, 83, North Western Railway, Ingleton to Tebay branch, map, 1855, and book of reference, 1856
WPR/9/1, Orton parish register, 1596–1646
WPR/9/2, Orton parish register, 1654–1744
WPR/9/01, Orton churchwardens accounts, 1777–
WPR/9/Z10, Orton enclosure award, 1769
WPR/9/Z11, Orton enclosure maps, 1779
WPR/9/25, Dillicar enclosure award, 1853
WPR/9/31, Grayrigg enclosure award, 1868
WPR/9/90, Fawcett Forest enclosure award, 1870
WQ/R/LT, Orton land tax assessments, 1773, 1790, 1823, 1829
WQ/SR/182, Sessions Rolls, 1726–37
WQ/SR/83173, Sessions Rolls, 1737–44

Lancashire Record Office

DRB, Over Kellet tithe map, 1840

Addyman, P V, 1972 *The Anglo-Saxon house: a new review, Anglo-Saxon England*, **1**, Cambridge

Alcock, J P, 1980 Classical religious belief and burial practice in Roman Britain, *Archaeol J*, **137**, 50–85

Allan, T M, 1985 *Cumberland Westmorland Antiq Archaeol Soc Newsletter*, **4**, Spring 1985

Allen, J L, and Holt, A St J, 1986 *Health and safety in field archaeology*, Southampton

Andrews, G A, Fitzpatrick, A P, and Mould, Q, forthcoming *The Romano-British cemetery at Brougham, Penrith, 1966–7, English Heritage Archaeol Rep*

Anstee, J W, 1975a The bath-house of Low Borrow Bridge Roman fort, Tebay, *Contrebis*, **3** (2), 77–85

Anstee, J W, 1975b An aqueduct in the Tebay gorge, *Contrebis*, **3** (2), 74–5

Anstee, J W, 1986 *Some sites and an excavation near Brockholes Farm, Low Borrowbridge, Tebay*, unpubl report

Armstrong, P, Tomlinson, D, and Evans, D H, 1991 *Excavations at Lurk Lane, Beverley 1979–82, Sheffield Excav Rep*, **1**

Arnold, C J, 1988 *An archaeology of the early Anglo-Saxon kingdoms*, London

Arthur, B V, and Jope, E M 1962–3 Early Saxon pottery kilns at Purwell Farm, Cassington, Oxfordshire, *Medieval Archaeol*, **6–7**, 1–14

Ashmore, O, 1982 *The industrial archaeology of North West England*, Manchester

Atkin, M A, 1989 Hollin names in North West England, *Nomina*, **12**, 77–88

Atkinson, J C, 1923 *Forty years in a moorland parish*, London

Austen, P A, 1991 *Bewcastle and Old Penrith, A Roman outpost and a frontier vicus, excavation 1977–8, Cumberland Westmorland Antiq Archaeol Soc Res ser*, **6**

Bailey, J and Culley, G, 1805 *General view of the agriculture of Northumberland, Cumberland and Westmorland*, 3 edn, London (1972 facsimile reprint, Newcastle upon Tyne)

Baker, A R H, and Butlin, R A (eds), 1973 *Studies of field systems in the British Isles*, Cambridge

Baldwin, J R, and Whyte, A D (eds), 1985 *The Scandinavians in Cumbria*, Edinburgh

Bass, W M, 1987 *Human osteology, Missouri Arch Soc*, Columbia

Bennett, J, and Turner, R, 1983 The *Vallum* at Wallhouses, Northumberland; excavations in 1980 and 1981, *Archaeol Aeliana*, 5 ser, **11**, 61–78

Bergstrom, T, 1984 *Hadrian's Wall*, New York

Bewley, R H, 1986 Survey and excavation in the Solway plain, Cumbria, 1982–4, *Trans Cumberland Westmorland Antiq Archaeol Soc*, **86**, 19–40

Bewley, R H, 1992 Excavations on two crop-marked sites in the Solway plain, Cumbria: Ewanrigg settlement and Swarthy Hill, 1986–8, *Trans Cumberland Westmorland Antiq Archaeol Soc*, **92**, 23–48

Birley, A R, 1979 *The people of Roman Britain*, London

Birley, E B, 1932 Materials for the history of Roman Brougham, *Trans Cumberland Westmorland Antiq Archaeol Soc*, **32**, 124–40

Birley, E B, 1947 The Roman fort at Low Borrow Bridge, *Trans Cumberland Westmorland Antiq Archaeol Soc*, **47**, 1–19

Birley, E B, 1953 The Roman milestone at Middleton in Lonsdale, *Trans Cumberland Westmorland Antiq Archaeol Soc*, **53**, 52–63

Blackett-Ord, M, 1986 Lord Wharton's deer park walls, *Trans Cumberland Westmorland Antiq Archaeol Soc*, **86**, 133–9

Blagg, T F C, and King, A C (eds), 1984 *Military and civilian in Roman Britain, cultural relationships in a frontier province, BAR Brit Ser*, **136**

Bonser, K J, 1970 *The drovers*, London

Boon, G C, 1977 Gold-in-glass beads from the Ancient World, *Britannia*, **8**, 193–207

Bouch, C M L, 1955 A Dark Age coin hoard from Ninekirks, Brougham, *Trans Cumberland Westmorland Antiq Archaeol Soc*, **55**, 108–11

Bouch, C M L, and Jones, G P, 1961 *A short economic and social history of the Lake Counties, 1500–1830*, Manchester

Boyer, L L, and Grondzik, W, 1987 *Earth shelter technology*, Texas

Branigan, K (ed), 1980 *Rome and the Brigantes*, Sheffield

Breeze, D J, Close-Brooks, J, and Ritchie, J N G, 1976 Roman soldiers' burials at Camelon, Stirlingshire, 1922 and 1975, *Britannia*, **7**, 73–95

Breeze, D J, and Dobson, B, 1987 *Hadrian's Wall*, London, 3 edn

Bruce, J Collingwood, 1925 *The hand-book to the Roman Wall*, Newcastle, 8 edn

Brunskill, R W, 1974 *Vernacular architecture of the Lake Counties*, London

Brunskill, R W, 1978 *Illustrated handbook of vernacular architecture*, London, 2 edn

Bulmer, T F (ed), 1885 *History, topography, and directory of Westmoreland*, Manchester

Burleigh, G, and Stevenson, M, forthcoming *The excavations at Baldock*

Buxton, K M, and Howard-Davis, C L E, forthcoming *Ribchester graveyard excavations 1980 and 1989–90, Engl Heritage Archaeol Rep*

Buxton, K M, Lambert, J K, and Olivier, A C H, 1990 *North Western Ethylene Pipeline (English section): Report on 15 trial excavations in Cumbria and Lancashire*, Lancaster University Archaeological Unit , unpubl report

Charlesworth, D, 1965 A Roman milestone near Overtown, Lancashire, *Trans Cumberland Westmorland Antiq Archaeol Soc*, **65**, 427

Charlton, B, and Mitcheson, M, 1984 The Roman cemetery at Petty Knowes, Rochester, Northumberland, *Archaeol Aeliana*, 5 ser, **12**, 1–31

Cherry, J, and Cherry, P J, 1987 *Prehistoric habitation sites on the limestone uplands of eastern Cumbria, Cumberland Westmorland Antiq Archaeol Soc Res Ser*, **2**

Clack, P, and Haselgrove, S (eds), 1981 *Rural settlement in the Roman North, CBA Group 3*, Durham

Clare, T, 1981a *Archaeological sites of the Lake District*, Ashbourne

Clare, T, 1981b The evidence for the continuity of settlement in Cumbria, in P Clack and S Haselgrove (eds), *Rural settlement in the Roman North, CBA Group 3*, Durham, 43–56

Clarke, G, 1979 *Pre-Roman and Roman Winchester. Part II: The Roman Cemetery at Lankhills, Winchester Studies*, **3**

Cleasby, I, 1991 Early sites on the western Howgill Fells: a preliminary survey, *The Sedbergh Historian*, **2** (6), 1–8

Clifford, D J H (ed), 1990 *The diaries of Lady Anne Clifford*, Stroud

Codrington, T, 1903 *Roman roads in Britain*, London

Coggins D, Fairless, K J, and Batey, C E, 1983 Simy Folds: an early medieval settlement site in Upper Teesdale, County Durham, *Medieval Archaeol*, **27**, 1–26

Collingwood, R G, 1933 Prehistoric settlements near Crosby Ravensworth, *Trans Cumberland Westmorland Antiq Archaeol Soc*, **33**, 201–26

Collingwood, R G, and Wright, R P, 1965 *The Roman inscriptions of Britain, 1: Inscriptions on stone*, Oxford

Collingwood, W G, 1908 Report on an exploration of the Romano-British settlement at Ewe Close, Crosby Ravensworth, *Trans Cumberland Westmorland Antiq Archaeol Soc*, 8, 356–8

Colvin, H M, 1951 *The white canons in England*, Oxford

Cook, A M, and Dacre, M A W, 1985 *Excavations at Portway, Andover 1973–5, Oxford Univ Comm Archaeol Monogr*, 4

Corder, P, and Birley, E B, 1937 A pair of fourth-century Romano-British pottery kilns near Crambeck, *Antiq J*, 17, 392–413

Crossley, D W (ed), 1981 *Medieval industry, CBA Res Rep*, 40

Crummy, N, 1983 *The Roman small finds from excavations in Colchester 1971–85, Colchester Arch Rep*, 2

Cumbria Family History Society, 1991 *Transcript and index for the 1851 Census for Town Angle, Fellend Angle, Bowderdale Angle, Newbiggin Angle, Orton, Birkbeck Fells, Bretherdale, Raisbeck, Tebay, Langdale, and Asby (HO 107/ 2439 Folios 418–532)*

Cundill, P R, 1976 Late Flandrian vegetation and soils in Carlingill valley, Howgill Fells, *Trans Inst Brit Geogr*, n ser, 1, London

Cunliffe, B, 1975 Excavations at Portchester Castle: Vol II, Saxon, *Soc Antiq London Res Rep*, 33

Curwen, J F, 1913 *The castles and fortified towers of Cumberland, Westmorland and Lancashire North-of-the-Sands..., Cumberland Westmorland Antiq Archaeol Soc Extra ser*, 13

Curwen, J F, 1926 *Records relating to the Barony of Kendal, 3, Cumberland Westmorland Antiq Archaeol Soc and Westmorland County Council*, Kendal

Dent, J S, 1983 The impact of Roman rule on native society in the territory of the Parisii, *Britannia*, 14, 35–44

Denyer, S, 1991 *Traditional buildings and life in the Lake District*, London

Dickinson, S, 1985 Bryant's Gill, Kentmere: another 'Viking-period' Ribblehead? in J R Baldwin and I D Whyte (eds), *The Scandinavians in Cumbria*, Edinburgh, 83–8

Dixon, P, 1982 How Saxon is a Saxon house?, in P J Drury (ed), *Structural reconstruction, BAR Brit Ser*, 110, 275–88

Drury, D, 1991 *North Western Ethylene Pipeline (English section): Hadrian's Wall excavation*, Lancaster University Archaeological Unit, unpubl report

Drury, P J, 1981 The production of brick and tile in medieval England, in D W Crossley (ed), *Medieval industry, CBA Res Rep*, 40, 126–42

Drury, P J (ed), 1982 *Structural reconstruction, BAR Brit Ser*, 110

Duckett, G F (ed), 1882 *Description of Westmoreland, by Sir Daniel Fleming of Rydal, AD 1671, Trans Cumberland Westmorland Antiq Archaeol Soc Tract ser*, 1

Dunning, G C, Hurst, J G, Myres, J N L, and Tischler, F, 1959 Anglo-Saxon pottery: a symposium, *Medieval Archaeol*, 3, 1–78

Earle, J, and Plummer, C (eds), 1892 *Two of the Saxon Chronicles*, Oxford

Edwards, B J N, 1971 Roman finds from Contrebis, *Trans Cumberland Westmorland Antiq Archaeol Soc*, 71, 17–34

Ekwall, E, 1960 *Concise dictionary of English place-names*, Oxford, 4 edn

Elliott, G, 1973 Field systems of Northwest England, in A R H Baker, and R A Butlin (eds), *Studies of field systems in the British Isles*, Cambridge, 42–92

Elphick, D, and Lancaster, K J, 1989 Excerpts from the cartulary of Cockersands Abbey, *The Sedbergh Historian*, 2 (4), 2–7

Ely, S, and Lambert, J K, 1990, *North Western Ethylene Pipeline (English section): Phase II interim report supplement*, Lancaster University Archaeological Unit, unpubl report

English Heritage, 1989 *The management of archaeological projects*, London, 1 edn

English Heritage, 1991 *The management of archaeological projects*, London, 2 edn

Evans, J, 1989 Crambeck: Development of a major northern pottery industry, in P R Wilson (ed) *Crambeck Roman Pottery Industry*, Leeds

Evans, J G, Limbrey, S, and Cleere, H (eds), 1975 *The effect of man on the landscape: the Highland Zone, CBA Res Rep*, 11

Evison, V I, 1987 *Dover: The Buckland Anglo-Saxon Cemetery, Engl Heritage Archaeol Rep*, 3

Ewbank, J M, 1963 *Antiquary on horseback, Cumberland Westmorland Antiq Archaeol Soc Extra ser*, 19

Faraday, M A (ed), 1971 *The Westmorland protestation returns 1641/2 Cumberland Westmorland Antiq Archaeol Soc Tract ser*, 17

Farrer, W (ed), 1898 *The chartulary of Cockersand Abbey*, 1, *Chetham Society*, n ser, 38

Farrer, W (ed), 1905a *The chartulary of Cockersand Abbey*, 3 (1), *Chetham Society*, n ser, 56

Farrer, W (ed), 1905b *The chartulary of Cockersand Abbey*, **3** (2), *Chetham Society*, n ser, **57**

Farrer, W (ed), 1923 *Records relating to the barony of Kendale*, **1**, *Cumberland Westmorland Antiq Archaeol Soc Rec ser*, **4**

Farrer, W (ed), 1924 *Records relating to the barony of Kendale*, **2**, *Cumberland Westmorland Antiq Archaeol Soc Rec ser*, **5**

Farrer, W, and Brownbill, J (eds), 1914 *Victoria County History of Lancashire*, **8**, London

Fell, C I, 1972 Neolithic finds from Brougham, *Trans Cumberland Westmorland Antiq Archaeol Soc*, **72**, 36–43

Fell, C I, 1973 Dark Age to Viking times, in W H Pearsall and W Pennington (eds), *The Lake District: a landscape history*, London, 237–49 (1989 edn)

Fellows-Jensen, G, 1985a *Scandinavian settlement names in the North-West*, Copenhagen

Fellows-Jensen, G, 1985b Scandinavian settlement in Cumbria and Dumfriesshire: the place-name evidence, in J R Baldwin and I D Whyte (eds), *The Scandinavians in Cumbria*, Edinburgh, 65–82

Ferguson, R S, 1886 The Roman camp at Low Borrow Bridge, *Trans Cumberland Westmorland Antiq Archaeol Soc*, **8**, 1–6

Ferguson, R S, 1889 The retreat of the Highlanders through Westmorland in 1745, *Trans Cumberland Westmorland Antiq Archaeol Soc*, o ser, **10**, 186–228

Ferguson, R S, 1892 On the Roman cemeteries of Luguvallium, and on a sepulchral slab of Roman date found recently, *Trans Cumberland Westmorland Antiq Archaeol Soc*, o ser, **12**, 365–74

Ferguson, R S, 1893 *Testamenta Karleolensia (The series of wills from the pre-Reformation registers of the bishops of Carlisle), 1353–86*, *Cumberland Westmorland Antiq Archaeol Soc Extra ser*, **9**

Ferguson, R S, 1894 *A history of Westmorland*, London

Ferguson, R S, and Cowper, H S, 1897 Ancient and county bridges in Cumberland and Westmorland; with some remarks upon the fords. And Lancashire-North-of-the-Sands, *Trans Cumberland Westmorland Antiq Archaeol Soc*, o ser, **15**, 114–32

Fowler, P J (ed), 1975 *Recent work in rural archaeology*, Bradford-upon-Avon

Fowler, P J, 1983 *The farming of prehistoric Britain*, Cambridge

Fraser, C M, 1966 The Cumberland and Westmorland lay subsidies for 1332, *Trans Cumberland Westmorland Antiq Archaeol Soc*, **66**, 131–58

Frere, S S, 1967 *Britannia*, London

Garnett, F W, 1912 *Westmorland agriculture 1800–1900*, Kendal

Gejvall, N G, 1981 Determination of burnt bones from prehistoric graves, *Ossa Letters*, **2**, 1–13

Gelling, M, 1984 *Place-names in the landscape*, London

Gibbons, P, and Olivier, A C H, 1989 *North Western Ethylene Pipeline (English section), Archaeological assessment: Trial excavation of Hadrian's Wall*, Lancaster University Archaeological Unit, unpubl report

Giles, J A, 1876 *Chronicle of the kings of England*, London

Gillam, J P, and Davies, C M, 1961 The Roman mausoleum on Skorden Brae, Beaufront, Corbridge, Northumberland, *Archaeol Aeliana*, 4 ser, **39**, 37–62

Goodall, I, 1991 The iron, in Armstrong, P, Tomlinson, D, and Evans, D H, *Excavations at Lurk Lane, Beverley 1979–82*, *Sheffield Excav Rep*, **1**, 131–47

Gough, R, 1780 *British topography*

Graham, T H B, 1909 Six extinct Cumberland castles, *Trans Cumberland Westmorland Antiq Archaeol Soc*, **9**, 209–24

Gray, H, 1977 *Anatomy*, New York

Green, C J, 1974 Interim report on the excavations at Poundbury, Dorchester, 1973, *Dorset Nat Hist Archaeol Soc*, **95**, 97–100

Greene, K, 1978 Imported fine ware within Britain to AD 350: a guide to identification, in P Arthur and G Marsh (eds), *Early finds in Roman Britain*, BAR Brit Ser, **57**, 15–30, Oxford

Grew, F O, 1980 Roman Britain in 1979, *Britannia*, **11**, 358

Guido, M, 1978 *The glass beads of the prehistoric and Roman periods in Britain and Ireland*, *Soc Antiq London Res Rep*, **35**

Hadfield, C, and Biddle, G, 1970 *The canals of North West England*, Newton Abbot, **1, 2**

Hall, R A (ed), 1978 *Viking Age York and the North*, CBA Res Rep, **27**

Hall, R A, 1982 Tenth century woodworking in Coppergate, York, in S McGrail (ed), *Woodworking techniques before AD 1500*, BAR Int Ser, **129**, 231–44

Hall, R A, 1984 *The Viking dig: the excavations at York*, London

Hamerow, H, 1993 *Excavations at Mucking. 2: the Anglo-Saxon settlement*, *Engl Heritage Archaeol Rep*, **21**

Harkness, R, 1873–6 On a cist found at Brougham, *Proc Soc Antiq London*, 2 ser, **6**, 270

Harkness, R, and Stalker, V, 1880 Notice of the discovery of a cist and its contents at Moorhouse Farm, Brougham, Westmorland, *Archaeologia*, **45** (2), 411–16

Harley, J B, 1970 Cartographical notes, *OS Old Series 1″ map, Sheet 98 (Kendal)*, (1970 facsimile edn, Newton Abbot)

Harper, C G, 1924 *The Manchester and Glasgow road*, London, 2 edn

Harris, A, 1977 A traffic in lime, *Trans Cumberland Westmorland Antiq Archaeol Soc*, **77**, 149–55

Harrison, D, 1956 *Along Hadrian's Wall*, London

Harrison, P A, 1976 *Norman castles in Lonsdale*, unpubl dissertation, Lancaster University

Harrison, S M, 1981 *The Pilgrimage of Grace in the Lake Counties, 1536–7, Royal Hist Soc*, London

Hattatt, R, 1982 *Ancient and Romano-British brooches*, Sherborne

Haverfield, F, 1895a Report of the Cumberland Excavation Committee 1894, *Trans Cumberland Westmorland Antiq Archaeol Soc*, o ser, **13**, 453–69

Haverfield, F, 1895b A fourth century tombstone from Carlisle, *Trans Cumberland Westmorland Antiq Archaeol Soc*, o ser, **13**, 165–71

Haverfield, F, 1897 Report of the Cumberland Excavation Committee 1895, *Trans Cumberland Westmorland Antiq Archaeol Soc*, o ser, **14**, 185–97

Haverfield, F, 1899 Report of the Cumberland Excavation Committee for 1898, *Trans Cumberland Westmorland Antiq Archaeol Soc*, o ser, **15**, 345–64

Herring, E, and Howard-Davis, C, 1992 High intensity field collection at the site of the cemetery at Fondo Paviani, September 1990, *Quaderni di Archeologia del Veneto*, **8**, 180–3

Higham, N J, 1979 An aerial survey of the upper Lune valley, in N J Higham (ed), *The changing past*, Manchester, 31–8

Higham, N J, 1980 Native settlements west of the Pennines, in K Branigan (ed), *Rome and the Brigantes*, Sheffield, 41–7

Higham, N J, 1986 *The northern counties to AD 1000*, Harlow

Higham, N J (ed), 1979 *The changing past*, Manchester

Higham, N J, and Jones, G D B, 1975 Frontier, forts and farmers: Cumbrian aerial survey 1974–5, *Archaeol J*, **132**, 16–53

Higham, N J, and Jones, G D B, 1985 *The Carvetii*, Gloucester

Hildyard, E J W, and Gillam, J P, 1951 Renewed excavation at Low Borrow Bridge, *Trans Cumberland Westmorland Antiq Archaeol Soc*, **51**, 40–67

Hindle, B P, 1984 *Roads and trackways of the Lake District*, Ashbourne

Hindle, B P, 1989 Roads, canals and railways, in W Rollinson (ed), *The Lake District: landscape heritage*, Newton Abbot, 130–56

Hirst, S M, 1985 *An Anglo-Saxon inhumation cemetery at Sewerby, East Yorkshire, York Univ Archaeol Pub*, **4**

HMSO, 1908 *Calendar of Inquisitions Post Mortem*, Edward II, **5**, London

HMSO, 1912 *Calendar of Inquisitions Post Mortem*, Edward I, **3**, London

HMSO, 1913 *Calendar of Inquisitions Post Mortem*, Edward III, **8**, London

Hodges, R, 1989 *The Anglo-Saxon achievement*, London

Hodgson, J, 1820 *A topographical and historical description of the county of Westmoreland*, London

Hodgson, T H, 1907 Notes of excavations along the Roman Wall in Cumberland, 1894–1906, *Trans Cumberland Westmorland Antiq Archaeol Soc*, **7**, 296–301

Holdsworth, P, 1983 The Anglo-Saxon period, in M Morris (ed), *Medieval Manchester, The Archaeology of Greater Manchester*, 1, 6–15, Manchester

Holt, G O, 1986 *A regional history of the railways of Great Britain: 10, The North West*, Newton Abbot, 2 edn (rev G Biddle)

Hope-Taylor, B, 1977 *Yeavering: an Anglo-British centre of early Northumbria, Department Environment Archaeol Rep*, **7**

Horsman, V, Milne, C, and Milne, G, 1988 *Aspects of Saxo-Norman London: 1, Building and street development near Billingsgate and Cheapside, London Middlesex Archaeol Soc Spec Pap*, **2**

Howard, P, 1990 *North Western Ethylene Pipeline (English section): Geophysical survey report*, Lancaster University Archaeological Unit, unpubl report

Howard-Davis, C L E, 1983–4 Lancashire Sites and Monuments Record and its computerisation, *Contrebis*, **11**, 3–25

Howard-Davis, C L E, forthcoming The stone artefacts, in R M Newman and R H Leech, *The early Christian site at Dacre, Cumbria: excavations 1982–5*

Howard-Davis, C L E, and Quartermaine, H, forthcoming The glass, in R M Newman and R H Leech, *The early Christian site at Dacre, Cumbria: excavations 1982–5*

Howe, M D, Perrin, J R, and Mackreth, D F, 1981 *Roman pottery from the Nene valley: a guide, Peterborough City Museum Occas Paper*, **2**

Hurst, J G, 1959 Middle-Saxon pottery, in G C Dunning *et al*, Anglo-Saxon pottery: a symposium, *Medieval Archaeol*, **3**, 13–31

Hurst, J G, 1981 The pottery, in D M Wilson (ed), *The archaeology of Anglo-Saxon England*, Cambridge, 283–348

Hutchinson, W, 1794 *History and antiquities of Cumberland*, Carlisle

Iles, P D, Lambert, J K, and Olivier, A C H, 1989 *North Western Ethylene Pipeline (English section), Archaeological assessment: Stage 2 revision*, Lancaster University Archaeological Unit, unpubl report

Isings, C, 1957 *Roman glass from dated finds*, Groningen

Jackson, M J, 1990 *Castles of Cumbria*, Carlisle

James, S, Marshall, A, and Millet, M, 1984 An early medieval building tradition, *Archaeol J*, **141**, 182–215

Jarvis, R A, Bendelow, V C, Bradley, R I, Carroll, D M, Furness, R R, Kilgour, I N L, and King, S J, 1984 *Soils and their use in northern England, Soil Survey of England and Wales*, **10**

Jefferson, S, 1840 *The history and antiquities of Leath Ward, in the county of Cumberland*, Carlisle

Johnson, S, 1983 Burgh Castle, excavations by Charles Green 1958–61, *E Anglian Archaeol Rep*, **20**

Jones, G D B, 1974 *Roman Manchester*, Altrincham

Jones, G D B, 1975 The North-Western interface, in P J Fowler (ed), *Recent work in rural archaeology*, Bradford-upon-Avon, 93–106

Jones, G D B, and Shotter, D C A, 1988 *Roman Lancaster*, Manchester

Jones, M J, 1975 *Roman fort defences to AD 117, BAR Brit Ser*, **21**, Oxford

Jones, M J, 1977 Archaeological work at Brough-under-Stainmore 1971–2: 1 The Roman discoveries, *Trans Cumberland Westmorland Antiq Archaeol Soc*, **77**, 17–47

Jones, M U, 1979 Saxon sunken huts: problems of interpretation, *Arch J*, **136**, 53–9

Jones, R F J, 1984 Death and distinction, in T F C Blagg and A C King (eds), *Military and civilian in Roman Britain, cultural relationships in a frontier province, BAR Brit Ser*, **136**, Oxford

Joy, D, 1967 *Main line over Shap*, Clapham

Kapelle, W E, 1979 *The Norman conquest of the North*, London

Keevil, G, forthcoming *Excavations to the west of Carlisle Cathedral*, Carlisle Archaeological Unit

Kelly, 1858 *Post Office Directory*

King, A, 1978 Gauber High Pasture, Ribblehead: an interim report, in R A Hall (ed), *Viking Age York and the North, CBA Res Rep*, **27**, 21–5

Kirby, D P, 1962 Strathclyde and Cumbria: a survey of historical development to 1092, *Trans Cumberland Westmorland Antiq Archaeol Soc*, **62**, 77–94

Krupa, M, 1994 *Topographical survey of features at Crosdale, near Sedbergh*, Lancaster University Archaeological Unit, unpubl report

Lambert, J K, 1990 *North Western Ethylene Pipeline (English section): Phase II interim report*, Lancaster University Archaeological Unit, unpubl report

Lambert, J K, 1991 *North Western Ethylene Pipeline (English section): Report on surveys and excavations in Cumbria, Lancashire and Cheshire*, Lancaster University Archaeological Unit, unpubl report

Lambert, J K, 1993 *North Western Ethylene Pipeline (English section): Final report*, Lancaster University Archaeological Unit, unpubl report

Lambert, J K, forthcoming *The distribution of charcoal burners' pitsteads in Furness Fells, Cumbria*

Lambert, J K, and Quartermaine, J, 1990a *North Western Ethylene Pipeline (English section), Archaeological studies: Phase I interim report 1 (Rapid field scan)*, Lancaster University Archaeological Unit, unpubl report

Lambert, J K, and Quartermaine, J, 1990b *North Western Ethylene Pipeline (English section), Archaeological studies: Phase I interim report 2 (Rapid field scan)*, Lancaster University Archaeological Unit, unpubl report

Lambert, J K, Olivier, A C H, and Quartermaine, J, 1990a *North Western Ethylene Pipeline (English section), Archaeological studies: Phase I final report*, Lancaster University Archaeological Unit, unpubl report

Lambert, J K, Middleton, R, Olivier, A C H, and Quartermaine, J, 1990b *North Western Ethylene Pipeline (English section), Archaeological studies: Phase I revised final report*, Lancaster University Archaeological Unit, unpubl report

Long, C D, 1988 The Iron Age and Romano-British settlement at Catcote, Hartlepool, *Durham Archaeol J*, **4**, 13–36

Lowndes, R A C, 1963 'Celtic' fields, farms and burial mounds in the Lune valley, *Trans Cumberland Westmorland Antiq Archaeol Soc*, **63**, 77–95

Lowndes, R A C, 1964 Excavation of a Romano-British farmstead at Eller Beck, *Trans Cumberland Westmorland Antiq Archaeol Soc*, **64**, 6–13

Macfarlane, A, 1981 *The justice and the mare's ale*, Oxford

MacGregor, A, 1985 *Bone, antler, ivory and horn. The technology of skeletal materials since the Roman period*, London

Maltby, M, 1983 The animal bone, in M Millet with S James (eds), The excavations at Cowdery's Down, Hampshire, 1978–81, *Archaeol J*, **140**, 151–279

Mannex, P J, 1849 *History, topography, and directory of Westmorland; and Lonsdale north of the sands*, London

Manning, W H, 1975 Economic influences on landuse in the military areas of the Highland Zone during the Roman period, in J G Evans, S Limbrey, and H Cleere (eds), *The effect of man on the landscape: The Highland Zone, CBA Res Rep*, **11**, 112–16

Manning, W H, 1986 *Catalogue of the Romano-British iron tools, fittings and weapons in the British Museum*, London

Margary, I D, 1957 *Roman roads in Britain*, **2**, London

Marshall, W, 1808 *The review and abstract of the county reports to the Board of Agriculture*, **1**, Northern Department, York (reprint, nd, Newton Abbot)

Mason, D J P, 1985 *Excavations at Chester, 26–42 Lower Bridge Street: 1974–6, The Dark Age and Saxon periods, Grosvenor Museum Archaeol Excav and Survey Rep*, **3**

Mawson, D J W, 1980 Agricultural lime burning—the Netherby example, *Trans Cumberland Westmorland Antiq Archaeol Soc*, **80**, 137–51

McCarthy, M, 1979 The pottery, in J H Williams, *St Peter's Street Northampton: Excavations 1973–6, Northampton Development Corporation Archaeol Monogr*, **2**, 153–240

McDonnell, J, 1988 The role of transhumance in northern England, *Northern History*, **24**, 1–17

McGrail, S (ed), 1982 *Woodworking techniques before AD 1500, BAR Int Ser*, **129**

McKinley, J I, 1989 Cremations: expectations, methodologies and realities, in C A Roberts, F Lee, and J Bintliff (eds), *Burial archaeology: current research, methods and developments, BAR British Series*, **211**, 65–76

McKinley, J I, 1993a Cremated bone, in Timby, J, Sancton, **1**. Anglo-Saxon cemetery excavations, 1976–80, *Archaeol J*, **150**, 287–95, 300–11

McKinley, J I, 1993b Bone fragment size and weights of bone from modern British cremations and its implications for the interpretation of archaeological cremations, *Int J of Osteoarcheology*, **3**, 283–7

McKinley, J I, 1994a The Anglo-Saxon cemetery at Spong Hill, North Elmham, **8**: The cremations, *East Anglian Arch*, **69**

McKinley, J I, 1994b Bone fragment size in British cremation burials and its implications for pyre technology and ritual, *J Arch Sci*, **21**, 339–42

McKinley, J I, forthcoming The Romano-British cemetery at St. Stephen's, St. Albans: The cremations and inhumations, *St Albans Museum*

McMinn, R M H, and Hutchings, R T, 1985 *A colour atlas of human anatomy*, London

McWhirr, A, Viner, L, and Wells, C, 1982 *Romano-British cemeteries at Cirencester, Cirencester Excavations*, **2**

Millet, M, with James, S (eds), 1983 *The excavations at Cowdery's Down, Hampshire, 1978–81, Archaeol J*, **140**

Ministry of Public Building and Works, 1967 *Excavations Annual Report 1966*, HMSO, London, 12

Ministry of Public Building and Works, 1968 *Excavations Annual Report 1967*, HMSO, London, 17

Moore, D T, and Oakley, G E, 1979 The hones, in J H Williams, *St Peter's Street Northampton: excavations 1973–6, Northampton Development Corporation Archaeol Monogr*, **2**, 280–3

Moore, P D, Webb, J A, and Collinson, M E, 1991 *Pollen analysis*, Oxford

Morris, J (ed), 1978 *Domesday Book*, Chichester

Morris, M (ed), 1983 *Medieval Manchester: a regional study*, Greater Manchester Archaeol Inst

Murray, H, 1983 *Viking and early medieval buildings in Dublin, BAR Brit Ser*, **119**

Newman, R M, and Leech, R H, forthcoming *The early Christian site at Dacre, Cumbria: excavations 1982–5*

Nicholls, W, 1877 *The history and traditions of Ravenstonedale, Westmorland*, Manchester

Nicholson, J H, 1891 The parish registers of Orton, Westmorland, *Trans Cumberland Westmorland Antiq Archaeol Soc*, o ser, **11**, 250–65

Nicolson, J and Burn, R, 1777 *The history and antiquities of the counties of Westmorland and Cumberland*, London (1976 facsimile edn, Wakefield)

O'Brien, C, and Miket, R, 1991 The early medieval settlement of Thirlings, Northumberland, *Durham Archaeol J*, 7, 57–92

Oldfield, F, and Statham, J C, 1964–5 Stratigraphy and pollen analysis on Cockerham and Pilling Mosses, North Lancashire, *Manchester Memoirs*, **107** (6), 1–16

Oliver, R, 1993 *Ordnance Survey maps: a concise guide for historians*, London

Olivier, A C H, 1987 Excavation of a Bronze Age funerary cairn at Manor Farm, near Borwick, North Lancashire, *Proc Prehist Soc*, **53**, 129–86

Olivier, A C H, 1991 *A study of certain types of one–piece brooch in southern Britain during the first century AD: aspects of form, distribution, and chronology*, unpubl PhD thesis, Nottingham University

Park, C (ed), 1990 *Field excursions in North West England*, Lancaster

Parker, F H M, 1909 Inglewood Forest, **IV**—The revenues of the Forest, *Trans Cumberland Westmorland Antiq Archaeol Soc*, **9**, 24–37

Parson, W, and White, W, 1829 *History, directory, and gazetteer of the counties of Cumberland and Westmorland*, Leeds

Partridge, C, 1981 *Skeleton Green: a late Iron Age and Romano-British Site, Britannia Monogr Ser*, **2**

Peacock, D, and Williams, D F, 1988 *Amphorae in the Roman economy*, London

Pearsall, W H, 1961 Place-names as clues in the pursuit of ecological history, *Namn och bygd*, Uppsala, 72–89

Pearsall, W H, and Pennington, W, 1973 *The Lake District: a landscape history*, London

Peers, C, and Radford, C A R, 1943 The Saxon monastery of Whitby, *Archaeologia*, **89**, 27–88

Philpott, F A, 1990 *A silver saga. Viking treasure from the North-West*, Liverpool

Philpott, R, 1991 *Burial practices in Roman Britain: A survey of grave treatment and furnishing AD 43–410, BAR Brit Ser*, **219**

Pigot, J, 1829 *Pigot and Co's new commercial directory, for the counties of Cumberland, Durham, Northumberland, Westmoreland, and Yorkshire, for 1828–9*

Poole, A L, 1955 *Domesday Book to Magna Carta, 1087–1216*, Oxford, 2 edn

Potter, T W, 1979 *Romans in North West England: excavations at the Roman forts of Ravenglass, Watercrook, and Bowness on Solway, Cumberland Westmorland Antiq Archaeol Soc Res ser*, **1**

Price, A J, and Cottam, S, forthcoming The glass, in K M Buxton and C L E Howard-Davis, *Ribchester graveyard excavations 1980 and 1989–90, Engl Heritage Archaeol Rep*

Pringle, A, 1805 General view of the agriculture of Westmorland, in J Bailey and G Culley, 1805 *General view of the agriculture of Northumberland, Cumberland and Westmorland*, 3 edn, London (1972 facsimile reprint, Newcastle upon Tyne), 274–361

Pringle, A W, 1990 Landform development in the eastern and central Lake District, in C Park (ed), *Field excursions in North West England*, Lancaster, 20–33

Quartermaine, H, forthcoming The loomweights, in R M Newman and R Leech, *The early Christian site at Dacre, Cumbria: excavations 1982–5*

Ragg, F W, 1908 The feoffees of the Cliffords, from 1283 to 1482, *Trans Cumberland Westmorland Antiq Archaeol Soc*, **8**, 253–330

Ragg, F W, 1909 Charters to Byland Abbey, *Trans Cumberland Westmorland Antiq Archaeol Soc*, **9**, 252–70

Rahtz, P A, 1981 Buildings and rural settlement, in D M Wilson (ed), *The Archaeology of Anglo-Saxon England*, Cambridge, 49–98

Raistrick, A, 1967 *Old Yorkshire Dales*, Newton Abbot

Raistrick, A, 1978 *Green roads in the mid-Pennines*, Ashbourne

Ramm, H G, McDowall, R W, and Mercer, E, 1970 *Shielings and bastles, Roy Comm Hist Monuments Engl*, HMSO, London

Reece, R (ed), 1977 *Burial in the Roman world, CBA Res Rep*, **22**, 44–6

Richardson, G G S, 1976 Observations on the Natural Gas Pipeline through North Cumbria, *CBA Regional Group 3 Archaeological Newsbulletin*, **12**, 8–10

Richardson, G G S, 1979 Kings Stables, an early shieling on Black Lyne Common, Bewcastle, *Trans Cumberland Westmorland Antiq Archaeol Soc*, **79**, 19–29

Roberts, C A, Lee, F, and Bintliff , J (eds), 1989 *Burial archaeology: current research, methods and developments, BAR British Series*, **211**

Rollinson, W (ed), 1989 *The Lake District: landscape heritage*, Newton Abbot

Ross, P, 1920 The Roman road north of Low Borrowbridge to Brougham Castle, Westmorland, *Trans Cumberland Westmorland Antiq Archaeol Soc*, **20**, 1–15

Royal Commission on the Ancient and Historical Monuments of Scotland, 1990 *North East Perth, an archaeological landscape*, HMSO, London

Royal Commission on the Historical Monuments of England, 1936 *Westmorland*, HMSO, London

Salway, P, 1967 *The frontier people of Roman Britain*, Cambridge, 2 edn

Salway, P, 1993 *The Oxford illustrated history of Roman Britain*, Oxford

Satchell, J E, 1989 The Bretherdale wool weight, *Trans Cumberland Westmorland Antiq Archaeol Soc*, **89**, 131–40

Sawrey, H, 1967 *The history of a country parish*, Orton

Scull, C, 1991 Post-Roman Phase 1 at Yeavering: a reconsideration, *Medieval Archaeol*, **35**, 51–63

Searle, C E, 1993 Customary tenants and the enclosure of the Cumbrian commons, *Northern History*, **29**, Leeds, 126–53

Sharpe France, R, 1955 Two custumals of the manor of Cockerham, 1326 and 1483, *Trans Lancs Cheshire Antiq Soc*, **64**, 38–54

Shell Chemicals UK Ltd, 1989 *Environmental statement: The North Western Ethylene Pipeline*, Aberdeen

Shell Chemicals UK Ltd, 1993a *Archaeological studies along the North Western Ethylene Pipeline*, Ellesmere Port

Shell Chemicals UK Ltd, 1993b *The environment along the North Western Ethylene Pipeline*, Ellesmere Port

Shipman, P, Foster, G, and Schoeninger, M, 1984 Burnt bones and teeth: an experimental study of colour, morphology, crystal structure and shrinkage, *J Arch Sci*, **11**, 307–25

Shotter, D C A, 1974 Observations in the Sedbergh area of Cumbria, *Contrebis*, **2** (2), Lancaster

Shotter, D C A, 1990 *Roman Coins from North West England*, Lancaster

Shotter, D C A, 1993 *Romans and Britons in North West England*, Lancaster

Shotter, D C A, and White, A J, 1990 *The Roman fort and town of Lancaster*, Lancaster

Shotter, D C A, and White, A J, 1995 *Romans in Lunesdale*, Lancaster

Simpson, F G, 1913 Excavations on the line of the Roman Wall in Cumberland during the years 1909–12, *Trans Cumberland Westmorland Antiq Archaeol Soc*, **13**, 297–397

Simpson, F G, Richmond, I A, and St Joseph, J K S, 1936 Report of the Cumberland Excavation Committee for 1935, *Trans Cumberland Westmorland Antiq Archaeol Soc*, **36**, 158–91

Simpson, W D, 1958 *Brocavum*, Ninekirks, Brougham: a study in continuity, *Trans Cumberland Westmorland Antiq Archaeol Soc*, **58**, 68–77

Smith, A H, 1961 *The place-names of the West Riding of Yorkshire*, **6**, Cambridge

Smith, A H, 1967 *The place-names of Westmorland*, **1**, **2**, Cambridge

Smith, G H, 1978 Excavations near Hadrian's Wall at Tarraby Lane 1976, *Britannia*, **9**, 19–56

Sparey-Green, C, 1987 *Excavations at Poundbury, 1964–80, 1, The settlements, Dorset Natural History and Archaeological Society Monogr*, **1**

Stead, I M, 1991 *Iron Age cemeteries in East Yorkshire. Excavations at Burton Fleming, Rudston, Garton-on-the Wolds and Kirkburn, Engl Heritage Archaeol Rep*, **22**

Stead, I M, and Rigby, V, 1986 *Baldock. The excavation of a Roman and pre-Roman settlement, 1968–72, Britannia Monogr Ser*, **7**

Steane, J, 1985 *The archaeology of medieval England and Wales*, London

Stenton, F M, 1947 *Anglo-Saxon England*, Oxford, 2 edn

Swan, V, G, 1984 *The pottery kilns of Roman Britain, Roy Comm Hist Monuments Engl*, London

Tanner, V, 1986 Northgate excavations, in J S F Walker (ed), *Roman Manchester —A frontier settlement, The archaeology of Greater Manchester*, **3**, 21–61

Taylor, B J, Burgess, I C, Land, D H, Mills, D A C, Smith, D B, and Warren, P T, 1971 *British regional geology: Northern England*, HMSO, London, 4 edn

Taylor, C, 1974 *Fieldwork in medieval archaeology*, London

Taylor, C, 1975 *Fields in the English landscape*, London

Timby, J, 1993 Sancton, **1**: Anglo-Saxon cemetery excavations, 1976–80, *Archaeol J*, **150**, 243–365

Topping, T, 1989 Early cultivation in Northumberland and the Borders, *Proc Prehist Soc*, **55**, 161–79

Toulson, S, 1983 *Lost trade routes*, Aylesbury

Turnbull, J, 1984 *An economic and social study of Orton (Westmorland) between 1650 and 1850*, unpubl dissertation, Lancaster and Liverpool Universities

Tweddle, D, forthcoming The fine metalwork, in R M Newman and R Leech, *The early Christian site at Dacre, Cumbria: excavations 1982–5*

Van Beek, G C, 1983 *Dental morphology: an illustrated guide*, Bristol

Wainwright, A, nd *Walks on the Howgill fells and adjoining fells*, Kendal

Wainwright, A, 1988 *Westmorland Heritage*, Kendal

Walker, D, 1966 The late quaternary history of the Cumberland lowland, *Phil Trans Roy Soc London*, B, **251**, 1–210

Walker, D, 1964 Post-glacial deposits at Tarn Wadling, Cumberland, *The New Phytologist*, **63**, 232–5

Walker, J S F (ed), 1986 *Roman Manchester—a frontier settlement, The archaeology of Greater Manchester*, **3**

Watkin, W T, 1883 *Roman Lancashire: a description of Roman remains in the County Palatine of Lancaster*, Liverpool

Webb, P, Owings, A, and Suchey, J M, 1985 Epiphyseal union of the anterior iliac crest and medial clavicle in a modern multiracial sample of American males and females, *American J of Physical Anthropology*, **68**, 457–66

Webster L, and Backhouse J, 1992 *The making of England: Anglo-Saxon art and culture, AD 600–900*, London

Webster, P V, 1976 Severn Valley ware: a preliminary study, *Trans Bristol Gloucestershire Archaeol Soc*, **94**, 18-46

Wenham, L P, 1968 *The Romano-British cemetery at Trentholme Drive, York, Ministry of Public Building and Works Archaeol Rep*, **5**, HMSO, London

West, S, 1955 Romano-British pottery kilns on West Stow Heath, *Proc Suffolk Inst Archaeol Hist*, **26**, 35–53

West, S, 1985 *West Stow, the Anglo-Saxon village, East Anglian Archaeology*, **24**

Weston, G F, and Hope, W H St J, 1889 The Praemonstratensian abbey of St Mary Magdalene at Shap, Westmorland, **1**: historical, *Trans Cumberland Westmorland Antiq Archaeol Soc*, o ser, **10**, 286–314

Wheeler, H, 1985 The racecourse cemetery, *Derbyshire Archaeol J*, **105**, 222–80

Whellan, W, 1860 *History and topography of the counties of Cumberland and Westmorland*, Pontefract

Whitaker, T D, 1823 *An history of Richmondshire, in the North Riding of the County of York; together with ... Lonsdale, Ewecross and Amunderness*, **2**

White, R H, 1988 *Roman and Celtic objects from Anglo-Saxon graves: a catalogue and an interpretation of the evidence, BAR Brit Ser*, **191**

Whiteside, J, 1904a Orton, Westmorland: the church and some documents in the chest, *Trans Cumberland Westmorland Antiq Archaeol Soc*, **4**, 154–82

Whiteside, J, 1904b *Shappe in bygone days*, Kendal

Whyte, I D, 1985 Shielings and the upland pastoral economy of the Lake District in medieval and early modern times, in J R Baldwin and I D Whyte (eds), *The Scandinavians in Cumbria*, Edinburgh, 103–17

Wightman, E M, 1970 *Roman Trier and the Treveri*, London

Willan, T S, 1951 The navigation of the River Weaver in the eighteenth century, *Chetham Soc*, 3 ser, **3**

Williams, D F, 1977 Black Burnished Ware from Mumrills; a reappraisal of sources by heavy mineral analysis, in J Dore and K Greene (eds), *Roman pottery studies in Britain and beyond*, BAR Int Ser, **30**, 177–188

Williams, J H, 1979 *St Peter's Street Northampton: excavations 1973–6, Northampton Development Corporation Archaeol Monogr*, **2**, 280–3

Williams, J H, 1988a *Proposed ethylene pipeline, Grangemouth to Stanlow (English section), Archaeological assessment: Stage 1*, Lancaster University Archaeological Unit, unpubl report

Williams, J H, 1988b *Proposed ethylene pipeline, Grangemouth to Stanlow (English section), Initial archaeological assessment: Hadrian's Wall*, Lancaster University Archaeological Unit, unpubl report

Williams, J H, 1989 *Proposed ethylene pipeline, Grangemouth to Stanlow (English section), Archaeological assessment: Stage 2*, Lancaster University Archaeological Unit, unpubl report

Williams, J H, and Howard, P, 1989 *Proposed ethylene pipeline, Grangemouth to Stanlow (English section), Archaeological assessment: Hadrian's Wall, Stage 1*, Lancaster University Archaeological Unit, unpubl report

Williams, L A, 1975 *Road transport in Cumbria in the nineteenth century*, London

Wilmott, A, forthcoming Birdoswald excavations 1987–92, *Engl Heritage Archaeol Rep*

Wilson, D M (ed), 1981 *The archaeology of Anglo-Saxon England*, Cambridge

Wilson, D R, 1967 Sites explored in Roman Britain in 1966, *J Roman Stud*, **57**, 174–202

Wilson, D R, 1968 Sites explored in Roman Britain in 1967, *J Roman Stud*, **58**, 176–206

Winchester, A J L, 1979 Deserted farmstead sites at Miterdale Head, Eskdale, *Trans Cumberland Westmorland Antiq Archaeol Soc*, **79**, 150–5

Winchester, A J L, 1984a Peat storage huts in Eskdale, *Trans Cumberland Westmorland Antiq Archaeol Soc*, **84**, 103–17

Winchester, A J L, 1984b Shielings in upper Eskdale, *Trans Cumberland Westmorland Antiq Archaeol Soc*, **84**, 267

Winchester, A J L, 1987 *Landscape and society in medieval Cumbria*, Edinburgh

Wright, T B, 1936 E U Savage (ed), *The watcher by the bridge*, Kendal

INDEX

recording system 6
rents and entry fines 173–5
shieling 26, 57, 58, 173, 188, 189, 190
site stratigraphy 181–7
tenants of Brockholes and Powsons 173–5
topographical survey 178–9
trackways 23, 65, 67, 76, 173, 177, 178, 181, 182–3, 188
trial excavation in 1990 5, 6, 24, 181
Priest Hutton, Carnforth 31
Priories
    Conishead, Lancashire 56
    Coverham, Yorkshire 56
    Watton, Yorkshire 56
Quarries 63
    Roger Howe 63
    Gelstone 63
    Hadrian's Wall 81, 82, 83, 84, 85, 86
    Hardendale 22
    Trainriggs 22
Quernmore, Lancaster 33, 91
Railways
    at Tebay and in the Lune gorge 45, 46, 63, 64, 71, 73, 74, 76, 77, 78
    Caledonian 74, 76
    Eden Valley 21
    Garstang and Knott End 37
    Ingleton to Tebay Branch 27, 73, 177
    Lancaster and Carlisle 66, 70, 73, 74, 76, 177
    Little North Western 33
    Liverpool to Manchester 40
    Liverpool, St Helens, and South Lancashire 40
    North British 10, 12
    Ormskirk to Rainford Junction Branch, Liverpool, Ormskirk, and Preston 40
    South Durham 67, 73, 78
    West Lancashire 38
Rainford Moss, West Lancashire 5
Rapid field scan 2–3, 4, 8, 191, 192
Rapid response team 6, 7
Ravenstonedale, Kirkby Stephen 55, 56, 59, 173
Rawbusk Farm, Tebay, deserted farmstead 51, 57, 58, 61, 66, 75
Rawcliffe Moss, Fylde 5
Recommendations to SCUK 4
Recording system 6
Redgill, Tebay 51, 61, 62, 67
Rheged 49, 50
Ribble, River 5, 38, 43, 49
Ridge and furrow 10, 12, 14, 16, 17, 21, 22, 23, 24, 26, 27, 28, 31, 32, 33, 35, 36, 37, 38, 42, 63, 65, 171, 177
Rispa Pike, Howgills 51
Ristewald, landholders in Tebay 55
Roads
    Drove 27, 28, 69–70, 74
    Packhorse 28, 67–9
    Roman *see also Roman roads* 1, 2, 5, 6, 7, 12–13, 15, 17, 22, 26, 27, 40, 45, 46, 67, 74, 78, 87, 91, 95, 96, 109, 118, 127, 130, 165
    Turnpike 67, 70, 73, 74, 77
Roger Howe, Tebay 23, 53, 54, 63
Roman aqueduct, Low Borrowbridge 95, 96
Roman bathhouse, Low Borrowbridge 74, 95

Roman cemeteries
    Brough under Stainmore 123
    Brougham 5, 17, 19, 123, 127, 160
    Low Borrowbridge 7, 8, 27, 46, 50, 87–125
    York 123
Roman coins, Low Borrowbridge cemetery excavation 93, 106, 108, 113
Roman forts 1, 2, 5, 7
    Bainbridge 94
    Birdoswald 130, 169
    Brough 17
    Brougham 1, 17, 19, 22, 91, 127, 130, 134, 160, 165
    Low Borrowbridge 1, 2, 5, 22, 26, 27, 46, 48, 50, 51, 53, 74, 77, 78, 87, 90, 91, 92, 93–6, 109, 124, 127, 173, 191
    Old Penrith (*Voreda*) 1, 2, 15, 17
    Vindolanda 94
    Watercrook 48, 95
Roman marching camps 2, 15
Roman milestones 91
    Cowan Bridge 91
    Middleton 91
Roman occupation 48, 61, 78, 90–96
Roman roads
    Brougham 91, 127, 130, 165
    Crosby Ravensworth Fell 78
    Howgill Lane 26, 67, 91, 96, 109
    Lodge Lane 40
    Low Borrowbridge 26, 27, 74, 87, 91, 95, 96, 109, 118
    Lune Valley 91
    Main route north to Carlisle 7, 15, 17, 22, 26, 45, 46, 67, 74, 78, 87, 91, 96, 109, 127, 130
    Sproatgill vii, 6, 7, 22, 26, 67, 91
    Stanegate vii, 2, 5, 6, 7, 12–13, 79
Roman tombstones, Low Borrowbridge
    of a mounted soldier 94
    of *Aelia Sentica* 27, 93, 103, 104, 109, 115, 118, 123
Romano-British civilian or extramural settlement 2, 5, 7, 17, 26, 87, 91, 93, 94, 95, 109, 124, 127, 130, 134, 165
Romano-British or Iron Age settlements
    Brockholes 26, 46, 173
    Brougham 1, 2, 17, 127, 165
    High Carlingill 48, 173
    Lazonby Fell 2, 16–17
    Low Carlingill 48
    Lune gorge 24, 26, 46, 48, 173
    Over Kellet 32
    Sceugh Farm 2, 17
    Sealford 173
    Tebay 23
    Whins 48
Romans in the Lune Valley 90–3
Roundthwaite
    cow pastures 61, 66
    drove road at 69
    enclosures 61
    farm rents 62
    farmhouses 75
    highwaymen at 70, 77
    lordship 55
    manorial watermill 64
    medieval settlement 54, 55
    Norse settlement 50, 51
    place name 50, 51